P9-EEB-319

SATHER CLASSICAL LECTURES

Volume Forty-Nine

Poetry into Drama

POETRY INTO DRAMA

Early Tragedy and the Greek Poetic Tradition

By JOHN HERINGTON

UNIVERSITY OF CALIFORNIA PRESS
Berkeley · Los Angeles · London

University of California Press
Berkeley and Los Angeles, California

University of California Press, Ltd.
London, England

Library of Congress Cataloging in Publication Data
Herington, John.
Poetry into drama.

(Sather classical lectures; v. 49)
Bibliography: p.
1. Greek drama (Tragedy)—History and criticism.
2. Greek poetry—History and criticism. 3. Performing
arts—Greece—History. 4. Tragic, The. I. Title.
II. Series.
PA3135.H47 1984 882'.01'09 83-9146
ISBN 0-520-05100-9

Printed in the United States of America

1 2 3 4 5 6 7 8 9

Contents

List of Illustrations

Preface

During the past century and a half, Attic tragedy has presented itself in exceedingly varied guises. We have seen it as *ritual*, deriving its mysterious hold over us from beliefs rooted deep in human prehistory and the human subconscious—belief in the wild god of all liquid life-forces, or in the death and rebirth of the crops, or in the need to reanimate from time to time the slumbering powers of the heroic dead. More recently (especially since its restoration to the repertory of the live theater and its consequent incorporation into the syllabuses of Drama Schools) we have seen Attic tragedy approached and criticized in purely aesthetic terms, as just one facet of a vast and ill-defined phenomenon called *drama*, to which Shakespeare, Racine, and Beckett all equally belong. Both these extreme approaches, as well as the many approaches that are possible between the extremes, have sharpened our understanding of the plays and have enhanced for us what Aristotle called "the pleasure of tragedy." Yet none of them seems quite adequate, singly or in combination, either to account for the character and makeup of the Attic tragedies we have or to explain why the tragic art should have come into being just when and where it did. The aim of this book is to consider in some depth an approach to the history and nature of tragedy that seems at least as legitimate as the approaches just mentioned and is certainly far older. Indeed, it is implicit in most discussions of tragedy at all periods of classical antiquity and can be traced back into the era when the great surviving tragedies themselves were being composed and first performed. In brief, the tragic art as the Greeks themselves saw it was not primarily a religious ritual, nor was it a totally unprecedented artistic phenomenon that had miraculously sprung into being at Athens in the later sixth century B.C.; rather, it was a species of the genus *poetry*. Rooted in the entire Greek tradition of poetry from Homer onward, tragedy was that tradition's final, hybrid flower. It too was poetry, poetry enlarged by a dimension. Strangely enough, this ancient perception of tragedy seems not to have been comprehensively described or assessed in recent times. Any student of Greek classical literature must have been aware of it from the moment of first reading Plato's *Republic* or Aristotle's *Poetics* (unless the theories developed about tragedy over the past century and a half have prevented him or her from assimilating the actual views of those philosophers on the subject). Very many modern scholars, naturally, have dealt with this or that aspect of the question. Their names, for the most part, must be left to emerge in the course of the following pages, but here I would mention Wilamowitz-Moellendorff (passim, but particularly in the *Einleitung in die griechische Tragödie*) in an earlier generation and, among contemporaries, Gerald Else.

Probably the chief block to our full comprehension of the ancient view that *tragedy, and, indeed, all drama, is a species of poetry* is the chasm that has opened up between these two arts in modern times. For us (with very few exceptions), "poetry" is a solitary, individualistic activity resulting in a number of irregular printed lines which are destined to be read by solitary individuals; nothing could be more different from our contemporary drama, a performing art involving the cooperation of several ancillary arts (acting, music, costuming, painting) and enacted before a large group of human beings, their eyes undistracted by print, capable of interacting with the performers and even, in subtle ways, molding the performance. So sharp has this distinction become in our practical experience that perhaps even the professional classicist, let alone the Common Reader who seeks to make sense of early Greek literature, may have some difficulty in fully realizing that it scarcely existed in archaic and classical Greece. To approach the main theme of the present book, therefore, we must first radically redefine our idea of *poetry*. We must learn to hear and see Greek poetry as a performing art, in some of its manifestations capable of extremely complicated musical, histrionic, and balletic effects, almost, indeed, as a kind of drama-before-drama. The business of chapters 1 and 2, therefore, will be to present the evidence in support of this fundamental generalization.

In Chapter 3 we turn from external conditions of performance to content: to the imaginative world on which both Greek nondramatic poetry and Greek tragedy equally drew. In this matter the modern reader once again needs violently to readjust his ideas about both arts. Over the last two centuries, but especially over the past fifty years or so, we have become used to a poetry and to a somewhat lesser extent a drama that express the lonely individual artist's comforting fiction—the structure that he has built for himself (and possibly for a vaguely perceived audience) to stand solid and coherent in an otherwise fluid and inexplicable universe. In approaching early Greek literature, however, we have boldly to imagine the now almost unimaginable: a world of heroic and divine myth, in part at least as old as the Bronze Age, which is the common property and theme not only of poetry, not only of tragedy, but of the very audiences, the very society, within which these arts had their being. In this respect, as in respect of their manner of performance, the ancient poetry and the ancient drama were far closer together than they have been at any time since. It was not difficult for the one to merge fairly smoothly into the other.

And that, in fact, is very much what they seem to have done in sixth-century B.C. Athens. Chapter 4 surveys the conditions—conditions apparently the result of a long series of deliberate political acts—under which their merging came about. It will be understood that for simple lack of evidence we cannot reconstruct the precise moment when tragedy was born: the moment when the characters of the ancient poetic tradition took on *separate* voices and *visible* forms and when the dance floor on which they moved ceased to be a mere patch of tamped soil and became an imagined space, a space located anywhere in the world known to the Greeks. We can, however, reconstruct the musical and poetic environment within which, and perhaps because of which, that miracle took place.

In Part III of the book, chapters 5 and 6, we shall turn our attention to the extant or partially extant tragedians of the fifth century B.C.; primarily to the earliest of them, Aeschylus, since he stands closest to the origins. The aims here may be described fairly simply. They are, first, to examine those features of Attic tragedy, metrical and thematic, that clearly derive from the pretragic poetic tradition; second, and no doubt more hazardously, to inquire what new techniques, unknown to that tradition, emerged as the new art of tragedy matured and slowly distanced itself from its immeasurably ancient background. The hope here is not by any means to "explain" the infinite complexity or the deep humanity of Greek tragedy. Rather, it is to send the contemporary reader back to confront those texts for himself or herself, perhaps with a clearer sense of what to expect and what to hear and see: indeed I know of no other good reason for writing about great literature. Finally, the Epilogue will emphasize once more the question that will have pursued us in one way or another throughout the book—the question of *performance*, be it of Greek poetry or of Greek tragedy. Rather late in the history of both arts a strange, a fantastic lyric poem was performed in Athens by a good friend of Euripides'. It happens that this is the only surviving Greek poetic text the performance of which can be at least partly reconstructed in detail. Such a reconstruction, which seems never to have been attempted before, is presented in the Epilogue.

This book is a rewritten and expanded version of the lectures that I had the honor to present as Sather Professor of Classical Literature at Berkeley in April and May, 1978. It is a great pleasure to thank the members of the Berkeley Department of Classics for their hospitality during that visit: as so many others have found before me, they are, indeed, *ξείνοισι θαυμαστοὶ πατέρες*. Among the many people, inside and outside the university community, to whom I am grateful for advice, encouragement, and fresh points of view, I wish in particular to name Elaine and Carlo Anderson, Donald Mastronarde, Michael Nagler, Thomas Rosenmeyer, and Philip Stanley. Here in New Haven, the following colleagues and friends have generously provided advice on various points: Thomas Cole, Diana Kleiner, Naphtali Lewis, Sarah Morris, Hayden Pelliccia, Jerome Pollitt, and Diana Stone. Donald Kagan and Sheila Murnaghan not only taught me much in conversation, but also had the great kindness to read the work in typescript; they have eliminated a number of errors in style and fact. I further thank Yale's Whitney Humanities Center for an A. Whitney Griswold award, which enabled me to have my manuscript professionally typed, and Jane McHughen, Sally Moran, and Jean Edmunds, the elegance of whose typing has been matched only by their skill in decipherment.

Certain features of the book require some explanation here. The first is a matter of nomenclature: the Greek words *aulos* and *aulētēs* are throughout represented by "oboe" and "oboist" respectively, not by the conventional translations "flute" and "flautist." For although there is no modern English word that will really fit the double *aulos*, an instrument that became obsolete some fifteen centuries ago, my translation at least brings out its one indisputable feature: it belonged to the reed family (compare, for example, Landels [1968], where further references will be found). We still know all too little about the sound of the *auloi*, but to translate as "flutes" is to negate even that which we do know. Both the analogy of modern reed instruments and the ancient literary testimonies suggest that the *auloi* possessed a warm and vibrant timbre that, especially in the lower registers, was quite unlike the tone of the flute family.

In rewriting the text for publication I have tried, as I tried in the original lectures, to address myself not merely to the classical specialist but also to the Common Reader. So far as possible, therefore, I have unloaded technical discussion and documentation into the Notes and Appendices. Inevitably, some technicalities had to intrude here and there into the text (especially in Chapter 5), but even in such passages I hope that the nonspecialist will be able to follow the drift of the argument without much difficulty. A word needs to be said on the nature and scope of the Appendices, especially those that attempt to collect the evidence concerning the performing conditions of Greek poetry. Part of my preparation for the lectures was the agreeable task of reading or rereading (aloud, so far as possible) all the Greek poems and poetic fragments that date from earlier than about 400 B.C. and noting such evidence as I could see that might throw light on their performance. To this I added a search for relevant material, first, in Plato, Aristotle, Athenaeus, Pollux, and the pseudo-Plutarchan *De Musica*, as well as a number of other prose works, and second, in all the modern collections of *testimonia* to the Greek poets that I could lay hands on, notably the rich storehouse contained in Edmonds (1928). Concurrently I put together a fairly extensive secondary bibliography relating to the subject, from which I learned a number of other ancient literary references and almost all the references to archaeological material that are collected in this book (especially at the end of Appendix V). I do not claim that the material in the Appendices is complete. For one thing, I have deliberately excluded from them much trivial, repetitious, and dubious matter. For another, it would be unrealistic to suppose that the collection of evidence that I assembled in my private notebooks could be without serious gaps. The area ideally to be searched is coextensive with the entire literature of classical antiquity and partly even with that of mediaeval Byzantium, not to mention the inscriptions and visual monuments of those periods. It is to be hoped that some scholar—or some team of scholars—may one day undertake such a search, for which I know of no precedent. The most that the present collection may claim is that it includes most of the relevant pre-Hellenistic passages and a reasonably extensive sampling of the later Greek and Roman evidence: enough, it may be, to substantiate in general my account of the performing aspect of Greek poetry during the city-state era, even if more details remain to be discovered. As for the Bibliography: a complete guide to the secondary literature on all the topics and authors discussed in this inquiry would plainly be impracticable on grounds of space alone. The purpose of my list of books and articles is simply to supply details of those works that are referred to, normally in abbreviated form, in the text, Notes, and Appendices.

All the translations from Greek and Latin are my own, with the exception of the passage from Pherecrates quoted in the Epilogue.

John Herington
New Haven, Connecticut

September 1982

PART
ONE

Pretragic Poetry in Greece

1. Poetry as a Performing Art

THE SONG CULTURE

> I discovered that I could get [the songs] I wanted from pretty nearly everyone I met, young and old. In fact, I found myself for the first time in a community in which singing was as common and almost as universal a practice as speaking. . . . So closely, indeed, is the practice of this particular art interwoven with the ordinary avocations of everyday life that singers, unable to recall a song I had asked for, would often make some such remark as: "Oh, if only I were driving the cows home I could sing it at once!"

Such were the delighted words of an English collector of folk song in the southern Appalachians during the early part of this century. He was confronted, in a purer form than he had ever seen before, with something that we may call (for convenience) a song culture: a society whose prime medium for the expression and communication of its most important feelings and ideas was song.[1]

Certain accidents of history and scholarship long ago conspired to obscure the fact that well into the fifth century B.C. Greece also was essentially a song culture, although of a far more sophisticated and complex kind than that of southern Appalachia. Poetry, recited or sung, was for the early Greeks the prime medium for the dissemination of political, moral, and social ideas—history, philosophy, science (as those subjects were then understood), and indeed of what Socrates was later to call "human wisdom." Even today, with all the information that is now available about the practice of oral poetry at various dates and places (including early Greece itself), it is not easy for a scholar to assimilate this fact or fully to imagine its consequences. On the shelves, chronologically arranged, sit the silent ranks of conscientiously edited poetic texts, from Homer through the Attic tragedians. To restore them all, in the mind's ear and eye, to *performance*—and to contemporaneous, even mutually competitive, performance at that—requires an exceptional effort of the historical imagination. Yet that effort seems worth making, not merely for the immediate purposes of this inquiry, but also for a better understanding of the entire poetic and dramatic tradition of classical Greece.

Three sources are available for a reconstruction of the performing aspect of early Greek poetry. First: the evidence embedded in the poetic texts of the song-culture era itself, supplemented here and there by contemporary works of art, especially vase-paintings, that show the performers in action. Second: statements by writers of the later fifth and of the fourth century B.C. (notably Plato and Aristotle), who were still in close touch with the song culture, even though it was disintegrating rapidly in their time. Finally: reports by writers who lived in an era when the song culture had been almost entirely replaced by a culture much more similar to our own, and which we may call (again, for the sake of convenience), the book culture; that is, from about the last years of the fourth century B.C. until the fall of the Roman Empire (or, in a few cases, even later than that). This last class of evidence is naturally the most difficult to assess. Many of the ancient writers involved were, indeed, professional scholars or antiquaries with access to infinitely more evidence about the song-culture era than is available to us. But scholars will be scholars, then as now, and all too often we must remain uncertain whether we are dealing with neat academic conjectures and combinations or with statements that were firmly based on genuine documents of the song-culture era—early poems now lost to us, for example, or the official records of the ancient poetic and dramatic contests. The reader will therefore approach this last class of evidence cautiously, testing it as well as he can case by case. But I shall not exclude it from my account where there seems to be a reasonable likelihood of its accuracy.

Our evidence from all three classes is inevitably scattered and fragmentary. Sustained ancient accounts of the performance of poetry are very rare, and our reconstructions will usually rest on numerous glancing allusions in a variety of authors, helped out where possible by archaeological material. For this reason, much of the evidence has been relegated to appendices, where the reader may check it for himself or herself at first hand; as a rule, only the most significant documents will be quoted and discussed in the text of each chapter.

Even when all difficulties are taken into account, the general picture presented by the scattered evidence is clear beyond any doubt. The Greek nondramatic poetry that covers the period from Homer and Hesiod (perhaps in the late eighth century B.C.) to at least about the time of the death of Pindar (ca. 438 B.C.)—the main subject of these first three chapters—reached its public *through performance*. The manner, and the social context, of performance varied immensely; to some degree but not entirely, they can be correlated with the *genre* of poetry involved—epic, choral lyric, solo lyric, elegy, and iambic. To explore these varieties in more detail will be the business of the rest of this chapter.

PERFORMANCES AT PUBLIC RELIGIOUS FESTIVALS

Where temples were, there, as a rule, poetry was performed as well as sacrifice.[2] At most of the innumerable temple-sites from end to end of the Greek world, the poetry no doubt was of a simple and traditional kind: a processional as the worshipers approached the shrine; a hymn round the altar for the moment of sacrifice itself.[3] From the earliest times, however, certain sanctuaries encouraged the production of far more elaborate and sophisticated performances, not as a part of the ritual, as cult song in the strict sense, but to do honor to the god of the sanctuary and to rejoice his heart.[4] Performances of this kind, on the whole, seem to have borne no closer relationship to the ancient *ritual* of the god than did the sculptured offerings (*agalmata*, "delights")[5] that were dedicated in his sanctuary, or even than the athletic games that often also formed part of the festival. Nor was the content of a poem so performed necessarily restricted to the praise of the sanctuary's god or the narration of his exploits. It could draw, like any other Greek poetry, on the entire world of divine and heroic myth which will be outlined in Chapter 3. (This distinction between cult poetry and poetry performed as part of a religious festival should above all be borne in mind when the time comes for us to examine the origin and nature of tragedy.) Finally, these poetic exhibitions, like the athletic games, were normally organized in the form of contests between performers or groups of performers. There is even some evidence that the results of the contests were felt to be of such public importance that they were recorded in the local official archives, just as were the results of the major athletic games (and, as we shall see, the results of the tragic contests in Athens).[6]

It is into the context of such religious festivals that we have to replace the performance of some of the most important kinds of nondramatic Greek poetry that have survived to us, above all the Homeric epics. Two ancient passages best recreate the general atmosphere in which the festivals took place. The third Homeric Hymn, which by most reckonings dates at the latest from the seventh century B.C., describes the gathering of the Ionians for an Apollo festival on the sacred island of Delos thus (lines 146–55):

> But it is in Delos, Apollo, that your heart most delights; that is the place where the Ionians assemble for your glory, wearing their long robes, together with their children and their honored wives. Having you in mind, they delight you with boxing and dancing and song, each time they set up their gathering [?].[7] A man who came upon the Ionians at that time, when they were all together, would say to himself that they were immortal and forever ageless; for he would see then the charm of them all, and his spirit would delight as he looked at the men, and at the beautifully-girt women, and at the swift ships, and at the many possessions of them all.

This description, like so many descriptions embodied in the early epic poetry (the banquet, the sacrifice, the welcoming of a stranger, the ship putting to sea) is surely meant to be paradigmatic. This is not just *one* great festival, the periodic gathering of the Ionian Greeks from the islands and the Asiatic coast, but in a sense it is *all* such festivals: a festival as it should be. The passage therefore seems crucial to our understanding not merely of the spirit in which the poetic contests were held, but also of Olympian religious worship in general. The modern reader, especially if he has been brought up in the Judaeo-Christian tradition, will probably note with some surprise the inextricable mixture of what we would see as religious and as quite secular motives. Side by side with the glorification of the god—or, rather, a necessary part of that glorification—stand human beauty, dignity, accomplishments, and even material wealth. The keynote of the entire happening is *delight*, human and divine: the god delights, the pilgrims delight in honoring him, even the casual visitor delights in what he sees. In that reciprocal joy, for a passing moment, the worshipers earn the surprising epithets of "immortal and forever ageless," which are normally reserved for the gods alone. But this comes about through no mystic sacrament or ancient cult-ritual. It comes about when the humans show the god the best they can be or do "in boxing and dancing and song."

Our second general description of a Greek religious festival relates to a more parochial celebration than the great Panionian gathering described in the hymn. At the same time, however, it is more specific and gives a clearer idea of the context within which the poetic events took place. The location is Sparta; the occasion, the Hyakinthia, a three-day festival of Apollo; the narrator (who gives the impression that he has been an eyewitness), a certain Polykrates.[8] The first day, he says, is a day of mourning for the fate of Hyakinthos, Apollo's favorite, whom the god accidentally killed with a discus. On this day the Spartans wear no garlands, eat frugal meals, and omit from their sacrifices the paean—the hymn sung to Apollo—and all other festive trappings.

> But on the middle day of the three there is a colorful spectacle [*thea*; this description emphasizes the visual throughout] and a great and notable public gathering (*panegyris*). Boys wearing girt-up tunics play the lyre, sweeping all the strings with the plectrum as they sing the god in the anapaestic rhythm and at a high pitch.[9] Others pass through the viewing area (*theatron*)[10] on finely caparisoned horses. Massed choruses of youths now enter and sing some of the national songs, while dancers mixed in with them perform the ancient dance-movements to the oboe (*aulos*) and the singing. Next maidens enter, some riding in richly adorned wicker cars, while others make their procession in chariots yoked with mules [?];[11] and the entire city is astir, rejoicing at the sight (*theōria*). On this day they sacrifice an abundance of victims, and the citizens feast all their acquaintances and their own slaves. And no one is left out of the sacrifice, but it comes to pass that the city is emptied for the spectacle (*thea*).

Apart from the surprisingly Keatsian ending (is it conceivable that the poet had perused Athenaeus before he composed his *Ode on a Grecian Urn*?), one notices in this account also the atmosphere of public joy and excitement in which the poetic events take place and the distance at which they stand from the strictly ritual elements in the Hyakinthia festival; those seem to have been reserved for the somber first day of the three.[12]

An up-to-date and comprehensive study of the Greek divine festivals that included poetic events—*agōnes mousikoi*, to use the ancient term

TABLE 1. *Greek Divine Festivals with Poetic Events*

	Peloponnese	*Central Greece & Attica*	*Aegean Islands*
800 B.C.	OLYMPIA: Zeus; 776 B.C.*		
	ITHOME, Messenia: Zeus; eighth century? (Choral lyric).		DELOS: Apollo; eighth century? (Rhapsody? Choral lyric).
700 B.C.	SPARTA: Karneia festival for Apollo, 676–73 B.C. (Kitharody); several other festivals (involving choral lyric), seventh century.		
600 B.C.	SIKYON: before ca. 600 B.C. (Contests in Homeric rhapsody: "tragic choruses" for Adrastos); then, early sixth century ("tragic choruses" for Dionysos).	DELPHI: Pythia festival for Apollo, from remote antiquity. (Hymns, kitharody); reorganized 582 B.C. (Kitharody and aulody).	
		ATHENS: (1) Panathenaia, 566 B.C. (Kitharody and Homeric rhapsody, at some point between 566 and 514 B.C.)	
500 B.C.		(2) Great Dionysia, ca. 535–33 B.C. (Tragic contests at that time; dithyrambic choral contests, 508 B.C. at latest; comic contests, ca. 486 B.C.).	

* Poetic events were never officially included here, but Olympia served as a center for unofficial poetic performances (see evidence for this and for other data in this table in Appendix I).

—seems to be lacking. It would be an attractive project in itself, and its results would certainly illuminate the political, as well as the artistic, history of archaic and classical Greece. It would also, however, be a vast project, far beyond the scope of the present book, for it would have to take into account not merely the long-known literary sources but also the archaeological evidence, notably in the form of inscriptions, that has accumulated over the last fifty years or more. For our present purposes, fortunately, we may be content to outline the chronological and geographical distribution of the main festivals that had come into being before the Great Persian Wars. The table opposite gives the approximate order in which these festivals were founded (or first surface in history) and the main geographical areas into which the sanctuaries concerned fall—Peloponnese on the left, Central Greece and Attica in the middle, the Aegean islands on the right. In parentheses are named the poetic events known to have been included in each festival. For the sake of perspective I have included the Olympia festival, although it must be stressed that poetic events were never officially included there. (For the evidence that Olympia served as a center for *unofficial* poetic performances, and for the other evidence on which the table in general is based, see Appendix I.)

That is the simplified picture. In detail, much of the evidence is obscure and doubtful, and will have to be considered more closely in Chapter 4. Yet certain preliminary observations may be made at this point. First, the institution of the tragic contests at the Athenian Great Dionysia is, in one sense, very far from being the radical innovation that it is often represented to be. Rather, it marks an end, for it is the last important member of a long series of archaic *agōnes mousikoi* stretching back at least into the eighth century B.C. The features in Attic tragedy that most surprise the innocent modern observer—the fact that it was a competitive sport, the fact that its performances were limited to certain periodic divine festivals, and, indeed, the fact that it was composed throughout in verse—all fit perfectly into a very ancient pattern. Second, the institutions of quite a large proportion of the *agōnes mousikoi* listed can be dated with tolerable accuracy. The implication is that, in contrast to strictly cultic practices, they are the result of deliberate administrative action, whether on the part of the sanctuary's priesthood or (as seems very likely in the sixth-century instances at Sikyon and Athens) on the part of the political authorities. Finally, we should here take note of the three main kinds of poetic event represented in the *agōnes mousikoi*: *rhapsody*, the unaccompanied delivery of stichic verse (mostly, but not exclusively, epic verse); *kitharody*, the solo singing of stichic or lyric verse to the singer's own accompaniment on the *kithara*, the concert lyre; and *choral lyric*, the performance of lyric verse by a choir, always accompanied instrumentally and usually reinforced by the power of the dance.[13] Even in this regard, it will be observed, the Attic tragic contests do not entirely fall out of the ancient pattern. They involve the same varieties of performance; the difference is that they mix all of them together in a single work. Such ancient evidence as has survived about the manner of performance of each kind will be considered in the following sections.

RHAPSODIC PERFORMANCE

Plato's little dialogue *Ion* provides the most vivid and detailed surviving evidence about the rhapsodic performances—or, indeed, about the performance of any kind of Greek poetry whatsoever. The player of the title role, Ion of Ephesus, is a professional rhapsode who travels around Greece reciting poetry (*Ion* 541b8). He appears to earn his living, at least in part, from the prizes he receives at rhapsodic contests (535e4–6). Indeed, at the dramatic date of this dialogue he has just carried off first prize in the Asklepieia festival at Epidaurus and has arrived in Athens to compete at the Panathenaia (530a–b). He is a fanatical admirer of Homer (whose poems he claims to interpret better than any man: 530c–d and passim), to the exclusion of all other poets. It appears, however, from remarks made by his interlocutor, Socrates, that the standard repertoire of a contemporary rhapsode, and probably of Ion himself, includes a number of those other poets also (530b8–9, 531d4); Hesiod and Archilochus are specifically mentioned (531a1–2, 531c2, 532a5–6). It is the rhapsode's proud privilege, we learn, "to interpret the meaning of the poet to the audience" (530c3–4), and in this he is compared to an actor: "you are wise, I dare say," says Socrates (not without irony), "*you rhapsodes and actors*, and those whose poems you chant" (*aidete*, 532d6–7). The rhapsode's external circumstances match the importance of his function. In reciting, he stands on a platform (535e2), gorgeously dressed and adorned with golden garlands (530b6–8, 535d2–5). Finally, the audience before which he performs is said, perhaps with some exaggeration, to number more than twenty thousand people (535d4–5).

For our purposes, the most important passage in the dialogue occurs at 535b–e. Socrates is here pressing his point that the rhapsode's art, like that of the poet or the seer, is a matter of inspiration, of possession by some divine force, rather than of a communicable skill.

> SOCRATES: Let us take the times when you are speaking (*eipēis*) the epic verses splendidly and most deeply astounding the spectators: for instance, when you are chanting (*aidēis*) the passage where Odysseus is jumping onto the threshold and being revealed to the Suitors and pouring out the arrows before his feet [*Od.* 22.2–4]; or Achilles charging against Hector [*Il.* 22.312 ff.]; or again, one of the pathetic episodes that involve Andromache, or Hecuba, or Priam [cf. *Il.* 6, 22, 24]. At those times, are you in your senses? Or do you become outside yourself, so that your soul is possessed, and thinks that it is present at the actions about which you are speaking (*legeis*), whether those are in Ithaca or in Troy, or in whatever situation the verses require?
>
> ION: For me, Socrates, that proves your point most vividly. I will not hide it from you: when I speak (*legō*) one of the pathetic episodes, my eyes brim over with tears; and when I speak one that is filled with fear or dread, my hair stands on end with fright, and my heart pounds.
>
> SOCRATES: Really! Ion, can we maintain that this man whom you describe is in his senses at that point? Here he is, adorned with colorful clothing and golden garlands, and yet he is crying, although he has lost none of these things, and in that atmosphere of sacrifice and holiday! Or else he is frightened, standing among more than twenty thousand friendly people, although no one is trying to rob him or do him wrong!
>
> ION: No, Socrates, we certainly can't say that he is in his senses, to be quite honest about it.
>
> SOCRATES: Well, now, do you realize that you rhapsodes produce just the same effects in most of the spectators, too?
>
> ION: I most certainly do realize it! Each time, from up there on the platform, I spot them crying, and taking on dreadful expressions, and matching all that is spoken (*tois legomenois*) with their wonder. In fact, I'm obliged to pay the closest attention to them, the reason being that if I make them cry I shall laugh, because I get money; but if I make them laugh I shall cry, because I lose money.

Such other evidence as survives about the rhapsodes' manner of performance tends to confirm the picture drawn in the *Ion*. Plato himself, in other dialogues, and his approximate contemporary Alcidamas simi-

Plate I: Rhapsode by the Kleophrades Painter (courtesy of British Museum).

larly treat the performances of the rhapsode and of the dramatic actor as practically identical. Aristotle, a generation later, also brackets the two arts together, but in chapter 26 of the *Poetics* (an important passage for the history of both) he draws a distinction, too: rhapsodic delivery involves less outright imitation than tragic performance, since it depends far less on gesture, "although even in rhapsodic delivery people may overdo the gestures, as Sosistratos did."[14] Finally, the type of oral delivery adopted by the rhapsodes can probably be deduced from Plato's choice of verbs to describe it, both in the *Ion* passage and elsewhere. The reader will have noticed that he uses the verb *legein/eipein* (which simply means "speak") and *aidein* (which can mean anything from "intone" to "sing") interchangeably. It seems a fair conclusion that the rhapsode's delivery of verse had a certain incantatory quality, above the level of ordinary colloquial utterance but well below the level of song.[15]

We can thus reconstruct a rhapsodic performance of Homer (or indeed of several other nonmelic Greek poets) with a tolerable fullness of detail, as it was enacted in the early fourth century B.C. or even within the last three decades of the fifth century.[16] It is very difficult to decide how far our results can be applied to rhapsodic performances at earlier periods. Can we project something like Ion's manner onto the rhapsodes at the first Panathenaic contests in the sixth century B.C.? Or onto the Argive rhapsodes at Sikyon, perhaps before 600? There are two possible arguments against doing so. First, Plato, like his contemporary Xenophon,[17] is clearly scornful of the rhapsodes and could well have exaggerated the emotionalism of Ion's performance. Second, even if Plato's account is perfectly accurate, we have to reckon with the fact that in the last third of the fifth century the old artistic restraints were generally tending to break down—in metrics, in music, in acting styles, and, perhaps, one might add, even in the visual arts;[18] should we not expect that the art of rhapsody (closely associated, as it was, with the art of acting) would have suffered the same fate? The solitary counterargument is empirical and subjective, but perhaps none the less powerful for that: one has only to recite Homer aloud, before a real or imagined throng of people, to reexperience the emotions described by Ion. That Homeric poetry (and, as we shall see later, a good deal of other Greek nonmelic poetry too) seems to have been designed from the first to be *acted*. It demands impersonation; it demands skillful variations in tone, tempo, and dynamic; and there are some points, also, where it seems imperiously to exact from the speaker some form of physical gesture. One is prepared to believe that in all these respects the sixth- or seventh-century rhapsode may have been less violent, less emotional, than Plato's Ion. One is not prepared to believe, on the basis of experience, that he stood there like a treetrunk and recited "the pathetic episodes that involve Andromache, or Hecuba, or Priam" at an even speed and in a monotone.[19]

The only pre-Platonic evidence for the manner in which the Greeks performed their epic poetry tends, perhaps, to confirm this view. It is the well-known vase painting by the Kleophrades Painter (Plate I), datable probably in the decade 490–480 B.C.[20] The painting shows a bearded man in profile, facing right, and standing on a platform; his only garment is a plain cloak, a *himation*; and his only property of any other kind is a long stick, the handle of which he holds in his outstretched right hand, while the base rests close to the toes of his right foot. His mouth is open, and near it the Kleophrades Painter has drawn letters which, transliterated into our modern conventional Greek script, read: *ὧδέ ποτ' ἐν Τύρινϑι*. The figure is usually taken to represent a rhapsode. The main reasons are that (like Ion) he stands on a platform, which suggests that this is to be thought of as a formal poetic recital before a considerable audience; and that the words proceeding from his mouth constitute metrically half an epic hexameter, and also have a suitably epic content ("Thus, on a time, in Tiryns . . ."). But there are difficulties. The reciter, whoever he is, cannot be performing at the most famous of Athenian rhapsodic contests, that of the Panathenaia; for at that festival only the *Iliad* and *Odyssey* were performed, and this half-hexameter belongs to neither poem.[21] The absence of any kind of personal adornment (one remembers the brilliant clothing and golden garlands worn by Ion; compare also the costumes of competing kitharodes, to be discussed later) may suggest, indeed, that the occasion is not a public festival at all. The staff which the figure holds perhaps leads to the same conclusion; it is nothing other than a walking stick, with a short handle set at a right angle to the long and heavily knotted stem. Just such walking sticks were used by elderly Athenians to support their steps, and by the younger set as a kind of swagger cane, to fool around with at parties.[22] In short, the figure shown by the Kleophrades Painter is wearing the ordinary civil dress of an Athenian gentleman. We do best to conclude, until and unless further parallels are noticed among the vase paintings, that he is not a professional rhapsode at all but, rather, a poet or an amateur reciter of poems, performing in a private context.[23] Even so, we are still privileged to be present at a recitation of epic verses, whatever its precise status, in the period of the great Persian Wars. The performer stands upright, in a relaxed, somewhat statuesque posture; the right leg is advanced and slightly bent, the left evidently straight. We cannot see his left arm, but it is probably to be thought of as held still under the ample folds of the *himation*. The right arm, as already mentioned, is held out straight in a magnificent gesture, so that the stick grasped in its hand inclines sharply forward. Is this a gesture of emphasis, perhaps to stress the ὦδε? One cannot help recalling the Homeric description of Odysseus's peculiar speaking style: before Odysseus opened his mouth, says Antenor (*Il.* 3.216–20), you would have thought him a person of no knowledge or sense, because he stood stock still with his eyes on the ground, "*and did not keep moving his staff either backward or so as to lean forward.*" Our reciter seems to be of the contrary and more popular persuasion: he is not afraid to look up and out into the world, or to accompany his words by a restrained gesture with his staff-holding hand.

KITHARODIC PERFORMANCE

At least in ancient poetry, there is nothing equal or close to the description of a kitharode—one who sings to his own accompaniment on the lyre—that is presented in the fourth Homeric Hymn, lines 418–33. The moment there described is a marvelous one in divine (and human) history: the young Hermes has just invented the lyre, and demonstrates it to Apollo, the god whose property it will shortly become.[24] Yet the passage, like the passage on the Delos festival quoted earlier from the second hymn, is also paradigmatic. Here stands a kitharode for all time:

> Hermes took the lyre on his left arm, and tried it out with the plectrum, part by part. At the touch of his hand, the lyre rang out with a tremendous sound, and Phoebus Apollo laughed with joy, for the lovely breath of its marvelous voice went through his heart, and sweet desire took hold of his spirit as he listened. Then Hermes was encouraged, and took his stand on the left side of Apollo, playing in lovely notes on the lyre. Soon, as he touched the piercing-toned strings, he began to utter speech in a prelude (lovely was the voice that attended him): he wrought the undying gods and the black Earth, telling how first they came to be, and how each of them received by lot his share ⟨in the order of things⟩. First among the gods he honored Memory (*Mnemosyne*), mother of the Muses; for

> Hermes has fallen to her share. Next Hermes, glorious son of Zeus, honored the immortal gods in order of their age, telling how each came to be. All this he told in order, still playing the lyre held against his forearm, and Apollo's spirit in his chest was gripped by irresistible yearning."[25]

Such lyre-singing, according to some later Greek historians of music, was the oldest branch of Greek poetry. Thus it was that Demodocus, the Phaeacian bard, had performed (as we can still read for ourselves in the *Odyssey*); and thus, even before him, had figures of heroic legend like Orpheus, Thamyris, and Amphion.[26] Here, however, our business is with the professional kitharodes of the historical era, from the seventh century B.C. to about the middle of the fifth. After the Homeric Hymn, the most important literary testimony is a famous passage in Herodotus (1.23–24). The fabulous character of the incident, or at least of its ending, should not distract us from the fact that we here have a vision of a great kitharode described by a historian who was still living just within the song-culture period (Herodotus probably wrote his work between about 450 and 430 B.C.) and whose sympathies with the song-culture were deep, even influencing his manner of composition. Arion of Methymna, says Herodotus, "a kitharode second to none among the kitharodes of that time" (i.e., in the reign of Periander, about 600 B.C.), was once returning to Corinth from a tour in Italy and Sicily, in which he had made a great deal of money. On the high seas the sailors conspired to seize his goods, giving the artist himself the choice of committing suicide or jumping overboard. In response, Arion simply asks their permission first to sing, "in all his outfit," *tēi skeuēi pasēi*, standing on the poop-deck. Bloodthirsty though they are, the pirates are delighted by the thought of hearing a free concert by "the best singer among men" and they retire from the poop. Arion then "dresses in all his outfit," performs the Orthian nome, and jumps into the sea "with all his outfit." It is a relief to learn from Herodotus that he is saved by a dolphin, and thus finally appears in Corinth (need I say?) "with his outfit" to confront the malefactors. It is perhaps significant that only once elsewhere in his *Histories* does Herodotus employ the phrase "all his outfit," and that is in a description of the ceremonial costume of the Persian king (7.15.3). To the resulting picture of the professional kitharode in his gorgeous attire,[27] we can add one further item of literary evidence. One Phillis of Delos, a Hellenistic antiquarian, is reported as writing that "the ancient kitharodes allowed few movements of the features, but more movements of the feet, marching and dancing."[28]

Kitharodes are represented quite often on the Attic vase-paintings, and with especial frequency in the late archaic period. Probably the finest representation so far known is that by the Berlin Painter on an amphora in New York (Plate II), which not merely records with great beauty the external trappings of the kitharode (many other contemporary vase-paintings do that), but somehow, as far as drawing can, captures the very spirit of the singing and playing.[29] There are in fact two figures on the amphora, which is datable to the early years of the fifth century. On the reverse side stands a stately, bearded man, garlanded, wearing a *himation* and carrying a long forked wand in his left hand; his right hand is outstretched. Similar figures are found on other vase-paintings in the presence both of kitharodes and of athletes, and are naturally interpreted as trainers or judges, the wand being presumably used to inflict mild corrections.[30] The kitharode himself holds the ornate concert-lyre,[31] with a long embroidered and fringed flap hanging below it like a banner (and like a banner, too, it must have waved in performance, echoing and reinforcing the movements of the performer). He supports it partly in the crook of his left arm, partly by means of a strap athwart the left hand, whose fingers touch the strings. He has just completed a sweep of these strings with the plectrum in his right hand. His mouth is wide open, and his head is thrown back in the rapture of the song; his whole body is astir with the "marching movement" that was remarked on by Phillis of Delos. On his head is a garland. His costume is less spectacular than Herodotus's description would have led us to expect, but it is highly elegant, and quite unlike the costume of the contemporary Athenian-in-the-street; we should also allow for the fact that the red-figure technique has only the most limited resources for depicting variety of color. This vase, like many of the Berlin Painter's most brilliant works, permits no base lines. Absolutely nothing is to distract the eye from the human figures themselves, which float in the infinite curving space of the black-glazed ground. It is therefore only from other vase-paintings that we discover a further detail about the archaic kitharode performances, not recorded either here or in the literary sources: the performer (like the rhapsode Ion) was mounted on a platform.[32]

The question of what poems were actually performed by the kitharodes at the archaic festivals—of what words we should imagine to be

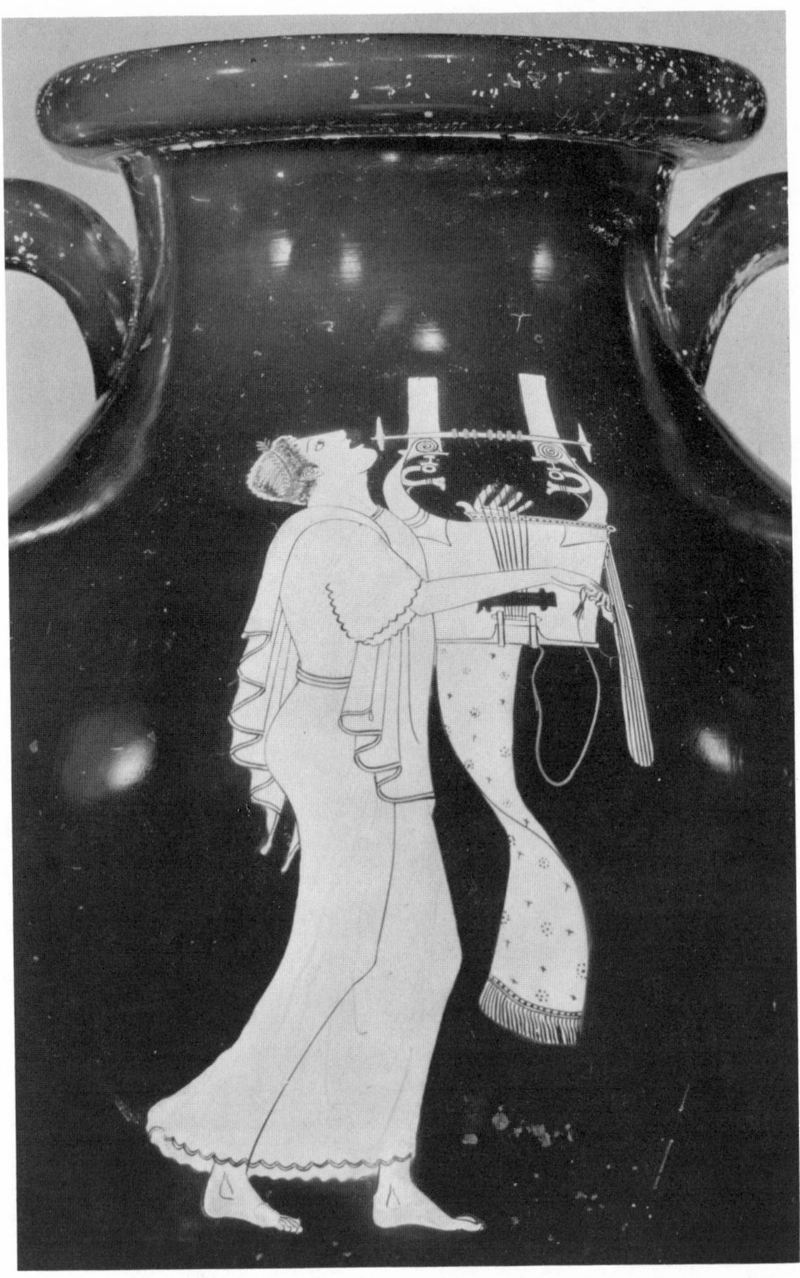

Plate II: Kitharode by the Berlin Painter (The Metropolitan Museum of Art, Fletcher Fund, 1956).

issuing from the mouth of the Berlin Painter's performer, for example—is extremely difficult to answer. The indirect testimony on the subject is late and highly confusing, and not a single undisputed verbal fragment has survived from the songs of the earlier kitharodes. References to the ancient evidence and to modern discussions of it will be found in Appendix III; in this place it seems best merely to state the salient points that seem to emerge, although in no case except the first can we assert their historical accuracy with great confidence.

All the ancient authorities agree that the work performed by the kitharode was called, for whatever reason, a *nomos*; in this musical-poetic context we translate the word as *nome*, although of course it is precisely the same as the Greek word for "law." In its purely musical aspect, the nome seems usually to have been a traditional melody; the rather restricted repertoire of such nome melodies was ascribed to the invention of certain early poet-musicians, above all to the renowned Terpander of Lesbos, who worked mainly in Sparta during the early to mid seventh century B.C. The words of a nome could be either traditional or composed by the kitharode himself. It is recorded of Terpander that "being a composer of kitharodic nomes, he set to music in each nome hexameter verses of his own and of Homer's, and sang them in the contests"[33] (Heraclides Ponticus *ap.* ps.-Plutarch, *De Musica* 1132c); he also composed "kitharodic preludes (*prooimia*) in hexameter verse" (ps.-Plutarch, ibid. 1132d). If this information is trustworthy, two points of considerable interest emerge from it: first, that the Homeric poems (or parts of them) were performed to lyre accompaniment in early times, as well as in the unaccompanied delivery of the rhapsodes;[34] second, that the characteristic meter of the early nomes was the hexameter.

Such seems to be the state of our knowledge, or perhaps, rather, our ignorance, about the earliest kitharodic poetry. If a contemporary scholar's suggestion is right, however, we possess relatively extensive fragments of such poetry from about the second quarter of the sixth century B.C., in the works of Stesichorus of Himera. M. L. West has argued, convincingly to the present writer, that both the fragments of this poet and the indirect tradition concerning him make best sense on the assumption that he worked primarily as a kitharode. The epic content and narrative manner of his compositions[35] and the almost epic scale of some of them[36] seem to fit more neatly into what we know of the earlier kitharodic tradition than into the practice of any other so-called lyric poet whose fragments survive, whether choral or monodic. Further, the overwhelmingly dactylic character of his verse, throughout the extant fragments, likewise sets him apart from the other "lyric" poets and may be thought to align him, rather, with the earliest kitharodes.[37] For something like a century after Stesichorus, we hear very little about the *creation* of poetry for performance in the kitharodic nomes, and it may well be that during that period the kitharodes mostly contented themselves and their audiences with virtuoso performances of already existing poems. In that case, it is not absolutely forbidden to imagine that the Berlin Painter's kitharode may be performing a poem by Terpander, Arion, or Stesichorus—his *Oresteia*, perhaps, or his *Helen*?[38] It is unlikely that in the Athens of that date he would be performing any part of the Homeric epics, since the *rhapsodic* performances of them were by then well established.

The second half of the fifth century saw a spectacular revival in the art of kitharody, but at the same time a revolution in the style, first of its music, and then of its poetry. The evidence both about the manner and about the content of this later kitharody is relatively abundant; it even includes over two hundred lines of the text of a famous nome by a very famous performer, the *Persians* of Timotheus. Discussion of this work, however, would take us well beyond the chronological limits of the present chapter: it will be reserved until the Epilogue.

THE PERFORMANCE OF CHORAL LYRIC

Two great poets provide by far the greatest proportion of our direct evidence concerning the performance of choral lyric: Alcman, who worked almost at the beginning of the tradition (at least, so far as it is preserved in writing; we have no way of telling how long it had existed before him), and Pindar, who culminated the tradition and saw it end.[39]

Alcman, who worked in Sparta about the middle of the seventh century B.C.,[40] gives the more vivid picture of the two, and that for a very strange reason. It is clear from the surviving fragments that some of his choral lyrics, at least, involved not merely the representation of divine and heroic legends, nor merely the measuring of human events against the lessons to be drawn from those legends (features we find in all the major genres of classical Greek poetry from Homer through tragedy). They involved also the dramatization—there can be no other word for it—of the poet himself in his aspect of composer and producer of the lyric, and of the chorus members who participated in it. These are lyrics, indeed, and lyrics of haunting beauty if not perhaps the most profound content; yet at the same time they are also dramas that represent the performance and even the rehearsal of lyrics. This aspect of Alcman's work comes out most clearly in those poems that he composed for performance by choruses of young women, the *Partheneia*, but there is some slight evidence that it may also have appeared in other classes of poem by him.[41]

Most students probably make their first acquaintance with Alcman (and often their first acquaintance with Greek choral lyric) in the great song partially preserved by the Louvre papyrus (fr. 1 *PMG*). From the first, tattered column of that papyrus (lines 1–34) they will hear, with many interruptions in the singing, what all their prior knowledge of archaic Greek poetry and art would have prepared them to hear. This is a song of heroes, of the great fight between Herakles and the sons of Hippokoon, and it is interspersed and concluded with general reflections on the rules that constrict mortal life (lines 13–21[?], 34–39). In principle, the student will later find that the choral lyric of Pindar and of Bacchylides works by similar means, and that the Attic tragedians themselves still stand within that same tradition, however subtly and magnificently they develop it. But at line 39—just after the midpoint of the song as it stood entire, on the most plausible reconstruction[42]—something amazing happens: the chorus begins to sing to itself, and about itself. Individual personalities emerge with extraordinary vividness from among the group of ten dancer-singers (the text allows us to know the number of the chorus also). We hear their names; we learn of their beauty, especially that of their leader (*chorāgos*, *chorostatis*) Hagesichora. They even confide to us their fear about the outcome of this lyric contest (for so it seems to be) with another, eleven-member, chorus: can they compete with them in the splendor of their beauty and adornments? In lines 64–68 we seem actually to glimpse some of their finery: the purple dress, the intricate snake-bangle of solid gold, the headscarf brought across the seas from Lydia. Yet against all that rival splendor, it seems, we must weigh the perfection of Hagesichora's singing voice. . . . And so the papyrus fades out, depriving us only of the last four lines of the song.[43]

A similar effect is found in the papyrus fragments of another song by Alcman (fr. 3, *PMG*), which is also presumably a *Partheneion*; at any rate the singing voice is feminine (lines 81, 83; cf. line 10). Here it happens that no trace has been preserved of any heroic narrative, and we are involved almost at once in the situation and the feelings of the chorus. In the present state of the papyrus, the singing comes across to us at first only fitfully: for example, in lines 5–8:

> Of women hymning in a lovely song . . . shall scatter the sweet sleep from [my?] eyes . . . drives me to go to the contest [*or* "gathering", *agōna*], just where I shall toss my yellow hair . . . delicate feet. . . .

Only at lines 61–72 does the papyrus let us hear the singing in all, or almost all, its fullness:

> and with shattering desire, more meltingly
> than sleep and death she[?] looks at me[?]:
> and not at all in vain her sweetness[?],
> but Astymeloisa answers me nothing,
> only, wearing her garland,
> like a star shooting through the brilliant sky,
> like a golden leafspray, or the delicate wing of . . . ,[44]
> on slender feet she has passed through and gone.
> The liquid charm
> of Kinyras[45] rests on her young-girl's hair. . . .

Here, where the song again fades into semi-intelligible fragments, it is worth pausing. The two *Partheneia* that we have considered present the girl dancers of Alcman's choruses with an astounding clarity, not only physically but psychologically: their garlands, their dress, their jewelry, their heads tossing in the dance, even the perfume wafted from the hair of the *assoluta*; their anxieties and their loves. We have to repeat that these poems are not just choral lyrics; they are *lyric dramatizations of lyrics*, and of extraordinary power. But the story does not stop there: the dramatizations embraced not merely the dancers, but also the composer himself. Thus it comes about that from Alcman we obtain the clearest picture we have of the choral lyric poet's profession. In the songs he presented himself as librettist and composer: in fragment 39 we hear:

> These words, this song
> Alcman discovered,
> piecing together
> the tongued[46] voice of partridges;

an idea apparently echoed, so far as the music goes, in fragment 40: "and I know the melodies of all the birds."[47]

But the choral poet's task did not end at warbling his wood-notes wild. Before him lay the practical problems of rehearsal and production, in which both dancers and musicians must be disciplined into bringing about the total effect that he was seeking, in a combination of words, music, and song. Alcman's poetry contained epithets, apparently of his own devising, for girls who performed the dance in their correct station, *homostoichoi* (fr. 33, literally "in the same line together"), and for the kind of chorister, still not unknown in modern choirs and ballets, who "likes to stand at the edge of the chorus," *philopsilos* (fr. 32). It seems not impossible that fragment 31, "you will destroy the Muse," was addressed to an errant singer, but this must remain a conjecture, since the source gives no context. There are bland or complimentary references to oboe accompaniment of the lyrics in fragments 37b and 87b, but fragment 109 gives three epithets, apparently highly derogatory, which the poet applied to bad oboists. The lyre, the *kithara*, was used for accompaniment too—"all of us that are girls praise our lyre player" Alcman puts, perhaps as a hint to the instrumentalist, into the mouth of a chorus (fr. 38)[48]—but we cannot tell whether Alcman ever used oboe and lyre together to accompany one and the same lyric (some of Pindar's lyrics certainly required this, as we shall see later). But there still remains to be quoted one of the most extraordinary of all the passages in Alcman, fragment 26:

> No longer, sweet-singing girls with holy voices,
> no longer can my legs bear me; gods, if I were a kingfisher,
> flying along with his halcyons over the whitecap wave,
> a bird, no sorrow in my heart, sea-purple, holy!

According to Antigonus of Carystus, the chief ancient source for this quotation, the speaker of these lines is Alcman himself, "weak with old age" (to quote Antigonus) "and unable to whirl around along with the choruses or with the dancing of the girls." We have no way of deciding whether Antigonus (or his source) found solid evidence for this statement elsewhere in the song from which he preserves these marvelous lines, or whether he has fallen for the temptation—which besets so many other scholars, both ancient and modern—of routinely identifying the "I" of a poem with the historical personality of the poet. Perhaps the latter is more likely; but anyway there seems little room for doubt that in these lines Alcman dramatized, whether or not in his own person, that melancholy role: the great ballet-master who has grown too old to keep up with his own class.[49]

The scanty external evidence about Alcman adds little to the vivid picture of archaic choral lyric *in performance* that emerges from the fragments of his own poetry. Only two later testimonies deserve discussion here. The first is a passage from the somewhat mysterious treatise which Page has entitled *Commentarius in Melicos* and which is preserved on an Oxyrhynchus papyrus datable roughly to the first or early second century A.D.[50] The author is discussing, with commendable evenhandedness, the old question of whether Alcman was a Lydian or a Spartan by birth.

> [It need cause no surprise][51] that the Lakedaimonians of that time should have appointed one who was a Lydian as *didaskalos* of their daughters and youths in their traditional choruses . . . but not yet to engage in contests[52] . . . ; and even now they employ an alien as *didaskalos* of their choruses.

There are several puzzles here, but the point immediately relevant to us is beyond doubt. To the anonymous and undatable (but evidently well-informed) writer, Alcman's position in Sparta was that of *didaskalos*, teacher or trainer of choruses; and this position had been retained in that highly conservative society until the writer's own day (or at least until that of his source). From our point of view, the title *didaskalos* is highly suggestive. It well denotes Alcman's function as we have seen it described in Alcman's own words: he must not only create the poem, the melody, and presumably the choreography; all of that is useless unless he can also realize the artistic totality by molding the performers to his will, by drilling them patiently in words, music, and dance. Further, the later history of the word (and of its related words, the verb *didaskein* and the abstract noun *didaskalia*) is of considerable interest to our entire inquiry. From the early fifth century onward it is in regular use as a technical term to denote (a) the poet-producers of the kind of lyric poetry called dithyramb, and (b) the poet-producers of tragedies and of comedies. In later writers the word is used to describe the poet-producers of other kinds of choral lyric also, and it may well be mere accident that we have no classical instances of this usage.[53] In any case, its history emphasizes rather strikingly the continuity and the similarity between the professions of pretragic poet and of tragedian. We probably have to imagine a Phrynichus or an Aeschylus as proceeding in much the same way and as facing many of the same difficulties in the rehearsal of a tragedy, as did Alcman in the rehearsal of a choral lyric some one hundred and fifty years before them. (Since, obviously, tragic poetry was not self-referential in the sense that Alcmanic lyric was, we have no firsthand evidence about the tragedians' methods of rehearsal. The only substantial item of indirect evidence about them known to me is late, and impossible to verify. I quote it here because it is not commonly known and, to me at least, has the ring of truth:

> Euripides the poet was rehearsing (*hypolegontos*) to his chorus members an ode that he had composed to music. When one of them laughed, Euripides said: "If you weren't insensitive and ignorant, you wouldn't be laughing at me for singing in the Mixolydian mode.")[54]

The second external testimony to be discussed is a passage from a book *On the Sacrifices in Lakedaimon* by the historian Sosibius. Sosibius was an expert both on Sparta and on Alcman (he is known to have written a treatise *On Alcman* in at least three books, and he is also cited in the papyrus scholia to the poet), and there is, further, reason to think that he was himself a Spartan; his date cannot be precisely fixed but may lie between about 250 and 150 B.C.[55] He here presents an account—which, considering his probable nationality and date and the conservative practices even of Hellenistic Sparta, could well be an *eyewitness* account—of certain ceremonies performed at the time of the Spartan festival of the Gymnopaidiai. A certain kind of garland called *Thyreatic*, he says, is carried by the leaders of the choruses in memory of the great Spartan victory over the Argives in the battle of Thyrea (datable to about 546 B.C.).

> And the choruses are: in front, boys, ⟨on the right, old men⟩, and on the left, grown men; they dance naked and sing songs by Thaletas and Alcman, and the paians of Dionysodotos the Laconian.[56]

What is interesting about this passage is not only the somewhat startling manner of performance (it is a pleasing, if fruitless, pastime to conjecture which if any of the extant fragments were thus delivered by rank upon rank of naked dancing males), but also the fact that some at least of Alcman's compositions were still being re-performed well into the

Hellenistic era. (This matter of re-performance will occupy us again in the next chapter.)

The Theban Pindar, our other major source of information about the performance of choral lyric, is immediately seen to differ from Alcman in two significant respects. In his extant poems and fragments he never dramatizes his own role as *didaskalos*;[57] and only in a few poems (none of them epinician odes) does he dramatize the role of the chorus. One reason for the former omission seems clear from the evidence of the primary texts alone: Pindar did not normally, and in practice often simply could not, undertake the actual rehearsal and production of his poems. His work was in demand in places as far apart as Tenedos, Rhodes, Cyrene, and Sicily. He might simply "send" (*pempein*) a minor poem for performance in the home of the person who had commissioned it; on one occasion at least he seems to have dispatched a *chorodidaskalos* to supervise the performance of an important ode (*Ol.* 6: see Appendix IV for details of this and of the other matters discussed in this section). The ancient biographical tradition adds to this the fact that he couldn't sing,[58] which would certainly have been a grave disadvantage in rehearsal.[59] We have to turn to the same tradition for the information, which seems in itself credible enough, that Pindar was a trained oboist and lyre player, having been taught the former of these arts by his uncle, and the latter by Lasus of Hermione.

Our only quite certain information, however, must come from the surviving texts of Pindar's poetry. It is natural to begin with the fragments of his *Partheneia*, which at least one ancient critic already recognized as standing apart, stylistically, from the rest of his work.[60] On our more limited knowledge, at least one of them also stands apart in that it dramatizes the chorus almost in the Alcmanic fashion; modern students have suggested, reasonably, that Pindar here consciously follows the precedent set by Alcman.[61] It is the *Partheneion* numbered II in Snell's edition,[62] designed to be sung in a procession to a shrine of Apollo, presumably the Ismenion, in Pindar's own city of Thebes. As in so much other Pindaric singing, the glory of the immortal god is here—momentarily—fused with the glory of a mortal community and a mortal family, in this case the noble house of Aioladas.

For Apollo comes, gladly,
to blend his immortal charm with Thebes.
But quickly I shall gird my robe,

and in my gentle hands
holding a glorious (*aglaon*) branch of bay,
I shall hymn the famous house of Aioladas
and of his son Pagondas;
I, a girl, my head flowering with garlands,
miming the splendor of a siren song
to woodwind melody . . . (lines 3–15)[63]

After, in fact, singing the praises of that house, the chorus returns to its own situation in the streets of Thebes; we seem actually to be present at the marshalling of the procession, now that the girls are properly adorned for it. They address the boy who is to lead them, and mention the girl, a relative, who is to follow in his steps:[64]

Son of Damaina, lead my way!
Step on with happy omens!
First on the road your[?] daughter, full of gladness,
will follow you, close by the bay-tree's noble leaves,
marching in sandalled feet;[65]
she whom Andaisistrota
trained with her counsels[?] . . . (lines 66–72)

In Pindar's *Partheneion* II, as so often in Alcman, we are brought very close to participation in the production of a choral lyric; missing is only the vivid presence of the *didaskalos* himself.[66] But that remains the only passage of the kind in the extant work of Pindar. In two of his *Paeans*, the choruses have a national identity and to that extent may be said to be dramatized,[67] but to that extent alone.

And what of the performance of the most familiar poems by Pindar, the epinician odes? Here the evidence is extraordinarily scanty—far more scanty than is perhaps generally recognized—and for that reason what there is of it seems worth considering in some detail. We have to concede at once that the voluminous ancient scholia on the epinicians contain no more authentic information about the locations where the odes were performed, or about their manner of performance, than we moderns can deduce from the bare texts themselves. On other questions the scholia or, rather, their Hellenistic sources have preserved invaluable factual information; but what external evidence could even the most industrious Hellenistic researcher possibly have uncovered about the actual production of the songs? The kind of person who produced or witnessed a victory ode, whether in a Sicilian tyrant's palace or on some aristocratic estate in Orchomenos or Rhodes, was not the kind of person (particularly during the first two-thirds of the fifth century) to leave a written record about it.[68] To my knowledge, there exists only one reliable external testimony to the manner in which an epinician ode might be performed in the classical period, and that is not in the Pindar scholiasts but in Aristophanes, *Clouds* (produced in 423 B.C.) 1355–58. Here Strepsiades tells the audience that after dining with his son (who has just been instructed in the New Learning by Socrates), he told the young man "to take the lyre and sing a song by Simonides, 'How the Ram Was Shorn'; but he at once began to say that it was out of date to play the lyre and sing over the drinks, just like a woman grinding barley." Simonides' "Ram" poem was in fact an epinician ode for the Aeginetan wrestler Krios (Simonides, fr. 507 *PMG*). The circumstances, obviously, are not like those in which the epinician would originally have been performed; and yet it seems of some interest that by 423 B.C.[69] a middle-aged Athenian can expect, apparently as a matter of routine, to hear the song performed by a soloist accompanying himself on the lyre.[70]

We shall return to that point at a later stage. First, however, it will be worthwhile to summarize the information about the performance of epinician odes that can be more or less certainly deduced from the Pindaric texts themselves (the references in detail are collected in Appendix IV). That the odes were normally performed in the hometown of the victor is a natural assumption which is not contradicted by the texts. Only quite rarely, however, are we given any more precise information about the place of performance. Tolerably certain instances are the eleventh Pythian, sung in the Ismenion at Thebes, toward nightfall (lines 1–10); the first and ninth Nemeans, designed for performance in the banqueting-hall of Chromios at Aitna (*Nem.* 9.1–3; 9.48–52 suggests fairly strongly that the occasion is a symposium); the tenth Nemean, performed in or near the prytaneum at Tenedos (lines 1–7); and the eighth Isthmian, before the house of the victor's father (line 3). Somewhat fewer than half of the odes contain information about their own instrumental accompaniment (we may note, without comment for the moment, that of these only one happens to be addressed to a victor whose hometown is on the Greek mainland). The lyre, the *phorminx* (less often, *lyra*), is mentioned in almost all of these cases; both lyre and oboe are mentioned as accompanying five odes, all of them of considerable length;[71] the oboe as sole accompaniment is mentioned only in *Ol.* 5, which is probably not Pindar's work, but we may perhaps guess at its presence in the performance of *Pyth.* 12.[72] We may tentatively conclude that in the accompaniment of an epinician ode the lyre was de rigueur, the combination of lyre and oboe reserved for the more elaborate and costly productions, the solo oboe unusual. Finally, eight of the odes (only one of them for a mainland client) appear to incorporate information about the musical style in which they are to be performed: "in Aeolic song," for example (*Ol.* 1.102), or "in the Lydian fashion" (*Ol.* 14.17).

In a few famous passages two or more of the components in a choral lyric production—words, instrumental music, and dance—are presented together, and we gain some faint idea of the relationship between them.

> The garlands pressed like a yoke on the hair exact from me payment of this debt laid up by the gods: to blend together properly the lyre with her intricate voice, and the shout of oboes, and the placing of words. (*Ol.* 3.6–9)[73]

> Lyre of gold! . . . to which the dance-step, beginning of joyful triumph, listens; and singers obey your signals, each time you fashion, quivering, the opening notes of the preludes! Why, you even quench the thunderbolt, with his lance of ever-streaming fire . . . and your arrows bewitch the hearts even of gods. (*Pyth.* 1.1–6, 21)

It should be noted that that marvelous passage describes the situation only at a specific moment, the instrumental prelude to the choral lyric. At this stage, certainly, the lyre issues "signals" to the dancer-singers, who wait as modern athletes wait for the starter's gun (and probably with similar tensions). Thereafter, however, there is no question as to which of the three elements in the performance is to rule: it is the poetry. *Anaxiphorminges hymnoi*, "songs lords-of-the-lyre," is the famous phrase that opens the second Olympian ode; and both the majestic adjective and the idea seem to be echoed, a few years later,[74] in an epinician ode by Bacchylides.

Somewhat surprisingly, the Pindaric texts present, on examination, only the vaguest picture of the singer-dancers themselves. There is no indication whatsoever of their number in any given ode; we know that they are plural, but beyond that we can only conjecture at what point the number may have fallen within the extreme ranges that are attested for choral lyrics other than epinicians: ten, and a hundred (see Appendix IV). Wherever their sex is mentioned they prove to be men, and where their age is mentioned they prove to be young. They wear garlands, they step springily; in four passages they appear to sing as a body, besides dancing; in an epinician ode by Bacchylides they are "fair-limbed." One has the impression that they are probably gentleman amateurs, friends and relatives of the victor and of his family. This impression is perhaps confirmed by the rather surprising fact that they are not once referred to collectively as a *choros*, or individually as *choreutai*, although Pindar uses both words (and Bacchylides uses *choros*) often enough with reference to nonepinician performances. The word most commonly used to describe them collectively is *kōmos*, which elsewhere in Greek denotes a wild, rather disorganized, and often intoxicated revel. In one relatively early passage it is in fact distinguished from a *choros*.[75]

That is all, or practically all, the solid evidence about the performance of epinician choral lyric that can be collected from the texts themselves. I have to admit that when I set out to collect it I had expected to arrive at a far more distinct picture. What we have, in fact, allows much room for speculation; and to speculation the remainder of this section will now frankly be devoted. In view of the evidence and, equally, the lack of evidence, about epinician performances, two questions seem at least worth posing.

First, what exactly happened on the occasions when Pindar "sent" an ode to a distant recipient? We have seen that on one occasion he probably dispatched a trusted *chorodidaskalos* from the studio in Thebes (*Ol.* 6.87–100): the entire production, music, dance, and all, would then presumably conform to Pindar's own design. It seems unlikely, however, that this expensive procedure would be followed in all cases. We then have to consider the possibility that the recipient of the ode would be sent simply a bare text and that the performance (in Aitna, or Akragas, or Cyrene, or Tenedos) would be evolved on the basis of the indications in that text alone. *Musical* notation almost certainly did not exist at this period (the question will be further considered in the next chapter);[76] no *choreographic* notation of much practical value was to be devised until the work of Rudolph Von Laban in the early twentieth century A.D. We are left, it seems, with the strong possibility that a local *didaskalos* would work up a production, devising the music and choreography in accordance with the indications embodied in the script received from Pindar. Such indications were not few. The meter itself no doubt dictated with absolute precision the rhythms of the music and dance. We have already seen how a number of the texts contain built-in directions on the instrumental accompaniment and even on the musical mode. It is also worth recalling that the vast majority of the odes that contain such directions are destined for overseas recipients.[77]

The second question is this: who actually sang the epinician odes? It is usually assumed without question that the entire chorus delivered the poems in unison; and four of the odes in fact contain allusions which, on the most reasonable interpretation, seem to suggest this, even if they do not quite prove it.[78] I confess, however, that my imagination falters before the vision of a performance of (say) the fourth Pythian ode in unison from end to end. Perhaps it is worth considering the possibility that in this and some other cases the poem was delivered by a solo voice—or an alternation of solo voices?[79]—while the *corps de ballet* (or better, *corps de kōmos*) danced in sympathy with the poetry. Performances of that mixed kind were certainly known to Greek practice from the time of Homer[80] down to Hellenistic Sparta; compare Polykrates' account (above, p. 7) of the dancers weaving in and out among the choruses who sang "the national songs." One may further recall the solo performance of a Simonidean epinician, attested in Aristophanes' *Clouds*. But at this point even speculation about the epinician odes reaches its justifiable limits.[81]

THE PERFORMANCE OF OTHER KINDS OF POETRY

After we have considered the kinds of early Greek poetry that figured most prominently in the great festival contests—Homeric epic, kitharodic poetry, and choral lyric—we are still of course left with a vast body of poems of most varied form, manner, and content. If we contemplate these remaining poems simply as texts lying etherized on the paper (or vellum, or papyrus), the only common factor that we shall find in them is that they are for the most part comparatively *short* pieces: few, if any, seem to have attained to the length of Pindar's fourth Pythian ode or Stesichorus's *Oresteia*, and none whatever to the amplitude of the epic. In most, so far as our admittedly very imperfect evidence goes, the limits seem to have varied between about ten and one hundred lines.

When we proceed to the next (and, for the really conscientious inquirer into early Greek poetry, the inevitable) step of contemplating them not as *texts* but as live *performances*, we find, first, that their running time was thus remarkably brief—between a couple of minutes and a quarter of an hour.[82] A second factor common to the poems under consideration will be found to be that all, as far as we can see, were designed for delivery by a solo voice. Finally, with the exception of one notable early group of the poems, all appear to have been composed for relatively small private gatherings, especially symposia; and, as a matter of history, to have been normally performed in such gatherings by the later date at which the evidence permits us to see them in performance at all. That evidence, unfortunately, is exceptionally fragmentary and diverse in nature. It is scattered here and there not only among our primary texts and secondary ancient literary sources, but also among the vase-paintings. Even so, it seems to add up to a tolerably reliable picture, of which the outlines will be drawn here. For the details, the reader is referred to Appendix V.

We may begin with the notable exception, mentioned above, to the rule that the poetry under consideration was designed for private gatherings. Certain early poems, mostly of the seventh century B.C., seem to have been composed and received as instruments of war or of politics. A poem (or poems) by the mid-seventh-century elegist Callinus of Ephesus exhorted his fellow citizens to rouse themselves to war in the face of the Cimmerian invasion; and there are traces of poems that may have had a similar tendency in the fragments of the elegist Mimnermus of Smyrna, a younger contemporary, perhaps, of Callinus. These Ionian poems, however, have reached us (as usual) without any external indications of the context within which they were performed, and we cannot exclude the possibility that they were composed (e.g.) for symposia attended by somewhat militaristic persons (the Veterans of Cimmerian Wars, it might be). It is the analogy presented by the work of yet another mid-century elegist, the Spartan Tyrtaeus, that may incline us to think otherwise. The internal evidence of Tyrtaeus's poems and the unusually solid external evidence about their function in later Spartan life leave little room for doubt: *these were instruments of civil and military policy*. How and where his elegiac poem entitled, at least later in antiquity, the *Eunomia* (frr. 1–4W) was published to the Spartan community, we can only conjecture. It is difficult to believe, however, that this firm reminder of the Spartan system of government was not addressed to that community as a whole, and there is no reason to doubt Aristotle's inference from the poem that it was meant to reconcile a dissension between the haves and have-nots among the citizenry (*Politics* 5.1306b, 1307a). The bulk of the remaining elegiac fragments contain reminders of earlier Spartan successes, and stern exhortations to further war and to heroism in battle; those who wish to imagine what it felt like to be a Greek hoplite waiting in the line for the enemy to attack will find no more vivid or terrifying descriptions than those in frr. 10.15–32W, 11.21–34, 12.10–22. Such poems can hardly have been chanted by the soldiers on the march (as anyone who has tripped over his own feet while trying to recite an elegiac couplet on the march will know to his cost!), or in the battle line itself. Here, however, some external testimonies may perhaps safely be invoked. Although both are much later than Tyrtaeus, they are credible in themselves; and once more we should remember that in the conservative society of Sparta, institutions were apt to be perpetuated unchanged for many centuries. The fourth-century B.C. Athenian orator Lycurgus (*in Leocratem* 107), in quoting the long fragment 10W for the edification of his audience, observes that the Spartans have a law that

> when they are on a military expedition they are to summon all the soldiers to the king's tent to hear the poems of Tyrtaeus, being of the opinion that by these means the soldiers would be most ready to die for their country.

About a generation later another Athenian, the historian Philochorus, recorded that it was the custom of the Spartans on campaign each in turn to chant (*aidein*) the poems of Tyrtaeus, after dinner; and for the general to give a prize of meat to the winner in that contest (Philochorus *ap.* Athen. 14.630f). It is in such circumstances that we may imagine the delivery of Tyrtaeus's elegiacs. That he also wrote "war songs" (*Souda*, s.v. *Tyrtaios*) or "march songs," *embatēria* (Athen., loc. cit.), seems certain; these can probably be identified with the "poems" by him which "the Spartans in their wars recite from memory, marching in rhythm to them" (ibid.). Unfortunately, no texts of this kind certainly attributable to Tyrtaeus have survived.[83]

The latest and in many ways the most extraordinary of this series of poets is Solon the Athenian. His earliest known poem was a major political act: the hundred-line[84] elegy *Salamis*, in which he urged his fellow citizens to go out and renew their war for the island, then occupied by the Megarians. It is difficult to know what weight to attach to the circumstantial stories told by much later authorities, who have Solon feign madness, "leap out" into the Athenian Agora, and declaim the *Salamis* (or have it declaimed by a herald), with completely successful political and strategic results.[85] But fortunately the opening lines of the poem itself seem to embody the information that it was designed for a public gathering of the Athenians; and what more likely place for that, at any date, than the Agora? "I came as a herald in my own person from lovely Salamis, putting the glory of verses in place of public speech."[86] In this earliest poem Solon seems to follow directly in the footsteps of Tyrtaeus, using the poet's art as an instrument of war; although it may be significant that, in the less austere and regimented society of Athens toward the year 600, his appeal (at least in the extant fragments) is to the citizens' sense of bitter shame rather than to the prospect of winning death or honor in the hoplite line. But if the *Salamis* anticipated, in purpose and function, Demosthenes' *Philippic Orations* of two and a half centuries later, a large proportion of Solon's subsequent poems anticipated, rather, such speeches as *On the Crown*. In elegiacs, for the most part, he diagnosed the state of Athenian society and warned against the growing threat of tyranny.[87] In two meters which had long been cultivated also by the Ionian poets and were to surface again as the staple dialogue meters of Attic tragedy well within a century—the iambic trimeter and the trochaic tetrameter catalectic—Solon explained and justified his policy as lawgiver. One would give much to know the circumstances in which this group of poems was performed. In one case, only, a late external testimony survives. Diogenes Laertius (1.49) has him "rush" into the Assembly, the *Ekklesia*, with spear and shield (Solon's entrances appear to have been nothing if not dramatic!), and, on being accused of madness, retort with the elegiac couplet, fragment 10W. Again, there is no knowing how such information is to be evaluated, and the fragments of the poems themselves give no hint on their circumstances of performance. We can only surmise that in them too, Solon employed "the glory of verses in place of public speech" and that they were probably meant for declamation in some public place. We must also note that the iambic and tetrameter poems are pervaded by the *first person singular*. Whether they were declaimed by Solon himself or by a professional declaimer, a herald (we have seen how one version of the

Salamis incident has a herald pronounce that poem), the effect must have been that of a formal dramatization. The meditated verses, wrought with amazing skill—above all, the great iambic fragment 36 seems technically and stylistically far ahead of its time[88]—read aloud, leave us with the impression not quite of the living and breathing Solon but of a majestic, grave persona considerably larger than life. If a Lawgiver had had any place among the heroic cast of Attic tragedy, it would be in these tones, in this manner, and in this very meter that he would speak. Hardly a change would be necessary.

The nonpolitical poems of Solon, in contrast, fit naturally into the vast body of archaic solo poetry—elegiac, iambic, and monodic lyric—which is now to be considered from the point of view of performance. Indeed, a number of these Solonic works (frr. 6.3–4, 15, 24) were later incorporated into the elegiac "songbook" that we now know as the *Theognidea*, in which context they are perfectly at home, indeed, not easy to distinguish from the surrounding poems.[89] In general, it is safe to say that practically all the diverse kinds of poems now to be examined have this in common: they were designed for performance at informal private gatherings, as opposed to the formal setting of the agora, the civic assembly, or the festival-contest. We must certainly allow for possible exceptions; but that is the inference to be drawn at once from the content and tone of the overwhelming majority of these poems.

The literary evidence about the precise manner of performance of these various kinds of poem is very scanty, as one might expect from the mere fact that the circumstances were private. For example, the only external testimony that I have come across to the performance of the works of a poet as great as Sappho is a passage from Aelian (*ap.* Stobaeus, *Florilegium* 29.88):

> Solon's nephew Exekestides once sang a song by Sappho over the wine. Solon was delighted with the song, and told the boy to teach it to him. When asked why he was so keen on this, Solon answered: "So that I may learn it and die."

One would dearly like to believe this charming anecdote, which sounds so true to life: that is how monodic lyric (as we shall see) was often performed in Athens at a later date; that is how one would expect Solon to respond to a good song. But if it is true to life, the overwhelming odds are that the truth has been hit by fortunate guesswork, for it is hard to see from what genuine sixth-century source Aelian (*floruit* ca. 200 A.D.) could have picked up such a story.[90]

The remaining literary evidence concerning the performance of monodic poetry is distributed casually among many late sources, but its only firm results can be summarized in a single sentence. The monodic lyricist sang her (or his) poetic-musical composition to her (or his) own accompaniment on a stringed instrument, usually the lyre or its somewhat less respectable relative the *barbitos*; and the occasion of the performance was apt to be a wine party. The tradition mentions by name Sappho and Anacreon as composers of their own lyre music, and also as lyre players; it happens to mention Alcaeus and Ibycus merely as lyre players, but we may plausibly guess that in fact they too were their own composers. So far as the lyre-playing goes, the literary evidence is corroborated by surprisingly ample evidence in late archaic and early classical art (see Appendix V). As early as the last decade of the sixth century B.C. a woman bearing a lyre and inscribed PHSAPHO (= Sappho) appears on an Attic vase. Between then and the middle of the fifth century, we have other certainly identifiable representations (mostly on the vases) of Sappho, Alcaeus, Anacreon (cf. Plate III), and Anacreon's much less famous contemporary Cydias, of whom the majority are depicted carrying lyres. In further confirmation of the literary indications, the last two of the poets named are shown on the vases as energetic participants in the revels of the symposium. There are even a few vases, all showing symposia, on which inscribed scraps of monodic-type lyric proceed from the mouths of the reclining participants. On one vase the author of the fragment can be identified with a fair degree of certainty as the Argive poet Praxilla (fr. 754 *PMG*); on another, the fragment is new to us (fr. S317 *SLG*; there placed among the *adespota*, although Vermeule's interesting suggestion that Anacreon could possibly be the author is also noted). Of both these vases it should be observed that (a) the performer is not the poet,[91] but simply a member of a symposium, Boeotian in the former vase (datable to about 470), Athenian in the latter (datable to the late sixth century); and (b) both singers appear to be accompanied not by the expected lyre but by the oboe. We have to allow, it seems, for the possibility that monodic lyric (like much eighteenth-century *Tafelmusik*) was so composed that it could be performed with any instrument that came to hand, ad lib.

Such evidence as the vase-paintings provide on gnomic elegiac poetry

Plate III: Anacreon with his lyre, by Oltos (courtesy of British Museum).

suggests that this genre, also, was normally performed in the symposium or in some private party of a similar kind. In the tondo of an Attic kylix of about 490 B.C. a bearded man reclines on a cushioned couch, as one did at a symposium.[92] From his open mouth proceed the words ὦ παίδων κάλλιστε, "O most beautiful of boys," which are identical with a half-line in the *Theognidea* (1129W); in his left hand he holds a pair of castanets, with his right he fondles a hare (destined as a present to the object of his song?), which sits below his couch. On a fragmentary calyx crater in Copenhagen by the early Kleophrades Painter, Immerwahr has read the word [π]ενίης, "of poverty," apparently proceeding from the mouth of a lyre player in a symposium, and has suggested, with some plausibility, that we may be present at the delivery of *Theognidea* 1365. Finally, one side of the Boeotian vase of about 470, already mentioned, shows a symposium scene at which one reclining participant is playing the lyre while another, two places away from him, is apparently uttering the words φασὶν ἀληθῆ ταῦτα, "they say that this is true"; the phrase does not occur in extant Greek poetry, but the meter and the sense together are consistent with the probability that it is a fragment of gnomic elegiac poetry.

This visual evidence, so far as it goes, is confirmed by several passages in the corpus of *Theognidea* itself (e.g., 239–40), as well as by some of the later external testimonies. We are reasonably safe in assuming that from the beginning the natural habitat of elegiac poetry was the symposium or similar gathering. It is in this context that we had best imagine (for instance) the performance of the nonpolitical elegies of Solon, the gnomic poetry of the *Theognidea*, Mimnermus's poems about love and death, and at least some of Xenophanes' elegiacs (for example, fr. B1W, which incidentally embodies one of the richest extant descriptions of the external apparatus and the general tone of an archaic symposium). The mere enumeration of these varied poets, and of the monodic poets whose work we saw earlier to have been performed in the same milieu, should be enough to suggest that the institution of the symposium may have been of crucial importance in the genesis, dissemination, and transmission of archaic Greek poetry. Unfortunately, neither the visual nor the literary evidence allows us to be sure exactly how the elegiac poems were normally delivered in the symposia. The old notion that they were regularly delivered to oboe accompaniment can no longer be sustained in the light of all our evidence.[93] Indeed, that evidence rather suggests that practice varied from occasion to occasion: one might utter them now to the rhythmic clack of castanets, now to the strumming of the lyre, now (perhaps) to no accompaniment at all. Only one point seems reasonably sure, and that is that the mode of delivery in the sixth century, at least, is much more likely to have been unadorned speech (*legein*) or nonmelodic chant (one sense of *aidein*) than fully melodic *song*. Whatever may have been the practice of the very earliest elegiac poets, it is probably significant that our sources never speak of Solon, Theognis, or Xenophanes as lyre or oboe performers, still less as composers; the contrast with the traditions about the monodic lyricists is very striking in this respect.

From our point of view, the *iambic* poets of archaic Greece present a complicated problem. In general, one would be inclined to assume from the content and manner of their extant fragments that their works were performed (like those of the elegists) primarily at symposia, and that their iambics, choliambs, and trochaic tetrameters, at least, were delivered without musical accompaniment. No evidence, internal or external, survives to control this subjective impression where Semonides,

Hipponax, and Ananius are concerned.[94] Archilochus is another matter. Later tradition is unanimous in attributing to him—just as it does to the great monodic lyrists—the use of the lyre to accompany his own poems; and an Attic vase-painting in Boston of about 460 B.C. seems to indicate that this tradition already existed in the Greek classical period. Against that must be set the relatively early evidence which indicates that on occasion some of his poems were delivered by rhapsodes (and therefore, almost certainly, without musical accompaniment); and perhaps also the observation made in modern times that certain of the fragments are reminiscent of the "political" poems of Solon and might well have been spoken at public gatherings. Provisionally, our only safe conclusion from all this must be that Archilochus was just as versatile and innovative in the matter of performance styles as he quite evidently was in metrics and subject matter. Beyond that is guesswork only, but a fair guess might be that his iambic trimeters were designed for unaccompanied delivery, his epodes for (sporadic?) accompaniment on the lyre.

CONCLUSION

In this chapter I have concentrated simply on the evidence that relates to the performance of the major kinds of Greek nondramatic poetry. Many details, undoubtedly, will need to be modified in the light of future inquiries, but the general picture of what I have called, for short, the "song culture" which prevailed in archaic and early classical Greece will perhaps still be acceptable. Even a brief contemplation of that picture will be enough to make the reader realize the scale and nature of the problems it presents to a modern inquirer into Greek literary (so-called) and dramatic history. Some of these problems will be faced in the following chapter. Here it will be convenient to summarize the bearing of what has been said so far on our overall theme, the relation between Greek poetry and Attic tragedy.

First, and above all, there is seen to be no unbridgeable gap between the poetry and the drama of the Greeks, as there is between our poetry and our drama. Both were performing arts. At least one variety of poetic performance, the rhapsodized epic, probably involved scarcely less histrionic ability than was required of the Greek tragic actor; and the same may well have been true of Archilochian and Solonian iambic delivery. Another variety of poetic performance, the choral lyric, drew, as tragic drama was later to draw, on the arts of dance and music as well as on verbal art, and (notably in Alcman's hands) had a strong tendency to become a kind of drama in itself. The tragic poet seems also to have inherited the function and the very title of *didaskalos* from the choral lyricists. Finally the tragedies, like rhapsody, kitharody, and several kinds of choral lyric, were performed in officially organized contests, *agōnes mousikoi*, which were attached, mostly at quite definable dates, to certain of the great religious festivals. Many of the poetic elements that later, combined, will surprise and charm us in Attic tragedy have already come into being in the Greek song culture by the middle of the sixth century B.C., but still remain separate. To blend them into a single art, which in that very process will become a *new* art, will be the achievement of Athens in the time of her tyrants.

2. Text and Re-performance

The previous chapter attempted a survey of archaic Greek song as it must have appeared, so to speak, from the outside: from the point of view of the audiences who watched and heard performances of the various kinds of poetry. Here we shall try to probe more deeply and to ask certain questions about the way in which the poems were composed and transmitted. In this matter, for lack of evidence, few of our answers can be altogether dependable and none can be precise. Yet the questions at least have to be posed if we are to grasp the extraordinary situation of the archaic poet and of his heir, the Attic tragedian.

The archaic Greek song culture differed most radically from the song cultures of Appalachia, or of most others known to history, in this: although its *performances* were universally oral, it rested on a firm substructure of carefully meditated written texts. Only the existence of written texts can account for its astounding sophistication, refinement, and variety and also for the transmission and preservation of its songs in reasonably uncorrupt form. When one turns from a Border ballad or an Appalachian song, however moving in content, to a song by Sappho or Alcman, one is taken captive by the sheer craftsmanship of the archaic Greek verses. Like the marble sculptures of the same era, they combine two apparently opposite qualities: they are cut with absolute precision and yet are vibrant with spontaneous life. In contrast, the English songs picked up for us by the folklorists come in different versions from different settlements, and in all of them the original edges seem to have been rubbed away by centuries of truly illiterate transmission. I do not feel competent to pronounce a dogmatic judgment on the question of whether Homer's poetry itself was composed (and so transmitted) in writing. Very great scholars have taken flatly opposed positions on that for the last two centuries. Yet it is only fair to the reader to record here my own working hypothesis that the Homeric epics too must have been embodied in a text (perhaps, as Wade-Gery[1] and others have suggested, the first of all book texts in the Western tradition) from the beginning. Otherwise we should hardly be fortunate enough to find in them something like those contrasting qualities that we find in Sappho and Alcman.

We begin with two interlocking questions which concern, in a word, transmission. First, what were the form and the function of the written texts of Greek nondramatic poetry generally, before the Hellenistic era? Second, how were the music and (in some cases) the choreography of early lyric poetry preserved, as they seem to have been, well into the fourth century B.C., if not later?

THE NATURE AND FUNCTION OF THE ALEXANDRIAN EDITIONS

It is of course a crucial fact for the Greek scholar (and indeed for the historian of European civilization) that almost all the classical Greek poems we still have, both dramatic and nondramatic, owe their present form to the learned men who worked, mostly in Alexandria, from the third to the first century B.C. They brought together the scattered texts from all over the Greek world, sorted them out, and disposed them in editions that for the most part are the direct textual ancestors of our own. Thanks to the scholiastic material preserved in the mediaeval manuscript tradition and to the great numbers of papyri that have come to light in the present century, it is now possible to form quite a clear idea of the appearance of such an Alexandrian edition.[2] We can obtain an equally clear idea of the most usual function of such a book, whether in the schoolroom or in the salon: it was to be *read aloud*, with all possible attention to appropriate delivery, *hypokrisis*. What is the very first part of literary study, *grammatikē*? It is, says the Alexandrian-born scholar Dionysius Thrax in the second century B.C., the proper distinguishing and pronunciation of the written letters in the text

> in order that we may read aloud tragedy heroically, comedy in the voice of ordinary life, elegiac poems in clear and plaintive tones [*ligyrōs*, a word never easy to translate], epic forcibly, lyric poetry melodiously.[3]

The Alexandrian poetry book, in short, has begun to approach the function of a mediaeval or modern poetry book, to the extent that it expects its reader to treat the poems simply as *verbal* structures and to ignore the elements of gesture, dance, melody, and musical accompaniment. At least, however, those verbal structures were still to be translated into sound before the poem truly achieved its being (for only through *hypokrisis*, adds Dionysius Thrax, shall we attain to "the specific excellence, the *aretē*, of the poets"). The final step toward our present condition, the treatment of a literary text as something to be gathered by the eye from the surface of the page, was not generally taken until the end of antiquity.[4]

For our immediate purpose, the important point that clearly emerges from all our present knowledge is that the Alexandrian editions of the lyric and dramatic poets *included no musical notation*. This is now a generally accepted fact: the question is, why?

Several students have assumed that the lyrics of Pindar, for example, were musically notated from the first, and some have believed that musically scored texts arrived in Alexandria at the time when the library was forming its collection, in the early third century B.C. Pfeiffer, in his great *History of Classical Scholarship*, goes so far as to criticize the Alexandrian scholars for concentrating purely on the letters of the *text* in their editions, and thus consigning the heritage of Greek lyric and dramatic music to oblivion.[5] With great deference, both to Pfeiffer's learning and to the historians of Greek music, one must submit that there is another and, on our present evidence, a more likely explanation for the Alexandrian scholars' omission. There is as yet no convincing proof that any form of practical musical notation existed in Greece before the late fourth century B.C. The fifth-century vase-paintings, according to a distinguished student of these matters,[6] show no trace of any such thing, nor is there any mention of it in the numerous writers of the late fifth and the fourth centuries B.C. who touch on music, from Aristophanes through Aristotle. Only in the latter part of the fourth century do we find a passage in Aristoxenus that clearly refers to some kind of musical notation (*parasēmainesthai*, *hē parasēmantikē*), but the exact significance even of that may be disputed.[7] And when we are at last in a position to inspect an actual Greek musical score, approximately in the middle of the third century B.C., what we find is not so much a score in the modern sense (for example, the score of a Schubert song, from which any competent performer can produce a tolerably faithful rendition at sight) as what appears to be a rough and inadequate outline of a melody.

In short, even if the lyric texts of Sappho, Pindar, and the rest actually had reached the Alexandrian library equipped with musical notations, those notations would scarcely have been worth incorporating in a scholarly edition. They would have been useless to anyone who possessed no prior training in the practical rendition of the songs concerned. Surely the most probable inference from our available evidence is that no such musically notated texts existed in archaic or classical Greece. While conceding, as any prudent person must, that this inference could be refuted tomorrow by the turn of an archaeologist's spade anywhere in the lands surrounding the Mediterranean, we may at least provisionally consider its consequences. They are as follows. Just as the pitch accents of the spoken Greek language never needed to be written down until after Alexander the Great's conquests, so the music of the archaic and classical Greek lyrics required no notation until about the same period. Neither written accentuation nor written musical notes were wanted so long as the Greek-speaking world remained an ethnic and cultural unity, so long as its city-states maintained their traditional institutions, transmitted from father to son and teacher to pupil, and so long as its poetry remained essentially a performing art, whether in the great festival or in the symposium. The written texts of the poems could and did survive the disintegration of the classical Greek political and cultural structure and were duly rescued by the Alexandrians. Their accompanying melodies and dance steps, on the other hand, had been preserved entirely in practical performance. Once the continuity of the performing tradition of any given song had been snapped, the music and dance of that song would be lost forever. There can be little doubt that this was the fate of the majority of archaic and classical Greek songs during the transition from the classical to the Hellenistic era. There must of course have been exceptions. For example, there was no apparent break in the performing tradition of Attic tragedy, and no doubt it is to this fact that we owe our two musically notated papyri of classical tragic lyric.[8] It is worth noting that both the tragedies concerned belong to Euripides' latest period (the *Orestes*, produced in 408 B.C., and the *Iphigeneia in Aulis*, produced posthumously), when his lyrics seem to have been heavily under the influence of the so-called New Music. It is probably no coincidence that the only classical lyric poet whose work we know to have been reperformed well into the Hellenistic period was the high priest of the New Music movement, Timotheus.[9] One may suspect that the majority of those classical tragedies and lyrics that continued to be re-performed in the third century B.C. and onward were examples of this relatively late musical style, which retained its popularity with the Hellenistic Greeks.[10]

THE NATURE AND FUNCTION OF THE PRE-ALEXANDRIAN TEXTS

It has been pointed out time and again that the Homeric epics make no allusion to written poetic texts,[11] and the conclusion has often been drawn that for that reason the composer or composers must have been ignorant of their existence. It is not so often observed that the post-Homeric Greek poets, down to the last quarter of the fifth century B.C., are almost equally reticent about written poetic texts. The reason is surely not that they did not know of their existence. Rather, the texts were no part of the performed poem as such, but merely a mechanical means of preserving its wording between performances. You could hardly expect the archaic poem to allude to its own written text any more than you could expect a violinist in the concert hall to interrupt the music with an allusion to his printed score. That is the fundamental difference between the poetic text as we have known it from the Alexandrian editions onward and the poetic text as it existed in the Greek song culture.

None the less, there *were* texts, from the early archaic period onward. This is suggested by the general consideration that without texts the early poems could never have reached the Alexandrians (and hence us) in such relatively uncorrupt and unified condition as they did. It is almost proved by certain allusions in the poems of Pindar and Bacchylides, and also by a fifth-century reference to the practice of a much earlier poet, Alcaeus. And unless we are to dismiss a larger number of independent and scattered post-fifth-century testimonies as simply a conspiracy to hoax posterity, those testimonies provide absolute proof. In addition, the vase-paintings provide ocular proof that book texts of poetry were in use in the Athenian schools from no later than circa 490 B.C., and even in private circles from about the middle of the fifth century.

As usual, I reserve the detailed primary evidence for an appendix (Appendix VI). Let it suffice here to summarize the various ways in which literary texts can be shown to have been preserved in the period that ends with the late fifth century.

1. *Temples*: there are tolerably credible accounts of the preservation of Heraclitus's book in the Artemision at Ephesus and of Pindaric texts in temples at Rhodes and Thebes; less certain, perhaps, are the reports of an ancient leaden copy of Hesiod's *Works and Days* in or near the sanctuary of the Muses on Mount Helikon and of the third Homeric Hymn preserved on a white tablet in the Artemis temple on Delos.
2. *Family archives*: there is good fourth-century evidence that a noble house might preserve the writings, *grammata*, of a poet who was of family interest—because of his relationship with the family or because of the contents of his poems—for as long as 150 years.[12]
3. *Schoolteachers*, as mentioned in the previous paragraph (see also Appendix VI): their collections of poems for instructional use were surely of extreme importance in the transmission and diffusion of the texts.

Without doubt there were many other ways in which the texts were preserved, since our information even on the above three is scanty and haphazard; in particular, one would imagine that a performer of poetry by *métier*, whether rhapsode, kitharode, or *chorodidaskalos*, would possess his own texts and would transmit them to his pupils. How far such performers would have constituted what we call (somewhat misleadingly?) guilds, I cannot say; certainly such "guilds" existed from the fourth century onward.[13] We may conjecture that those professional associations also would possess collections of texts.

We must emphasize once more that on our present evidence the archaic and classical poetic texts, however and wherever preserved, are most unlikely to have been anything more than mere rows of capital letters without word division, without line division (except, probably, where stichic meters were concerned),[14] without accents, with no more than a minimum of punctuation, and without musical or choreographic indications in any form.

A final question relating to the poetic texts is at least worth raising here: how and at what point in the process of composition did the archaic and classical poets commit their words to writing? Just where did our texts begin? I can find only two passages before the fourth century in which the composition of a poem is apparently described. Both are in Aristophanes. In *Acharnians* 383–479, Euripides is revealed in the very act of composing a tragedy (*poiei tragōidian* 399–400; cf. 410, 464,

470). The equipment mentioned for this purpose is a wardrobe of ragged clothes apt for distressed heroes and a number of minor stage properties such as a chipped mug (459), but there is no mention in the long scene of writing materials or the act of writing. Similarly in *Thesmophoriazusae* 25–265, the tragedian Agathon is described as composing a lyric (*melopoiein* 67; cf. 42, and the passage 48–57) in the form of a hymn to the Letoids, although it is evidently meant to be part of a tragedy (cf. 149–51). In order to "round off his stanzas" in this cold season, he must come out into the sunshine when he "begins to compose lyric" (67–68). When the great *tragōidodidaskalos* (88) appears, he does indeed render a lyric (101–29) to a melody which has a most powerful effect on one of the other characters (130–33). Opinions differ about the actual method of rendering, but it seems most likely that Agathon himself sings both the solo parts and the parts designed for a female chorus; for this reason, indeed, he turns out to be wearing female dress, it being necessary to his art to empathize with the sex of the characters described. We seem to be witnessing a quite early stage in the composition both of words and melody, before they have reached the point when they can be "taught" to the chorus and actor. Again, the scene contains no hint of writing.

Even when we make full allowance for the whimsical distortions of Aristophanic comedy, the probable conclusion from both scenes is that the late-fifth-century tragedian did not take to his pen or stylus until late in the composition or even until after the process was finished. Indeed, when he had the music, dance, and blocking to consider simultaneously with the words, he would be unwise thus to concentrate his attention on the words alone.[15] It is a fair inference from Plato (*Laws* 7.817d)[16] that he (or an amanuensis?) would have to prepare a written version of his tragedy before it could be accepted by the archon for staging, but that is as far as we can go.

Such are the admittedly faint indications of the manner in which a dramatic text might come into being in the last quarter of the fifth century B.C. We may guess that at least the lyric poetry of archaic Greece, and perhaps its poetry in all kinds, was composed by a similar process, with the act of writing down occurring toward the end or at the end rather than toward the beginning.[17] In any case, it seems most likely that the resultant text showed no directions for the accompanying music or dance.

RE-PERFORMANCES

If the conclusion drawn in the preceding section is correct, then how was an extensive and subtle knowledge of the music and even the choreography of many archaic Greek poets transmitted well into the fourth century B.C.? We cannot doubt that it was indeed so transmitted, unless we are to accuse such authorities as Plato and Aristotle and their immediate pupils of mystification or outright charlatanism. Appendix VII includes select passages from these fourth-century writers that can only be interpreted as implying familiarity with Greek music up to three centuries older than their time.[18]

If (as we have assumed) this knowledge was not transmitted by written symbols, it can only have reached the fourth century through an uninterrupted succession of *re-performances*. There is in fact nothing intrinsically improbable in this supposition, and we have already seen a good deal of positive evidence in its favor. At Sparta in particular the tradition of re-performance was very strong. "Above all the Hellenes," says Athenaeus (14.632f; unfortunately he does not name his source here) "the Spartans maintained *mousikē*, making the most use of it, and many lyric poets arose among them. And even now[19] they preserve the ancient songs with great care, being widely learned and accurate (*akribeis*) with regard to them." An example of choral re-performance of songs of Alcman and other early poets at Sparta down into Hellenistic times was cited in the first chapter (p. 25), and some further evidence to the same effect is collected in Appendix VII. We have further seen reason to believe that re-performances of kitharodic lyrics were long normal at the kitharodic contests, notably those of the Pythia and the Panathenaia.

Professional musicians no doubt were important links in the chain of accurate transmission of the music. A very striking instance is preserved by Aristoxenus, writing in the fourth century B.C.: his contemporary, Telesias of Thebes, he said,

> had been brought up as a youth in the finest kind of music, and had learned the well-reputed works, among others, of Pindar, Dionysios of Thebes, Lampros, Pratinas, and the other lyricists who had been good composers of lyre music (*poiētai kroumatōn agathoi*); he had also been a fine oboist. . . . When, however, he had passed his prime, he was so deluded by the elaborate music of the theater that he scorned the noble

works on which he had been brought up and began to learn by heart the works of Philoxenus and Timotheus. (fr. 76 Wehrli = ps.-Plut. *De Mus.* 31.1142b–c)

He tried, adds Aristoxenus, to compose music in the styles both of Pindar and of Philoxenus, but could not succeed in the latter, "and the reason for this was his admirable training (*agōgē*) in youth." Here, then, we have the certain case of a practicing musician toward the end of the city-state epoch whose musical repertoire ranged from the beginning of the fifth century (Pratinas, Pindar) approximately through the period of the Peloponnesian War (Dionysios, Lampros) to the work of the great exponents of the "New Music" (Philoxenus, Timotheus: the latter died circa 360 B.C.).

In the transmission of the ancient music, just as in the transmission of the words, the work of the schoolmaster must have been of extreme importance. There are famous passages in Plato's *Protagoras* (325e–326b) and Aristophanes' *Clouds* (964–71) that show how instruction in singing earlier poetry to lyre accompaniment was a major component in traditional Athenian education. In the *Clouds* passage, the Just Logos tells how the boys used to march in good order to the school of the lyre master, who would "teach them to learn a song by heart—'Dread Pallas City-Destroyer' or 'Far-echoing Cry'[20]—*keeping to the musical modes which our fathers handed down to us.*" Here, quite evidently, the instruction is oral and practical; and that this is no product of Aristophanic whimsy is shown not merely by other, non-comic literary passages (see the Appendix) but also by the famous "school cup" of the painter Douris, where a similar educational process seems to be operating in the Athens of about 490 B.C.[21]

That strict discipline in the art of re-performing the ancient songs did not go wasted in the boy's later life; it must have come to highest fruition in the symposium. Both the literary evidence (notably in Old Comedy) and the vase-paintings testify to the importance of symposiac singing, in chorus and solo. They also testify to the very wide range of songs that might be sung. There was not only the repertoire of short patriotic and gnomic lyrics, the *skolia*, which is partially preserved by Athenaeus and of which some pieces may date from as early as the last decades of the sixth century; we learn also that songs by the great choral lyricists and kitharodes (Alcman, Stesichorus, and Simonides are named), by the monodic lyricists (Alcaeus, Anacreon, Praxilla), and by the comic poet Cratinus might also be rendered in the symposium. Such evidence (collected in Appendix VII) throws a startling light on the musical and poetic knowledge possessed by the private Athenian citizen during the fifth century. It also suggests once more that the institution of the symposium may have been of enormous significance to the diffusion and transmission of Greek poetry with its accompanying music at all dates.

So far in this section we have discussed only the re-performances of lyric poetry, in an attempt to show how the fourth-century writers could perfectly well have acquired their knowledge of early Greek music and dance even if (as we have assumed) the archaic and classical poetic texts contained only the bare words of the songs. To complete the general picture of constant re-performance in the city-state period, we may also recall here the evidence for re-performance of unaccompanied poetry, cited in Chapter 1 and its appendices: the public rhapsodic re-performances of the Homeric epics (notably at the Panathenaia), of Hesiod, Archilochus, and Empedocles; the semipublic re-performances of Tyrtaeus's elegies at Sparta; and the re-performances of the Theognidean elegiac poems in the symposia. And it should be noted that these are only scattered instances, surviving by hazard in our very fragmentary sources, of the re-performances of works by identifiable poets. There is every reason to suppose not merely that all the archaic and early classical poetry that survived into the Hellenistic age was originally performed orally and before audiences, large or small, but also that most of it was often re-performed subsequent to the first production. Otherwise, what would be the point of the poets' universal claim, from Homer to Pindar, that they conferred lasting and widespread glory, *kleos*, on the subjects of their songs?[22] And, indeed, in the era before private reading became a habit, what would be the point of making or preserving a written poetic text at all, if the papyrus was destined only to decay in a closet, voiceless?

APPROACHES TOWARD DRAMA IN PRETRAGIC POETRY

Fully to envisage the consequences, literary, cultural, and social, of the picture that has emerged from this and the preceding chapter is perhaps one of the most difficult tasks that a student of Greek poetry can set himself; perhaps, also, it is one of the most urgent. We have to imagine our way into a unique song culture that began to disintegrate as long ago as the second half of the fifth century B.C., had become a mere memory (though a powerful one) by the third century, and finally faded out of the Western tradition with the collapse of Rome. Between us and it lies a monstrous barrier: two thousand years' accumulation of books, books which while preserving the memory of that culture have simultaneously distorted it. There is a story that Sir Walter Scott once

> thought to flatter an old Scotswoman from whose singing he had taken down a number of ballads, by showing her printed texts of the pieces she had sung to him. But the old woman was more annoyed than amused. He had spoiled them altogether, she complained. "They were made for singing and no for reading, but ye hae broken the charm now and they'll never be sung mair. And the worst thing o' a', they're nouther right spelled, no right setten down."[23]

A disaster of that kind, but on a cataclysmic scale, befell the Greek song culture in the library of Alexandria, although (as we have seen) through no fault of the devoted scholars there: the fault was history's. All we can do now is try to repair the damage so far as the evidence allows.

Here I would consider only one consequence of the practice of performance and re-performance as the sole method of publication in the period of the song culture (others will be reserved for the third chapter): *in several respects much pretragic poetry will have already been very close to drama in the sense in which we now understand that word*, far closer, certainly, than one can realize if one merely contemplates the poems on the printed page.

We have already seen how Plato, Aristotle, and others habitually pair the art of the rhapsode with that of the actor, just as they habitually pair Homeric epic with tragedy. One obvious resemblance between the two arts is that they both involved the skilled delivery of verse, from memory, in such a way that it should be audible to great crowds of people; to some extent the delivery was reinforced by bodily movement, although the rhapsode of all dates will naturally have made far less use of this than the actor. A less obvious resemblance—less obvious until one has experimented with delivering the nondramatic poetry aloud before a real or imagined audience[24]—is the very high degree of *impersonation* that the rhapsode's art involves. Since Aristotle (and, no doubt, since the time of Homer himself) it has been acknowledged that one of the peculiar excellences of Homeric epic is the high proportion of speeches in the mouths of characters other than the narrator.[25] In delivering all such speeches the rhapsode (even if he was not quite such a temperamental and passionate virtuoso as the Ion of Plato's dialogue) must have become to some extent an impersonator, distinguishing at least between the tones, pitches, and tempos appropriate to the various speakers. And to this day, as a matter of practical experience, anyone who sets himself seriously to declaim a Homeric episode—for instance, the debate in the Greek camp near the opening of the *Iliad*—will be led almost without noticing it into acting out the very different voices and emotions of Agamemnon, Achilles, and Nestor; Homeric verse is built that way.[26] He may even find himself led into physically miming certain of their actions: the half-drawing and then the slamming home of Achilles' sword (*Il.* 1.194, 219–20), or the magnificent gesture of the hurling of the scepter to the ground after the hero has sworn by it (245).[27] In such passages as these, to be found in any book of Homer, we come very close to drama in the fifth-century and later senses. It is not a very long step from the debate in the camp, properly acted out by a good rhapsode, to, for example, the *agōn* in the *exodos* of Sophocles' *Ajax*, even though in the latter the speeches are uttered by separate voices.

At this point we must remind ourselves that the Homeric epics were not by any means the only poems recited by the rhapsodes before their crowded audiences. Most of the surviving evidence about the rhapsodes, understandably, concerns their renderings of the prince of poets, but (as was seen in Chapter 1 and Appendix II) rhapsodic recital also happens to be attested for unnamed works by Hesiod and Archilochus and for the *Katharmoi*, "Purifications," of Empedocles.[28] As it stands, this is a surprising assortment, but in the very fragmentary state of the evidence we must assume that many other hexameter and iambic poets were included in the classical rhapsode's repertoire. Even the works named, however, have something in common: in a great part of Archilochus, in the *Katharmoi* of Empedocles, and in the *Works and Days* of Hesiod, the poet speaks loud and clear in the *first person*: he builds up a dramatic character for himself and a dramatic situation to go with it. The *Works and Days*, delivered aloud, is particularly striking for the variety of tone and ethos which it demands from the reciter. It is a joy to act: the verses invite one to sense one's way into the persona of Hesiod and to follow his moods, which vary from angry denunciation, through self-deprecating humor, to the triumphant pride of the accomplished bard (661–62). This experimenter soon found himself addressing the kings and berating the delinquent Perses almost as if those characters were present in the room. Much less, obviously, can be said about Empedocles' fragmentary *Katharmoi*, but the fragments suffice at least to show that this poem too opened in the "I–you" mode, with a passionate call to his fellow citizens in Akragas, and may well have continued in that mode throughout.[29] Perhaps the most interesting case of all is that of Archilochus.[30] The majority of Archilochus's poems seem to have been relatively short and were concerned, as we know, with various situations arising in battle, in storms at sea, in partying, and (most notoriously, but by no means only, in the recently published Cologne papyrus) in uninhibited lovemaking.[31] In our attempt to reconstruct how these poems may have come across to an audience unprovided with books and, at least on some occasions, in rhapsodic recitals at the great poetic contests, it is convenient to begin by looking at those poems whose original initial lines happen to have been preserved.[32] Of the nine instances of initial lines that I count among the fragments, only one is not cast in the first or second person singular.[33]

One must imagine the rhapsode, presumably wearing his splendid robe and garland and with his staff of office in his hand, mounting his platform and gesturing for silence. Then the poem simply jumps out at the audience:

> I don't care for all the riches of Gyges!
> I never yet felt envy, nor can marvel at
> the works of gods, or lust for mighty tyranny. (fr. 19W)

Or:

> Your skin is soft and ripe no longer!
> It is seared by furrows already, and [the curse?]
> of old age is destroying you! (fr. 188W; cf. S478b *SLG*)

The spectators are granted no immediate information about the identity of the speaker. Sometimes this will emerge in the course of the performance; we happen to know, for instance, that the "I" who doesn't care for riches will turn out to be an individual named Charon the Carpenter. It is likely, however, that many poems contained no identification of the speaker from end to end. The effect, either way, is that of a highly dramatic monologue which develops a personality and a situation out of nothing.

Archilochus himself, in performing the monologue of Charon the Carpenter, must have become an impersonator, a character actor, at least in the opening lines and perhaps throughout.[34] Whether Archilochus felt himself (and meant himself to be felt by his audience) as impersonating another character or simply as the poet Archilochus when he was performing a poem in which the "I" was not identified is an intriguing question:[35] were such poems to be taken as autobiographical records, a kind of seventh-century *True Confessions*? This question, however one may feel inclined to answer, is probably insoluble in strict method. What is certain is that any rendering of such a poem not performed by Archilochus in person (such as the rhapsodic renderings apparently referred to by Heraclitus and Plato more than one and two centuries respectively after the poet's death) will necessarily be a dramatic impersonation. Either the rhapsode will be miming Archilochus himself, or he will be miming the unidentified "I" created in the poem; in either case his function will essentially be indistinguishable from that of an actor.[36]

It is worth spending a few moments (even though here, again, we are in no position to obtain very firm results) to pursue this line of questioning with regard to other kinds of early Greek poetry, for instance, choral lyric. On the assumption that all this poetry was constantly re-performed through the classical period, and indeed only for that reason survived to reach the Alexandrians,[37] the re-performance of an Alcmanian *Partheneion* will present us with some exceedingly interesting problems. For example, what will be the status of the following lines from the first *Partheneion* if we suppose the song to be re-performed perhaps a century after the poet's death—and also, therefore, after the death of the girl choristers who performed in the original production?

> My cousin Hagesichora's hair
> flowers on her like pure gold;
> silver, her face—why must I tell you clearly?
> This is Hagesichora! (fr. 1.51–56 *PMG*)

Or of these?

> We have not Nanno's hair,
> we have not Areta the goddess-like,
> we have not Sylakis and Kleesisera. (fr. 1.70–72 *PMG*)

These lines, and indeed almost the whole of the song from line 39 onward, might seem at first sight to represent a single, unrepeatable historic moment, sometime in the middle of the seventh century B.C. on a Spartan dancing floor. Taken literally, this poem can only be performed *once*, or at most a few times during the brief period before the maidens who are named and described in it become the brides of Spartiates. If it was re-performed after that period (and can we really believe that the Spartans would carefully preserve the text of such a song for four centuries while allowing it to remain silent?), the re-performance must automatically have become a kind of impersonation, a highly dramatic recreation of that original moment and of those women. Theoretically, of course, another interpretation of the *Partheneion* is possible, and that is that Hagesichora and her fellows are beauties who never were, that all these singer names were fictitious from the beginning. In that case the poem will have been a quite complex and sophisticated drama even at the moment of its original performance.[38]

Pindar's choral lyrics present a much more difficult case. We have already seen evidence that some of his music was very familiar in the musical schools down into the fourth century (above, pp. 48–49), and on our adopted hypothesis this can only have been due to an uninterrupted succession of re-performances. We happen to know, indeed, from an Athenian poet that people (presumably in Athens) had given up performing Pindar's work during the late fifth century, but that is hardly surprising in view of the intellectual and artistic atmosphere in late fifth-century Athens and in view of the nature of Pindar's poetry.[39] I would be inclined to guess (and obviously no more than guesswork is possible here) that many of his works indeed continued to be re-performed in the more conservative places and social circles for which they were originally composed: that the Theban house of Aioladas, for example, would not lightly have allowed such a monument to its glory as the second *Partheneion* (quoted in Chapter 1, in the section on "The Performance of Choral Lyric") to be left unsung and undanced forever after the original production. A similar guess might apply to many, or most, of the epinician odes. It is perhaps too easy, even for experienced scholars, to forget that the epigraphs which appear in such impressive capital letters at the head of each ode in our modern texts (e.g., "FOR PHYLAKIDAS OF AIGINA IN THE BOY'S PANKRATION," *Isthm.* 6) are additions, and shamefully simplistic additions at that, by the Alexandrian editors. Their practice apparently was to seek out from the text the name and athletic skill of the victor immediately concerned in the ode (with luck, the name could then be identified in the appropriate victor lists, and so provide a *terminus post quem* for dating) and to place them at the head for ready reference. Again and again, unbiased inspection of the text itself will remind us that not merely the current victor is being glorified, but also his family (the dead as well as the living), his city, his city's heroes, and its major gods. *Isthmian* 6 is a good case in point.[40] The glory and virtue of an entire community of men, heroes, and gods are normally at stake in a Pindaric ode, and one would conjecture that so long as that community lasted intact there would be a pressing demand for the ode's re-performance, perhaps on the anniversary of the victory that had originally occasioned it. If so, each re-performance would again be a kind of play, a dramatic re-creation of the momentary joy of the victor and of his family and city.

There remain to be mentioned two passages of early lyric in which the boundary between performed or re-performed poetry on the one hand and drama on the other (ill-defined as that boundary is now seen to be) seems to have been crossed, far away from Athens and long before the first tragic contests at the Athenian Dionysia. Both are fragments of Sappho (who worked in Lesbos in the decades around 600 B.C.); each of them apparently comprises a *verse dialogue* between two separate voices of which at least one impersonates a fictitious character. The first instance (fr. 114 *PLF*; cf. Page [1955], pp. 118–19 notes, and p. 122) is not entirely certain because of the circumstances of its preservation, but seems more probable than not.[41] It is a dialogue between a bride and Virginity:

(*First voice*:) Maidenhood, you have left me, Maidenhood, where are you gone?

(*Second voice*:) I'll not come again to you, love, I'll not come again.

More certainly attested as a dialogue for two voices, and also more intriguing in content, is the second example (fr. 140a *PLF*) preserved by Hephaestion in his metrical handbook; and Hephaestion's practice is such that we have no reason to suppose that he would have omitted an intervening line between the two which he quotes:

(*First voice*:) Oh Kytherēa, he is dying, the delicate Adonis! What should we do?

(*Second voice*:) Beat your breasts, maidens, tear up your robes!

In the first line Kytherea (i.e., of course, Aphrodite) is addressed in the vocative singular by a first-person-plural subject; the second line appears to answer that appeal with a command uttered in the imperative plural. We are made to be present at a mythical happening, the death of Adonis from the boar wound, which is not being narrated but immediately presented. A group of female voices (possibly impersonating Nymphs?) appeals to Aphrodite for instructions and is answered by a single imperious voice which can only be impersonating the goddess herself.[42]

From the bare text of fr. 140a, which is all that is left, we can deduce no more about that eerie performance. It could well have been a truly ritual drama, a reenactment of Adonis's death-in-life for a group of his devotees, just as fragment 114 might well be interpreted as a sort of ritual drama for performance at wedding ceremonies. But drama of some kind it may certainly be called, and it long anticipates such scenes in Attic tragedy as the lyric finale of Aeschylus's *Persians*, where another imperious voice (that of Xerxes) commands the chorus of Persian nobles to lament and tear their robes. If these considerations are correct, we have to credit none other than Sappho with the earliest fragment of verse drama that survives in the entire European tradition; even though that drama was of a kind that, so far as we know, was not developed later and had little or no influence on the genesis of Attic tragedy.[43]

No doubt much more could be inferred from the pretragic Greek practices of performance and re-performance than has been inferred in this chapter; no doubt many of the inferences that we have tentatively made will be subject to correction. Yet the general lesson to be drawn from it is plain. The ultimate task of the student who seeks to understand the early Greek poems as they actually were is, paradoxically enough, to reverse the terms of Mallarmé's fearsome saying: *Tout, au monde, existe pour aboutir à un livre.* On the contrary, he or she must *begin* with a book, a cold text "nouther right spelled, no right setten down," as the old Scotswoman put it to Sir Walter. The first and obvious duty is indeed to repair and explain that text by the best philological means available. Yet accompanying that duty and transcending it may be the duty of envisioning and hearing the text, so far as possible, as the thing it was designed to be: the promptbook for a live performance, before living human beings, under the sun.

3. The Forests of Myths

The present chapter concludes our survey of the archaic Greek song culture. It will necessarily be of a different character from its predecessors, which treated in some detail the performance of the poems, their peculiar relationship to the written texts, and their approximation in some instances to what we should now think of as drama. For here we are to consider, primarily, the content and some of the major themes of pretragic poetry, subjects so vast that (given the framework and scope of this book) they can only be dealt with in rather sweeping generalities. The excuses are two. First, some such survey seems indispensable if the reader is adequately to grasp the continuity between Greek pretragic and tragic poetry, which is our central subject. The second excuse is that, after all, it does no harm occasionally to stand well back and contemplate the enormous scale of the historical and spiritual phenomenon with which we students of classics have to deal; indeed, I suspect that to induce such contemplation was one of the main purposes for which the Sather series was originally instituted. Specialists, however, may wish to skip this chapter, since much or all of it should long have been familiar to them. Nonspecialists, I hope, may wish to check its generalizations for themselves by returning to the ancient poetry.

THE APPEAL TO THE MUSES

A convenient starting point is one of the most familiar of all the features of early Greek poetry, yet a feature that at once differentiates it very sharply from modern poetry—and indeed from any intellectual or artistic practice known to modern urban humanity. It is the early poet's constant insistence that what he sings comes from outside himself, from some divine being, usually the Muse. Perhaps the most emphatic and most moving instance is the invocation that opens the Catalogue of Ships in the *Iliad* (2.484–86):

> Now speak to me, Muses, who hold your homes in Olympos; for you are goddesses, and are present, and know all, whereas we hear only the fame (*kleos*), but know nothing.

The most lengthy and elaborate description stands in the opening of Hesiod's *Theogony* (1–115). Similar claims, explicit or implicit, for the Muses' power and knowledge are made throughout the poetic tradition, even by those composers whom we call "personal" poets (although the ancients did not, and it is a term we could very well do without): Archilochus, Sappho, Ibycus, and Anacreon, for instance.[1] The series of such claims culminates, perhaps, in a fragment of Pindar (150 Snell):

> *μαντεύεο, Μοῖσα, προφατεύσω τ' ἐγώ*
>
> You be the oracle, Muse; and I will be your interpreter.

For our purposes it is irrelevant to inquire whether such passages are assertions of a firmly held belief in divine inspiration or merely polite gestures to an established convention. In most cases—if I know anything about that delicate balance between imaginative acceptance and hard-headed realism which is so characteristic of the ancient Greeks' attitude to their divine and mythical world[2]—the truth probably oscillates between those extremes at all dates from Homer onward. Our concern is with the mere fact that the belief or convention prevailed in every kind of Greek poetry before about the mid fifth century B.C., for it emphasizes an important aspect of that poetry's character. By appealing to the Muse the Greek poet deliberately distances himself from his subject matter. He deliberately proclaims the opposite of what any modern poet since the Romantics would ever dream of proclaiming: that which the Greek poet's audience is now about to hear will *not* be some transient private insight, which is all a mortal individual is good for; rather, it will be a facet of a fixed truth, of a fixed world that is known to the immortal Muses and must be communicated by them to singers, for "we hear only the fame, but know nothing." Thus Greek poetry from the first has a strong and explicit universalizing tendency. Its appeal is to a sphere beyond the transient present and beyond the mortal individual. We do not wonder that such a song culture was in the long run to provide the conditions not merely for a Sophocles but also, paradoxically, for a Plato.

KLEOS

The poets at all periods in the tradition advance a further, and closely related, claim: their song extends the fame, the *kleos*, of its subject; and indeed, if that subject is a mortal individual—as in a love song or an epinician ode—that the song will bring him as near as an early Greek can hope for to a release from death. Granted the poet's relationship to the Muse, this claim makes perfect sense. The fleeting moment of mortal beauty or success, when enshrined in the song and thus adopted by the Muses, will be assumed into a greater and more lasting sphere, taking its place alongside the deeds of the gods and of the ancient heroes. It will enter the province of the Daughters of Memory.

"I gave you wings," said the sixth-century elegist Theognis in a poem to Kyrnos, "and with them you will fly over the endless sea and all the earth." You will be sung at parties everywhere, the poem goes on, and even when you die, you will not lose your *kleos*, but you will still travel over Hellas and the islands. For "the glorious gifts of the violet-garlanded Muses will send you on; and to all who care for song, even those who are yet to come, you will alike be a song, so long as there shall be earth and sun" (*Theognidea*, 237–52). Against that gift of fame, which thanks to the Muses will triumph over space as well as time, the poet bitterly sets the ephemeral, mortal situation: what was probably the final couplet of his poem (253–54) runs: "And yet from you I receive no respect, not even a little, but with your words you deceive me as if I were a little child."

Passages of this kind are known to any casual reader of the early poetry,[3] and it is unnecessary to cite them at length. But there is surely an important inference to be drawn from them, the practical consequences of which are perhaps not always clearly envisaged. It is that the Greek poet might regularly expect that his poem would be re-performed later and elsewhere; that it would eventually be taken up into a Panhellenic repertoire. Otherwise, in a culture that knew nothing of published texts or of a reading public as we know them, a culture in which performance was the only form of publication, what possible sense could there be in the poet's claim to confer widespread and lasting *kleos* through his work? A claim like that of Theognis to Kyrnos seems to reinforce the conclusions that were drawn from other evidence in the preceding two chapters. The poet's—at least, the good poet's—work was not destined for a single performance only, nor might he expect to die merely "leaving great verse unto a *little* clan." Rather, he might expect that a successful poem would eventually find its way, as Theognis promised, over Hellas and the islands, whether by private channels (traveling from symposium to symposium?), or through solemn re-performance at the great religious festivals. In some such ways a vast poetic and musical dialogue seems to have been set up, in which poets conversed with poets who might not merely live far away but might in some cases long be dead. So Simonides (fr. 581 *PMG*) corrects in song the author of the magnificent, and evidently much earlier, hexameter epitaph on King Midas.[4] Or again: in the early sixth century we find an elegiac poem by the Athenian Solon that explicitly responds to an elegy composed by Mimnermus of Smyrna, perhaps a generation earlier and on the other side of the Aegean. "May the fate of death come upon me at sixty years," the melancholy Mimnermus had chanted. "Remake those words, Mimnermus!" the optimistic Solon chants back; "This is how you should chant it: May the fate of death come upon me at EIGHTY!"[5] It should be added, of course, that these and a few similar passages are only overt examples of the great poetic dialogue which flourished in the song culture; covert examples, that is, references by one poet to another without the mention of names, are far more numerous.[6]

CONTEMPORANEOUS PERFORMANCES

In the succeeding chapter reasons will be adduced for thinking that this poetic dialogue may have reached its most complex stage and its climax in Athens during the second half of the sixth century B.C. (when the city welcomed and concentrated into one place so many different kinds of performance from all over the area in which the song culture flourished) and that it is not quite coincidental that Attic tragedy arose within that particular milieu. We may usefully pause at this point to consider in just what guise the accumulated poetry of the archaic period would have presented itself to a late sixth-century Athenian, whether an ordinary citizen or a youthful Phrynichus or Aeschylus. The effort to imagine this confronts us with a question which may be of profound importance for our understanding of early Greek literary (as we must call it by convention, for want of a better word) and intellectual history. Since Western culture became subject to linear chronology and to some form of the idea of progress—a revolution that, like so many others, began to take place in the later decades of the fifth century B.C.—it has become very difficult for the intellectual historian to envisage even for himself a song culture like that of archaic Greece, which simply did not respond to *time* in the way we do. A closely related difficulty meets the literary student when he tries to make sense of the time dimension in the works of Aeschylus, Pindar, or of that late outrider of the song culture, Herodotus. For these men, time did not necessarily run in a straight line, and consequently there was no sharp division between the old and the new.[7] Even if the intellectual or literary historian succeeds in assimilating this fact, he may not find it easy to communicate his vision to his public in the era of the paper cup and the paperback. If that public thinks about the history of literature at all, it inevitably tends to think of it as a long row of books arranged in chronological order, the oldest ones being decrepit and disposable, and becoming increasingly so as each new and shiny acquisition is added to the right-hand end of the infinite shelf. And even the thoughtful literary scholar, trained as he should be to value all human products by their quality and not by their age, will still mentally order his books (and actually arrange them in his library) chronologically.

But that is just how things cannot have been in the period of the song culture. In a society where libraries—at least, libraries in any modern sense—did not exist[8] and in which for all practical purposes the only publication was performance or re-performance, *the poetry composed in all previous eras coexisted at any given moment.* The poems, from the Homeric epics to the latest song by Anacreon to hit the symposia, were all around their hearers, not stretching away into the chronological distance. No doubt, as the repertoire of poems increased with time, new meanings would be imported into earlier songs in the light of more recent ones and of more recent political and intellectual experience.[9] But the fact remains that for the Greek poet at any time in the song-culture period, Homer and all the line of great singers who followed him were in constant re-performance before the community: as alive, as available, and as potent in rivalry as any contemporary poet.

With that compact and omnipresent tradition, and in it, the beginning poet lived, as did his prospective audience. His task, both for his own sake and for that of his clients, was nothing less than to achieve incorporation into that tradition, or, in other words, to compose poems good enough to merit re-performance. This intense competitive pressure may be partly responsible for the extraordinary combination of vitality and technical excellence which amazes us in the archaic poems that reached the Alexandrian library and thence (mostly, alas, in fragments) the modern world. A clumsy or dull poem could not then, as such a poem can now, expect even a dubious survival in the dry dock of a printed book; it would founder without trace at first performance. That was the fate, for example, of the poems by Dionysius of Syracuse which were performed before the crowds attending the Olympic Games of 388 B.C. According to Diodorus Siculus (14.109), the tyrant sent a squad of the best rhapsodes to Olympia to recite them, along with several four-horse chariots and some gorgeous tents, all to his own greater glory. At first the excellence of the rhapsodes' voices drew a throng of listeners; when, however, the audience realized how awful the poetry itself was, they laughed at Dionysius "and so despised him that some even went so far as to tear the tents apart." A late incident, admittedly, and preserved to posterity only because of the political importance of the poetaster concerned; but even at the height of the song culture a similar fate must have awaited any poem that didn't work.

THE SHARED WORLD OF MYTH

Everything that has been seen so far in this book of the conditions under which the early Greek poet worked reveals him as tied inseparably to a community or, rather, to a concentric pattern of communities. First was the living community, whether private or public, before which his poem was performed. Second was the community of the earlier and contemporary poets whose works constituted the Panhellenic repertoire and were regularly in live performance around him and his audience. Third, and now to be considered, was a community that for him, his rivals, and his audiences was scarcely less alive than the other two: the vast realm of mythical and legendary beings presided over by the Muse whom the poet invoked. Again, one must pause to consider the enormous contrast between these working conditions and the conditions under which poets have worked in recent times. The poet of the song culture had his problems, no doubt; but solitude, alienation from the society and the shared dreamworld of the mass of his fellow beings, was not among them. As we should expect, it is in the second half of the fifth century B.C. that we find the first major Greek poet in whom we can clearly make out the symptoms of that familiar modern disease: Euripides. For it was only during that period, above all in Athens, that the solid and immemorially ancient realm of myth began rapidly to fall apart.[10] Seen in the context of our entire history and prehistory, this collapse was a cultural and psychological event scarcely less significant than the more publicized political collapse of the Roman Empire. Before it happened, the great mass of inherited stories was not just the property of a relatively small and relatively educated class (as Aristotle already represents it in a famous passage of the *Poetics*, 1451b25–26),[11] but a world shared in and imaginatively lived in by virtually every member of society—a world in which the dreams, the hopes and fears, and the moral searchings of unnumbered human generations had acquired vivid expression. One might almost describe it as a shared subconscious, were it not that the myths presented themselves in vivid shapes perfectly assimilable by the conscious mind and perfectly communicable in words or pictures.

That all this was so in the song-culture period could be adequately shown merely from the practice of the early poets. Its most overwhelming proof, however, lies scattered in thousands upon thousands of tactile objects in clay, stone, and metal, from sites all over the Hellenic world, which represent mythical scenes and beings.[12] This archaic visual culture, like the archaic song culture, is seen to have been for all seasons and for all levels of activity. An enormous range of myths, some of them scarcely known to the modern scholar, stared down from the glowingly painted pediments and metopes of the temples; or, equally, stared up at the same observer through his wine, from the tondos of the spreading drinking cups. Of that society it can be said (to adapt a famous couplet from Baudelaire) that:

> There a man passes through forests of myths,
> Who watch him with familiar looks.[13]

It must be stressed once more that the poet and his audiences alike were at home in those forests. This becomes particularly clear from the practice of the choral lyricists, above all of Pindar. The poet can shift with marvelous freedom from myth to myth, sometimes introducing only a fleeting extract from a given story but evidently confident that his audience will pick up its resonances. There are passages in Pindar where he almost seems to be feeling his way into the right myth, the one that will say what he wants to say, somewhat as one has heard an extemporizing musician searching out the key that just fits.[14] There must have been other students besides myself who have experienced the shock that I did when I approached the Greek text of Pindar in all innocence for the first time, with nothing to guide me (it so happened) but an unfortunate statement in some old-fashioned handbook that the central feature of a Pindaric ode was something called The Myth. Repeatedly, instead of the expected self-explanatory narrative, I encountered at best a series of bright facets of a single myth, not necessarily in linear-chronological order; at worst (so it seemed then), a shifting kaleidoscope of luminous mythical fragments, the pattern collapsing from Pelops into Herakles into Pyrrha-and-Deukalion into Protogeneia into Patroklos—while a mortal victor, "beautiful and noble, worker of noblest deeds," played in and out of this heroic throng.[15] Only gradually did it dawn on me that for Pindar, and for Pindar's audiences, the procedure made perfect sense: to people who carried the whole world of myth in their heads these transient glimpses of one legend or another must have had the immediate intelligibility and impact of a family joke.

Pindar is admittedly an extreme example. Perhaps no other composer ever walked the forests of myth so freely or so alert to all the presences there, benign, hostile, monstrous, yet all eternal—the Muse's domain of things that *are*, against which we can measure and understand the acts of things that pass. Aeschylus (one surmises as one contemplates the fragmentary as well as the extant dramas) may have run him very close in this regard, but the different nature of his art, and even more the different composition of his vast audiences, precluded such virtuoso displays of allusiveness as those of Pindar.

THE ANTIQUITY OF THE INHERITED MYTHICAL WORLD

The mythical tradition is, I suppose, the most obvious of all the elements that are common to pretragic poetry and to tragedy. It is indeed so obvious, so central, that because of the specializing and centrifugal tendencies of modern professional classical studies, it is actually liable to be overlooked in practice, especially in discussions of the origin and nature of Attic tragedy. I therefore do not much apologize for contemplating yet again the antiquity, the extraordinary character, and the pricelessness of the Greek mythic tradition as a whole.

It is possible to view the history of all Greek poetry, pretragic and tragic, as the direct continuation of an unimaginably older history that reaches far back into the Greek Bronze Age and even beyond, into civilizations that antecede the coalescence of a Greek people and lie outside the borders of Greece. It is the record of a quest for patterns of conduct, patterns of narrative, and types of human character, a record embodied in a repertoire of stories. The repertoire seems already to have been complete in all essentials well before the earliest extant Greek poetry. By the time of Homer, not merely was the entire Matter of Troy evidently so well known that much of it is touched on merely by allusion in the *Iliad* and *Odyssey*, but so also were the other major sagas. For example, Oedipus was already known to have killed his father and married his mother (*Od.* 11.271–80), and Niobe to have boasted of her children, seen them die, and been turned to stone for sorrow (*Il.* 24.602–17); and already in Homer some of these legendary incidents are being adduced as paradigms and precedents for certain human situations occurring within the poems.[16] The most recent major accession to the mythical repertoire seems to have come about some centuries before the Homeric epics, in the shock of a cultural catastrophe of world-historical significance: the collapse of the Bronze Age civilizations of the Mycenaeans and of the other peoples who inhabited the Near East and the shores of the Aegean, and the transition to the Iron Age, beginning approximately in the twelfth century B.C.[17] How much of the repertoire is yet older than that—how much had been created by the Mycenaeans while their culture flourished, well back in the second millennium, or by their remote Indo-European ancestors, how much had originated in the non-Greek Bronze Age peoples, Anatolian and Mesopotamian—that is not easy to define at this late date, although steady progress is being made in the understanding of this question.[18] What is clear in general is that by the time the repertoire reached the earliest extant Greek poets (and Greek artists), it carried with it the accumulated thinking, expressed in story form, of the early Iron Age and an immeasurable tract of the Bronze Age too. One way to look at archaic and classical Greek poetry is as the culminating phase—a phase which happens by a miracle to have been captured and preserved in alphabetic writing—in a long accumulation of highly sophisticated preliterate wisdom: the wisdom that results from leisurely, sharp-eyed observation of the way human beings act, in lively communities totally undistracted by books. The extraordinary power and charm that extant Greek poetry exerts over us—whether as historians, as literary students, as anthropologists, as psychologists or, in a word, as humanists in the broadest nonprofessional sense, as searchers of ourselves—is surely in part attributable to those fathomless human depths from which it draws. Greek poetry holds a lofty mountain pass between two great epochs in the history of mankind, looking at least as far backward into the experience of being human as it looks forward.

SOME CHARACTERISTICS OF THE INHERITED MYTHICAL WORLD

On present evidence it seems that the Greek poets whose works were preserved in writing received the mythical world complete in all its major outlines from a remote preliterate past. Some of them, without doubt, contributed much to the organization and articulation of that world (the Cyclic poets; Hesiod, especially in the *Theogony* and *Catalogues*); others succeeded in realizing certain of its characters and events with a clarity and force rare in the annals of any literature (Homer; and in his following, the Attic tragedians); all of them (and here we must not forget the elegiac and choral lyric poets, in particular) revealed or at least reemphasized certain messages, implicit in the stories, about the way human life is. And under the song culture that world of myth, we must remind ourselves again, was not simply a poets' world; it was shared equally by the Greek visual artists and by the public for whom both poet and artist created their work.

The mythic world was a kind of encyclopaedia, in the etymological as well as in the restricted modern sense. In it you could find not only the past of your nation (and indeed of the human race), but also the geography of your landscape and the nature of your gods. Further, you didn't have to believe literally in any of it; you only had to share in imagining it, to be able to share in the rich intellectual and artistic life of an early Greek community.[19] What is perhaps less often observed but is almost equally important if we are to account for the nature and limits of all extant Greek poetry down through tragedy, is the enormous range of characters, story patterns, themes, and tones that was apparently to be found already in the inherited legendary repertoire. The result was far more than a mere factual encyclopaedia: it was truly an "all-round education," for the literary composer no less than for the inquirer into moral or political conduct.

Here I would briefly survey some of the features just mentioned, only warning the reader that my examples, necessarily and obviously, will be drawn from extant poetry (although from one of the earliest strata, the hexameter poems). Any given instance will therefore be open to the objection that it may have been the creation of the individual literate poet concerned, but I believe that on balance this may seem to be the less likely alternative.

In this mythic world we can find the very pattern of virtue: one thinks of the blameless seer Amphiaraos, who already appears in Hesiod's *Eoiai* (fr. 25.37–38 M-W) as "good in the debate, good in the fighting, noble in mind, beloved of the immortals." We cannot tell, on our data, who first saw what we should now call the profoundly *tragic* implications of the contrast between such a noble nature and the premature fate that befell Amphiaraos before Thebes, as Homer already knew, "because of gifts to a woman" (*Od.* 15.146–67). It is very probable that someone had already seen it before a Corinthian vase-painter drew the scene of the hero's departure from his home in the middle years of the sixth century. It is certain that the tragedian Aeschylus had seen it by 467 B.C. in composing his *Seven Against Thebes*, where Amphiaraos appears as one who "wishes not to *seem* the noblest, but to *be* it" (line 592) and yet arms himself for the battle, well knowing his fate. And all the world knows how, paradoxically but characteristically, Plato seized on this creation of the song culture to illuminate a crucial passage of his *Republic*.[20] Beside that pattern of virtue the sagas could show male and female characters who illustrated almost every tint of the moral spectrum, through a Penelope, a Hector, and an Aegisthus to an Atreus (shade of what ancient Mycenaean tyrant?). No less diverse were the moods and attitudes to the world that were implicit in the various legends, from the high-tragic stories of Niobe, of Achilles, of Priam, of Troy herself, through the light comedy of Hermes and the infant Apollo retold in the fourth Homeric Hymn, to the satirical and often outright bawdy motifs found in the *Kerkōpes*, the Hesiodic *Melampodia* (notable here is the outrageously witty story of Teiresias and his sex-changes, fr. 275 M-W), and the pseudo-Homeric *Margites*, as well as several episodes in the Homeric epics themselves.[21] Eustathius's remark on that last group of examples is worth considering here: commenting on the episode of the foolish Elpenor in the *Odyssey*, he notes that

> the ancients bring such matters also into their writings for the sake of wide learning (*polymatheia*), that there may be abundance of such matters also for those who wish to find out.[22]

This catholicity of the early epic (which presumably reflects a similar catholicity in the preliterate mythical repertoire) is apparent in other ways as well. The repertoire included the elements, and in some cases more than the elements, of the spy story, the ghost story, the novella, and even a kind of science fiction.[23] Also notable is the strong interest in the romantic geography of the half-known or unknown world, which surfaces not merely in *Odyssey* 9–12 but also in the Argonaut saga (e.g., *Carmen Naupactium* frr. 7–8 Kinkel, Hesiod frr. 63 M-W, 241[?], 263); and in that world's exotic inhabitants—Graiai, Gorgons, Harpies (*Theog.* 265–83, etc.), Griffins, Half-Dogs, Long-Heads, Pygmies (all these in the *Eoiai*, frr. 151–53 M-W). But surreal and monstrous episodes are also introduced nearer home: they are more prominent, perhaps, even in the *Iliad* than good Homerists like to think (the *machē parapotamios* of Book 21 is surely one of the most surreal incidents in all Greek literature before Old Comedy); but outside Homer they are certainly more frequent, notably in Hesiod and the Epic Cycle.[24]

The mythic corpus known to the earliest Greek poets, and by them transmitted to the poets and public of archaic and classical Greece,[25] thus constituted a "universe of every kind of poetry," *epeōn kosmon pantoiōn* (to adapt the wonderful phrase Democritus applied to Homer's epics).[26] It was almost a complete moral and imaginative universe in its own right, shared by all, at once close to an audience because of its familiarity, and distanced and authoritative because of its antiquity. As will appear in more detail in a later chapter, its extraordinary richness needs to be borne in mind particularly when we approach the study of Attic tragedy. The more one surveys Attic tragedy *as a whole*, including the titles and fragments of the lost dramas, the more one is struck by the catholicity of that art form, both in content and in tone, especially in its earlier phases. That catholicity Attic tragedy seems to have inherited directly, along with so much else, from the traditional mythic world. Our perception of this may have been seriously distorted by the solemnity of the critics and educators of the post-tragic age, especially those unknowns who were responsible for the selection of the relatively few tragedies that have reached us complete. Indeed, our resultant expectation of the lofty and serious tone that later came to be felt as uniquely appropriate to tragedy may sometimes blind us to certain features—especially fantastic and comic features—in the extant tragedies themselves.

THE POET AS INTERPRETER OF LIFE

The mythic world, then, comprised somewhere within it almost every aspect of human experience, but the poet's function was not confined to vividly enacting aspects of that world. His function was also to interpret the myths: to elicit from them general conclusions about the way life is, the way death is, and above all the ways in which mortality relates to the divine and eternal. This function is for the most part implicit in the Homeric epics; it becomes explicit in the *Works and Days* of Hesiod and in choral lyric. In one important branch of early poetry, the elegiac, the commentary on life to some extent detaches itself from the mythic corpus and the advice is given directly, although even here the myths are fairly often invoked as exemplars, to make vivid a given teaching.[27] This gnomic element, whatever form it takes, is central to the pretragic poetic tradition. The Greek poet claimed, and was felt, to be *a teacher of how to live*; we should not blind ourselves to that fact, academically convenient though it may be to judge his work purely from an aesthetic, or philological, or historical point of view. This appears not only from the poets' own practice at all periods but also from the bitterness of the opposition that they met with in the late fifth and the fourth centuries at the hands of the philosophers, above all Socrates and Plato. The philosophers' objection was not (like the objection heard so often from modern philosophers and from the modern public at large) that what the poet did was socially irrelevant, a mere matter for aesthetes and literary critics to squabble over in the darkened cloisters of academe. Rather, it was that poetry claimed to teach an art of crucial importance to all human beings, whether as individuals or as citizens, the art of right living; but that the poets went about it in altogether the wrong way, drawing not on rational principles but on that age-old reservoir of human experience, the myths. "We [the philosophers and the poets] are rivals in the same trade" is Plato's famous statement, near the end of his life, about the roots of the quarrel between them, "we are competitors in the noblest drama of them all" (*Laws* 7.817b). Even in his lifetime and after we can still hear many voices maintaining the traditional view of the poet's social effectiveness. It is true that some of those voices may sound somewhat shrill (they are the desperate and confused cries of a rear guard in the final retreat of the song culture), but their message surely represents the practice and belief of the whole line of major Greek poets from Homer through the tragedians. "The *Odyssey* is a fine mirror of human life (*καλὸν ἀνθρωπίνου βίου κάτοπτρον*)," said Alcidamas the Sophist, an older contemporary of Plato (*ap.* Aristotle, *Rhet.* 3.1406b12); and an almost exact contemporary, Xenophon, has this to say about the elegiac poetry of Theognis: "This poet has made his theme none other than the excellence (*aretē*) and the viciousness of humanity. His poetry is a treatise about humanity, just as if an expert on horses were to write a treatise about horse-training."[28] Thus even in the period of the final disintegration of the song culture there were still well-informed Greeks who recognized its claim to teach the art of living as true, or if not true, still as centrally important. This claim, too, was directly inherited by Attic tragedy from the song culture, and perhaps we should not neglect it if we are to see that art in its proper historical, social, and literary perspective. Whatever the claim's actual merits, it is of course a claim so unfashionable nowadays that many will find it hard to take seriously. But that seems to be another of those fundamental differences between the conditions of ancient Greek and modern poetry that we can only assimilate with an imaginative effort.

A NOTE ON THE METERS OF PRETRAGIC POETRY

Finally, before taking ship to Athens (our destination in the next chapter), we must consider yet another fundamental difference between ancient Greek and contemporary English poetry. This is the matter of metrics. For it is probably the Greek meters that provide our most important and objective clue to the genesis of Attic tragedy and to the nature of its relationship with the pretragic poetry. Unfortunately, Greek metrics is a technical subject, not easily surveyed either briefly or in such terms as will be intelligible to an educated but "Greekless" reader (and it was for such a reader, I take it, that the Sather series was originally designed, quite as much as for the professionals). It is also difficult to expound, even at best, without inducing mortification in persons who do not know Greek. I can never forget experiencing a similar feeling in a chapel in Wales (one of the last European strongholds of the song culture, complete with *agōnes mousikoi*), where a series of *pennillion* were being performed—extemporized Welsh songs sung against instruments playing a traditional melody. At the end of each, the presiding clergyman would rise and say pointedly: "What a pity you English in the back there don't understand Welsh! You miss all the beauty of it!" Nonetheless, some of the metrical background must here be sketched in if we are to follow the next stages in the story.

The essential points to be grasped are two: first, the profound difference between the quantitative verse with which the ancient Greek poet worked and our contemporary verse shapes; second, the rigorous distinctions that were maintained between one type of meter and another during the pretragic period.

If all poetry in all languages is (or has been until recently) in one aspect a glorious game with patterns of sound, the early Greek poet enjoyed exceptional opportunities for playing that game to the limit. It has been said by one of the most learned of all modern writers on the subject—and a writer least of all given to incautious generalizations—that the potentialities of ancient Greek in this respect far exceed those of any other language.[29] The basic principle on which ancient Greek versification depends, *syllable quantity*, already brings it closer to the precision and variety of sound attainable in music than is possible for most of our modern languages. English-speaking poets (to take the comparison nearest home) live primarily on *word accent*. Until early in the present century, English poetry was a matter of stressed syllable alternating with unstressed syllable(s) in a certain number of regular and recognized patterns—a very limited number, in practice. There must be many besides myself who have heard Robert Frost wryly remarking: "There are two things you can do in English verse: you can do strict iambic or loose iambic," with "loose iambic" defined as "two shorts between the longs."[30] In much of the most interesting contemporary poetry, of course, even the convention that the stresses should recur in fixed patterns has fallen away. That is testimony, one will believe, to our poetry's prime merit, honesty, since a shapeless society probably exacts a rhythmless poem, but unfortunately for our present purposes it sets poetry as now understood even further apart from the poetry of the ancient Greeks, which is essentially rhythmic, singable, danceable—a matter of the pulse.[31] And perceptible rhythm here does not entail monotony, any more than it does in music. For the ancient Greek versification did not depend on simple alternations of stressed and unstressed syllables, nor indeed, in most of its forms, did it depend on the inflexible and mechanical alternation of anything. It was built on complex patterns of long and short syllables—long and short, that is, in duration, a long syllable standing to a short as a quarter-note in music stands to an eighth-note. This allows a very large number of patterns, none of which can be precisely reproduced in an accentual language like ours, and most of which are easier conveyed in music than imitated in any modern speech. To take only one example of a simple pattern common in Greek versification: the Greek proper name whose beauty obsessed Keats above all, *Endýmion*, was pronounced by him, as it is by us, with a stress on the second syllable and no particular emphasis on the other three.[32] In the quantitative Greek this name becomes a quite different sound, *Ēndўmĭōn*: long, two shorts, long—a choriamb. That marvelously musical pattern is difficult to reproduce even once in the English language, let alone in sequences of any length. Here, by contrast, is the Greek of a line by Sappho that was already quoted in the second chapter: "Maidenhood, you have left me, Maidenhood, where have you gone?"[33] "Maidenhood" is *pārthĕnĭā*, exactly the same pattern as *Endymion*; in this line Sappho puts together three such choriambic units in succession, and rounds them off with a bacchius (⏑ – –), like this:

pārthĕnĭā, pārthĕnĭā, pōı mĕ lĭpōıs' ăpōıchēı?

That example of the built-in musical quality of Greek versification must suffice for the moment. We need only add that so far as is known the melody (if a poem was sung) and also the dance (if it was danced) conformed to the same pattern of longs and shorts as we can still read in the Greek texts of the poems. Thus those texts, both of poetry and of tragedy, at least preserve some idea of the rhythms of the otherwise lost music and dance that accompanied them. Only with the advent of the so-called New Music in the later decades of the fifth century was this close partnership broken up.[34]

The outcome of this quantitative principle of versification is a poetic art of marvelous variety and beauty, but also an extremely exacting one.

As anyone who himself has tried to compose in the Greek meters will know, the words (or, in the earliest hexameter poetry, the phrases, the "formulae") each with its inexorably fixed musical shape, have to be fitted into whatever metrical pattern the composer has committed himself to; a Roman poet, working in the same metrical tradition, was not far out when he compared the process to mosaic work, the words being slotted tightly, like tesserae, into their inevitable places.[35] It is thus small wonder that the poets of the archaic period tended to specialize in certain types of meter, much as their contemporary fellow craftsmen, the sculptors, tended to specialize only in one or two postures for the free-standing figure. In fact, an archaic poet would normally restrict his main output to only one of the following major classes of meter (and hence, of course, to the kind of theme and subject matter that traditionally went with each class): dactylic hexameter, elegiac (sometimes adding the practice of iambics, sometimes not),[36] solo lyric, and choral lyric. There were occasional minor exceptions; for example, Anacreon composed some iambics and some elegiacs, in addition to the solo lyrics for which he was most famous (West, *Iambi et Elegi Graeci*, vol. II, pp. 30–34); Simonides, besides his main work as choral lyricist, composed many elegiacs (ibid., pp. 112–17).[37] But one practice that is never found in any serious poem of the pretragic era is the mixture of any two or more of those major classes of meter within a single poem. Not only the several classes of meter in themselves but also the manner of performance, the dialect, and to a great extent the subject and tone associated with each of them, were apparently felt as too different to be brought together in the same piece; to the archaic ear that would be as disconcerting as, say, the intervention of a trombone in a string quartet. Thus, to take a somewhat extreme example, you never find a pretragic poem that modulates from iambic speech to the sung rhythms of solo lyric, let alone from those into the song and dance of choral lyric. You never even find an extensive elegiac poem that modulates into iambics (or vice versa), even though, as we have seen, these two meters seem to have been felt as rather similar media; several early poets, notably Archilochus and Solon, composed extensively in both. The only apparent exception to this rule in the archaic period was a mild one, and the poem concerned was comic. It was the lost *Margites*, long attributed to Homer himself, composed partly in dactylic hexameters and partly in iambic trimeters. Since it told the story of a totally incompetent man, a kind of anti-hero (the *Silliad* has been suggested as the best translation of its title), the mixture of heroic hexameter and down-to-earth trimeter must have greatly reinforced the deliberate bathos at which it evidently aimed. I wish we had the whole of it, instead of only a few intriguing fragments;[38] but even if it were recovered complete it certainly would not affect our general picture of the strict distinction between the various metrical genres that obtained in serious pretragic poetry.[39]

There is much more yet to be said on the metrical aspect of our subject as a whole, but it will be more conveniently placed in a later chapter. I will make only one remark in anticipation. From a metrical point of view, the great innovation of Attic tragedy was definitely not the discovery of new kinds of meter; every major variety of Greek meter, with only one probable exception, had already been highly developed in archaic nondramatic poetry—but separately, and often in separate areas of the Hellenic world. The unprecedented achievement of Attic tragedy was its fusion of the known metrical genres within the compass of a single work. Only when we realize this can we fully understand both the enormous popular success of tragedy in the fifth century (to the extent that for a time it came near to killing off the composition of any other form of song),[40] and the unparalleled technical complexity of the tragedian's craft. The tragedian was to emerge as the Greek poet par excellence, and tragedy was to become the architectonic art under which almost all earlier Greek poetic techniques were to be subsumed. Nor, finally, was this true only of metrical and performing techniques. It seems to have been true also (although the matter is obviously harder to demonstrate objectively) of the subject matters, themes, and tones associated with each separate technique during the pretragic period; here again, one of tragedy's mightiest achievements was to fuse what had formerly been distinct.

* * *

In this first part of the book I have tried to reconstruct certain of the conditions under which the pretragic Greek poet worked. The reconstruction has necessarily been less complete than one could wish, largely because of the fragmentary condition both of the early poets' works as we now have them and of the secondary ancient sources, mostly belonging to the Hellenistic period, on whom we have to depend so heavily for information about the performance of poetry. Very many details must remain in the dark or half-dark. Yet some fairly certain conclusions can be drawn. The early Greek poet differs from his modern homonym above all in that his work is not a private book-art but a performing art which in one way or another extends into all society. A contemporary American poet has written, sadly:

> As for the poetry
> it works wonders like a space agency
> and saves no one,
> not even poets.

and has mentioned in correspondence that what he really wants to do is to compose such a poetry as will reach *the people who don't read books*.[41] That marvelous ideal was a simple reality for the poet of the Greek song culture. Besides that, he shared with his society something that no writer may dare hope for now or in the imaginable future: an immemorially ancient mythical world in which he and his society might discover universally applicable patterns of human character and behavior. Finally, his art, metrically considered, was something far nearer music than any poetry has managed to be since. Rhythm was essential to his utterance, rhythm in almost innumerable forms; and often the verbal rhythm was reinforced by melody and the dance.

T. S. Eliot divided poetry into three voices:

> The first voice is the voice of the poet talking to himself—or to nobody. The second is the voice of the poet addressing an audience, whether large or small. The third is the voice of the poet when he attempts to create a dramatic character speaking in verse.[42]

The first voice, as we have seen, was an impossibility under Greek conditions. The second is heard loud and clear all across the early Greek landscape; and often, already, it sounds so like the third, the dramatic voice, that distinctions are hard to draw. One or two poems of Sappho seem to have pitted two dramatic voices against each other within the same performance. Yet even that achievement, although very close to drama in the modern sense, is not like tragedy in the ancient sense. It is not that unprecedented mixture of all the early poetic genres—that compound which unites and transcends all the elements of which it is formed. No such thing, as far as we know, was to be found until the middle years of the sixth century B.C. or elsewhere than in Athens, which will be the scene of Part Two.

PART
TWO

The Confluence

4. Poetry in Sixth-Century Athens

It has long been observed that in general the Athenian thinker or artist tends to enter the Panhellenic arena relatively late,[1] but that once he has entered he works rapidly and singlemindedly, exploiting many techniques developed abroad and ultimately creating out of them an art that transcends all its foreign models. For example, philosophy had been practiced in one guise or another on the eastern and western borders of the Greek world for a century before any of its major exponents even came to reside in Athens, and for a century and a half before the Athenian Socrates began his career. Somewhat similar stories can be told of historiography and oratory and—the most obvious instance, perhaps—architecture. The Parthenon itself, and the other buildings of the fifth-century Acropolis, present a style that is foreign in its origins and yet not foreign as a whole. It is Doric and Ionic and . . . an interesting question, what exactly is the *Athenian* element there? Perhaps the short answer might be: daring; and a few extraordinary individuals who saw how to exploit the entire Hellenic architectural tradition and how to break it wide open at the same time. We might borrow an epigrammatic phrase from Aristotle to describe this peculiar Athenian gift: *τοῖς παραδεδομένοις χρῆσθαι καλῶς*, "to apply the traditions finely" (*Poet.* 1453b25–26).[2]

It has equally long been suggested that the art of tragedy is another, and perhaps the extreme, example of this Athenian tendency; that in some respects, at least, tragedy was a conscious and deliberate synthesis of most of the previously independent genres of Greek poetry into a new art, accomplished by a few individuals between the middle of the sixth century and the beginning of the fifth. Wilamowitz himself maintained a version of this assumption, especially in his writings on metrics, and it seems to be adopted, whether openly or by implication, by several other modern writers on Greek meter. A somewhat similar assumption underlies the (to me, at least) epoch-making studies by Gerald F. Else.[3] There have been objections, of course, to Else, of which the following is an example: "We cannot separate Greek Theatre from Greek rituals in order to interpret it as the result of a *literary* synthesis of two *literary*, *nonmimetic* forms" (my emphasis).[4] But a serious difficulty seems to lie in the absolute distinction thus drawn between the supposedly "literary" and "nonmimetic" poetry of the pretragic period, and the "mimetic" art of tragedy. As the preceding chapters have attempted to show (and as a glance at Aristotle's *Poetics*, for instance, will confirm) such a distinction will not apply to the poetry and drama of archaic and classical Greece: both arts were mimetic, and even Aristotle still had no word for *literary* in anything like the modern sense, with its evocation of silent written words confined in books. What Else thinks of, and what I think of, is no abrupt jump from the nonmimetic into the mimetic, but a synthesis of live performing arts. There is in quite recent history at least one close analogy to such a rapid synthesis of diverse arts (as will be suggested at the end of this chapter); further, it seems difficult on any other hypothesis to account for those characteristics of Greek tragedy (especially the *metrical* characteristics) which will be considered in the ensuing chapters.

I am not here concerned, however, to attempt yet another blow-by-blow reconstruction of the origins of Attic tragedy. There exists of course abundant speculation on this intriguing subject, and I have contemplated much of it; but I have concluded that the evidence is simply insufficient to allow the application of rational methods. The problem has sometimes presented itself as comparable to that of reconstructing an outsize vase out of a score or so of microscopic shards, given that half of them may well never have belonged to the vase in the first place; but which half, you cannot tell. The aim of the present chapter is more modest. It is primarily to reconstruct *the artistic environment within which Attic tragedy, as we know it, arose*, by surveying the history of the song culture in Athens during the sixth and early fifth centuries. To do so will certainly not be to explain or to describe the ultimate origins of tragedy. Nor will it be to deny the possibility, or even here and there the probability, that many of the theories so far published about those origins may have correctly identified certain altogether nonpoetic elements in tragedy's formation: agricultural rituals, for instance, or ancestor-cult, or Dying-God rites, or any of the various masques and mummings that are shown on the Attic vases of the relevant period. The trouble with all of these theories is that we cannot verify them; we can only guess with more or less plausibility, for there is just not enough evidence. On the contrary, there exists a very substantial body of evidence, namely, the entire corpus of classical Greek poetry from Homer onward, by which we can control the hypothesis that one of the most important elements in the formation of Attic tragedy as we know it, in matters both of technique and of content, was the predramatic poetic tradition. There is, further, overwhelming evidence that this view was held by a majority of the classical Greeks themselves. At this point, for brevity's sake, we need only mention the simple matter of nomenclature. In our book sources from Aristophanes, through Plato and Aristotle, to the end of classical antiquity, tragedy is invariably treated as a species of *poetry*, and the tragedian is referred to as a *poet* (*poiētēs*) hardly less often than he is referred to as a tragedian (*tragikos*, *tragōidopoios*, *tragōidodidaskalos* or, in later times, *tragōidos*). Even Thespis himself is named a *poiētēs* in what is usually considered the most reliable testimony that we have concerning him, the entry in the Parian Marble that records the earliest official tragic contest at Athens.[5] Oddly enough, not a single ancient source ever alludes to him or any of his successors as (for example) a fat dancer or a hairy satyr or a stiltwalker or an ancestor worshiper. The word is *poet*.

* * *

What songs the lyre players sang, or the passionate mourners chanted, who are seen on Attic geometric and subgeometric vases, is beyond conjecture.[6] The vase-paintings are evidence that the Athenians of the ninth to the seventh century B.C. were no strangers to mime, dance, and (presumably) song; indeed, we should expect to find as much in any Greek community from then until now. Yet it is remarkable how little is heard of Attica as a center of song before about 600 B.C. So far as our information goes, there were no widely known musical festivals within its borders, and no famous schools of poets either. In Boeotia, in Lesbos, in East Greece and the islands, in Laconia, and even perhaps in the Sicilian colonies, the various genres of Greek poetry were being practiced and developed well before the end of the seventh century, but the Athenian contribution to the Panhellenic song culture up to that time seems to have been little or none. The only *named* Athenian pretragic poet is of course Solon, who lived in the generation before Thespis; his career extended probably from a little before 600 B.C. to the fifties of the sixth century.[7] Even that extraordinary man, however, for all his originality, composed in metrical forms—elegiac couplets, trochaic tetrameters, and iambic trimeters—which had been in use among the Ionic-speaking Greeks for at least a century;[8] and Solon even followed them in composing in the Ionic/epic language, not in the Attic dialect. The anonymous fragments of presumably Athenian poetry, such as the famous hexameter inscription on the Dipylon jug of the second half of the eighth century B.C., are again in a metrical form long developed elsewhere.[9] The same is true of the Homeric Hymns to Demeter and Athena, which some have assumed to be Attic works, but largely because of their Attic subject matter—hardly a safe criterion in itself, since it would apply equally to (say) the seventeenth and eighteenth poems of the Keian Bacchylides.[10] In brief, there seems to have been no poetry earlier than Thespis that could have been identified by a listener as distinctively Attic, in meter or in dialect. The only native Attic poetry was to be tragedy; perhaps it was not entirely coincidental that the three-dimensional kind of poetry which we call Attic tragedy should have come into being in a city whose early artistic tradition had been almost exclusively visual. Before then, Athens seems on our evidence to have been a poetic backwater.

We are now to examine the extraordinary reversal of that situation which occurred in the period between the latter part of Solon's lifetime and the Persian Wars, that is, from about 570 to 490 B.C. By the latter date, the city which had earlier played almost no part in the song culture had become that culture's hub and center, not merely attracting to itself most of the great contemporary singers from other regions of Greece but also producing an incomparable school of native singers—the tragic poets. To identify all the underlying causes of this cultural revolution would be to write a perfect history of sixth- and early fifth-century Athens in all its aspects, economic and political as well as artistic; for the ancient city-state was a tight-knit organism, its activities far more interdependent than those of any modern community. One would, for instance, have to weigh the effects of the upsurge in Athenian industry (especially among the pottery kilns), the influx of non-Attic workers, and the concomitant development of foreign trade. For all such matters, however, as for so many aspects of archaic Greek history, the evidence is insufficient to allow very precise conclusions. Only one factor in the Athenian poetic revolution seems fairly clearly identifiable at this date, but it is perhaps the most important of them all: that revolution was actively encouraged, if not inspired, by the political leadership of the city. In part, at least, it seems to have been due to a policy, a deliberate effort of will, which was sustained throughout the period, notwithstanding several changes of regime: from the obscure period of political confusion in the wake of Solon's reforms, to the tyranny of Peisistratos (which lasted, with interruptions, from 561/60 B.C. until his death in 528/27),[11] to the tyranny of his sons (which ended with the expulsion of the dynasty in 511/10), into the Kleisthenic democracy that succeeded it. The policy was implemented in at least two ways, to judge from the record: by the official institution or remodeling of *agōnes mousikoi* at two of the Athenian religious festivals; and by personal acts on the part of the political leaders, especially during the regime of Peisistratos's sons.

At this point (as so often in the course of our study) the modern reader may perhaps need to overcome some preconceptions. Anyone who has lived through the middle years of the twentieth century may well shudder at the mere thought of "political intervention" in the artistic life of a community, remembering the resultant paintings and sculptures of musclebound ideological paragons, the public buildings whose lifeless geometry is only accentuated by incrustations of totalitarian symbol and misapplied classical motif. If, however, he is to sympathize with events in a sixth-century B.C. city-state, his model should rather be the mediaeval French cathedral city or Renaissance Florence: the political authority provides the framework necessary for massive artistic achievement and certainly reaps some political prestige therefrom in its time, but the work of art itself, in its time and forever after, is directed elsewhere, to the glory of God and the delight of man.

In archaic Athens, the process seems to have begun (as we shall see), with a reorganization of the Panathenaic festival perhaps datable to 566/5 B.C. By that time there already existed at least one, and perhaps two, precedents elsewhere in Greece. Both are worth mentioning briefly.[12] It seems likely that the tyrant Periander, who ruled Corinth in the decades around 600 B.C., encouraged the kitharode Arion in his productions of a new form of dithyramb, a poetic genre that was elsewhere associated with Dionysos.[13] However that may be, the tyrant Kleisthenes of Sikyon, whose regime is datable approximately to the first quarter of the sixth century, intervened with undoubted effect in the poetic life of his city: first negatively, by abolishing the existing Homeric rhapsode contests at Sikyon; second, by transferring certain performances which Herodotus calls *tragikoi choroi* from the tomb of the hero Adrastos to (a festival of?) Dionysos. Both acts were overtly political, according to Herodotus, being aimed against the supremacy of Kleisthenes' great enemy, Argos.[14] It is further noteworthy that certain of the Athenian nobility in the first half of the sixth century had close family connections with both the Corinthian tyrant and the Sikyonian. Megakles, of the great house of the Alkmaionids, married Kleisthenes' daughter, Agarista (Herodotus 6.130–31). Even more suggestive, however, is the case of Hippokleides, a member of the Philaid house. Not only was this man related by marriage to Periander (Herodotus 6.128.2) and on close terms with Kleisthenes (until the unfortunate breach of etiquette narrated in Herodotus 6.129); but there is also some evidence that he was archon of Athens in the very year, 566/5 B.C., in which the Panathenaic festival was reorganized.[15] If true, surely not quite coincidental?

THE GREAT PANATHENAIA

For time out of mind the Athenians had honored their city goddess with an annual festival, the Panathenaia. Already in the fifth century the historian Hellanicus attributed its foundation to the ancient Athenian king Erichthonios, and in this he was followed by several later writers, for example the mythographer known to us as Apollodorus, who says that Erichthonios "established the image (*xoanon*) of Athena on the Acropolis and organized the festival of the Panathenaia." The only significant variant is one found in Pausanias, to the effect that under Erichthonios the festival was called simply *Athenaia*, the name *Panathenaia* being substituted at the time of Theseus's synoecism. By any reckoning, however, the annual ceremony was exceedingly ancient.[16] From the classical evidence concerning it we can infer that the proceedings were primarily ritual in nature, focused upon the primeval *xoanon* of Athena that was housed on the Acropolis; essentially it was a sacrifice on the rock, preceded by a procession and followed by a feast.[17]

Quite suddenly, sometime in the second quarter of the sixth century B.C., a new and more spectacular Panathenaia was superposed on the old. The *annual* rites for Athena continued (how could they not?), under the name of *Little Panathenaia*, but every fourth year an enlarged version of the ceremony was now to take place, the Great Panathenaia.

Although 566/5 B.C., the date of this innovation given in Jerome, cannot be accepted as certain, it can hardly be much more than a decade or so out;[18] for the earliest group of the official Panathenaic prize-amphoras, all of them showing athletic and equestrian events, are stylistically datable in the second quarter of the sixth century. The prize-amphoras also confirm Jerome's other item of information, namely, that an important feature of the new quadrennial celebration was an *agōn gymnicus*, a contest in athletics, and they add the information that there were equestrian contests also.[19] So much is certain about the new festival, and it is already interesting enough in itself for the student of Athenian politics, culture, and religion, and of their perpetual interaction. By a deliberate (and more or less datable) civic act a primeval religious cult has been enlarged by an essentially secular addition. As a result the Great Panathenaia ranges itself alongside the preexisting Panhellenic quadrennial festivals at Olympia, Delphi, Nemea, and the Isthmus;[20] and incidentally the fame of the goddess of Athens, the skill of her potters, and the excellence of her main agricultural product, olive oil, are advertised across the Mediterranean area by the Panathenaic prize-amphoras the victors carry home from the contests.[21]

Unfortunately for our purposes, the literary and archaeological evidence about other aspects of the new quadrennial festival is much less clear. Two questions, above all, have occasioned great debate: who was responsible for the reorganization? And at what date were contests in poetry and music attached to the festival? To a certain extent, as will appear, these questions are interrelated. For a thorough and, to me, generally convincing analysis of the complicated evidence, I would refer to the article by Davison cited in note 16 above, to which I have little to add but a minor suggestion here and there. In brief, the problems present themselves as follows.

Among our ancient sources, only one expressly names any individual as responsible for the institution of the Great Panathenaia, and that individual is Peisistratos. A scholium on Aristides' *Panathenaicus* remarks: "He [Aristides] refers to the Little Panathenaia. That is the older, having been instituted in the reign of Erichthonios, son of Amphiktyon, on the occasion of the death of the Giant Asterios; but it was Peisistratos who established the Great Panathenaia."[22] A second source, Marcellinus in his *Life of Thucydides*, mentions Hippokleides, son of Tisandros, as the man "in whose archonship the Panathenaia was established"; that, if true, leaves open the possibility that Hippokleides' relationship to the event was simply chronological, but in view of his status and known connections (see above, p. 84) one would rather expect that he would have participated actively.[23] Finally, the sources mention two other important political names, not in connection with the establishment of the Great Panathenaia as a whole but in connection with one of its most extraordinary features, the contest between Homeric rhapsodes—the feature that marks it off most sharply from the other major Hellenic quadrennial festivals, even the Pythia at Delphi. Diogenes Laertius, in his account of Solon, says that "he [Solon] moved a law that the poems of Homer should be delivered rhapsodically on cue (*ex hypobolēs*), that is, that where the first rhapsode ended, the next should begin."[24] If that information is accepted, the rhapsode-contests at the Great Panathenaia must date back to the earliest years of the festival, if not to its very beginning; for Solon can hardly have lived past the middle of the sixth century. On the other hand, the unknown author of the pseudo-Platonic dialogue *Hipparchus* says that this son of Peisistratos "first brought the poems of Homer to this land [of Attica] and compelled the rhapsodes at the Panathenaia to go through them in order, picking up one from the other [*ex hypolēpseōs*], even as they still do now."[25] If there is truth in this, the institution of the rhapsode-contests should date from the last decade or two of the Peisistratid tyranny, the *terminus* being provided by the assassination of Hipparchus in 514 B.C.—at the Panathenaia festival, it happens.

It will be seen that not one of these ancient sources is particularly early or notably trustworthy on questions of archaic history; much depends on the quality of *their* sources, a question we now are in no position to determine. They do, however, conspire to suggest the existence of a strong tradition that the rhapsode-contests were incorporated into the Great Panathenaia at some period between 566 and 514 (at the very latest) and that the Peisistratean house was in some way involved with them. The alleged involvement of Solon, if taken seriously, might incline one to date the rhapsode-contests in 566 or not long thereafter, and to assume that the story about Hipparchus actually reflects a *reorganization* of them about a generation later; but certainty is not to be had on this evidence alone.

By the classical period, the musical contests attached to the Great Panathenaia certainly included not merely Homeric rhapsodizing but also kitharody, aulody, and unaccompanied lyre- and oboe-playing.[26]

Again, there has been much debate as to exactly when these contests were originally incorporated, but the ceramic and inscriptional evidence adduced by Davison strongly suggests that they go back well into the sixth century and in some cases almost as far back as 566.[27] Unfortunately, victors in the musical contests were not normally rewarded with large quantities of Attic oil, as the athletic and equestrian competitors were, but with gold crowns and/or cash; in this case, therefore, we cannot check the early record with the aid of a long and fairly well datable series of official Panathenaic prize-amphoras.[28] Nonetheless, on present evidence it seems reasonable to conclude, with Davison, that the four strictly musical contests at the Great Panathenaia were in being quite early, before the time of the institution of the Great Dionysia. The exact date of the rhapsode-contests must be left open.[29] But the effect of them all must from the first have been similar to that of the athletic and equestrian contests, in that they would have attracted skilled performers from all over the Greek world.[30]

THE CITY DIONYSIA

A generation after the establishment of the Great Panathenaia, but still within the lifetime of Peisistratos, another contest was instituted at Athens: a contest between tragic poets. All we can certainly know about this momentous innovation is that it occurred in one of the years 536/5, 535/4, or 534/3,[31] and that the contest was attached to a festival of Dionysos subsequently known as the *Διονύσια τὰ ἐν ἄστει* or *Διονύσια τὰ μεγάλα* or simply *Διονύσια*.[32] All the other ancient evidence that bears on it, or has been supposed to bear on it, continues to be disputed by reputable students of the subject.[33] This applies even to that document which, on the face of it, might seem to have the strongest claim to our respect, the famous entry in the Parian Marble: "Thespis the poet first [acted?], who taught (*edidaxe*, i.e., "produced") a drama in the City; [and as prize] was set up the goat. . . ."[34] The word *edidaxe* may be thought to have the ring of authenticity, since this same term is used of the competing poets in all the subsequent (and certainly authentic) records of the Athenian dramatic contests.[35] There thus seems to be no great obstacle to accepting the first two clauses of the entry (down to "the City") as derived ultimately from an official record. The last clause is infinitely more problematic; in form it bears no resemblance to anything found in official *didaskaliai* at any date, and its goat lies under suspicion for a number of reasons.[36]

That much, and in my opinion nothing more, can be obtained with a fair certainty from the ancient documentary evidence that refers to the establishment of the tragic contests at the City Dionysia. From evidence of other kinds, three inferences may reasonably be made. The first is that the small archaic temple in the precinct of Dionysos, just south of the existing theater, may have been founded in connection with the same event.[37] The second is that Peisistratos (now nearing the end of his life) and/or his sons must have been involved in the innovation, if not actually its initiators. No ancient source actually says so; but (as we have seen) our definite ancient information about the founding of the City Dionysia happens to be remarkably scanty, and there is much evidence, to say nothing of general probability, that the ruling house was very much concerned both with the temples and with the festivals of Athens.[38] Indeed, in the circumstances of a sixth-century city-state, to neglect those matters would have been to neglect the art of politics itself.

The third inference that may be made about the nature of the earliest official contests in tragedy is perhaps more solidly based than either of the other two. It is, in brief, that *from a strictly religious and ritual point of view* those contests were the least significant event in the least significant festival devoted to Dionysos in Attica. However great their importance in the artistic and intellectual history of the city (and, indeed, of Western civilization), they had little to offer a devotee of the god's cult as such.

The primary evidence about the various Attic festivals of Dionysos has been collected and analyzed by the late Sir Arthur Pickard-Cambridge in the most masterly of all his books.[39] To this the reader must be referred for details; all that will be attempted here is to summarize his results as faithfully as possible and to consider them from our present perspective. The "oldest and most holy" shrine of Dionysos in Athens was that named *en Limnais*; its location is still debated, but it was almost certainly not in the Theater precinct.[40] This shrine was the focus of the strange, and in some respects even eerie, rites of the three-day festival named the *Anthestēria*, generally acknowledged in ancient as well as modern times to have been the oldest Athenian Dionysiac festival.[41] Less is recorded about a second major Athenian Dionysiac festival, the *Lēnaia*,[42] but the following facts are beyond doubt: its focus was not in the Theater precinct but in a sanctuary called the Lenaion, the whereabouts of which is still debated; it involved a *pompē*, a procession; and it was administered by the *archōn basileus* (a point to which we shall return). There are indications that the Lenaia festival was extremely ancient in origin[43] and that either at it or at the Anthesteria maenadic rites were celebrated in the presence of a Dionysos-mask affixed to a pillar;[44] and one late authority has even been thought to speak of a song performed by its celebrants "which involved the tearing apart (*sparagmos*) of Dionysos."[45] Of the *Rural Dionysia*, the Dionysiac festivals celebrated in the various Attic demes, little need be said from our point of view, except that they, again, seem to have been of very ancient origin and rich in agricultural ritual: "closer to the earth than the great festivals of the city," as Pickard-Cambridge put it.[46]

Against this background, we may now consider the ritual aspects of the City Dionysia festival. There is no evidence about it dating from as early as the Peisistratid regime but documents of the fifth century B.C. and onward permit a fairly full reconstruction of the proceedings in the classical period, and in matters of ritual (as opposed to *contests attached to ritual*) there are not likely to have been radical changes since Peisistratos's day.[47] We may observe first of all that the City Dionysia was administered by the *archōn epōnymos*, a detail that is significant in itself. The most venerable office in the Athenian state was that of the *archōn basileus*, among whose prime duties was the supervision of the Eleusinian Mysteries and of the Lenaia; after that came the management of "practically all the ancestral sacrifices"; after that, the hearing of legal cases involving impiety, the allocation of priesthoods, and murder. The *archōn basileus* was in fact concerned with most matters of deep religious significance in Athens. The office of the *archōn epōnymos*, by contrast, was later in creation and essentially political in function.[48]

The festival of the City Dionysia was formally in honor of Dionysos Eleuthereus, and the most striking ritual element in it was devoted to the god in that aspect. In the archaic temple within the Theater precinct was preserved an image, a *xoanon*, of Dionysos, which was said to have been brought to Athens from the deme Eleutherai on the Boeotian frontier.[49] This image was taken from its temple and transported to a temple near the Academy (on the route, in fact, to Eleutherai), where sacrifice and song were offered to it; finally it was brought back in a torchlight procession to the Theater precinct, where it was set up to witness the dramatic performances.[50] The date of this ceremony's origin is unknown, but the primitive character of the image (see note 49 above) and of the rite might suggest that it was ancient; certainly the event it was supposed to commemorate, the bringing of the image from Eleutherai to Attica by one Pegasos, was apparently believed to have taken place in the time of the kings. It does not seem likely that the image, the rite, and the aetiology for both were all fabricated ad hoc in ca. 534 B.C. to suit the institution of the Great Dionysia (who would have been taken in by such a fabrication?), and I am therefore inclined to think that they were very much older.[51]

The second element in the annual proceedings was a magnificent procession through the city, in which bulls were escorted for sacrifice in the temple in the Theater precinct; there also marched men and women carrying a variety of objects—baskets and trays of offerings, wine skins, long loaves of bread, and, not least, phalloi. This *pompē*, "the central rite of the Dionysia" as Parke calls it, was succeeded by a *kōmos* or revel.[52] Again, the origin of this second element cannot be dated by external evidence, and yet, again, it has the air of an ancient religious ritual rather than of a performance arbitrarily invented in ca. 534 B.C. Indeed, its essential components are precisely those of the immemorially old Rural Dionysia celebrated in the Attic demes. As indicated in a brilliant passage of Aristophanes' *Acharnians* (237–79), where Dikaiopolis performs this rural rite, they were: a *pompē* (line 248) leading up toward a sacrifice (240) in which were carried a basket of offerings (242, 253) and a phallos (243, 259–60), and there are hints of a *kōmos* to follow (277). Clearly the two rites, *τὰ κατ' ἄγρους Διονύσια* (*Ach.* 202, 250), and the element of the *Διονύσια τὰ ἐν ἄστει* (e.g., Dem. *Meid.* 10) which we are now considering, are identical except as regards magnificence. It is open to us to suppose either that this element of the Great Dionysia had anciently been performed at Athens, as the city counterpart of the ceremony performed in the rural demes, or that it was instituted in ca. 534 on the model of the Rural Dionysia. Perhaps the former alternative may seem more probable; but in either case the ceremony is essentially a religious rite for the god, with roots deep in the Attic past.

We come now to the third and last element in the festival, the tragic contests. Unlike the other two elements, this was established at a known moment in history (i.e., within a year or two of 534 B.C.), and its traditional ritual content, so far as our sources go, was minimal; the only ritual activity, in the strict sense, directly associated with the contests was the purification of the theater at some point by the offering of a piglet.[53] Certainly they took place within Dionysos's sacred precinct (of which the theater was a part), and the god's ancient image, as well as his priest, were given front seats in the performances. Certainly, also, the period of the contests was perceived as sacred to the extent that prisoners might be temporarily released and legal suits and distraints for debt forbidden while it ran its course.[54] Otherwise, the nondramatic activities in the theater were notably secular and political in nature, at least by the latter half of the fifth century: the display of the allied tribute moneys, the parade of orphaned children in armor, the proclamation of honors decreed to citizens and foreigners.[55] As for the contests themselves, their analogy is to be found not in any native Attic or even Hellenic ritual, but, rather, in the long series of *agōnes mousikoi* which were discussed in Chapter I (pp. 7–10).

When one surveys this Dionysiac festival as a whole, one is struck by its resemblances to the Great Panathenaia of a generation earlier. The same modus operandi, almost, perhaps, the same personal style (the style of Peisistratos?), seems to be traceable in both. In each, the contest element appears to result from an administrative act, datable within close limits. In each, a *pompē* and sacrifice belonging to age-old Attic ritual is enlarged and made more spectacular. In each, also, a rite centering on a primitive image of the deity concerned (an image of the kind which the worshiper feels free to treat as a child treats a *doll*: clothing it or making it move from this site to that) is worked into the new celebration. Finally, each seems designed, at least in part, to encourage musical-poetic activities in Athens: the Panathenaia largely by attracting foreign performers to the city; the Dionysia by providing a meeting point both for Athenian and for foreign exponents of the relatively new art of the *tragōidoi*. (Perhaps it is worth recalling that out of the first twenty-five tragedians listed more or less chronologically in Snell's *Tragicorum Graecorum Fragmenta*, no fewer than seven are non-Attic, and four are from the northeast quarter of the Peloponnese: Pratinas and his son Aristias, both of Phleios; Aristarchus of Tegea; Neophron of Sikyon; Ion of Chios; Achaios of Eretria; and Akestor, an alien of uncertain race.)

HIPPARCHUS

Although solid facts about either the Great Panathenaia or the City Dionysia are few and hard to come by (but the nature of our sources is such that the same is true of every aspect of Athenian history in the sixth century), all the indications are that the two festivals represent a deliberate policy on the part of the Peisistratean regime. The motives of the tyrants are not likely to have been pure and unmixed. Political and economic considerations clearly played a very significant part, both in the establishment of these festivals and in the establishment or reorganization of a number of other festivals in which the regime is surmised to have had a hand: centralization of the political system, popularity with the merchants and artisans who formed the tyrants' power base, and the attraction of external trade and labor to Athens are only a few of the advantages that one can imagine.[56] But in our two festivals it seems fairly clear that one important motive was the encouragement of music and poetry at Athens, in the first instance by the attraction of performers from other areas of the song culture where these arts had already been more highly developed.

The recorded activities of one member of the Peisistratid family, Peisistratos's son Hipparchus, may be thought to confirm this view of the regime's policy. The question of whether this man was responsible for the official introduction of Homeric rhapsode-contests into the Great Panathenaia must, I think, remain undecided (see above, p. 86). There can be no doubt, however, about his personal interest in the attraction of non-Attic poets to the city. Indeed, Hipparchus appears to have collected live singing poets with the same ruthless determination which we later see displayed by wealthy connoisseurs in their pursuit of those inanimate objects, books. The pseudo-Platonic *Hipparchus* records that he dispatched a naval vessel (a *pentekonter*, roughly the equivalent of a destroyer) to fetch the most charming and gifted of all Greek solo lyrists, Anacreon of Teos, from the isle of Samos; the date of this may have been about 522 B.C.[57] The same source reports that he paid heavily to retain the services of the greatest choral lyrist of his age, Simonides of Keos.[58] He seems to have collected other performers also, to judge by Aristotle's remark that "he sent for Anacreon and Simonides, and for *the other poets*."[59] Who those "other poets" for whom Hipparchus sent may have been, we cannot now say for certain. It is not impossible that they included Lasus of Hermione (in the northeast Peloponnese), a man famous in his time both as a poet and as a highly innovative musician.[60] Certainly there is early and dependable evidence of Lasus's presence in the Peisistratid court.[61] His possible role in the introduction of the dithyramb into the Dionysiac contests will be discussed below. Finally, in this context, we should recall a passage which if taken at face value would provide the most enlightening evidence of all about Hipparchus's activities and motives. The pseudo-Platonic *Hipparchus*, after its mention of Anacreon and Simonides, continues: "And he [Hipparchus] did these things because he wished to educate (*paideuein*) the citizens, so that those subject to his rule might be as good as possible . . . and when the citizens in Athens and its neighborhood had been educated to his satisfaction . . . , with the intent to educate those in the countryside also, he set up Herms along the roads between the city and each of the demes" and inscribed specimens of his wisdom on them in pentameters. On one side of the Herm was a statement that it stood midway between Athens and such and such a deme; on the other, a gnomic pentameter. Two examples of the pentameters are quoted in the dialogue: *μνῆμα τόδ' Ἱππάρχου· στεῖχε δίκαια φρονῶν*, and *μνῆμα τόδ' Ἱππάρχου· μὴ φίλον ἐξαπάτα*.[62] There is every reason to believe the unknown author's statement that Hipparchus set up a number of these poetical milestones (indeed, an example of one of them may have survived).[63] His account of Hipparchus's motivation for so doing can scarcely have rested on any explicit external evidence, but it seems a legitimate (if somewhat exaggerated) inference from the known facts.[64]

THE CONTESTS IN DITHYRAMB

We have seen that there is excellent reason to believe that Lasus of Hermione was closely associated with Hipparchus. It is also certain that one of Lasus's main interests as poet and composer was the dithyramb, the circular chorus of fifty accompanied by an oboist.[65] That he produced some of his dithyrambs in Athens during the Peisistratid regime is therefore likely enough, and there is even some evidence that suggests (although it cannot be said to prove) that he introduced dithyrambic *contests*.[66]

Whether or not in consequence of a precedent set by Lasus and Hipparchus, however, the Athenians certainly instituted an official contest in dithyramb within a couple of years after the expulsion of the tyrants.

The date of the institution, as given in the Parian Marble (Epoch 46; again, presumably, derived ultimately from the official contest records), appears to have been 509/8 B.C., and there can hardly be any question that the festival to which the contest was attached was the City Dionysia.[67] This was not, in fact, the last addition to be made to the contest element in that festival; yet a third kind of contest, in comedy, was added in or about 486 B.C., but that event lies outside the period with which we are immediately concerned.[68]

In this case, even more clearly than in those of the Great Panathenaia and the tragic contests at the City Dionysia, we are able to verify the importance of these festival contests in attracting foreign poets to perform at Athens. The fragmentary annals of the dithyrambic contests (derived ultimately, no doubt, like those of the tragic contests, from the official archives) show that the winning poet in 509/8 was a foreigner, Hypodikos of Chalcis.[69] It is known from a papyrus first published in 1961 that the Theban Pindar competed and won in about the year 496. Pindar also competed on at least one other occasion.[70] Other foreign competitors during the generation after 509/8 were Melanippides of Melos, victor in 494/3;[71] the great Simonides of Keos (whom we have earlier met at the court of Hipparchus), who seems to have competed in Athens many times, until as late as 477/6 B.C.;[72] and Bacchylides, also of Keos, on at least two occasions, not exactly datable.[73] By contrast, the only known *Athenian* dithyrambists of the same period are the obscure Agathocles and Apollodorus, and the only slightly more celebrated Lamprocles.[74]

EFFECTS OF THE POLICY

Thus by about 500 B.C., at the moment when Aeschylus was about to begin his career as a tragedian, Athens had become an important center of the song culture; indeed, as far as we can now see, it had become the most important of all. At least in part, this revolution must be attributed to the successive institutions of *agōnes mousikoi* at the great festivals: at the Great Panathenaia from an early date (and perhaps as early as 566 B.C.), at the City Dionysia in ca. 534, and again at the same festival in 509/8. Aeschylus and his somewhat older contemporary Phrynichus[75]—the poets who were believed by later antiquity to have raised tragedy into a major art[76]—could witness annually or quadriennially performances in Athens such as their grandfathers might never have seen in a lifetime, unless they had traveled widely overseas. For almost all the arts now performed in the Athenian contests had been developed, and long practiced, far away from Athens: kitharody (in Lesbos and Sparta above all, and later apparently in Sicily), aulody (the tradition points to Phrygia and later to Argos[77]), rhapsody (in East Greece), and dithyramb (traceable earlier in the Aegean islands and the northeast Peloponnese). Even the apparent exception to this rule, the art of the *tragōidoi*, is said in later sources to have been practiced elsewhere in Greece before and during the lifetime of the Athenian Thespis; in what form we can hardly tell (any more than we can really obtain a clear idea of its form in the hands of Thespis himself), but the high proportion of non-Attic contestants at the Great Dionysiac tragic competitions may perhaps confirm the tradition.[78]

A further important effect of the policy initiated by the tyrants must have been the personal meetings that resulted between the major living exponents of the hitherto separate genres of Greek poetry. In the years around 500 B.C., an Aeschylus or a Phrynichus could have met two of the leading choral poets of the time (and indeed, of the entire tradition), Simonides and Pindar, as well as many less famous dithyrambists from abroad, and the great solo lyrist Anacreon. Only a few years earlier, during Aeschylus's teens, they might have met the great musician and dithyrambist Lasus. So far we have only spoken of the chronologically possible, but there is a little evidence to suggest that such personal encounters took place. The relationship between Aeschylus and Anacreon will best be discussed in the following chapter. There are testimonies, admittedly in very late sources, to an association between Pindar and Aeschylus,[79] as a result of which Pindar profited from Aeschylus's celebrated *megalophōnia*, his majesty of utterance.[80] We shall, of course, treat such evidence with reserve—the Greeks of all periods were too fond of inventing anecdotes which brought together famous thinkers or artists—but the solid evidence that Pindar was present in Athens for the City Dionysia in or about 496 B.C. (p. 94 above, with note) now suggests the possibility that some historical truth underlies these stories. Even more intriguing (and less suspect, because its circumstantial details are not of the kind that late anecdotists were liable to invent) is a story preserved in the ancient *Life of Pindar*: "They say that his [Pindar's] teacher at Athens was, according to one account, Agathocles, according to another, Apollodorus; and that the latter, being in charge of cyclic [i.e., dithyrambic] choruses and having to travel away from the city, entrusted the training (*didaskalian*) of them to Pindar, who was still a boy; and that Pindar, by managing them well, became famous." If this is true, then by the late sixth century Athens was becoming not merely a focus for the performances of nondramatic poetry, but also a center of instruction—a kind of *conservatoire* for student composers of lyric poetry.[81]

The institutions of the tragic and dithyrambic contests must also have had an immense effect on the musical culture of the Athenian citizenry in general, as a simple calculation will suggest. For each annual production of the City Dionysia from at least 508 B.C. onward, a total of 500 choristers will have been required for the ten competing dithyrambic choruses of boys; another 500 for the men's dithyrambic choruses;[82] and an unknown number, but almost certainly not less than thirty-six, for the choruses of the competing tragedians.[83] The dithyrambic choruses were drawn from the ten tribes of the Athenian citizenry; we do not know exactly how the tragic choruses were selected, but it is to be presumed that in the early years they, too, consisted of ordinary citizens.[84] Thus a cadre of trained singer-dancers and connoisseurs of poetry must have been built up fairly rapidly in the early years of the democracy.[85] But the evidence for a growing interest in poetry and music among the Athenians about the turn of the sixth and fifth centuries does not stop at such abstract calculations. We have already seen (pp. 49–50 above) how the vases and skolia of the same period tell a similar story, this time in vivid detail: the multiplication of scenes from Homer (especially from the *Iliad*), the evidence of acquaintance with (and sometimes actual quotations from) the solo-lyrists and Theognis.

We know little enough about the nature of tragedy in this same period, about 500 B.C.; but we can state as a historical fact that the earlier works of Phrynichus and the first essays of Aeschylus were composed at a time when the society around them was passionately preoccupied, as it had never been before, with most of the major genres of Hellenic poetry from Homer through Simonides and Anacreon. There had probably never been before, in the Greek world, such a concentration of diverse musical and poetic talent within a single city as now existed in Athens. And in reflecting on this fact, we should not forget the message of chapters 1 and 2: poetry, like music, could be and was realized only in *performance*. All this had come about, as far as we can tell, within the two or three generations since the foundation of the Great Panathenaia. The concentration of the Hellenic song culture in Athens was no less sudden and swift a miracle than the rise of tragedy is often represented to have been. In fact, the two miracles (if miracles they are to be called, rather than deliberate exertions of human will and invention) took place almost contemporaneously; and in some ways, as the following chapters may suggest, were so closely connected as to be almost one miracle and one alone.

INTERMEZZO: THE EARLY FILM-MAKERS

As was mentioned near the beginning of this chapter, it is no part of the present inquiry to attempt yet another reconstruction of the origins of tragedy or of its development from Thespis's first official performance in ca. 534 down to the beginning of the fifth century B.C. Nor are we concerned to polemicize against those theories which trace tragedy back to this ritual practice or that, or to Arion's dithyrambs, or to satyr drama. There may well be some truth in any or all of these theories; though it is a very different question how far they can properly be applied to the criticism and interpretation of the extant fifth-century tragedies. Our business is with the relationship between tragedy as we perceive it dimly in the work of Phrynichus and more clearly in Aeschylus's plays and fragments on the one hand, and nondramatic Greek poetry on the other.

In view of what is to come later, it may be worth drawing attention to the extraordinary story of the rise of a comparatively modern art, that of film. We shall not, of course, claim that the analogy proves anything scientifically; we shall only suggest that it provides an acceptable model for our reconstruction of tragedy's development during the early decades.

Most students, however much they differ on the remote and immediate origins of Thespian tragedy, will probably agree that, if we can trust any of the ancient statements about Thespis,[86] his most certain achievement was *to disguise his performers.* I, for one, find it hard to imagine fully the shattering impact of that single technical innovation, even in the first moments of the first performance, whatever its nature. The poem—and we are given good reason to suppose (especially by the Parian Marble's *poiētēs*)[87] that it was felt as a poem—abruptly took on three dimensions. Heroic and divine characters who in earlier poems had possessed only voices—and those transmitted only through the mouths of the undisguised performers—were now given their own faces, bodies, and movements. Equally important, they were now given their own appropriate location: the dance-floor, as well, would now begin (as it were) to impersonate, to pretend to be a different place.

The art of film, too, began with a single, but stunning, technical innovation.[88] This immediately set off an explosion of short-lived experimental works in the new medium. The technical device opened up all the possibilities of an unheard-of realism but was, after all, only a device; it was not an art and incorporated in itself no hints as to how it could or should be applied. For inspiration, therefore, the earliest experimenters mostly looked to a preexisting art, that of the short vaudeville sketch. This was natural and even necessary, for both they and (even more) their prospective public had to build on something that was already familiar to them in some degree. (At this point of the story one cannot help recalling Aristotle's mention of "the little plots and laughable diction" that characterized the earliest Attic tragedy.)[89] Yet with remarkable swiftness the film-makers proceeded from these short and naively reproduced farces to the exploitation of the new medium in ways that were simply impossible with the resources of the earlier artforms. The annals of film during its first years, like those of tragedy, are replete with "first inventors," *prōtoi heuretai*, of this technique or that. The first simulation of a beheading; the first closeups; the first cuts and dissolves; the first shots of adventures on a moving train; the first chase scene; above all, the increasing *lengths* of the productions, up to as much as a whole hour's run: all these innovations had appeared here and there within a mere ten years of Edison's first kinetoscope peepshow (1893). Concurrently, film became more and more clearly a separate art from vaudeville, and its ambitions widened. During the following decades (decades, incidentally, of exceptional social and military upheaval), it was to draw on serious live drama and serious literature in all their branches, until by the 1920s (just thirty or forty years after Edison's peepshow) it had produced cinematic masters in their own right, peers and rivals of the novelists and dramatists: a Griffith, an Eisenstein.

The analogy between film and tragedy might be pursued much further, both in its artistic and in its social aspects. Both, for instance, are essentially democratic arts: "the most people-pleasing and hypnotizing branch of poetry," growled the fourth-century author of the dialogue *Minos*, referring to Attic tragedy.[90] Certainly film, and possibly tragedy, seem first to have reached maturity at times of unprecedented world crisis.[91] And once they had reached maturity, both became so popular as entertainment with the masses of the citizenry that they tended to devour the traditional artforms that had begotten them and had continued to nourish them. By the outbreak of the Peloponnesian War, a century or so after the first official contests in tragedy, no first-rate poet in any of the traditional nondramatic genres was composing in Greece. By 1993, a century after Edison's peepshow, . . . but we had best refrain from speculating on the ultimate effects of film and television on their sister arts. The one result of the analogy that is perhaps worth bearing in mind, in our present context, is this. It suggests the possibility that tragedy may not only have been, in its origin, a natural continuation of pretragic poetry, but also that once tragedy had been born it continued to develop, surrounded by, influenced by, and in competition with, the chief poetic genres of the Hellenic song culture.

PART THREE

Tragic Poetry

5.
Some Features of Tragic Music and Meter

When the amateur of poetry in any language stands back and surveys extant Greek tragedy from a metrical point of view, his first reactions may well be neither pity nor terror but, rather, delight that there could exist any poetry like this: a poetry so close to music in its enormous variety and in its metrical precision; a poetry that is able to carry and metrically reinforce every mode of discourse, from narrative and argumentative in the iambic dialogue passages, to emotional in the anapaestic, to the language of our dreams at the lyric level. The Attic tragedian, from the moment in 472 B.C. (the production date of Aeschylus's *Persians*) when we can first clearly see and hear him in action, has in his hands an instrument for conveying all aspects of the human experience in words, such as the greatest masters in the modern European languages have yearned for ever since the tragedies became generally available again during the Renaissance. One thinks of the first Italian opera composers, of Milton's *Samson Agonistes*, of the German Romantic poets. Their longings are perhaps summed up in T. S. Eliot's words: "I have before my eyes a kind of mirage of the perfection of verse-drama, which would be a design of human action and of words, such as to present at once the two aspects of dramatic and of musical order."[1] For the Greek tragedian as we know him, that was no mirage; it was practical reality.

The aim of the present chapter is to inquire how this technical miracle may have come about. We cannot, of course, trace the history of the process step by step; all that we can be quite sure of is that it was complete, in most of its important aspects, by 472 B.C. A possible analogy from modern film for the evolution of the tragic art between Thespis and Aeschylus was put forward at the end of the preceding chapter;

such few tolerably certain facts as we know about that evolution will emerge in the course of this one. Our immediate concern will be with two topics: first, the views of the classical Greeks about the metrical and musical components in the fifth-century tragedian's craft, and about the relationship of those components to pretragic kinds of poetry; second, the evidence on these questions that emerges from a comparison between the tragic and the pretragic meters themselves.

SOME CLASSICAL VIEWS ON THE CRAFT OF TRAGEDY

Perhaps the most impressive evidence about the classical Greek opinion on the continuity between tragedy (as the classical Greeks knew it) and predramatic poetry is to be found in nomenclature. This point is no doubt sufficiently obvious and will not here be treated at length; yet a few striking instances may be worth recalling as a preliminary to our more detailed inquiries.[2] It seems to be the fact that all Greek writers before the Hellenistic period—that is, all Greek writers who composed during the time when Attic tragedy was flourishing as an important and a living art—refer to tragedy explicitly or implicitly as poetry; to them the tragic poet's craft appears not as a priestly ritual nor as any sacred or religious activity in some sense that did not apply to all other branches of poetry as well.[3] In them, the tragedians appear as an inseparable part of the song culture, fully accredited members of that ancient club and entering freely into its ancient dialogue, just as their nontragic predecessors had done. Herodotus, for instance, composing in the third quarter of the fifth century, remarks that Aeschylus, "unlike any of the poets (*poiētai*) who had preceded him," made Artemis the daughter of Demeter.[4] He thus lines up Aeschylus with the entire earlier poetic tradition. Equally, there are many passages in which some particular pretragic poet, above all Homer, is said to have provided a precedent for the tragedians: for example, Plato's famous remark (*Rep.* 10.607a) that Homer is "most poetic and first of the tragic poets," or the equally famous saying attributed to Aeschylus himself (we cannot tell with what reliability) that "his tragedies were slices from the mighty feasts of Homer."[5] Finally we may recall one rather less well-known passage of the kind which is perhaps the most concise summation of the pre-Hellenistic attitude to poetry and tragedy: Isocrates 2 (*Ad Nicoclem*)

48–49, probably composed within a year or two after 374 B.C. We love, says Isocrates, to hear the deeds of the heroes, and still more do we love to see the heroes in action. "For that reason," he continues, "it is proper to admire both the poetry (*poiēsin*) of Homer, and those who first discovered tragedy; because they realized the nature of human beings and made use of both these modes for their poetry. Homer turned into story [or "myth": *emythologēsen*] the contests and the wars of the demigods, and the tragedians rendered those stories into [real] contests and actions; the stories thus became for us not merely heard, but also seen."[6] There is no word here about ancestor-worship, goat-sacrifice, or ritual of any kind. The tragedians are seen as treating the same material as Homer had, and with the same motives, but as employing a new and more effective technique.

The *Frogs* of Aristophanes offers, among much else, an unrivalled view of the craft of tragedy as it was perceived toward the end of the fifth century, through the eyes of the greatest technical virtuoso of all the extant Attic dramatists; for Aristophanes, whatever may now be thought of the literary quality of his poetry, is demonstrably a connoisseur and a master of the entire range of Greek metrics and music up to his own time.[7] He can not merely quote, but brilliantly parody, anything from the solemn choral lyrics of Alcman or Stesichorus, through the solo lyricists and iambists, to the portentous hexameters of contemporary oracle-mongers;[8] to say nothing of his mastery of the New Music and of the iambic and lyric styles of the Attic tragedians—which is displayed perhaps most clearly in the comedy we are about to consider. As always, when we seek reflections of reality in the distorting mirror of an Aristophanic comedy, we must work cautiously. Much of that shocking fiction which occupies the second half of the *Frogs*, the contest between Aeschylus and Euripides, was never meant to be taken seriously by anybody. Yet it seems to be a fairly safe rule that any feature in Aristophanes which is not intrinsically comic and which must have been easily verifiable by his audience very probably represents serious fact.

One theme that persists throughout the entire comedy, but is never, that I can see, presented as something funny in itself, is the craft of tragedy. One must emphasize the word *craft*. Notoriously, the Greeks possessed no word that really corresponded to our *art*, just as they possessed none that really corresponded to our *literature*; and in fact, what Aristophanes offers in the *Frogs* is scarcely "literary criticism" in the sense in which that activity is nowadays understood. Although the discussion clearly has some literary-critical implications, its main emphasis is on musical and metrical *technique*. A partial exception to this rule is the great epirrhematic *agōn* (895–1098), but even this is concerned mostly with the moral effect of poetry (including tragedy) on society, rather than with strictly literary-critical issues. From end to end of the play the term most commonly used for tragedy is not, in fact, "tragedy" but "the craft," *hē technē*. "The craft" is referred to with enormous respect by all parties. It, alone, escapes any kind of mockery in this play, and indeed in Aristophanes' work generally. Students will debate eternally about Aristophanes' "real views" on morals and politics, on the New Learning, on the generation gap, on Kleon, on Euripides, and so on. Perhaps, in method, one can be sure of none of them; but it is a tenable thesis that if Aristophanes seriously cared about anything at all, he cared about the integrity of the poet's trade.[9]

Much of the debate in the *Frogs* has in fact the perennially fascinating air of any discussion between masters of a handicraft, whatever that handicraft may be: stonemasonry, say, or woodworking (a point that is reinforced by Aristophanes' own imagery in several passages).[10] The two great professionals are made to discuss the correct proportion of song to dialogue, and the character of that dialogue (905–91); then the moral impact of tragedy and poetry (1003–98: the two arts are not distinguished, at least by Aeschylus, who invokes the precedents of Homer, Hesiod, and other early epic composers); iambic prologues, together with the questions of clarity in diction (1119–99) and of the avoidance of metrical/syntactical monotony (1200–1247); choral lyric technique (1248–1329); solo lyric technique (1329–64); and weight of diction (1365–1414). All these topics, with the exception already noted (the passage 1003–98) are obviously in themselves of immediate concern to the poet qua craftsman. That the methods and arguments applied in debating them, and the decisions reached in each case, are mostly quite fantastic should be equally obvious. I cannot guess whether the shade of Aristophanes howls with laughter or with rage at the antics performed by some of his commentators on, say, his *lekythion* passage (1200–1247). Yet some good connoisseurs of Aristophanes have, I think rightly, braved the scorn of that irritable ghost so far as to suggest that there are certain details of the contest that can be treated as historical evidence for the early development of tragedy and for the methods of the tragedians. For they are details which, if known by the audience to be fictitious, would not only be unfunny but would also spoil the satirical effect of the passages in which they stand.

In lines 1264–95 of the *Frogs*, the stage Euripides sings two groups of samples from Aeschylean choral lyric. In both groups, the samples are metrically either iambo-dactylic or long rows of unmixed dactyls, of the type most familiar to the hearer of extant Aeschylus from the great lyric triad which opens the *parodos* of the *Agamemnon* (104–59). No fewer than three of the samples are taken from that very passage, being distributed between both of Euripides' groups;[11] the rest are taken from half a dozen now lost Aeschylean tragedies. At the pause after the singing of the first group (which Euripides accompanies by the noisy Aeschylean refrain *ἰὴ κόπον οὐ πελάθεις ἐπ' ἀρωγάν;*), Dionysos begs to be excused on the ground that all this thumping has given him a pain in the kidneys, but Euripides snaps: "No! Not until you've heard yet another stand(?) of songs contrived from the kitharodic nomes."[12] He proceeds to the second set of samples, only relenting to the extent that he now changes the refrain to *to phlattothrat, to phlattothrat*, in imitation of the monotonous strumming of a lyre. The passage as a whole is of great interest to the student of Greek poetry for two reasons. First, it indicates, if with considerable exaggeration, the rapid changes in musical and metrical taste that had taken place in Athens during the fifth century: one gathers that the rhythms of Aeschylean song must have sounded to certain connoisseurs in 405 B.C. as simplistic and repetitive as the clearly articulated patterns of Pope or Handel sound to people brought up on Eliot or Stravinsky.[13] Second, it charges Aeschylus with having imitated this particular kind of dactylic song from a long-established pretragic art, the art of the kitharode.[14] Now, what little information we have about the kitharodic nome suggests that this allegation is very probably true: as was seen above (pp. 19–20), the character of its music from the earliest times until after the death of Aeschylus was overwhelmingly dactylic.[15]

Furthermore, the stage Aeschylus himself admits the imputation without the least embarrassment. At line 1296 Dionysos sarcastically asks him: "What *is* this *phlattothrat*? Was it from Marathon that you collected these ropewinder's songs, or from where?" The exact meaning of this taunt is very doubtful indeed, but the context allows a fair guess at its drift: Aeschylus is a picker-up of old-fashioned and monotonous songs.[16] To this Aeschylus responds: "Well, anyway, I transferred them [the songs you mention] from beauty into beauty, so that I might not be seen harvesting the same sacred meadow of the Muses as Phrynichus did!" Here the "well, anyway," *all' oun*,[17] seems frankly to admit the charge of borrowing music, but an extremely interesting justification at once follows: Aeschylus did not want simply to follow the musical lead of his senior in the tragic art, Phrynichus; he therefore looked to a different source of music, and one apparently not hitherto exploited in tragedy. It is possible that we can catch Phrynichus himself at a similar game. We know in general, from several references in Aristophanes, that Phrynichus's choral music was so tuneful that it was still quite popular in the late fifth century.[18] Eduard Fraenkel, however, believed that on one point it was possible to be more precise than that. He pointed to a passage in Aristophanes' *Birds* (produced nine years before the *Frogs*) which resembles, especially in the imagery, the remark of the stage Aeschylus in our present passage. There the Bird Chorus sings:

> To Pan I open my sacred tunes (*nomous*),
> and solemn dances to the Mountain Mother,
> [here a bird-twitter:] totototototototinx,
> from which Phrynichus ever
> like a bee, grazing the harvest of immortal songs,
> brought home sweet music.[19]

From this Fraenkel guessed, with considerable probability, that Phrynichus too had been a music borrower in his time, turning for inspiration to kinds of tune and dance which Aristophanes associated with hymns to Pan and the Mountain Mother.

Now there seems to be no good comic reason for these Aristophanic indications about the procedures of Aeschylus, and of Phrynichus before him. In whatever fun and fantasy they may be wrapped, there is a fair case for supposing that in themselves they represent historic fact. In that case, they appear to allow a glimpse into that period of fervid experimentation with the possibilities of the new art of tragedy, which was theoretically postulated at the end of the preceding chapter on the analogy of the cinematic art. Phrynichus, who gained his first victory as far back as 511/508 B.C.,[20] is shown as the composer of a tragedy that was overwhelmingly lyrical (*Frogs* 909–915), the music of his choruses depending in some degree on certain cult hymns.[21] His junior, Aeschylus, who first produced in ca. 499/98 and first gained a victory in 484,[22] is represented as having continued the high proportion of lyric to dialogue but as having deliberately adopted a different lyric style; one art-form to which he turned (and which Phrynichus had evidently not exploited) was the kitharodic nome. It may reasonably be surmised that these are only two instances, the memory of which happens fortunately to have survived, of a constant process of borrowing which took place during the early years of tragedy. In that way we could perhaps best account for the extraordinary mixture of different meters, of quite diverse origins, that characterizes the first extant tragedy, the *Persians* of 472 B.C., which will be further considered in the second half of this chapter.

The *Persians* presents us with essentially the same range of meters as will be found in all subsequent extant tragedies. The great period of metrical borrowing and experimentation seems already to have been over by this time, and the repertoire was already established in its broad outlines. But in its broad outlines only: each of the two subsequent tragedians had his own preferences and made his own characteristic choices from within the repertoire. Nor did the practice of borrowing from nondramatic song entirely cease with Aeschylus. In the last decade or so of his life, Euripides began to take a great interest in the so-called New Music, a style of song that had been developed by the dithyrambists and kitharodes and that was to prove to be the popular music of the future. The evidence for his interest is to be found both in comparisons between his late works and the works of the New Musicians and in some passages in the comic poets.[23] Among the latter group, the most important is of course lines 1309–63 in the *Frogs*, where Aeschylus is made to parody the style. It is most unlikely that we can trust all the details of Aeschylus's accusation in *Frogs* 1301–3: "This person gets *his* honey from anywhere—from porn songs, from the drinking songs of Meletus, from Carian oboe tunes, from keenings, from the dance-halls"; but the general tenor of the charge, that Euripides has imported popular nondramatic music into "the craft," seems perfectly credible.[24]

The Aristophanic allusions to tragic borrowing from nondramatic poetry which we have discussed refer in part to music, in part to meter. It is worth comparing, at this point, a remark by a fourth-century B.C. writer that refers specifically to the borrowing of a musical style, this time from an archaic solo lyrist. According to this writer, Aristoxenus, Sappho "first discovered the Mixolydian mode, *and from her the tragedians learned it*; taking it over, they joined it to the Dorian mode, since the latter gives an effect of magnificence and nobility, the former an emotional effect; and tragedy is compounded from these two."[25] μέμικται . . . τραγῳδία, says the last clause: *Tragedy is a mixture!* These words might well serve as a motto for the present chapter.

There remains to be discussed a rather tantalizing ancient passage which might be interpreted as indicating that the metrical development of Aeschylus (or of the early tragedians generally) was influenced at an early stage by direct acquaintance with the great solo lyrist Anacreon. We have already met Anacreon at the Peisistratid court (p. 92 above), but the Attic vase-paintings strongly suggest that after the fall of the tyranny he either stayed on in Athens or returned there, becoming rather famous for his energetic participation in symposia.[26] On chronological grounds, therefore, it is possible, or even likely, that Aeschylus became acquainted with Anacreon during the years around and after 500 B.C., that is, just at the time when Aeschylus was beginning his career as a tragic poet. Now, there is an ancient scholium on Aeschylus's *Prometheus* 128 which, as it stands in the manuscripts, reads as follows:

> The rhythm [that is, the meter of *Prom.* 128] is Anacreontean, anaclastic, for an effect of lamentation. For he came to reside in Attica out of love for Critias, and he was greatly [here the MSS have an uncertain verb, in the aorist passive] with the songs of the tragedian. But they used them not in every place, but in contexts of lamentation, as also Sophocles in the second *Tyro* [fr. 595N, 656P]. And this passage is like the passage "And once more, won't you let me go home when I'm drunk?" [Anacreon, fr. 412 *PMG*].[27]

In this scholium we have the remains of an exceptionally learned ancient note: it is highly unusual among the Aeschylus scholia in that it displays an intelligent interest in the meter of the poetic text, and in order to illustrate its metrical point it adduces passages from Anacreon and Sophocles which are cited in no other source. Its information about the reason for Anacreon's residence in Attica is also unrecorded elsewhere.[28] Unfortunately, it is certainly corrupt in two places, one of them crucial, and is almost certainly abbreviated. Its general drift seems to be: "The anaclastic meter of *Prometheus* 128 (ff.) is characteristic of Anacreon, but is here employed in a mournful context. [How does the meter come to be found in tragedy?] The reason is (*gar*) that Anacreon lived in Attica for a time, and . . . [here the first corrupt passage]. [That is how the tragedians came to adopt it.] But (*de*) they did not use it in any context, but only in mournful ones. Here is an example [of which the actual words have been lost] from the second *Tyro*. Finally, here is an example of the meter from Anacreon himself, obviously not in a mournful context but in a sympotic one."[29] Here, if one were asked to supply the gap after "for a time, and . . ." simply to accord with the sense of its surroundings, one would surely write: "and the tragedians were (or: the tragedian, Aeschylus, was) much taken with Anacreon's songs." And in fact the corrupt wording of the manuscripts can without much difficulty be emended to mean this.[30] Much, of course, is in doubt; but provisionally the scholium may be accepted as further evidence of the earlier tragedians' practice of borrowing from the work of the non-tragic poets. It would further illustrate the extent to which Athens, by the turn of the sixth and fifth centuries, had become the center of a lively interchange between poets in different genres (cf. Chapter 4).

COMPARISON BETWEEN TRAGIC AND PRETRAGIC METERS

The classical testimonies examined in the preceding section have already produced a number of instances (some more certain, some less) of poetic or musical borrowings by the early fifth-century tragic poets: the sources mentioned are kitharodic nomes, hymns to Pan and the Mountain Mother, and the songs of two great solo-lyrists, Sappho and Anacreon. But such scattered testimonies can scarcely be expected to have preserved the whole story, and in fact there is a different kind of evidence which makes it certain that they do not. The general comparison between the meters of the extant tragedies of Aeschylus and those of the pretragic genres of poetry, which will be undertaken in the following sections, will show how by the time of Aeschylus Attic tragedy had absorbed practically every preexisting kind of Greek metric.[31]

To proceed directly from a reading aloud of the pretragic Greek poets to a reading aloud of the Aeschylean tragedies is an experiment which every student of Greek should make for himself as soon as he has acquired a fair knowledge of metrics. One's first impression is of an incredible opulence and diversity of rhythms; it is as if one had moved abruptly from the solo or chamber music of the Baroque into a Beethoven symphony. As one's ear becomes accustomed, however, to the new splendor, one realizes that almost all the basic elements composing this tragic verse are perfectly familiar. One has heard each of them long ago in widely separated parts of the Greek world and in very diverse circumstances: the festival-contest, the dance-floor, and the symposium. What the tragedians have done is to bring them together within a single poem and to reapply them in marvelous ways: here building a single element into majestic sequences of unprecedented length; there combining two, or many more, elements which have never been heard in juxtaposition before.

In general, we can no longer reconstruct the steps by which this came about; we can only postulate that it resulted from a long process of experiment in the last third of the sixth century and the first third of the fifth. By the time of the *Persians*, the main outlines of the tragic metrical structure have been fixed for all time. There are now, and will remain, three major *genera* of tragic verse: spoken; chanted to instrumental accompaniment; sung (and often, also, danced) to instrumental accompaniment—these are the same three *genera* that were performed, but separately, in the pretragic *agōnes mousikoi* (cf. pp. 7–10 above). It will be convenient first to examine, so far as our knowledge allows, the sources from which the tragedians may have learned each *genus*.[32]

PRETRAGIC HISTORIES OF DIALOGUE, ANAPAESTS, AND LYRIC

Certainly by the time of extant Aeschylus, and possibly by the time of Phrynichus, two meters are found in use for the dialogue passages of tragedy: the iambic trimeter and the trochaic tetrameter catalectic.[33] Both, of course, long antedate the rise of tragedy. There are good reasons to conjecture that they were developed far back in the preliterate period,[34] and there is an example of an iambic trimeter on a vase that may date from as early as ca. 720 B.C.[35] From then on throughout antiquity, and indeed beyond, they surface here and there as the meters of rituals, subliterary songs (notably children's songs), epitaphs and epigrams, and proverbs.[36] It was, however, the Ionic-speaking East Greeks and islanders who developed the two meters as vehicles for formal poetry: Archilochus, Semonides, the composer of the *Margites*, Xenophanes, Anacreon, and Simonides are all known to have composed in either one or both of them.[37] Trimeter and tetrameter poetry, in short, is almost exclusively an East Greek phenomenon during the archaic period. The solitary important exception to this rule is of course the Athenian Solon. His dependence on the East Greek tradition of this kind of poetry is made evident in many ways, not least by his use of the Ionic dialect rather than his native Attic; but we have already noticed how close some of his iambic verses come to the tone and manner of tragic dialogue.[38]

In its outlines, therefore, the pretragic history of these two important tragic meters seems fairly certain: already brought to a fine art during the seventh century by the Ionians on the other side of the Aegean, and transplanted to Attica by Solon in the early sixth, they have been adopted by the tragedians with relatively little change.[39]

There seems to be even less question about the source of the second major *genus* of tragic verse, the chanted "marching anapaests" arranged by dimeters. Virtually all the evidence points toward Sparta as its home from, at latest, the seventh century B.C. onward,[40] and there is very little trace of its use elsewhere until it appears again, on the grand scale, in the Attic tragedies.[41] By what route, and at what date, the marching anapaests came to be incorporated in the tragic repertoire can only be guessed.[42] But these Spartan rhythms are a very striking element in the metrical texture of the tragedies we have.

The third *genus* of tragic verse, the sung lyric, presents from our present point of view a far more complex problem than the other two. There can be no question of our deriving this *genus* in its entirety from any one school of pretragic poetry. We can only make two preliminary general observations. First, tragic lyric is sharply marked off from the other two *genera* by the exotic vowel sounds of the language in which it is composed. A prominent characteristic of the native Attic dialect is (to put the matter nontechnically) the regular appearance in it of long *ē* in words where most other Greek dialects have long *ā* (the so-called Doric alpha): *hēlios* "sun" for *hālios* of most other dialects, *gē* "earth" for *gā*, and so on.[43] Now, in the lyrics of Attic tragedy, and the lyrics alone, that non-Attic long *ā* is the norm. Thus when a tragedy shifts from either the dialogue meters or the marching anapaests to lyric, it carries its Athenian spectators not merely into a sphere of dance and melody but also into a language that has a perceptibly different coloring from their own. The explanation of this phenomenon has been much debated, but most authorities now agree that it cannot provide any useful evidence as to the regional origins of tragic lyric. The long *ā* in the places where Attic has long *ē* was characteristic of the dialects that prevailed in most of the major centers of nondramatic lyric—Lesbos, Boeotia, and Sparta—and may well have been accepted at an early date as an inseparable element of the genre;[44] in fact, even some nondramatic poets who were born and bred in the Ionic-speaking area (the dialect of which was in this respect akin to Attic) follow a similar practice in their formal public lyrics.[45] But the most we can profitably say here about the phenomenon is that the resultant alternation between different dialect characteristics *within the compass of a single poem* is unique to Attic tragedy. In this aspect, also, "tragedy is a mixture."

The second general observation that may be made about tragic lyric (as it appears in Aeschylus) is that it presents almost no kind of lyric meter, or metrical unit, that cannot be paralleled in earlier or contemporary nondramatic poetry. In this matter yet again, we find that Attic tragedy does not *invent*; rather, it *blends* and *redisposes* in such a way as to create totally new effects.[46] There is only one important exception to this rule, and even it is not quite certain: the strange and rather sinister rhythm called the *dochmiac*, basically ⏑––⏑– ("The wíse kángaróo, / She líves ín the zóo" gives a faint idea of the effect in English).[47] In extant Greek drama this makes its first hesitant appearance in *Persians* at 263 = 274 in the mouth of a distraught Persian chorus which has just learned of the disaster at Salamis; there is another probable example at 658 = 665 of the same play.[48] After that, Aeschylus used the meter on a monumental scale in the *parodos* of his *Seven Against Thebes*, produced in 467 B.C., and with somewhat more restraint, but still with powerful effects, in all his ensuing extant plays. Thereafter the dochmiac is firmly established in the tragic metrical orchestra as an instrument for moments of wild emotion—occasionally joy, more often rage, terror, and grief. It often marks the culminating point of the tragic narrative; this will be the meter, for instance, in which Kreon will lament at the end of the *Antigone*, and against which Euripides' Medea will slaughter her children offstage. Yet we have almost no clues to the origin of this important variety of tragic song. Certain students have identified isolated dochmiacs in the choral lyricists from Simonides onward, but the supposed instances all seem uncertain, at best.[49] Else has conjectured, interestingly, that the dochmiac was in origin a vernacular Attic rhythm employed in keenings for the dead, but no evidence can be produced in support of this.[50] On the evidence that we actually have, the earliest songs composed partly or wholly in the meter are those in the tragedies of Aeschylus. While Dale may be thought to have gone further than the facts warrant in suggesting that Aeschylus may have created dochmiac lyric, there is some case for supposing that either he or some earlier Attic tragedian was the first to exploit it on a large scale as a serious art-form.[51] Even if that is granted, however, dochmiac lyric will be the only important variety of Greek meter, lyric or other, that we owe to Attic tragedy; all the rest are borrowings.

As we have already mentioned, it seems a hopeless task to trace out the sources of all those borrowings; even if we still possessed the entire corpus of archaic nondramatic lyric as it once was, instead of a pitiably small selection from it, the picture would probably be too complex to allow many valid conclusions. Only in two special cases does the evidence seem enough to warrant some discussion of possible origins.

The first case is presented by a set of lyric forms that are already quite prominent in Aeschylus, and after him remain a standard element in the tragic metrical repertoire: (a) the so-called ionic-anacreontic rhythm, and (b) the combination glyconic-pherecratean. It may be stated without further ado that only one *nondramatic* poet can be found, in the entire story of Greek literature before the mid fifth century, who made any considerable use of either of these two forms; but in this poet's fragments both forms are very prominent indeed, to the extent that some of the later Greek metricians (followed by modern usage) actually named one of them after him. That poet is, of course, Anacreon. The rather complicated facts and figures on which I base this statement will be found in Appendix X. It seems, to me at least, that they cannot well be accounted for as mere coincidence. Rather, they seem to confirm quite elegantly the remarks about Anacreon's influence by the ancient commentator on *Prometheus* 128 that were considered earlier in this chapter.[52]

Our second specific instance of tragic borrowing from nondramatic lyric is the meter (or, perhaps better, *way of composition*) which in modern times has been rather cumbrously entitled "dactylo-epitrite." Of all the discoveries that await the amateur's ear when he approaches Greek metrics, dactylo-epitrite is one of the most surprising and one of the richest. At its simplest, this way of composing consists of taking two elements, a dactylic –⏑⏑–⏑⏑– and an epitritic –⏑–, and disposing them in an infinitude of ways, usually placing a single syllable as a kind of buffer between each element.[53] Although its earliest history is still debatable (some think foreshadowings of it occur in the asynartetic meters of Archilochus), there is now general agreement that Stesichorus is the first extant poet who uses it systematically.[54] The meter is heard loud and clear in several fragments of Simonides (a notable instance is fr. 581 *PMG*, the passage refuting Kleoboulos of Lindos), and in the extant poems of Pindar and Bacchylides it is the predominant meter: twenty-four of Pindar's forty-five epinician odes are composed in it, as are at least sixteen of the twenty more or less well-preserved songs in Snell's edition of Bacchylides.[55] The earliest datable song in dactylo-epitrites that is preserved complete is Pindar's twelfth Pythian Ode, composed for a victory in 490 B.C. In short, this way of composing seems to have been developed by a succession of great lyric poets from the first half of the sixth century B.C. and to have achieved overwhelming popularity by the first decades of the fifth.

In spite of that, dactylo-epitrite does not seem, on our evidence, to have established itself firmly in the tragic metrical repertoire until toward the middle of the fifth century. Three early tragic fragments have been read by Snell, apparently, as dactylo-epitrite; but of these Phrynichus fr. 9 and Pratinas fr. 6 really seem to have little in common with the meter as we know it in Pindar and Bacchylides, and Phrynichus's short fragment 13 can be interpreted equally well (or better) as a kind of verse that is already documented in Archilochus.[56] In the extant Aeschylean corpus there is not a single certain instance of the meter, until we reach the *Prometheus*.[57] In that play, however, we hear two choral odes (526 ff., 887 ff.) which are not merely composed in indisputable and fully developed dactylo-epitrites—that in itself is shock enough to anyone who has worked systematically through the meters of the rest of the corpus—but also show the meter in a remarkably pure form. As A. M. Dale has remarked, the second of the odes in question "is the only ode in drama which confines the colon-units to those found in the commonest and most straightforward of Pindar's dactylo-epitrites."[58] It thus seems possible that the *Prometheus* preserves for us the moment at which Attic tragedy incorporated into its repertoire this important branch of Greek lyric meter, borrowing it directly from the great choral lyricists whose achievement it was. Tragedy, as we shall see, had a standing tendency to modify and diversify the metrical forms that it borrowed, and this happened to the dactylo-epitrite meter in the hands of the subsequent tragedians; one thinks of its sustained use in (for example) Sophocles' *Ajax* and *Trachiniae*, and in Euripides'

Alcestis, *Medea*, and *Andromache*. The composer of the *Prometheus*, it appears, is scarcely yet ready to introduce innovations into the form which he has taken over from the choral poets. Even those who consider that that composer was not Aeschylus would probably put the play—and with it, possibly, the introduction of dactylo-epitrites into tragedy—not far from the middle of the fifth century.[59]

ADAPTATION OF THE BORROWED METERS

Once a given meter had been firmly incorporated into the tragedians' metrical repertoire, it tended to be more or less drastically adapted to its new environment, either in its form or in its poetic application or in both. We have already noticed, in the preceding section, how the *forms* of dactylo-epitritic composition were modified by the Attic dramatists during the decades following the *Prometheus*.[60] An example of a change in *poetic application* has already been provided by the anonymous (but evidently learned and acute) scholar whose work underlies the mutilated scholium on *Prometheus* 128. In spite of the textual difficulties, there can be no doubt that one of the points he makes is that the tragedians took over these anaclastic ionic measures directly from Anacreon, who notoriously had used them in sympotic and erotic contexts, "but they used them not in every place, but in contexts of lamentation."[61]

Although, obviously, there will be many uncertainties, it seems worthwhile at this point to survey what we know, or can reasonably infer, about the tragedians' adaptations of the other meters they borrowed from nondramatic Greek poetry.

First, *the spoken meters*: it would be difficult to judge *simply by ear* whether a given iambic trimeter or trochaic tetrameter catalectic actually composed by Archilochus, say, or Solon, did or did not come from Attic tragedy; the only immediate aural clue to its origin among the Ionian school of iambists would be a nonmetrical one, the dialect. The Ionian and the tragic trimeter share certain basic laws—notably the insistence on a caesura within the second metron, the restriction of resolution to certain places in the line, and the observance of Porson's law—which sharply distinguish them, as *Kunstdichtung*, from the far more loosely constructed trimeters we find in Attic and Sicilian comedy; and the same applies, *mutatis mutandis*, to the tetrameters. On the other hand, there is many a tragic trimeter, even in the earliest extant tragedies, which the practiced ear could not possibly mistake for a trimeter composed by an Ionian iambist. Already by the time of the *Persians*, in fact, the tragedians are seen to have introduced certain modifications into the trimeter (and tetrameter) which, although not affecting the fundamental artistic character of the verse, allow more variety and, perhaps, a somewhat closer approach to the rhythms of the ordinary spoken language.[62]

Of far greater significance for the entire character of Attic, and of all subsequent European, tragedy was the tragedians' adoption of the iambic trimeter as the prime medium for their actor episodes. This did not happen at a single blow. There was a time, according to Aristotle (unfortunately, he does not specify exactly *what* time), when the predominant tragic meter was the trochaic tetrameter; only "late," and concomitantly with the growing dignity of tragedy, did the iambics prevail.[63] It has often been suggested that our earliest extant tragedy, the *Persians*, represents the penultimate stage in that transition. Here three relatively long passages, all of a somewhat agitated nature, are in tetrameters. Thereafter, in the extant plays, Aeschylus employs the meter only at two exceptionally turbulent moments of the *Agamemnon*; it then disappears from tragedy until the last two decades of the fifth century, when Euripides revives it on quite a large scale for his own purposes.[64] There is thus some reason to think that the final triumph of iambic over trochaic as the tragic dialogue meter par excellence may be due to Aeschylus.[65] It was a momentous step; had it not been taken, Senecan and Elizabethan tragedy, in the verse forms in which we now have them, would scarcely be imaginable.

Here above all we should bear firmly in mind the results of the discussion in Part I (especially pp. 34–35): the works of the Ionian iambists and of their follower Solon were *performed*, and presumably were still to be seen and heard in performance during the formative years of tragedy. The manner of performance—often involving, it seems, impersonation—was such that the first tragic actors must have been able to take it over without any change in speaking their iambic scenes; it seems very likely, the more one re-imagines the situation, that the European histrionic art is ultimately the creation of the seventh- and sixth-century rhapsodes. Only a feature not directly connected with meter or delivery, the *mask*, revolutionized all: the performer now shed all vestiges of his rhapsode personality and merged visually as well as verbally into his speaking part.

Even the content and tone of the Ionian iambic poems were readily adaptable to dramatic situations. We noticed earlier (p. 35) how easily the great *rhesis* of Solon on the *Seisachtheia* (fr. 36 W) would fit into a tragedy, had tragedy permitted that kind of subject matter. Like so many of the Ionian-school iambic poems, the speech presumes—one might almost say *creates*—an unseen antagonist, who may be answered (as here) by stately moral and political rhetoric or (as often in Archilochus and Hipponax) by scathing invective. "One side of a dialogue" might be an apt description of many an Ionian iambic poem, perhaps of most. Some of those poems, indeed, embodied within themselves two-sided dialogues, on occasion remarkably snappy ones, such as this fragment of Hipponax, where a man and woman (it seems) contrive to exchange substantial insults within the compass of a single line:

ἀπό σ' ὀλέσειεν Ἄρτεμις – σὲ δὲ κὠπόλλων![66]

In the Ionian iambists, then, the first tragedians found ready to hand not merely a verse form but also a style of composition and performance that were superbly fitted to the argumentation, the clash of personalities, inherent in *drama* as we now understand it. Circumstances further forced them to assign to the iambic trimeter an important function which it had never served before in the history of Greek poetry: large-scale narrative.

Epic, above all Homeric epic, is almost omnipresent in Attic tragedy from the beginning to the end; of this more is to be said later. The chief exception to the rule is, of course, the almost total absence from the tragic repertoire of epic's characteristic meter, the dactylic hexameter.[67] One may conjecture that the chief reasons for this absence were (a) that the meter in itself is far removed from the rhythms of ordinary speech,[68] (b) that this very fact entailed composition in a highly artificial language, even if one did not resort to the ancient formulary which had been so well worked out by the epic poets, and (c) that speeches, long or short, in dactylic hexameters could offer nothing to the audience of an early tragedy that it could not hear in abundance at the contemporary rhapsode-performances of epic. On the other hand, throughout the Greek poetic tradition so far the dactylic hexameter had been the meter par excellence for extended and continuous narrative. Now, at some time during the formative period of tragedy—certainly before the *Persians* and probably long before it[69]—the dramatists came in fact to incorporate a very substantial element of straight narrative poetry into their plays—an element which, as we all know, is prominent in every extant tragedy from first to last, mainly (though by no means exclusively) in the messenger speeches.[70] To this function the tragedians adapted the iambic trimeter, which had never before, so far as our evidence goes, been used for anything of the kind.[71] The most we find in the Ionian iambists is the brief and lively anecdote (as, for instance, in the animal fables of Archilochus) rather than the flowing narrative. This assimilation of essentially epic matter (and possibly, to some extent, epic language and delivery also) to iambic metrical form is one of the most striking of all the early tragedians' innovations.[72] To the modern reader, fresh from contemporary drama, it may also be one of the most disconcerting, but consideration of this matter is best reserved until the next chapter.

The tragedians' adaptation of the *anapaestic* meter was less drastic than that of the iambics, but it is still of considerable interest. We saw above how, on our present evidence, they seem to have borrowed the meter direct from the Spartans. The evidence suggests that in Sparta it was primarily a marching rhythm, and this is not surprising: a very similar rhythm is used in the anapaestic drum-roll that is used to accompany military marching to this day. Perhaps one will not be too fanciful if one hears the formidable quickstep of the ancient Spartan infantry in such lines as these:

ἄγετ' ὦ Σπάρτας ἔνοπλοι κοῦροι
ποτὶ τὰν Ἄρεως κίνασιν.[73]

The earliest example in Attic tragedy probably occurs in Phrynichus (fr. 2 Snell, from *Alcestis*).[74] The fragment has reached us without a context and is in itself too short to provide much idea of the way in which Phrynichus applied the meter. Yet it does show a peculiar metrical feature which cannot be traced in pretragic anapaests: the emergence, no less than twice in a single dimeter, of a *dactyl* (–⏑⏑) to take its place alongside the anapaest (⏑⏑–) and spondee (––) which are the sole components of the meter in the pretragic examples. From line 2 of Aeschylus's *Persians* onward through all extant tragedy, this dactylic substitution is regular, giving a quite remarkable rhythmic effect. It would be over-bold, however, to assert that this important feature was an innovation of the Attic tragedians, since the examples of pretragic anapaests are so scanty; at this date we can merely note the facts and hope for the appearance of new evidence.[75] We have already observed how the dialect of the anapaests, like that of the iambics, was Atticized in the tragedians.

The poetic functions of the anapaestic meter, when we can at last fully observe them in Aeschylus's tragedies, are fairly easily defined. In three of the surviving plays, and probably in at least three of the lost ones, it accompanied the first entrance of the chorus, presumably being chanted as they filed through the *parodos* and circled the *orchēstra* before taking up station. The same rhythm accompanied the final exits of the choruses in the *Choephori* and (probably) the satyric *Diktyoulkoi*.[76] Thus the pretragic marching association of the anapaests is still very much alive in Aeschylean tragedy. From the beginning, however, their functions are seen to have been multiplied. Anapaests may be chanted by an apparently stationary chorus to accompany the entrance or exit of an actor,[77] or chanted by an actor himself as he enters or exits.[78] Even in these cases, of course, the anapaestic meter retains something of its original connection with *movement*. There remain some places in Aeschylus (and a good many more in the later tragedians) where that connection seems to be completely broken, and the meter seems to be used as an expression of emotional, as opposed to physical, excitement and disturbance. This is probably true of the numerous fairly short anapaestic passages that are prefixed to choral odes, as at *Persians* 532–47;[79] the intended effect seems to be, as it were, to gear up the emotions, to raise the level a step above that of the iambic verse by way of transition to the highest level, full song. Certainly it seems to be true in the *kommoi* of the *Oresteia*; it is into anapaests, for instance, that Clytaemnestra eventually moves (or, shall we say, is cornered?) in her great confrontation with the Chorus after the slaying of Agamemnon.[80] The tendency is carried to its extreme in that play of so many extremes, the *Prometheus*: this includes not only an anapaestic-plus-lyric *kommos* (128–92) of the type already heard in the *Oresteia*, but also an entirely anapaestic *kommos* (1040–93), and the speech—unique in all extant tragedy—in which Prometheus modulates from iambic to anapaest to iambic to lyric to anapaest again (88–127). There can, of course, be no question of physical movement in those anapaests that are chanted by

Prometheus himself in this play, since he has been firmly bound and skewered to a rock from line 55 onward. The debate will probably continue as to whether this is a sign that the play is spurious or is yet another proof of the versatility and creativity of the aging Aeschylus.[81]

The tragedians' adaptations of the inherited pretragic *lyric* meters were even more drastic. In this matter there is much that simply cannot be accounted for on our present evidence, as will be seen in the following section. Here one general observation may be made: "Tragedy is a mixture" in its lyric songs also. Within a single choral ode it can juxtapose discrete types of meter which so far as we know, had never been heard together before. Thus the tremendous *parodos*-song of the *Agamemnon* includes a lyric triad in the dactylic measures familiar since at least the days of Stesichorus (*Ag.* 104–59), four stanzas primarily in an iambo-trochaic meter which can already to some extent be paralleled in Alcman's first *Partheneion* (*Ag.* 160–91), and six stanzas in a predominantly iambic meter (*Ag.* 192–257). The nearest parallel I know to such a mixture in earlier or contemporary nontragic lyric is Bacchylides' *carmen.* 3 (honoring Hieron's victory at Olympia in 468 B.C. and presumably composed fairly soon after it, since Hieron died in the following year); here the strophes and antistrophes are in aeolic meters (with a first line that may perhaps be iambic), but the epodes are in dactylo-epitrite.[82] The *Agamemnon parodos*-song, however, is an unusually simple example of the tragedians' juxtaposition of different kinds of meter within a single ode and of the vast range of association, tone, and tempo which thus became possible in tragic song, as never before. Most tragic odes, in Aeschylus and his successors, are more complicated than this in that the kinds of meter used can vary widely *within the stanza itself.* One has only to listen to the first stanza of the "Helen ode" in the *Agamemnon* (691–98), which modulates from iambo-trochaic to ionic-anacreontic to aeolic—combining, that is, rhythms from almost all over the area of the archaic song culture, with unforgettable effect. Such modulation within the limits of the stanza is only faintly paralleled in one or two nontragic poems, none of them earlier than the career of Aeschylus. The best-known is Pindar's thirteenth Olympian Ode, composed for a victory of 464 B.C., but even that is temperate compared to most of the tragic songs, with their wild diversification of meters.[83]

CONCLUSION

Such statements as the ancient Greeks have left concerning the craft of tragedy, and inspection of the pretragic and tragic meters themselves, thus conspire to suggest that the early Attic tragedians were, and were thought to be, the heirs of the entire preceding poetic tradition, so far as verse technique was concerned. They were grasping and resourceful heirs. By the time of Aeschylus's extant plays they had brought together three previously separate *genera* of art-poetry, spoken, chanted, and sung; and within the sung category they had melded all sorts of previously separate metrical elements, both from monodic and from choral lyric. This metrical and musical accomplishment in itself may in great part account for the enormous popularity of the new art and for its overshadowing of the other major forms of archaic poetry in the course of the fifth century. Tragedy could offer all to the ear that those other forms of poetry could, and something that (as we saw at the beginning of this chapter) neither they nor any later forms of poetry can offer to this day: an infinite diversity of rhythms, adaptable to any level of reason or emotion.

Much in that process must still remain unexplained, since it took place for the most part during the scarcely documented period between Thespis and the production of the *Persians*. Here and there, as was seen earlier, we can still catch a glimpse of an early tragedian, a Phrynichus or an Aeschylus, at his work of developing the repertoire of tragic song, but our ignorance remains great and must probably always remain so. The same, unfortunately, must be said about the origin and early history of certain striking features of tragic verse at the level above that of the metrical unit: stichomythia, the *agōn* form, the arrangement of the lyrics in pairs of strophe and antistrophe (as opposed to the nonstrophic, monostrophic, or triadic disposition of pretragic lyric), the *thrēnos* or lamentation. In all these cases it is no doubt legitimate to seek explanations from outside the sphere of art-poetry, that is, in rituals or at least in subliterary performances; and this many students have done, although without results that have found general acceptance.[84] Even so, it must be acknowledged that where those features appear in extant tragedy they already conform in meter, in diction, and in style to the mainstream of the archaic Greek poetic tradition. Here again, tragedy must have borrowed and blended, gathering in a form from outside and turning it to tragedy's own artistic purposes. The results which we have before us, be they the great *thrēnos* that ends the *Persians*, the crucial stichomythia between Agamemnon and his queen in the Tapestry Episode, the Suppliants' great song of blessing on the Argives, or the *agōnes* in the last part of Sophocles' *Ajax*, can be counted neither as subliterary mummings nor as ritual. They seem already to be tragic poetry.

6. Old and New In Early Tragedy

THE TRAGIC CRUCIBLE

However many doubts may remain about this detail or that, the preceding chapter as a whole seems to have shown with reasonable certainty that early tragedy, metrically speaking, was like a crucible, ever on the boil, into which had been stirred, by the mid fifth century, almost every metrical element known to the pretragic tradition of poetry. Out of it emerged unheard-of compounds releasing explosive forces that might have astonished the original alchemists themselves and which continue to astonish us.

It may seem possible, and perhaps even likely, that the image will apply not merely to tragic metrics but to tragedy in all its dimensions. To demonstrate that, however, is infinitely more difficult on our available evidence. Even the metrical material, as we have seen, is scanty and elusive enough, but at least the phenomena are such that they can be described and compared with some degree of objectivity. It is obviously far otherwise with (shall we say?) the Attic tragedians' narrative technique and plot construction, their methods of closure, their dialogue technique, their characterization, their imagery, their moral and religious teaching, the appalling atmosphere of ambiguity and dread that shades and colors so much of the tragic landscape. For, first, to draw adequate comparisons between tragic and pretragic poetry from these points of view we should require many more *complete* examples of the pretragic works than have actually survived. Second, those features of tragedy in themselves, and still more in the profound effects that they had and will ever have on an audience, are hard to pin down and describe with precision, even under the most favorable circumstances.

Yet, here and there, something can be done in this nonmetrical area too. The present chapter considers continuity and innovation: first, certain nonmetrical features of Attic tragedy that seem clearly to have been inherited from the earlier poetic tradition; second, and more tentatively, certain features that seem to be wholly new in Greek and in Western literature. I do not pretend to be complete, or even near complete, and in some cases my treatment will be more an indication of areas to be explored than a systematic investigation. This is partly due to the limits imposed by the design and proportions of the present study, but also to the limits of my own knowledge; it seems that there is much spadework yet to be done on this whole question. As in the preceding chapter, most of my tragic instances will necessarily be taken from the work of Aeschylus, but I have also considered the fragments of the other early tragedians and shall draw upon them where appropriate.

DICTION AND STYLE

The fourth in the long line of tragedians who descended collaterally from Aeschylus,[1] Astydamas II, received the honor of a bronze statue, erected in the Theater of Dionysos during his own lifetime. The statue's inscription, a four-line elegiac epigram, ascribed to Astydamas himself, was rightly criticized in antiquity for its absurd immodesty, but is of interest to us here for the remarkable line in which it characterized the great tragedians of the past: "those who have the fame of winning first prize for the charm of their speech."[2] Even as late as 340 B.C.—the earliest date at which the verses can have been composed—there is no mention of their glory as dramatists or as evokers of pity or terror or whatnot; the sole characteristic of tragedy that is chosen for mention within the cramped space permitted by an epigram is the pleasure communicated by its *language*.

One of the many secrets of that pleasure seems to have been, once more, the mixture of elements diverse in origin. In its broadest outlines, the picture presented by Aeschylean style rather resembles that presented by Aeschylean meter. Aeschylean style, too, is a volatile compound of features drawn from all the pretragic genres, with all the range and flexibility of tone that this implies. At will, the tragedian can touch the epic, choral lyric, personal lyric, and iambic chords. The range is further extended by a new element which we must suspect—but, in the absence of contemporary prose documents, cannot absolutely prove—to be the style of spoken Attic, especially that of the law courts.[3]

In thinking of Aeschylus's style we usually, and naturally, recall Ben Jonson's "thund'ring Aeschylus";[4] but it is too easy to overlook passages in him, such as the Furies' opening examination of Orestes in the *Eumenides*, which show a lucidity and businesslike directness hardly to be paralleled elsewhere in Greek poetry or prose.[5] The hearer of Aeschylus, perhaps more than of any other ancient poet except Aristophanes, needs to be able to tune his ear to variations of stylistic tone which range from such passages as the wild dithyrambic style of *Choephori* 423–28 to the epic-lyric majesty of the opening triad in the *Agamemnon parodos*-song.

The language of Aeschylus, in short, comes to us (as was once said of Milton's verse) "freighted with the spoils of all the ages," from Homer down until his own time.[6] It is quite impossible to trace the steps by which this amalgamation of different styles had come about, but we may guess that the process was similar to that which (on the basis of a little more evidence) we have postulated for the tragic amalgamation of meters. It is certain that Aeschylus presents us with what, in all its essentials, was to remain the dialect of the Greek tragedians until the end of antiquity. The word *dialect* is used advisedly: this tragic language is a distinct and easily recognizable composite genre-dialect, comparable in many ways to that earlier amalgam which we traditionally, if inaccurately, call the *epic dialect*.[7] This is one of the truly insuperable difficulties that confront the translator of Attic tragedy into a modern language. There is much we can, or at least might, do with English. We can make speakable and actable verses; sometimes, with luck, we can even make singable songs; and to that extent we can match the effects of the ancient originals. What we cannot do is to reproduce a dialect which embodied and evoked an entire national poetic tradition, a dialect which was never spoken outside the theater but was mostly as remote from the *language* of the streets as the tragic masks and costumes were from the *dress* of the streets.[8]

A full examination of tragic—and especially Aeschylean—*verbal imagery* in its relation to pretragic Greek poetry might well reinforce the conclusions we have reached in the matters of meter and style. We might find once more an unrestrained eclecticism that issues in an essentially novel technique. This, however, would really require a separate monograph, and we must be content in this context simply to recall a very well-known generality about the pretragic poetic genres. In the epic, the element of comparison is mostly concentrated in the formal similes, introduced by "just as" and ending "just so"; metaphorical expressions—for our present purposes, the Aristotelian definition of metaphor as comparison not introduced or closed by comparative adverbs will be adequate—are rare, brief, and not striking, sometimes indeed having the air of clichés.[9] The extensive and creative exploitation of metaphorical language seems on our evidence to have been primarily the province of choral lyric poetry. From this point of view, surviving iambic poetry is plainer in texture than either of the two genres just mentioned, rarely admitting either simile or metaphor at any length whatever; its sister genre, elegiac, has a slight propensity to formal simile, as one might expect from its metrical ties to the epic.[10] In this matter again, it falls to the tragedians to scramble up the conventions previously reserved for this or that poetic genre. The language of Aeschylus's spoken and chanted, as well as of his choral, poetry may be extensively metaphorical; and while neither he nor his successors very often introduced a formal simile, they were prepared on occasion to do so (usually, it seems, in order to intensify an already epic atmosphere) in any variety of meter.[11]

ONCE MORE THE FORESTS OF MYTHS

The least innovative feature in the new art of tragedy was its repertoire of stories and characters. As one surveys the entire output of the tragedians—the titles and fragments of the lost dramas, as well as the extant works—one sees that they simply moved in and reoccupied the entire archaic forest of myth. In great part they seem to have drawn this basic material directly from the great corpus of hexameter epic that had come into being (or at least had been put into writing) from the eighth through the sixth century B.C. Homer, as we shall see later, is a very special case; here we may briefly recall some instances of the apparent contribution of other early epic to the story material of tragedy. For the influence of the Epic Cycle, the *locus classicus* is Aristotle's *Poetics*, 1459b4–7: "Many tragedies are made from the *Cypria*, and from the *Little Iliad* more than eight, such as the *Judgment of Arms*, the *Philoctetes*, the *Neoptolemos*, the *Eurypylos*, the *Begging* [of the disguised Odysseus in Troy], the *Laconian Women* [again, in Troy], the *Sack of Ilion*, the *Sailing Away*, and the *Sinon* and the *Trojan Women*."[12] Sophocles in particular, we are told by Athenaeus, "so much delighted in the

Epic Cycle that he composed whole plays in which he followed the mythmaking (*mythopoiia*) contained in it."[13] The Hesiodic epics likewise, although we have no such explicit ancient statements about their influence on the tragedians, are known or surmised to have served them as another great storehouse of myth; one thinks particularly of the Prometheus plays, which, with all their innovations, seem to depend ultimately on the *Theogony* for their story outline, and of the large number of plays based on mythic themes which first appeared, so far as we know, in the *Eoiai*.[14] One relatively early *lyric* poet, Stesichorus, seems to have ranked almost with the epic poets as a source of tragic myth and even, it seems, tragic treatment of myth. The very titles of his lengthy songs—for example, the *Helen*, the *Eriphyle*, the *Oresteia*—are suggestive enough in themselves, and we now have some direct ancient testimony to his influence on the tragedians.[15]

Only very rarely, it seems, did the tragedies cover mythological ground that had not been covered at all in the early epic corpus. The only fairly firmly establishable exceptions to this rule are the *Aitnaiai* and *Glaukos Pontios* of Aeschylus, each of which seems to have centered on a quite obscure local legend;[16] the *Archelaos* of Euripides, in which heroic myth seems to have been, to say the least, doctored somewhat for the greater glory of the reigning Macedonian king;[17] and the small early group of so-called historical tragedies, namely, Phrynichus's play on the fall of Miletus and his *Phoenissae*, and Aeschylus's *Persians*. That last group is perhaps not so startling an exception to the rule that tragedy's subject matter was myth as it is sometimes represented to be. As the present writer has argued elsewhere, the armed clash of the Persians and the Greeks in the early fifth century made so great an impact on the Greek imagination that this historical episode *alone* seems to have been accepted almost instantaneously into the corpus of inherited myth. Not only the early tragedians, but also the lyric poets, the vase painters, the wall painters, and the sculptors of the fifth century, all broke the Greek tabu against the artistic representation of contemporary events when it came to the Persian Wars.[18] And certainly in the extant examples of such work in any medium, above all in the *Persians* of Aeschylus and of Timotheus, the treatment is very far from "historical" in the modern, or even the Shakespearean, sense; it is almost indistinguishable from the fifth-century artist's treatment of any ancient, distanced myth. Finally, only once in the entire recorded history of tragedy did any playwright actually *invent* a story and characters for his play. That experiment was made, as we might have predicted, in the last decades of the fifth century, the very time when the inherited mythological world was beginning to lose its hold on society at large.[19]

THE CATHOLICITY OF EARLY TRAGEDY

Closer inspection of the fifth-century tragedies, especially the fragmentary ones, suggests that the tragedians' inheritance from the early epic by no means stopped short at mythological themes and characters. We have already discussed (pp. 67–70) the great range of the epic corpus in characters, story patterns, themes, and tones, and its admittance not merely of what we should, with hindsight, call tragic motifs, but also of the comic, the fantastic, the bawdy, the annalistic, and even the genealogical and the geographical. Attic tragedy, especially in its earlier phase, perpetuated all these characteristics in some degree.[20] The reader even of the extant tragedies (which have largely been selected for us by late-antique academics)[21] might be spared much bewilderment if he or she approached them in full recognition of this fact, instead of—as all too often happens—with the vague idea that any tragedy that doesn't behave like the *Oedipus Tyrannus* represents some kind of deviation. The long geographical speeches of the *Prometheus*, the drunken Herakles in the *Alcestis*, the monstrous Furies of the *Eumenides*, the Nurse bemoaning the task of washing Orestes' dirty diapers in the *Choephori*, the *Phoenissae* with its embodiment of almost the entire Theban saga—all these, whatever aesthetic or moral judgment one ultimately makes on them, stand firmly within the epic-tragic tradition as it actually was before the ravages of time.[22] The fragmentary tragedies, especially those by Aeschylus, present an even more striking picture.[23] Motifs, and even whole scenes, of a sort that struck some later Greek critics as *aprepeis*, unsuitable to the dignity of tragedy, are not infrequent among them: in the *Kabeiroi* the jesting gods, and Jason with his Argonauts brought drunk onto the stage (frr. 45, 46 M); the *Semelē*(?), in which all who touched the pregnant heroine's belly became inspired by the god (fr. 358); the stinking chamberpot, "smelling not of myrrh-flasks," described as slung at Odysseus by the drunken revellers in an unidentified play (fr. 486);[24] the homosexual love between Achilles and Patroklos in the *Myrmidons*, with the verbatim fragment of Achilles' passionate lament for his friend:

σέβας δὲ μηρῶν ἁγνὸν οὐκ ἐπηδέσω,
ὦ δυσχάριστε τῶν πυκνῶν φιλημάτων; (fr. 228)[25]

At least equally prominent in the dramatic work of Aeschylus, as it originally stood, were the monstrous, the fantastic, and the exotic elements, all of which were legitimate inheritances from ancient epic poetry, and especially from the Epic Cycle and Hesiod.[26] Although such elements are still traceable here and there in the lost plays of the subsequent tragedians,[27] they seem to have become much rarer after the mid fifth century. The reason for this is probably not far to seek, and is worth considering here, for it seems to have something to do with the extraordinary spiritual force which I for one feel in Aeschylean drama, and in no subsequent drama throughout the Western tradition. To the imagination of Aeschylus—as of Pindar, and of the great vase painters of the archaic age—the ancient forest of myth seems still to be utterly alive and numinous; even its most fantastic denizens watch the traveler "with familiar looks." The poet can summon any of them into his poem, and sometimes even onto his dance floor, without apparent self-consciousness or embarrassment. In this respect Aeschylus still remains squarely within the ancient poetic tradition, and within the even more ancient Indo-European way of thinking and seeing. His medium, the medium of myth, remains one old beyond our imagining; yet through it Aeschylus delivers a message that is new, analyzing a culture which was then evolving fast and in unprecedented ways into one that foreshadows our own. Nothing quite comparable has ever happened since in Europe or America, and in this fact may reside the greatest of the difficulties that face modern interpreters of Aeschylus. He stands on the other side of a gulf both from us and from the extant works of Sophocles and Euripides.

On the whole, those works emphasize the human and the credible aspects of the myths. The monstrous, the fantastic, and the surreal aspects they tend either to suppress, or to leave unseen on the periphery of the plot (*exō tou dramatos*, outside the action, as Aristotle puts it),[28] or to rationalize, or—as Euripides often does—to treat with a certain irony. Like their audiences, Sophocles and Euripides are gradually becoming intellectually detached from the ancient mythic world, whereas the imagination of Aeschylus, to the end, is totally and passionately involved with it. A few examples: as an infant, the Aeschylean Ajax in the *Thrēissai* had been made weapon-proof throughout his body except under his armpits; when he came to commit suicide, the sword doubled up against the invulnerable flesh (he was "like one bending a bow," said the Messenger who reported the scene), until at last some *daimōn* showed him where he must strike.[29] That strange, and surely ancient, aspect of the hero's death has of course been suppressed in Sophocles' extant treatment of it; just as his vision of the Oedipus story has filtered out the dark and primitive details (which apparently occurred in Aeschylus's *Laios*) that Oedipus was exposed for death shut in a jar, and that after murdering Laios he performed the apotropaic rite of tasting and spitting out his victim's blood.[30] Similarly, one might contrast the Furies whom Aeschylus brought into the *orchēstra* in the *Eumenides* with that supernatural female whom Euripides caused to appear at the top of the *skēnē* to madden Herakles: Lyssa, "Frenzy." The Furies are unabashedly monstrous, and confident of their status in the mythological cosmos, whereas poor Lyssa is made to take time off to explain that she comes of highly respectable parentage and really doesn't like doing this kind of thing at all.[31]

Perhaps the most interesting example of Aeschylus's total familiarity with the archaic mythical world—and of the extent to which that world had faded from the popular imagination by the end of the fifth century B.C.—occurs in Aristophanes' *Frogs* (930–33). In the *Myrmidons*, that same tragedy which included the lament of Achilles over Patroklos, Aeschylus had introduced reference to a "tawny cockhorse," a *hippalektryon*, painted as a device on a ship's stern (fr. 212f Mette). That puzzles even the god of tragedy himself. "A tawny cockhorse!" cries the stage Dionysos; "I've spent whole sleepless nights wondering what kind of a bird *that* was!" In the Athens of 405 B.C., such a monster has become an unintelligible absurdity. Yet in sober historical fact the cockhorse must have been a quite familiar figure to the archaic Athenian imagination. There are several extant pictures of it on late sixth-century vase-paintings, and a cockhorse in marble—a pleasing fowl with a horse's front, and actually bearing a neat little human rider—stood among the votive statues on the Acropolis until the Persians came in 480 B.C., when Aeschylus was already well into middle age—watching him with familiar looks?[32]

It is not surprising, then, that Aeschylus's repertoire of tragic themes contained some specially wild and exotic legends that were never, or very rarely, approached again in Greek tragedy, for the reason that they were not "human" enough and were too magical for later fifth-century taste. Such were the stories of the fifty Danaid sisters in the *Suppliants* (this had apparently also been treated by Phrynichus),[33] of the Phorkides (better known as the Graiai), of Orpheus on Mount Pangaion in the *Bassarides*, of Glaukos of the Sea. It seems possible that the same reason may account for the relatively high proportion of Dionysiac plays in the Aeschylean repertoire. Something like one-tenth of the poet's total output seems to have been devoted to Dionysiac themes.[34] Rather than think of this statistic as evidence for the derivation of tragedy from Dionysiac ritual, as has often been done, I would suggest that, like the cockhorse, it is evidence for the taste of Aeschylus's era; we can witness for ourselves an enormous passion for Dionysiac themes in the vase painters of his youth and middle age—the Kleophrades and Brygos Painters, and Makron, for instance. Only one other Attic tragedian is known to have composed more than one tragedy on a Dionysiac theme, and he was a contemporary of Aeschylus: Polyphrasmon. There are no certain examples by tragedians earlier than Aeschylus, and subsequent fifth-century tragedians seem to have treated the subject rarely, and never more than once in each case.[35] Euripides in his *Bacchae* seems deliberately to have set out to recreate some of the magic of the Aeschylean Dionysiac plays, and all the world knows how marvelously he succeeded.[36] Yet even there, as with his Lyssa in the *Hercules Furens*, the ancient magic is (again deliberately) diluted by modern doubts: while the Bacchantes reel inspired on the mountaintops, Teiresias is repeating the most up-to-date sophistical speculations in the town.[37] Something of what we may have lost with the disappearance of Aeschylus's Dionysiac plays may be indicated by the casual comment of an ancient critic. Aeschylus in his *Ēdōnoi* (the critic says) had written thus about the epiphany of Dionysos in King Lykourgos's palace:

> The house is full of god, the roof is revelling;

Euripides, however, "sweetened" (the critic's word is *ephēdynas*) this astounding line when he came to compose the *Bacchae* (line 726): his version runs "and all the mountain revelled with them."[38]

TRAGEDY AND HOMERIC EPIC

Aristotle's *Poetics* has for long been read, by literary and dramatic critics alike, primarily for its information about *tragedy*—to such an extent that the nonspecialist and even the classical beginner may be forgiven if he needs reminding that in this book Aristotle actually discusses the *two* kinds of poetry that in his view represent "serious" (*spoudaios*) people and actions, namely, tragedy and epic. In his general exposition and in his detailed illustrations he treats these arts as identical except in certain features that are determined by the manner and length of their performance: notably, epic lacks the musical and visual elements that are inseparable from tragedy and admits of digressions, "episodes," far more freely.[39] In a word, "anybody who can tell a good tragedy from a bad one can do the same with epics" (1449b17–18). There are, indeed, bad epics as well as good ones. In passage after passage Aristotle hammers home the point that artistically Homer (that is, for him, the poet of the *Iliad* and the *Odyssey*) is supreme, and the rest of the vast corpus of epic known to him is of little account.[40] Hesiod he never mentions; the Epic Cycle, and the early epics on Herakles and Theseus, he mentions only as examples of how *not* to compose. It is Homer alone who is the forerunner and evidently the model for the best in Attic tragedy, as Aristotle envisages it.[41] Homer showed how to construct a plot around an event of manageable scale (1451a16–35, 1459a30–b2; in both passages the practice of other early epic poets is contrasted with Homer's). Homer is "alone [among the early Greek poets] in that he not only composed well but also composed dramatic representations" (*mimēseis dramatikas*, 1448b35–6). "Homer deserves praise for much, but particularly because alone of the [epic] poets he is well aware of what he himself ought to do: the poet should speak as little as possible in his own person because in doing that he is not a representer. Now, the other [epic poets] act in their own persons throughout, and represent [other persons] briefly and rarely; but Homer, after a short proem, instantly introduces a man or a woman or some other character (*ēthos*)—no one without character, but each with character" (1460a5–11). His two great poems not only anticipate the major categories of tragic plot—"the *Iliad* is simple and 'pathetic,' the *Odyssey* is complex and 'ethic'"—but also excel in diction and thought (1459b13–16).

These Aristotelian passages, familiar and perhaps all too familiar though they are, have seemed worth recalling at this point because their collective significance for the *history* of Attic tragedy as we know it is perhaps not universally recognized. Aristotle was of course acquainted with great numbers of early epics, and of Attic tragedies, that are now lost to us. Armed with this knowledge, he observed (a) that, as we have seen earlier (p. 128), for their mythological subject matter the tragedians on the whole avoided the Homeric material, but made great use of the stories in the cyclic epics; and (b) that for almost every other aspect of their art that mattered in his eyes Homer—and no other poet known to him whatever—was their model.[42] These judgments, made by Aristotle himself under such favorable conditions, might well seem authoritative enough in themselves; furthermore, nothing in our admittedly scanty remains of early epic and tragedy seems to controvert them.[43]

The implications of all this for the history of tragedy, and indeed for the history of the European imagination, seem considerable. To view the story in its widest perspective: in almost all Greek poetry down to Aristotle's time, the basic narrative subject matter had been supplied by the vast and complex world of the myths. Only in two genres of that poetry, however, had the heroes and supernatural beings of the mythic world been fully realized, fully brought into the round in speech and action: in the eighth-century *Iliad* and *Odyssey* (which, as Aristotle saw, practically constituted a separate genre in themselves),[44] and in fifth- and fourth-century tragedy. The other epics offered on the whole flat, two-dimensional narratives about the heroes and gods, arranged on some mechanical principle, whether annalistic or genealogical; while the lyric, presupposing a full knowledge of such narratives in its hearers, offered only brief and vivid illuminations of them from this angle or that. In this matter, the early tragedians seem to have proceeded somewhat as we have already seen them proceed in the matters of meter and dialect. They *mixed*; they applied the techniques that they had learned from the Homeric epic to the story material they found in the cyclic epic. As one surveys the tables of Aeschylus's works arranged by mythological theme offered by Welcker and Mette,[45] a surprising possibility begins to shape itself: could the poet perhaps have set out systematically to rival or replace the entire corpus of cyclic epic, using a combination of the Homeric techniques with the new visual and musical resources of tragedy? To supersede the equably flowing cyclic narratives by a series of compactly constructed dramatic poems, centering each of them on one or at most a few of the heroes concerned in the story? Certainly the subject matter of the entire Trojan Cycle, from the *Cypria* to the *Telegonia*, seems to be represented among the extant plays and fragments of Aeschylus, with the sole exception of the *Iliou Persis* (and that gap was to be abundantly filled in time by Sophocles and Euripides; for instance, the former's *Laokoön*, *Sinon*, *Aias Lokros*, and the latter's *Troades* and *Hecuba*). So, too, does much of the subject matter of the

Theban cycle of epics, and the epic on the Danaid story, and less certainly, the Hesiodic corpus.

Year by year, Dionysia by Dionysia, as the fifth century advanced, we may imagine that process of *realization* of the non-Homeric myths and heroes continuing in the hands of Aeschylus and his successors. For contemporaries it must have been dazzling enough, especially in the early years, when each Dionysia might reveal to the audience for the first time ever an Orestes, say, or a Memnon, or a Niobe, or an Oedipus, who was no longer a mere mechanical component in a famous story but who breathed, walked, and, above all, spoke for himself. But the effects of the process are in fact felt to this day in European and American literature and culture. Certain of the figures of the ancient myths (as we all know) still somehow retain a clearly defined identity, a living personality, in the imaginations of educated people. On consideration it will be found that practically all such figures owe their continuing existence among us either to Homer's epics or to a *surviving* Attic tragedy. How much the hazards of preservation have to answer for may be illustrated by a passage in the *Poetics* (1453a20–21), where Aristotle lists the most frequently chosen tragic themes, as follows: "the actions and passions of Alcmaeon, Oedipus, Orestes, Meleager, Thyestes, and Telephos." Of those six heroes, the modern nonspecialist will at once know two, in the intimate way one knows a friend or enemy; but what of the other four, the four who happen not to have been treated in any of the tragedies that reached us through the Dark Age? Not even an Ovid or a Seneca possessed the art of restoring them to life and literature; they now remain much as they must have been before Attic tragedy came into being, "strengthless heads of the dead." Poring over the pitiable fragments of the lost tragedies that concerned them, one occasionally stops to wonder about the difference that they might have made, had they survived, to the texture of Renaissance and modern literature. Suppose Racine and Goethe, for instance, had known a *Meleager* or an *Alcmaeon*?

THE BEGINNINGS OF TRAGEDY AS WE KNOW IT

The Homeric techniques of plot concentration and of characterization by speech, considered in the preceding section, were obviously not assimilated at one blow by the tragedians instantaneously, nor homogeneously, nor even universally. Even in the extant works of the three great tragedians and in the *Rhesus*, we can see how unevenly and how differently each poet might apply the Homeric lessons. Aeschylus will be discussed in the following section from this point of view. Of Sophocles we may here briefly note that he applied those lessons most consistently and thoroughly. The ancient critics agreed that he was *Homērikōtatos*, the most Homeric of them all. Most of the grounds for that judgment are spelled out for us in Aristotle's *Poetics*, but one could easily find others.[46] It has often occurred to me that a major omission from J. Duchemin's valuable book on the *agōn* in Greek tragedy is any examination of the *Homeric* precedents for that form. She has pointed out that it first appears fully developed in the Sophoclean tragedies. Of course, there are differences here from Homer, most obviously the stichomythia which follows the interchange of long speeches in the tragic *agōn* and is rightly included by Duchemin in her definition of that phenomenon. Nonetheless, the basic idea of a highly dramatized debate between two or more speakers—the outcome of which may deeply affect both the progress of the plot and our understanding of their characters—is fully and richly anticipated in Homer.[47] It is a curious fact, which probably would repay further investigation, that in these debates Homer, rather like the tragedians, strictly limits the number of speakers taking part: there are often three, hardly ever more than four.[48] Euripides' relationship to Homer was the most complex and interesting of all. It might be summed up (and there is place here only for the barest and simplest of summaries) as: a strong tendency to prefer the Odyssean to the Iliadic model, not merely in plot construction but also in outcome and tone;[49] a tendency to introduce the *agōn* (in the looser, Homeric sense) much more frequently, if perhaps less successfully, than Sophocles had done;[50] and, unless I am mistaken, a reversion for his own ironic purposes to the Homeric habit of flatly juxtaposing divine characters and actions with mortal characters and actions—not seeking to explain or justify the divine, as the other two tragedians sought in their different ways, but simply allowing it to appear in its traditional guise and leaving the audience to draw its own conclusions about the rationality or otherwise of this life and this universe.[51]

Finally, before turning to Aeschylus from this point of view, we should acknowledge that not every fifth-century tragedy did in fact conform to the Homeric precedent in plot concentration and in characterization by speech. Even some of the extant tragedies (e.g., Euripides'

Andromache, *Troades*, *Phoenissae*) have to some modern critics seemed deficient in the former aspect. Aristotle, however, had witnessed some tragedies that flagrantly failed to conform either in characterization or in plot making: the *aētheis tragōidiai*, tragedies lacking *ēthos*, which were produced in quantities by the more recent (i.e., fourth-century?) tragedians (*Poetics* 1450a23–26); and the occasional annalistic, cyclic-style plots of which even Euripides was guilty in a lost treatment of the sack of Troy, and which were a major flaw in the work of Agathon. Tragedies of that kind, however, says Aristotle, "are either hissed off the stage or come out low in the competitions" (1456a18). Hence it is, no doubt, that we can point to no extant example.

In view of all this, it seems arguable that the origin of tragedy *as we know it* (tragedy as exemplified in the surviving dramas, which to a considerable extent, though not perfectly, overlaps with the kind of tragedy commended by Aristotle) must be datable to the moment when some tragedian decided to adapt the Homeric techniques, however hesitantly, to the dramatic realization of the Greek mythological heritage generally. For that decision beyond all others must have brought an end—no doubt a lingering end—to the pioneer phase of heady experiment, the phase of "little plots and laughable diction."[52] Can we date that decision or identify the tragedian who took it?

"AESCHYLUS HOMERICUS"?

In strict method, no; there is not now, and probably never will be, ample and solid enough evidence about the course of tragedy before 472 B.C. Yet certain well-known facts do converge toward the probability that the tragedian concerned was Aeschylus, and therefore that the decision was taken somewhere between the years 499/98 B.C. (at about which time Aeschylus first competed at the Great Dionysia) and 472 (the *Persians*). First, and probably the most reliable of them, is Aristotle's statement: "Aeschylus first brought the number of the actors from one to two, and diminished the part of the chorus, and contrived that speech [i.e., spoken, as opposed to sung, verse] should have the leading role."[53] To this may be added the universal ancient tradition, which surfaces already within the fifth century, that Aeschylus first raised tragedy to the level of a great art.[54] Next, and more doubtfully, we may cite the statement, attributed to Aeschylus himself, that his tragedies were slices from Homer's feasts, and the admiration for Homer that is attributed to him in the *Frogs*.[55] Some evidence in favor of our theory may also be drawn from the entire record of titles, fragments, and extant tragedies from the beginnings until the time of Aeschylus's death in 456/55 B.C. So far as that record goes, of the first nine tragedians as they are enumerated in Snell's *TrGF* I (the tenth is Sophocles) only one composed tragedies that centered on any hero of the Trojan War.[56] That solitary exception, Aeschylus, is an exception on a spectacular scale: his titles and fragments reveal three plays (almost certainly a connected trilogy) on Achilles; a possible trilogy on Odysseus and his return to Ithaca; a possible trilogy on Ajax and his suicide; four tragedies (*Memnon*, *Psychostasia*, *Telephos*, *Mysoi*) which have been conjectured to be the surviving remains of two trilogies, on Memnon and Telephos respectively; a tragedy on Palamedes; and a tragedy on Philoctetes.[57] To this list must be added the extant *Oresteia*.

On the facts as we have them, therefore, it seems probable that the first tragedian to realize dramatically the heroes of the Epic Cycle was Aeschylus. Two of his essays in this direction deserve special notice, for in them he seems to have confronted not just any poem in the chain of epics which narrated the Matter of Troy, but the Homeric poems themselves: to have challenged Homer, and the Homeric rhapsodes of the Panathenaic festival, on their own ground. In the Achilles trilogy and, less certainly, in the Odysseus plays the challenge was all the more audacious because of the scale of the Aeschylean works. It should not be forgotten that (at least to judge by the *Oresteia*) the running time of a trilogy could be more than a quarter of that of a full-length Homeric epic.[58] And if the sheer length of these trilogies to some extent rivaled the amplitude of Homer's poems, the ground covered by their narratives seems proportionately to have been even greater. It is certain that the Achilles trilogy treated at least of certain major episodes which Homer had treated of in books 16 to 24 of the *Iliad*, from the sending of Patroklos into battle until the ransoming of Hector's body—a third of the entire epic. The contents and order of Aeschylus's Odysseus plays are far less sure, but a fair case can be made for supposing that they may have extended from the visit to the dead (*Odyssey* 11) to the burial of the Suitors (*Odyssey* 24);[59] in that case more than half of the *Odyssey* was rivaled in this trilogy.

In these instances alone, it seems, an Attic tragedian ventured to set himself up for direct comparison with each of Homer's two great poems, in scale as well as in subject matter.[60] It is hard to imagine a riskier ploy than that, but apparently Aeschylus succeeded in his gamble, at least with the "*Achillēis*," as the number of later ancient references to it shows. A flood of light might be shed on the development of Aeschylus's art, and on that of tragedy itself, if we could only establish the date of these experiments. There is at present no way of doing that;[61] but the possibility is open that it was through them, in the very process of emulating the greatest of all epic poets, that Aeschylus discovered the peculiarly Homeric arts of concentration on one manageable, self-contained heroic episode, and on one or a few heroic figures. The possibility is also open that it was at this point that he devised the thematically connected trilogy/tetralogy, a form that seems to have predominated during the first half of the fifth century.[62] Then might follow the extension of these techniques to the dramatizing of other great heroes in the Trojan Cycle (the dramatic possibilities latent in the final days of Ajax, as told in the *Aethiopis* and *Little Iliad*, might have presented themselves next in order); then, or concurrently, to the dramatizing of heroes from other cycles, such as those of Thebes or Argos. Somewhat in that way, we may imagine, tragedy as we know it *might* have been born.

Many of the details in the above account must obviously be speculative, but the general probability remains: Aeschylus was the first tragedian to realize the importance of the Homeric model, and this realization to a great extent determined the subsequent course of Attic tragedy. We shall be far from supposing, however, that Aeschylus learned all Homer's lessons in a single flash of intuition or that he followed the Homeric precedents slavishly or even consistently. We have already seen how in his "*Achillēis*" he made Achilles and Patroklos passionate lovers, a change that must have profoundly affected the tone of the whole story; and several other innovations may be traced in the same trilogy, fragmentary though it is.[63] But those are, as it were, merely tactical matters. In the strategy of dramaturgy, also, Aeschylus's application of Homer was varied and, to the end, experimental. Else's view of Aeschylean tragedy as a continual process of experiment, right up to the poet's death, is surely justified; the extant dramas alone (all of them datable within the last sixteen years of his forty-three-year career in the theater) are evidence that Aeschylus never found and probably never sought a fixed formula for "Tragedy." And in this matter of the Homeric model there is some reason to agree with Else's epigrammatic statement: "Aeschylus was a devotee and follower of Homer, but in a thoroughly un-Homeric way."[64]

It is worthwhile to consider the implications of that paradox from our present point of view. Just what does Aeschylus seem to have learned from Homer, and to what degree did he apply, or modify, or occasionally slight, those lessons in practice? As Aristotle later saw, Homer's fundamental lesson to tragedy was that it should be *spoudaion*, serious (*Poetics* 1148b34–1149a6; cf. p. 134 above); there were to be no more of those "little plots and laughable diction" (ibid., 1449a19–1420) if tragedy was to realize its true potential. Aeschylus's extant dramas on the whole, of course, perfectly exemplify this principle, but we have seen evidence enough (pp. 130–31 above) to suggest that he by no means always adhered to it.[65]

Homer's second lesson was one that Aeschylus seems, on the extant evidence, to have assimilated fairly thoroughly: that the first step toward the construction of an aesthetically satisfying poem is *selection of a self-contained episode*, of manageable size and involving a manageable number of speaking characters, out of the endless string of heroic legends presented by the cyclic epics (or by the storytellers and singers who preceded them; or by that recent heroic myth, the Persian Wars).[66] As one reviews the individual Aeschylean tragedies, one sees how firmly he adhered to this practice. In each, what I may call the *here and now* of the stage action is centered on a crisis in the legend concerned: the impact of the news of Salamis on the Persian court, the death of the Theban brothers, the Argive acceptance of the Danaids as suppliants, the murder of Agamemnon, and so on.[67] Where Aeschylus differs radically both from Homer and from the subsequent tragedians is in the enormous proportion of the *there and then* that he is capable of incorporating into his poem, largely by lyric means. For example, the *here and now* of the *Agamemnon*'s action is a mere pinpoint compared with the great spheres of time and space opened up in the choruses and in some of the speeches too: the unspeakable scene at the altar in Aulis, the aromatic smoke rising from the faraway ruins of Troy, the nauseated Thyestes at the banquet-table long ago. Yet all these converge on Agamemnon's death-cry. Of this, more later.

The third Homeric lesson was one which not only all three tragedians but also the historian Herodotus seem to have learned thoroughly, to the profit of all subsequent narrative art. The heroic episode selected must be so treated that it will not flow at the same even pace but with mounting speed and excitement, toward a climax which will fall near or at its end. In a word, a good plot must involve *suspense*; the hearer must be so conditioned that he will feel no sense of completeness until the song dies away. (One has only to listen to any of the odes of Bacchylides or Pindar in which a single heroic legend is narrated at any length—the fourth Pythian, say—to realize the difference that this Homeric principle of construction makes, at least to a classical or modern hearer. By this comparison, of course, I imply no criticism of the choral lyric poets: they worked with a different vision of time and of causality in human life, and consequently with different principles of construction, which it is our main business as modern critics to restore and understand.) In general, a relatively actionless and expository beginning (e.g., *Iliad* 1–4.445, Herodotus 1–4.27), in which the issues and conflicts are presented, is succeeded by confrontation, leading on to a climax or crescendo of climaxes (e.g., *Iliad* 16 and 22, Herodotus 6–9).[68] At creating suspense in a plot, Aeschylus is by common consent one of the greatest masters of them all, and there is some slight reason to think that this crucial feature of drama (not merely of tragedy) may indeed have been introduced by him. Certainly Phrynichus, in the one tragedy of his that can be to any extent reconstructed—the *Phoenissae*, quite probably datable to 476 B.C.—seems to have ignored its possibilities entirely: in the *Phoenissae*, as we happen to know, the prologue to the tragedy already contained the announcement of the Persian defeat.[69] One has only to compare for a moment the way Aeschylus leads up to and introduces the same catastrophe in his own play, the *Persians*, to realize what a revolutionary effect this innovation must have had, not merely dramaturgically, but almost as it were theologically. We are plunged at once into a universe filled with dread, with ambiguous, unseen forces: the audience is held in constant suspense, as are the chorus and actors, by the question of whether or when those forces will strike. Yet that same example, the *Persians*, will at once remind us as clearly as any other play of Aeschylus's that his methods of creating suspense are very different from those of Homer before him or of Sophocles after him. In those two, on the whole, both the suspense building and the dénouement are carried by the progress of the human action in the *here and now*, before our eyes. In the *Persians* there is nothing of the sort; the suspense and the catastrophe are due to no action that takes place in the *here and now*; all is done by words, and much lies in the *there and then*. Even in the last two plays of his *Oresteia*, fourteen years later, where the trilogic action closes in increasingly to the *here and now*, and both a recognition and a peripety do occur before our eyes, Aeschylus does not manage these Homeric-Sophoclean techniques in anything approaching the Homeric-Sophoclean way. The recognition scene of the *Choephori* already seemed forced and artificial in the late fifth century (cf. Euripides, *Electra* 508–46), and critics still puzzle over the rationale of the ultimate peripety of the *Eumenides*, the conversion of the Furies.

Similarly, as we have seen (p. 137), it was reserved for Sophocles fully to master the Homeric arts of characterization by speech and (even more) by interchange of speeches, and of advancing the plot in that very interchange. As Duchemin saw, the extant works of Aeschylus contain no example of the fully developed tragic *agōn*, and indeed the Aeschylean world vision would scarcely permit such a phenomenon.[70] His characters speak only in part *to* each other; they seem also to speak *past* each other, into that infinitely complex divine and human universe from which no Aeschylean individual can really be isolated. It has been well observed that "despite the growing diversification of dialogue forms which characterize certain sections of the later plays of Aeschylus, . . . the most frequent means throughout the poet's work by which characters might be brought into close contact with each other remained consistently stichomythia"—that is, a form which for obvious reasons could have no precedent in Homer.[71]

Finally, Aeschylus's extant tragedies, at least, tend not to be concentrated on a single, towering heroic figure in the Homeric-Sophoclean manner. There is, as has often been pointed out, some approach to this technique in the *Seven against Thebes*, but not really a very striking one.[72] Only in the *Prometheus* does the approach become very close indeed.[73] It seems possible, however, that the recovery of some of the lost plays, particularly the presumed trilogies on Achilles, Ajax, and Odysseus, might alter this picture somewhat—one is never well advised to lose sight of the versatility of Aeschylus.

To sum up: the external evidence (especially Aristotle's) and the evidence provided by the titles and fragments of the lost tragedies, as well as the extant works, together amount to a fairly strong case for supposing that Aeschylus was the first tragedian to understand the enormous potential of the Homeric model. We have also, however, observed repeatedly that in applying any given Homeric lesson to practical dramaturgy he will suddenly, as it were, veer away or stop short, leaving the full realization of its possibilities to his successors in the art. To explore the reason for this apparent hesitancy might well take us into a second volume, a volume on Aeschylus. In the present context we can only sketch the outlines of a possible explanation; a few words on this will be said in the concluding section.

VERBAL AND VISUAL POETRY

With Homer we have reached our final, and surely our most significant, example of the all-pervasive presence of pretragic poetry in extant Attic tragedy. We have now seen how, in performance conditions, meter, diction, mythological subject matter, themes, tones, plot construction, and characterization by speech, the craft of tragedy represents no abrupt break with the past, as is so often assumed; rather, it represents a spectacular renewal and integration of all the finest elements in the archaic song culture. This *integration*, this syncretism of the genres, is one of the two greatest original achievements of the early tragedians.[74]

In this final section we shall survey their other great original achievement: the importation of a totally new element, the visual, into Greek poetry. Even in this brief consideration, however, we shall nowhere be quite free of the verbal, and it is worth pausing here, almost at journey's end, to look back on the importance of the *words* in Greek tragedy and in our appreciation of it. The words are certainly more important than most of our translations, or some of our dramatic criticism, might allow the nonspecialist to suppose. In Chapter 4 of this study we have seen how, in the era just before and during the formation of tragedy, the Athenian audiences were conditioned to become *hearers of poetry* in all genres, hearers possessed of an expertise such as can hardly be matched in the later history of the Western world. If we seek any modern analogy, we may find it, as so often, in music rather than in poetry. One may recall the audiences in the concert halls of late eighteenth-century and early nineteenth-century Vienna, trained almost to a person in musical practice and theory and able therefore to respond to the subtlest touch of musical wit or pathos; ready, also, to listen unwearied to those (by twentieth-century standards) formidably long programs of concerti and symphonies. Somewhat comparable to them must have been the Athenian audience whom the tragedians inherited from the pretragic performers of poetry, in whose presence they developed the art of tragedy, and whose expectations of consummate *verbal* poetry they continued to meet so long as "the craft" endured. Even in the latest and most mature Attic tragedies that are oftenest staged today—Euripides' *Hippolytus* or *Bacchae*, for instance—the unprepared modern spectator will be surprised (and often disconcerted, too) by the high proportion of the running time that is occupied by solitary speakers or by choral song. In such passages, as indeed in every passage, one must be prepared to listen to the words, their rhythms as well as their sound and sense, with the same sensitivity and attention that one gives to polyphonic music.

Before the time of extant Aeschylus, we know almost nothing of the ways in which the tragedians may have exploited the new visual dimension in poetry—essentially consisting in the disguise of the singer or reciter as someone else and the disguise of the dance floor as somewhere else[75]—which tradition attributes to Thespis. The solitary glimpse that we are allowed of a visual scene in any of the pre-Aeschylean tragedians is the opening of Phrynichus's *Phoenissae*, where a eunuch appeared draping the chairs for the counsellors of the Persian realm;[76] but since in Phrynichus certainly,[77] and by inference in his predecessors, there was a very high proportion of choral singing, not much room may have been left for a free exercise of the new technique. Once more, as in the matter of meter and language, we must postulate a fairly long phase of rather wild experimentation in the application and integration of the visual element. To that phase the extant plays of Aeschylus himself still seem to belong, as we shall shortly see. One general statement, however, may be made at once about all of them from the *Persians* onward. By some means Aeschylus has already acquired a truly unique mastery in the blending of verbal and visual poetry—a mastery that I cannot parallel in any other poet-dramatist known to me, of any date. The visual element in his work might perhaps best be characterized as a new dimension in poetical rhetoric, harmonizing so perfectly with the verbal poetry that the one leads smoothly and often imperceptibly into or out of the other; the regular order being first *words*, then, often as their culmination, *vision*. A simple example is the apparitions of Darius and Xerxes in the *Persians*, which relate as naturally (both in theme and in imagery) to the verbally developed first half of the play as the main statement of a periodic sentence relates to the preceding subordinate clauses. They clinch the period, complete the utterance.

In principle, a very similar technique appears in the *Oresteia*, although in practice its application is far more complicated in detail.

Before we proceed to that, however, it may be worth posing the question of why Aeschylus's visual-verbal technique differs so greatly from that of both his great successors in the art of tragedy. To those two poets, and surely rightly, is usually given the credit of developing tragedy into something approaching the form of drama which has been familiar to the Western world ever since. Why is Aeschylean tragedy so different? In this place I cannot do more than hint at an answer. If that answer is approximately correct, however, it will account not merely for our present problem but also for the problem raised toward the end of the preceding section: Aeschylus's apparent hesitation in applying the Homeric model to his tragedies. At the root of the whole matter, I suggest, is Aeschylus's total imaginative attunement to a certain archaic mythological and religious vision of the universe and of man's place in it. About this something has already been said (pp. 131–133); here, however, we should make a distinction which it was not necessary to make before, between one kind of archaic vision and another. Homer had set a magnificent and fateful precedent for the clear-cut, the humanized, in his treatment of gods, mortals, and their interaction. Both classes of being are sharply defined as individuals, and the relationships between them are equally clear: they interact in speech and deed much as we mortals interact with each other. Thus in Homer we already have the necessary ingredients for a representational fiction and drama *about individuals*. There was, however, another archaic vision probably much older in origin than Homer and perhaps even older than the coalescence of the Hellenic people. It is represented for us in Greek literature by certain archaic poets of the mainland: Hesiod, Pindar, and, above all, Aeschylus. In this other archaic tradition one might almost say that the divine is everything that is not human and that the relationship between it and the human is correspondingly ill-defined and complex. In such a mysterious and often terrifying universe everything, human or divine, interpenetrates. Sharp boundary lines are hard to draw around a god or around a mortal—particularly around a mortal. This is a universe in which a self-sufficient, isolated individual human being is not quite thinkable. Its contents may be patiently catalogued, as Hesiod did. A shaft of brilliant light may be projected into this part of it or that, as was done in the odes of Pindar. But how do you *dramatize* it? A tragedian with some such vision of the world as this must instantly have recognized the newly discovered visual dimension of poetry as a miraculous instrument for analysis, for clarification, and above all for the creation of a shattering climax to his poem. But he would not instantly, or easily, arrive at techniques of plot construction or of characterization by speech resembling the techniques of Homer or of Sophocles; for both of these poets presuppose a considerable degree of human individuality.

That said, we may return finally to the *Oresteia*, the only dramatic work by Aeschylus, besides the *Persians*, that we possess complete.[78]

The *Agamemnon* is overwhelmingly a *verbal* poem. The *visual* is applied more economically than in any other extant tragedy, and even where it is applied its effect is not yet to supply some climactic and definitive revelation but, instead, to clinch certain sinister and ambiguous themes that have been developed primarily by verbal methods. We need here say little of the supreme visual gestures which will surely be the first to occur to anyone who has studied the *Agamemnon*: the epiphany of the corpses (1372 ff.), toward which leads the episode of the purple tapestry along which the king walks to his murder in the palace (908–74). Characteristically, this latter is both a visual corroboration of all that is wrong in Agamemnon and the first in a chain of visual images that extends to the finale of the trilogy. Second in that chain is the bloody murder robe held high by Orestes' attendants near the end of the *Choephori* (963 ff.). Third are the crimson robes into which the Furies change during the last moments of the *Eumenides*; here the color, in a total reversal of symbolism, no longer signifies murder but an amnesty alike on the human plane and in the universe. Less often noticed, so far as I know, are two other applications of the visual element in the *Agamemnon*, each consummating a verbal theme with marvelous economy and force. As was observed above (p. 141), a very high proportion of the play is occupied with the *there and then*, with a research into time past. That research, necessarily developed in verbal poetry, uncovers in succession two major sequences of past events which converge on the king's death-cry in the dramatic *here and now* (1343–45). The first sequence, which may briefly be described as the "Troy Guilt," occupies the first half of the play through the end of the second stasimon (781), at which very moment *enter Agamemnon in great pomp, with Cassandra*; the king at once expounds, vividly and at length, his cruel vision of the sack of Troy. To this apparition responds the apparition of Aegisthus near the end of the play (1577), expounding in a long speech the story of Thyestes' exile, his banquet, and his fateful curse: in a word, the second major sequence of past events, which may be named for short the "Palace Guilt." The human link between those two sequences is Cassandra, who entered with Agamemnon at 782 and who, gazing at the palace with her gift of second sight, senses the horrors it has known.[79] From that point onward the play is increasingly preoccupied with the Palace Guilt, the cannibalistic banquet, and the vendetta carried on by the surviving child, Aegisthus, which has culminated in his adulterous union with Clytaemnestra and the murder of the king. We thus become conscious of quite another side to Clytaemnestra's murder plot: the Troy Guilt has made her seem, if not innocent, at least a terribly injured party; but the Palace Guilt reveals her adultery and treason.[80] The entrance of Aegisthus, visually and verbally responding to the earlier entrance of Agamemnon, sums up the moral dilemma of the play as a whole—the dilemma which, as the trilogy proceeds, will involve not merely the human participants in the story but the universe. Each side is right; each side is wrong. But this situation, so far, has mostly been expressed in verbal poetry, the visual poetry serving as an infrequent but powerful auxiliary.

"Utter disruption makes everything utterly clear, everyone knows who stands where," a comment by James Scully on the final earthquake scene of the *Prometheus*,[81] may well be applied to the progress of the *Oresteia* trilogy as a whole. From the moral and political disruption at the end of the *Agamemnon*, a play primarily of words, we shall proceed to a clear polarization of the human participants, very largely expressed by visual means, in the *Choephori*; and finally, in the *Eumenides*, to a polarization of the divine forces followed by a reconciliation between all classes of being in the last third of the play. By the very end, everyone indeed knows who stands where and there is utter clarity. As the trilogy advances, this development is brought about increasingly by visual as opposed to verbal means.

In the *Choephori* one notices at once how much more of the significant action is being concentrated in the *here and now*, onstage: the arrival of the travelers from Phokis; the offering at the tomb; the recognition scene; the intrigues and deceits at the palace door (a crucial moment in the plot, the interception and cancellation of Clytaemnestra's message to Aegisthus to come with his bodyguard, is enacted before our eyes); the final confrontation of Orestes with Clytaemnestra, which comes as near to onstage murder as any Greek dramatist ever ventured;[82] the revelation of the corpses and the robe (answering the revelation in *Agamemnon* 1372 ff.); and Orestes reeling before the unseen madness that strikes him before our eyes. At least on a superficial view, Aeschylus's application of the visual element in the *Choephori* anticipates the usage of Sophocles and Euripides.[83] And yet, while he is here almost inventing Attic drama in the sense that Aristotle and most other people have since understood it, Aeschylus is simultaneously preparing to pass through such apparently human-centered drama and out to the other side. This preparation is carried out entirely by verbal poetry. Still invisibly, the ancient divine universe is closing in on the human characters, pressing closer and closer against the frail dividing wall that separates god and mortal in Aeschylus. It is from Orestes' speech in 264–305 that we learn of the unseen presence of Apollo standing firmly behind the male killer; the great sung and chanted *kommos*, together with its spoken sequel (306–509), conjures the father, Agamemnon, out of the world of the dead and into the living action; finally, certain appalling female powers insinuate their way into the language of the *Choephori* to support the claim of Orestes' female victim.[84]

The full clarification of all these human and divine forces, and the final resolution of the issues, awaits of course the last play of the trilogy, the *Eumenides*. Here the visual element in Aeschylus's poetry triumphs as nowhere else in his extant work. It triumphs, indeed, to the extent that even his imagery, so richly developed, primarily in words, from the Watchman's speech in the *Agamemnon* onward, is now as it were drained out of the verbal poetry into the visible figures before us.[85] Throughout the *Eumenides*, but specially from the moment (235) when the scene of action is transferred to Athens from Delphi, we find ourselves watching one of the most action-filled dramas that have survived from classical antiquity, not excluding Old Comedy. In the Athenian two-thirds of the play, indeed, *all* the major decisions, *all* the significant steps in the progress of the plot, take place right before our eyes; it is hard to imagine a more complete contrast to the dramaturgy of the *Persians* (fourteen years before) or, come to that, of the *Agamemnon* (perhaps two hours before). From the trial scene onward (*Eumenides* 566 ff.) we are entirely and, it seems, uninterruptedly on the plane of the onstage *here and now*, and the *then and there* has fallen entirely away. The spectator's time, in other words, coincides exactly with the drama's time, a phenomenon rare in any theater of any date.[86] In the second half of the *Eumenides*, it seems fair to say, European drama achieves for the first time something approaching total illusionism.

But the *content* of the illusion here! That is another matter entirely. In this aspect Aeschylus's *Eumenides* does not look forward into the future, to the dramatic masterpieces of Sophocles and Euripides. Rather, it is the last and perhaps the most magnificent representative of a poetry, a mythological way of thinking, a song culture, that seem almost as old as time. The difference—and what a fateful difference, we feel as we look down the centuries that are to come—is that the ancient mythological figures have acquired legs and have moved onto the dancing floor. Poetry has merged, without any violent transition, into drama.

7. Epilogue: The Enactment of a Greek Lyric Poem

So far as my knowledge goes, there is only one classical Greek poem whose performance can be reconstructed with any degree of assurance, and that is the *Persians* by Timotheus of Miletus. Although this poem was composed some decades after our lower chronological limit, an attempt to hear it and visualize it as it was performed may be justified as a coda to the present study. It will bring together in one quite vivid instance a number of the points that were made in earlier chapters: the importance of the performing aspect of classical Greek poetry, the rather peculiar relationship of text to performance, the practice of re-performance, and the interplay (even at this relatively late stage) between tragedy and contemporary nondramatic poetry. As my final paragraphs will suggest, it may also serve as a fitting valediction to the entire tradition of classical Greek poetry, nondramatic and dramatic alike. Even here, my method must be in part conjectural, but only to the extent that some documented facts concerning late classical kitharodic performances, and Timotheus's general character as poet and musician, will here be applied to the specific text of the *Persians*. I hope, however, to present the evidence in such a way that the reader may nowhere be in doubt as to what is certain and what is due to conjecture of this limited kind.[1]

I envisage primarily the *first* performance of the *Persians*, but it is worth mentioning that there is a relatively full record of later performances of Timotheus's poems, extending over several centuries. For instance, there was a famous revival of this very poem at the Nemean Games of 207 B.C., in the presence of Philopoemen.[2] But the *Persians* seems first to have been presented to the public in a year not much earlier than 408 B.C.[3] The place was Athens, and the occasion was a competition in kitharody.[4] By far the most important of such competitions were those that formed part of the Panathenaia, and it is therefore very likely that this is the festival concerned here. If so, the season will be high summer[5] and the physical setting will probably be the Periclean Odeion just to the east of the Theater of Dionysos.[6] Present is an audience which we may imagine to have been large, and which we infer to have been irascible on this occasion.[7]

Timotheus is clothed and equipped in the traditional fashion of a kitharode (see pp. 16–17 above); as the event opens, he and his rival kitharodes—probably four in number at this date—are stationed somewhere on the floor of the spacious, high-roofed building.[8] When his turn comes, our poet will move forward and take his stand on a low platform (p. 17), probably not amid loud applause, but in a tense and hostile silence. "The red-head from Miletus" (his red hair, his pugnacity, and his pronounced egoism are the only strictly personal biographical data that have come down to us)[9] is a very controversial figure at this time. His musical revolutionism (*kainotomia*) has already gotten him into trouble with the Spartans at the most ancient and prestigious kitharodic festival of them all, the Karneia.[10] Here at Athens, too, it is a fair inference from the sources that his music up to now has been received rather unfavorably; Plutarch tells us that he has actually been hissed at some earlier performance.[11] We know of only one Athenian who positively supports Timotheus on this occasion, but that man is no less a connoisseur of music and poetry than the elderly but ever receptive Euripides. Euripides, we are told, has "recognized how great he [Timotheus] is in this branch of art,"[12] and there may even already be a rumor abroad that he has collaborated with Timotheus in composing the proem to this very production.[13]

The gorgeous figure on the platform raises its lyre high, and poises its plectrum. Its attitude from that moment onward until the end of the performance is that of Apollo, familiar in many paintings and sculptures of *Apollo Citharoedus*. Who knows? Perhaps the kitharodes, at least the earlier ones, were felt in some sense to be impersonating the god. But certainly the kind of poem about to be performed, the kitharodic nome, belongs in origin specially to Apollo, and at the end of the *Persians* (as we shall see) he will be summoned to bless both the song and the city, in turn.

At this hushed moment, before the notes of the lyre prelude break onto the air, we may pause to consider what is known or can reasonably be inferred about Timotheus's characteristics as an *artiste*. We have a good deal of literary information about his music but, as usual in this matter, it is of a kind that is almost impossible to translate into terms of modern musical experience. There is no question, however, that his music was revolutionary; that is attested on all sides.[14] Timotheus offended against the Greek musical tradition in his systematic employment of a lyre with eleven strings instead of seven;[15] in his abandonment of the modes traditional to each poetic genre, and even more in his modulation from mode to mode within the same poem;[16] and not least in his florid ornamentation of the music. The most graphic account we have of all this is by an older contemporary of Timotheus, the comic poet Pherecrates (*Cheiron*, fr. 157K). Music herself, personified, is the speaker: Timotheus, she says, has abused me by "turning from the common course and dragging me along crawling ant tracks, in shrill disharmonies with sinfully high-pitched and piercing notes and whistles (*niglarous*), cramming me with modulations (*kampai*) just as a cabbage-head is crammed with caterpillars."[17] Finally, in listening with the mind's ear to the *Persians* or to any other Greek lyric poem, we shall be justified in restoring an element that is perfectly within the range of our modern musical experience: that is, a clear, loud, superbly expressive singing voice. Plutarch, describing the re-performance of the *Persians* in 207 B.C., particularly mentions the effect produced there by the combined "brilliance of the singer's voice" and the "majesty of the poetry."[18]

Another important and well-attested aspect of Timotheus's performances was their highly mimetic character: their dramatic realism in music, voice, and gesture. We hear of his realistic storm at sea in the dithyramb *Nauplios*; the piercing screams of Semele in the dithyramb *Pangs of Semele*, and the ungainly walk of the accompanying oboist (apparently in imitation of the pregnant heroine) in the same poem; finally, in a famous passage of Aristotle's *Poetics*, the inferior oboist who mauled the chorus leader in the dithyramb *Scylla* (apparently in imitation of that monster's customary behavior toward mariners).[19] Naturally, there would be far less room for such extravagant miming in a kitharodic nome like the *Persians*, for here we have only a solo performer whose hands will be fully occupied with the management of his lyre and plectrum. But the generally mimetic character of the kitharodic nome, too, is attested in the Aristotelian *Problems*,[20] and we are probably justified in assuming at least a certain element of body language in the performance of the *Persians*. Still more clearly are we justified in assuming a great deal of highly realistic *vocal* mimesis. The poem in fact contains one passage, which we shall discuss in its place, where the evidence for such mimesis seems to be built into the letters of our surviving text.

And now we may return to the Odeion, and to Timotheus on his platform. Those members of the audience who have attended primarily in the hope of an instant artistic scandal (for such people are always with us) must be sorely disappointed by the poem's opening line:[21]

> Building for Greece the great and splendid beauty of freedom,
> *κλεινὸν ἐλευθερίας τεύχων μέγαν Ἑλλάδι κόσμον,*

For the style is as simple, the sentiment as wholesome, as those of an old-fashioned patriotic song, say by Lamprocles;[22] and the meter, the dactylic hexameter, is as old as time, as well as being the traditional meter of the archaic kitharodic nome.[23]

After that imposing start, the song eludes our modern hearing for a space of several minutes. Only a couple of one-line fragments break out of the silence, both of them evidently from speeches delivered to the Greek forces as they brace themselves for battle with the Persian fleet in Salamis Bay.[24] In these snatches of song, too, there is nothing to offend even the most die-hard traditionalist, either in the sentiment (an exhortation to valor), in the grave and simple diction, or in the iambo-trochaic meter. The shocks begin, for us, only where the more or less unbroken libretto of the performance becomes available, thanks to the Abusir papyrus, probably more than halfway through its original course.[25]

Such is the tattered state of the first and second columns of the papyrus that to begin with we can only hear the poem imperfectly; it is as frustrating as listening to a concert on the radio during a heavy electrical storm. Even so, one can already catch the theme and the manner. The singer is in the midst of a tempestuous rendering of the naval battle: triremes are colliding or shearing off each other's oars, while javelins, arrows, and what seems to be some otherwise unheard-of kind of incendiary missile[26] streak this way and that across the lurid scene. The meter is still iambo-trochaic, not essentially different from the iambo-trochaic to which our ears have been accustomed in the tragic theater since at least the time of Aeschylus, but with one crucial exception. This singing and this music *are not structured by strophe and antistrophe.* They run quite free, bunching and uncoiling according to the mood and course of the narrative at any given place. Just as striking is the diction. It is now quite altered from the archaic severity of the fragments belonging to the earlier part of the poem. If one can imagine a *verbal* equivalent to the trills, flourishes, and whistles that so offended some contemporaries in Timotheus's *music*, this might well be it. Translating such language is, I have found, a losing game, but here is an attempt to render a reasonably well-preserved passage from near the end of the sea-battle scene:

> The emerald-haired sea reddened in its furrows
> with rain of ship-blood. Babble of shouted orders
> filled it, and howls of pain.
> Again the Persian fleet,
> massed in disarray,
> swept into battle against them among the shining seafolds,
> the folds fishgarlanded.[27]

That is a fair specimen of the so-called dithyrambic style that colors the narrative part of the *Persians* (and the term is probably justified, from what we know of the new-musical dithyramb). Almost routinely, critics have scoffed at it, and indeed, viewed in the context of the other classical lyric poetry that has survived to us, its lack of restraint, its psychedelic coloring, must seem shocking enough. And yet, I have asked myself, do critics routinely scoff at such a passage as the following, by a different poet who was also trying to render a seascape?

> For the infinite air is unkind,
> And the sea flint-flake, black-backed in the regular blow,
> Sitting East-northeast, in cursed quarter, the wind;
> Wiry and white-fiery and whirlwind-swivellèd snow
> Spins to the widow-making unchilding unfathering deeps

That is of course from Gerard Manley Hopkins's *The Wreck of the Deutschland.* I do not pretend to place Timotheus at anywhere near those heights, but I do suspect that the two poets share a mode of poetic expression, and not necessarily an invalid or contemptible mode, which may occur at a certain phase of almost any culture, but which does not happen to surface very often in extant classical Greek. Perhaps critics might give Timotheus a second look from this comparative point of view.

Be that as it may, it will become increasingly clear as the kitharode's song proceeds that this dithyrambic style is very far from being the only style of the *Persians*. The poem in fact modulates from style to style within its course, just as it modulates freely from meter to meter, and just as (the ancient sources report) Timotheus's music varied from traditional mode to traditional mode. Even by this point of the performance we have moved from the heroic hexameter, through austerely composed iambo-trochaic, into freer iambo-trochaic in dithyrambic style.

From the sea-battle passage onward the song begins, as it were, to curve downward. The performer passes from the evenly balanced melee into the rout of the Persian armada. The growing atmosphere of defeat and desperation is created above all dramatically, in a sequence of four sharply characterized speeches, linked by quite brief narrative passages.[28] In turn the kitharode renders the speech of the drowning Persian magnate[29] (and here I frankly dread to imagine the mimetic bubblings, gaspings, and strangled shrieks that are all too clearly demanded by the libretto);[30] the wild lament of the naked castaways on the shore, and their passionate prayer to the Mountain Mother (exactly at the mention of her name, aeolic measures briefly appear in the song for the first time and are followed by the first appearance of lyric dactyls); finally, two amazingly contrasted speeches, the frantic supplication of the simple Phrygian captive, and the solemn lament by the Great King himself. Nowhere else in Greek poetry that I can think of, not even in tragedy, do we hear quite this Tolstoyan kind of realism. The common soldier, trapped in the inexorable machinery of war and babbling in pidgin Greek (as if this were a comedy, not a lyric), is juxtaposed with the generalissimo reflecting on his handiwork and issuing the only orders that he now can, back at Headquarters. It is perhaps worthwhile to reenact some parts of this passage in translation, however inadequately. First, the Phrygian, grabbed by his hair and menaced with a Greek swordpoint, desperately fumbling for just a few words in Greek, on which his life may hang (the kitharode's vocal mimesis may have reached its height here):

Me speak you how what use?
Never here me come again
this time lord of mine

brung me hither here
not for the rest no longer
honored sir
no longer me come here again to fight
but me sit still . . .
Me for
you
not
here!
Me
there
down to Sardi
down to Sousa
Agbatana be my home . . .
ARTIMIS
my big god
shall hold me safe
to Ephesos.

Against that we have to set the final dramatic speech of this performance, uttered by the Great King as he recognizes that his fleet has turned in irrevocable rout. As Korzeniewski has observed in the most illuminating study yet published on the metrical aspect of our poem, Xerxes' speech is quasi-antistrophic:[31] it divides into two halves which respond to one another in their number of verses, although not in their rhythms. The formality of the shape is (as we should by now expect of this singer) accompanied by stylistic formality. There is an almost archaic simplicity and majesty here.[32] Only at this point, perhaps, does the hearer realize that the dithyrambic diction of the main narrative has been insensibly fading out during the previous four or five minutes. There is absolutely nothing of it left in the King's speech:

Woe
for the wrecking of our House,
woe
for you searing ships of Greece,
ships who killed a generation,
young generation rich in manhood!
They'll not come home in Persian ships,
but angry smoking fire,
cruellest of elements, shall burn them:

Sorrow, sorrow and wailing
shall be for the Persian land!

Woe
for the deadweight of Fortune,
who brought me to the land of Greece!
Go, my servants, wait no longer:
Yoke the four horses
Under my chariot. And you,
Carry riches, untold riches
into our wagons!
Burn our pavilions!
Let no Greek enjoy our wealth!

There follows a very short conclusion to the narrative of the battle, in which the kitharode renders the triumph of the Greeks, and the dance they stamped out as they sang the paean of victory. There is much mimesis here, I imagine, recalling the "marching movements" which an ancient source attributes even to the earlier kitharodic performances (pp. 16 and 17 above).

The coda of the song is delivered in the persona of the poet himself, Timotheus; the dramatic illusion is abruptly dropped. Equally abruptly comes the last and greatest metrical (and musical?) transformation. Wilamowitz, the first Greek scholar privileged to hear this coda in modern times, was actually reminded of the singing style of Sophocles or of Anacreon before him.[33] It is cast mainly in that most singable and fast-moving of lyric meters, glyconic-pherecratean, in strict form with very little resolution; further, as Korzeniewski has observed, it is articulated by a rather complex system of quasi-responsions.[34] It too, therefore, has a traditional and even archaic air. Its opening and closing stanzas are, very properly, invocations of Apollo; but the bulk of it is occupied by Timotheus's defense against a Spartan charge of dishonoring the ancient musical craft. Not so, responds the singer: I stand in the direct line of great kitharodes that has descended to us from Orpheus through Terpander; and in my turn, like them, I have expanded the range of the craft.

The final quatrain of the song seems designed to be sung anywhere, any time, not merely at the premiere in Athens (once more we are reminded of the practice of *re*-performance; from now on the *Persians* will presumably become a standard item in our migrant poet's baggage), and it may fittingly be repeated here and now:

> But, far-shooting Pythian, come
> to this sacred city with happiness;
> send to this unscarred people peace,
> peace that flowers with harmony.[35]

With this performance of the *Persians* Timotheus won first prize in the contest.[36] He had succeeded in turning around an unfriendly audience in what was still the most musically sophisticated Greek city. He even succeeded in turning around Athenian musical taste for a few years, if we are right in taking certain of the songs in Euripides' later plays—most notably the extensive solo aria of the Phrygian in the *Orestes* of 408 B.C.—as evidence that the Timothean manner temporarily became acceptable in the tragic performances also.[37]

Who was right about the artistic quality of the *Persians*: Euripides and the late fifth-century Athenian audience, or Timotheus's modern academic critics? No doubt one would be misguided to attempt a decisive answer to such a question, in the absence not merely of (probably) about half the libretto, but also of so much else that must have played a part in the Athenian judgment: the music, the body language, the expert vocal and instrumental technique. Yet I may mention at this point two considerations that have caused me, for one, to feel a more sympathetic interest in Timotheus's work than I felt before I began to study him closely. The first consideration is merely historical: his is very nearly the last voice in a majestic tradition of *public poetry*, of poetry that directly and openly addressed the whole community, a tradition that had lasted unbroken from Homer and indeed from before Homer. That Timotheus was consciously striving to reassert that tradition's claims and to keep it alive is proved, I think, not only by the explicit statement in the coda but also by his poem as a whole. By the time we reach its end we have traversed almost the entire spectrum of archaic and classical Greek verse styles, from the Homeric epic, through personal lyric, through tragedy and even comedy, to the dithyramb of the New Music. If we were to seek historical parallels to such a bold, or desperate, attempt to prolong a noble tradition in a growingly anti-poetic environment, we might find them in two poets who were certainly greater than

Timotheus, but worked in a similar way and were criticized at first on similar grounds: Eliot and Pound.

The second consideration was already hinted at in the beginning of this chapter. In the *Persians* we are to some extent able to restore the silent printed letters to a performing context; and the outcome of the experiment has been, for me, not necessarily a finer work of art than that which appears in our literary handbooks, but certainly a different and more interesting one. I believe that the insights so gained might be transferable in some degree to other extant Greek lyrics. And, perhaps, to Greek tragedy and its history.

Appendix I

Performances (Especially *Agōnes Mousikoi*) at Religious Festivals

A: Bibliographical Note

As was observed on pp. 7–9 of Chapter 1, there seems to be no recent survey of this subject as a whole. The discussions by Reisch (1885) and Meier (1894), esp. cols. 853–57, were adequate for their time, but much evidence, especially epigraphical, has accumulated since. Subsequently there have been relatively brief treatments by Schmidt-Stählin (1929), pp. 23–24 and 332–35, and by Reinmuth in *Kleine Pauly*, art. *agones*, esp. col. 137. The purpose of this appendix is simply to bring together the main ancient accounts of musical performances at Greek festivals before ca. 400 B.C. (Section B, below) and to catalogue the sites at which such performances are known to have occurred before ca. 400 B.C. (Section C).

B: General Accounts of Musical Festivals

Arranged approximately in the chronological order of the sources.

1. Homeric Hymn 3, To Apollo, lines 146–78: the festival of Apollo on Delos. Lines 146–55 are quoted above, Chapter 1, p. 6; the passage continues with an account of the singing maidens of Delos, who can miraculously mimic the voices of all comers (156–64), and concludes with the blind singer's farewell to them (165–78, quoted in part by Thucydides, below, no. **2**).
2. Thucydides 3.104: in 426 B.C. the Athenians "purified" Delos by removing all the corpses buried on it; and after that (probably in 417; see below, Appendix IV, no. **16**) they established a quadriennial festival there. "In ancient times, also, there had been a great assembly on Delos of the Ionians and the neighboring islanders; they would attend the festival with their wives and children, just as the Ionians now attend the festival of Ephesia. Athletic and musical *agōnes* were

held on the occasion, and the various cities produced choral dances. Homer, above all, gives evidence that this was so, in the following verses, which are from his proem to Apollo." Thucydides then quotes lines 146–50 (see above, no. **1**), and proceeds: "And in the following words, which are from the same proem, Homer further gives evidence that there was an *agōn* in music and that people came there to compete. After singing of the Delian women's chorus, he ended his praise with these verses, in which he actually mentioned himself. 'But now may Apollo be propitious, and Artemis with him, and farewell to all you maidens. Make remembrance of me, whenever some other toiling stranger from among earthly men comes here and asks you, Maidens, who in your eyes is the sweetest of the singers who visit here, and in whom do you most delight? You must answer, all of you, in words of good omen: It is a blind man who lives in rocky Chios' (lines 165–72). That is the extent of Homer's testimony that in ancient times, also, there was a great gathering and festival in Delos. After that the islanders and the Athenians continued to send choruses and sacrifices; but the majority of the events, including the *agōnes*, were abolished, probably as a result of the island's misfortunes, until the time of which I am speaking, when the Athenians established the *agōn*. To it they added horse-races, which had not been held before."

3. Sosibius, *On the Sacrifices in Lakedaimon*, in Jacoby, *FGrH*, no. 595, fr. 5; quoted above, Chapter 1, p. 25, with note 56.
4. Polykrates in Jacoby, *FGrH*, no. 588 (his only surviving fragment); quoted above, p. 7, with note 8.
5. Ps.-Plutarch, *De Musica* 1134b–c: "The first organization of musical activities happened in Sparta, its author being Terpander. The main responsibility for initiating the second organization is assigned to Thaletas of Gortyn, Xenodamos of Kythera, Xenokritos of Lokroi, Polymnestos of Colophon, and Sakadas of Argos. It was on their proposal, people say, that the musical events at the Gymnopaidiai in Lakedaimon were organized, and those at the Apodeixeis in Arcadia, and, of the Argive festivals, that called Endymatia. Thaletas, Xenodamos, and Xenokritos and their followers were composers of paeans; Polymnestos and his school, of the compositions called orthian; Sakadas and his school, of elegiacs. Other authorities, however, say that Xenodamos composed hyporchemes, not paeans."

C: Alphabetical List of Places where Musical Festivals are Known to Have Existed before ca. 400 B.C.

6. *Arcadia*:
   Apodeixeis festival, known only from ps.-Plut. (above, no. **5**). Presumably seventh-century, at latest, in view of the poets named in connection with it.
7. *Argos*:
   Endymatia festival, known only from ps.-Plut. (above, no. **5**). Presumably seventh century, at latest (above, no. **6**).
8. *Athens*:
   Great Panathenaia: see the discussion in Chapter 4, pp. 84–87, and also Appendix II, nos. **4** (*Ion* 530b), **16**, **17**, **26**.
   The musical contests date probably from the mid sixth century, perhaps from ca. 566 B.C.
   Great Dionysia: see the discussion in Chapter 4, pp. 87–91 and 93–94. Tragic contests, ca. 534 B.C.; dithyrambic contests, no later than 509/8; comic contests, 486. Dithyrambic contests during the fifth century at the Thargelia and Lesser Panathenaia: Pickard-Cambridge, *DTC*², p. 37. For the conjecture that there may also have been dithyrambic contests at the Anthesteria, see note 70 to Chapter 4.
9. *Delos*:
   See above, nos. **1** and **2**, and below, Appendix IV, no. **16**. A very early musical festival, perhaps of the eighth century, is to be deduced (and was in fact deduced by Thucydides) from no. **1**. Supporting evidence may be found in the fragment of Eumelus's (eighth- to seventh-century) *Prosodion es Dēlon*, 696 *PMG*, with Paus. 4.4 init., cited by Page there. Hesiod *frag. dub.* 357 M-W (see App. II, no. **28**), although almost certainly not as early as Hesiod, may be evidence of a tradition current in classical times that there had been rhapsode-contests at Delos in the epic period. For the reinstitution of the contests in the late fifth century (418/17?), see above, no. **2**.
10. *Delphi*:
    Pythian festival: the main source for the history of the musical contests is Pausanias 10.7.2–8 (with Frazer's elaborate commentary ad loc.). This divides into two periods: an early period of kitharodic

contests, which has a legendary aura—involving as it does such names as Thamyris, Orpheus, Musaeus, Hesiod, and Homer—and a period for which Pausanias's ultimate evidence must have been the official victor-lists. The latter begins in the year 582 B.C., in which contests in aulody and unaccompanied oboe-playing were added to the preexisting contests in kitharody; Pausanias is able to identify the victors in all three events, and there is no reason to believe that the names he gives are fictitious. If we can trust the statement, in ps.-Plut. *Mus.* 1132e, that the mid-seventh-century kitharodist Terpander won four times in the Pythian contests, then records may have been kept for the earlier period, too; certainly it is reasonable to conjecture that it extended back at least into the early seventh century.

11. *Epidauros*:
Asklepieia: contests in rhapsodizing and "other musical events" are attested in Plato, *Ion* 530a, the dramatic date of which dialogue is probably to be placed in the last quarter of the fifth century. There is no information about the date at which they were instituted, but the festival itself was certainly much older than the *Ion*; it was already in existence by the time of Pindar, *Nem.* 3.84 (see schol. ad loc., and Nilsson [1906], p. 409).

12. *Ithome*:
Ithomaia, for Zeus: the existence of an *agōn mousikēs* in this festival at an early date is inferred by Pausanias (4.33.2) from fr. 696 *PMG* of Eumelus. As mentioned above (see no. **9**), Eumelus is datable in the eighth to seventh century.

13. *Olympia*:
The Olympic Games—founded, according to tradition, in 776 B.C. —included no official musical contests during our period. Unofficial performances of poetry at the *panegyris*, however, are recorded; cf. App. II, nos. **24**, **25**, **27**. Compare also the accounts of the literary displays at Olympia given by Hippias (Plato, *Hipp. Minor* 346a, etc.) and by a number of other sophists and prose composers (Lucian, *Herodotus seu Aetion*, 1–3).

14. *Paros*(?):
A poetic contest, possibly in honor of Demeter, in which Archilochus was the victor, is implied by schol. Aristophanes, *Birds* 1764. The entry is slightly corrupt, but the general drift seems certain; if its in-

formation can be trusted at all, this Parian festival must have been in existence by the mid seventh century B.C.

15. *Samos*(?):
Plutarch, *Lysander* 18.4, records that after the Spartan admiral's triumph over Athens in 404 the Samians changed the name of their festival Heraia to Lysandria. He then tells an anecdote about a competition between Antimachus of Colophon, the epic and elegiac poet, and one Niceratus of Heraclea, at the Lysandria in Lysander's presence. Thus a rhapsodic, or rhapsodic-like, contest at the Samian festival between 404 and Lysander's death (395 B.C.) seems certain. Whether this event had been carried over from the Heraia, there is no evidence to say.

16. *Sikyon*:
Rhapsodic contests at Sikyon, in being *before* the time of its tyrant Kleisthenes (early sixth century) are recorded by Herodotus 5.67.1; see App. II, no. 3. The name of the festival is not given. Performances (but not specifically contests) of "tragic choruses," first for Adrastos, then for Dionysos, are mentioned ibid., 5.67.5 (cf. *DTC*², pp. 101–7).

17. *Sparta*:
Karneia, for Apollo: the festival was established in Ol. 26, 676–73 B.C. (Sosibius *ap.* Athenaeus 14.635e–f). Either from the beginning or from very early in its existence, it included contests in kitharody, Terpander being the first recorded victor (Hellanicus *ap.* Athenaeus 14.635e). See Prehn, art. *Karneia* in *RE* 10 (1919), cols. 1986–88.
Hyakinthia: for Hyakinthos and Apollo: see above, no. **4** for the lyre-playing and choruses; Stengel, art. *Hyakinthia* in *RE* 9 (1916), cols. 1–2; Pötscher, art. *s.v.* in *Kleine Pauly.* The date of this festival's foundation is not recorded, but there is every reason to suppose that it was very ancient.
Gymnopaidiai: see above, no. 3, for the choruses of boys, men, and old men. Choruses at this festival are also mentioned by Xenophon, *Hellenica* 6.4.16 and Plutarch, *Agesilaus* 29, in wording that might imply that the festival included contests between choruses, but this is not certain (cf. Reisch [1885], p. 4, n. 2). The information given in ps.-Plutarch (above, no. 5) suggests that it was organized, at the latest, in the seventh century B.C. In general, see Hiller von Gaertringen, art. *Gymnopaidien* in *RE* 7 (1912), cols. 2087–89.

Alcman's *Partheneion*, fr. 1 *PMG*, seems to have been sung at a festival for the goddess Ortheia (Campbell [1967], on line 61), and his fr. 3 may have been sung at a festival for Hera (idem, p. 213); whether a contest was involved in either case is debated.

Appendix II

The Rhapsodes

A: Bibliographical Note

No detailed and comprehensive treatment of the Greek rhapsodes, from the beginnings through the Hellenistic period, seems yet to have been undertaken. For the pre-Hellenistic era (with which this appendix is primarily concerned), there are relatively lengthy discussions in Schadewaldt (1959), ch. 3, esp. pp. 55–61, and Pfeiffer (1968), pp. 8–12; and useful but inevitably brief articles by von Greisau in *Der kleine Pauly* and West in *OCD*[2] *s.v.* "Rhapsodes." On the (to me) still unsolved question of the history and meaning of the name *rhapsode*, see Fränkel (1925), pp. 3–6, Patzer (1952), and Tarditi (1968); on the vase representations (cf. Plate I), Webster (1972), pp. 61 and 171; on rhapsodic delivery, Nutzhorn (1869), pp. 74–99, Bölte (1907), and West (1981).

B: Pre-Hellenistic Testimonia

Arranged approximately in the chronological order of the sources.

1. Pindar, *Nem.* 2.1–2: "The sons of Homer, singers of stitched poems (*rhaptōn epeōn aoidoi*)." [For the ancient scholia on this passage, see below, no. **28**. Like most commentaries since, they assume that Pindar is alluding to rhapsodes.]
2. Pindar, *Isthm.* 4.38–39: Homer declared the valor of Ajax "by the rod (*kata rhabdon*), for posterity to delight in." [The ancient scholium comments: "that is, by *rhapsōidia*."]
3. Herodotus 5.67.1: Kleisthenes, the early sixth-century tyrant of Sikyon, "going to war with Argos, put an end to the rhapsode-contests in Sikyon because of the Homeric epics; for in them the Argives and Argos are celebrated almost everywhere."

4. Plato, *Ion*, passim: see Chapter 1, pp. 10–13.
5. Plato, *Republic* 2.373b: the specialist craftsmen who will be added in the second stage of the imagined city include "the representers (*mimētai*), many of them working in shapes and colors, and many in the musical arts: poets and their assistants, the rhapsodes, the actors, the choristers."
6. Plato, *Republic* 3.395a–b: just as it is difficult for the same men to succeed in both the apparently closely allied arts of tragedy and comedy, so it is difficult to be "at once rhapsodes and actors," or for the same actors to act both comedy and tragedy.
7. Plato, *Republic* 10.600d: "If Homer had been able to help his contemporaries toward *aretē*, do you think they would have allowed him or Hesiod to wander around as rhapsodes, and not rather have held on to them more tightly than to their gold?"
8. Plato, *Timaeus* 21b–c: Critias is recounting an episode that occurred when he was about ten years old (i.e., in the mid fifth century B.C.): "It was the day called Koureotis in the Apatouria. The custom of the festival was carried out for the boys on that occasion too: our fathers put up prizes for recitation (*rhapsōidia*). Many poems by many poets were spoken (*elechthē*); but many of us boys chanted (*ēisamen*) the poems of Solon."
9. Plato, *Laws* 2.658b–d: if someone were to announce an *agōn* in which prizes would be awarded simply for giving pleasure to the audience, "it is fairly likely that one contestant would produce an epic recitation (*rhapsōidian*), as Homer did, another a tragedy, and yet another a comedy; and it would be no surprise if another thought his best chance of winning would be to produce a puppet show." Little children would prefer the puppet show, older children the comedy, and the great majority, including youths and educated women, the tragedy; "but I dare say we old men would claim that a rhapsode who gave a fine recital of the *Iliad* or the *Odyssey* or one of the Hesiodic poems was easily the winner."
10. Plato, *Laws* 6.764d: the officers presiding over the *agōnes* of the ideal city will be "the same group for the athletic contests, both of men and of horses; but for the musical competition there should be one group in charge of solo and mimetic performances—such as those of the rhapsodes and kitharodes and oboists and all such people—and another group in charge of choral singing." [For the rhapsodic contests in the ideal city, see also *Laws* 8.834e.]

11. Xenophon, *Symposium* 3.5–6: Nikeratos has remarked that his father made him learn all Homer's works, and that even now he can recite the whole *Iliad* and *Odyssey* from memory.

"Antisthenes replied: 'But haven't you realized that the rhapsodes, as well, know these poems?'

'Of course I have! I listen to them practically every day!'

'Well, do you know any tribe sillier than that of the rhapsodes?'

'Really,' said Nikeratos, 'I don't believe I do.'

'Anyone can see,' said Socrates, 'that they don't understand the deeper meanings. But *you* have paid a good deal to Stesimbrotos and Anaximandros and many others, so that you have missed nothing of these valuable thoughts.'" [For Stesimbrotos as an interpreter of Homer, see Pfeiffer (1968), p. 35; Anaximandros is otherwise unknown.]

12. Xenophon, *Memorabilia* 4.2.10: Socrates, learning that Euthydemos has collected many books, asks him what he aims to be in life;

"'Not a rhapsode, surely? They say that in fact you possess all Homer's poems.'

'Good Heavens, no!' said Euthydemos. 'By my observation, the rhapsodes get the verses right, but in themselves they are completely silly.'"

13. Alcidamas, *De Sophistis* 14 Blass: improvised words (as opposed to written-out speeches) are more effective in practice, since "they closely resemble theatrical and epic delivery" (*hypokrisei kai rhapsōidiai paraplēsia*).

14. Isocrates, *Panegyricus* 159: "And I imagine that Homer's poetry obtained all the greater glory through its splendid praise of those who warred against the barbarians; and that this was the reason why our ancestors determined to have honor rendered to his art both in their musical contests and in the education of the young."

15. Isocrates, *Panathenaicus* 17–18: an incident just before the celebration of the Great Panathenaia. Certain sophists were sitting in the Lyceum "talking about poets, and especially about the poetry of Hesiod and Homer; they were saying nothing original, but were reciting (*rhapsōidountes*) their verses, and repeating the cleverest remarks that other people had made about them in the past."

16. Ps.-Plato, *Hipparchus* 228b: Socrates recalls Hipparchus, "the oldest and wisest of the sons of Peisistratos; among his many noble works of wisdom, he first brought the poems of Homer to this land [Attica], and compelled the rhapsodes at the Panathenaia to go through them in order, picking up one from the other (*ex hypolēpseōs*), even as they still do now." [Cf. Chapter 4, note 25.]

17. Lycurgus, *In Leocratem* 102 Conomis: the orator quotes Euripides' *Erechtheus* on patriotism, and then proceeds: "Next I wish to present to you some of the epic poetry of Homer. Your fathers took him to be so excellent a poet that they made a law ordaining that the epics of Homer, alone among all the poets, should be recited by rhapsodes (*rhapsōideisthai*) at every quadriennial recurrence of the Panathenaia. In this they gave proof to the Greek world of their preference for the noblest actions. It was a reasonable measure. For whereas laws, by reason of their concision, do not teach how one ought to act but simply command, the poets are representers of human life; and by selecting the noblest actions for their themes they persuade mankind to right action with reason and proof. Well, then: Hector, encouraging the Trojans on behalf of their fatherland, uttered these words. . . ." [Lycurgus then quotes *Iliad* 15.494–99.]
18. Aristotle, *Poetics* 1462a5–7: the philosopher is here countering the objection that tragedy is a more vulgar art than epic, since its effects depend so much on histrionic gesturing: "but this charge lies not against the poetic art [of tragedy], but against the art of the actors, for it is possible to overdo the gestures even in rhapsodic delivery (*kai rhapsōidounta*), as Sosistratos did; and in singing in a competition, as Mnasitheos of Opous did." [Nothing else is known of the rhapsode Sosistratos, or of Mnasitheos. Most commentators assume that the latter was probably a kitharode.]
19. Aristotle, *Rhetoric* 3.1403b–1404a: Aristotle here approaches the subject of *hypokrisis*, "delivery," in oratory and also in some related arts. His treatment deserves to be studied in full, but there is space here only to notice those passages in it which bear on the arts of acting and rhapsody. The systematic study of *hypokrisis*, he says, "arrived late in the arts of tragedy and rhapsody, for at first the composers themselves acted their tragedies." [The implication, apparently, is that early tragedy and epic did not require a professionally trained class of performers.] He then proceeds to define *hypokrisis*: "It is concerned with the right use of the voice for each emotion; for example, when it should be loud, when soft, when medium; and how one should apply the pitches, e.g., high, low, and medium; and

what rhythms one should use for each. These are in fact the three objects of current inquiry: intensity, pitch, rhythm. These are the qualities that receive the prizes from the competitions [in the theater]; and just as there the actors have more power than the poets in our time, so too in *political* contests, because of the poor quality of the political systems." Then, a little later: "Words are representations (*mimēmata*); and the voice is the most mimetic element in our makeup. That is why the arts of rhapsody and acting, etc., came into being."

C. Select Testimonia of the Hellenistic and Later Periods

Not arranged by chronological order of source.

20. Athenaeus 14.620b–d: a section on rhapsodes. A fair amount of the interesting information it contains clearly refers to the Hellenistic period or later, but the following extracts (nos. **21–24**) may refer to earlier times.
21. Athenaeus 14.620b: "Aristocles in his book *On Choruses* has stated that the rhapsodes were also called *Homēristai.*" [There seems to be no other evidence for the application of this term to rhapsodes in the strict sense; from the later fourth century B.C. onward (see Athenaeus's comment on this passage) it denoted actors or mimes of Homeric scenes. On Aristocles' *On Choruses*, see *RE* vol. 2, col. 936.]
22. Athenaeus 14.620c: "Clearchus in the first of his two books *On Riddles* says: 'Simonides of Zakynthos used to recite (*errhapsōidei*) the poems of Archilochus in the theaters, seated on a chair.'" [Clearchus of Soli, fr. 92 Wehrli; he flourished about 300 B.C. I have found no evidence to fix the date of the Simonides whom he mentions; West (1974), p. 23, puts the recitations in the fourth century B.C.]
23. Athenaeus 14.620c: "Lysanias in the first book of his *On the Iambic Poets* says that the rhapsode Mnasion, in his performances, used to act (*hypokrinesthai*) some of the iambics of Simonides." [Lysanias lived in the third century B.C.; nothing else is known of Mnasion.]
24. Athenaeus 14.620d: "Kleomenes the rhapsode recited (*errhapsōidēsen*) the *Katharmoi* of Empedocles at Olympia, as Dicaearchus

says." [Cf. below, no. **25**. Dicaearchus flourished in the latter part of the fourth century B.C.; this passage = fr. 87 Wehrli. We have no further information about Kleomenes.]

25. Diogenes Laertius 8.63: "It is said that Kleomenes the rhapsode recited (*rhapsōidēsai*) this same poem *Katharmoi* at Olympia, as in fact Favorinus states in his *Memorabilia*." [Cf. above, no. **14**.]

26. Diogenes Laertius 1.57: Solon "moved a law that the poems of Homer should be delivered rhapsodically (*rhapsōideisthai*) on cue (*ex hypobolēs*), i.e., that where the first rhapsode ended, the next should begin. Thus Solon did more to make Homer known than did Peisistratos, as Dieuchidas says in the fifth book of his *Megarika*." [For Dieuchidas, see Jacoby, *FGrH*, no. 485. Cf. also Chapter 4 of the present book, p. 86.]

27. Diodorus Siculus 14.109: in Ol. 98.1 (388 B.C.) the tyrant Dionysios I of Syracuse sent several four-horse chariots, and some gorgeous tents, to the Olympic Games. "He also sent the very best rhapsodes, so that by delivering (*propheromenoi*) his poems they might glorify the name of Dionysios; for he was wildly enthusiastic about poetry. To direct these rhapsodes he sent along his brother Thearides. On arriving at the panegyris, Thearides was the object of all eyes on account of the splendor of the tents and the number of the chariots. When the rhapsodes set themselves to delivering Dionysios's poems, the beauty of the actors' voices (*tēn euphōnian tōn hypokritōn*) brought the crowds running toward them, and everybody was amazed. Shortly after, however, the poor quality of the poems gave them second thoughts. They began to mock Dionysios and to despise him, to the extent that some people even tore the tents apart."

28. Scholia on Pindar, *Nem.* 2.1, pp. 28–32 in Drachmann, vol. III. [Like so many such entries, this is a mass of ill-digested material, of very diverse relevance, date, and quality. Here I extract those passages that bear directly on the rhapsodes or the history of their art. For the words of Pindar to which they refer, see above, no. **1**.]

Schol. 1a: Pindar's "singers of stitched poems" is interpreted by "rhapsodizers" (*rhapsōidountes*).

Schol. 1c: on Pindar's "sons of Homer" (*Homēridai*): "In ancient times they used to call by the name *Homēridai* those persons descended from Homer, who used to chant (*ēidon*) his poetry, it being handed down from one to the other; later the rhapsodes took over this function, although no longer claiming Homer as their ancestor.

Famous were the rhapsodes of the circle of Kynaithos; these, it is said, composed many of the epic poems and interpolated them into the Homeric corpus. Kynaithos was of a Chiote family; it was he who wrote that Hymn to Apollo which is now among the works which go under Homer's name, and ascribed it to Homer. Now this Kynaithos first recited (*errhapsōidēse*) the Homeric epics in Syracuse in the sixty-ninth Olympiad (504–500 B.C.), as Hippostratus reports." [On the *Homēridai* see, e.g., Pfeiffer (1968), pp. 11–12. Part of the information given about Kynaithos is repeated in schol. 1e (not reproduced here), and also by Eustathius; see the testimonia in Drachmann. For the historian Hippostratus, probably of the third century B.C., see Jacoby in *RE* vol. 8, col. 1922.]

Schol. 1d: here are discussed at length the principal ancient (and, indeed, modern) explanations of the name *rhapsode*. "Some etymologize them as 'rod-singers' (*rhabdōidous*), because they narrate the Homeric epics with a rod (*rhabdos*). . . . Others say that, Homeric poetry not yet being gathered into one . . . , when they rhapsodized it, they made something like a concatenation or stitching (*rhaphē*), thus unifying it. . . ." Then follow certain variants of the "stitch-singer" etymology, including this: "Philochorus says that the reason for their being so addressed was that they put together and stitched their song (*rhaptein tēn ōidēn*). And Hesiod shows this when he says:

> Then first in Delos Homer and I, the singers,
> stitching together our song in novel hymns,
> glorified Phoibos Apollo, gold-sworded, Leto's child.

And Nicocles says that Hesiod was the first to rhapsodize." [The alleged quotation from Hesiod is listed by M-W under *Fragmenta Dubia*, fr. 357. Few will believe in the authenticity of these lines, which seem designed to satisfy the deepest urges of any philologist: they bring together Homer and Hesiod in competition; and they triumphantly confirm the theory of the *rhaptein* school.]

29. Scholium on Plato, *Ion* 530a Greene: "'Rhapsodes' is the name for those who relate the Homeric epics in the theaters. They were so called because in relating them they held rods of bay wood (*rhabdous daphninas*). And 'to rhapsodize' is also used in the sense 'to talk nonsense.' . . ." [Greene, ad loc., cites a number of very similar

passages from late-antique lexicons. The "rods of bay wood" are clearly an inference—whether justified or not, is a difficult problem—from Hesiod, *Theogony* 30–34.]

30. Hesychius, *s.v.* Ōideion: "A place in which the rhapsodes and kitharodes competed before the theater was constructed." [On this problematic statement see Davison (1958), p. 29.]

D. Works Performed by the Rhapsodes

Homeric epic:

See above, nos. **3** (Herodotus), **4** (Plato, *Ion*: *Iliad* and *Odyssey*), **9** (Plato, *Laws*: *Iliad* and *Odyssey*), **11** (Xenophon: *Iliad* and *Odyssey*), **12** (Xenophon), **14** and **15** (Isocrates), **16** (ps.-Plato), **17** (Lycurgus), **21** (Aristocles *ap*. Athen.), **26** (Diogenes Laertius), **28** (Schol. Pindar: Homeric epics and Homeric Hymn to Apollo), **29** (Schol. Plato, *Ion*). To these add:

31. Hesychius *s.v.* Braurōniois: "Rhapsodes used to chant (*ēidon*) the *Iliad* in Brauron, a town of Attica."
32. Anon., *Certamen Homeri et Hesiodi*, lines 55–56 Allen (OCT of Homer, vol. V, p. 227): "Homer, after composing the *Margites*, traveled around from one city to another rhapsodizing [that poem?]."

Hesiodic epic:

See above, nos. **4** (Plato, *Ion*, esp. 531a, b, c and 532a), **9** (Plato, *Laws*), **15** (Isocrates), **28** (Schol. Pindar 1d; dubious).

Archilochus:

See above, nos. **4** (Plato, *Ion*: the rhapsode's close acquaintance with Archilochus's poems is assumed at 531a and 532a) and **22** (Clearchus *ap*. Athen.). The following passage may imply the rhapsodic delivery of Archilochus in early *agōnes mousikoi*, although we cannot rule out the possibility that its language is simply metaphorical.

33. Heraclitus, no. 22 D-K, B42: "Homer deserves to be thrown out of the *agōnes* and whipped; and the same holds good for Archilochus." [The word "whipped," *rhapizesthai*, seems to be the *vox propria* for the punishment of undisciplined athletes; cf. Herodotus 8.59. It is not impossible that Heraclitus also plays here on the word *rhapsōideisthai*; see above, no. **28**.]

Solon:

See above, no. **8** (Plato, *Timaeus*), for the "rhapsodizing" of Solon's poetry at an Attic family festival in the mid fifth century.

Simonides (or *Semonides*?):

See above, no. **23** (Lysanias *ap*. Athen.).

Xenophanes:

34. Diogenes Laertius, in his account of Xenophanes, 1.18 (21 Xenophanes D-K, A1): "Also, he recited (*errhapsōidei*) his own works." [Cf. Pfeiffer (1968), pp. 8–9, with n. 1 on p. 8.]

Empedocles:

See above, nos. **24** (Dicaearchus *ap*. Athen.) and **25** (Favorinus *ap*. Diog. Laert.); the *Katharmoi* is named in both passages.

Antimachus of Colophon(?):

See Appendix I, no. **15**.

Dionysios I of Syracuse:

See above, no. **27** (Diodorus Siculus).

E: Places and Occasions of Rhapsodic Performance

Athens, Panathenaia:

See Appendix I, no. **8**, and Appendix II, nos. **4** (Plato, *Ion* 530b), **16** (ps.-Plato, *Hipparchus*), **17** (Lycurgus), **26** (Diogenes Laertius).

Athens and Attica, elsewhere than in Panathenaia:

See above, nos. **8** (Plato; at the Apatouria), **11** (Xenophon; performances "almost every day"), **31** (Hesychius; at Brauron).

Crete(?):

35. Maximus of Tyre, 23.5: "Only late did Sparta and Crete take to rhapsodizing, only late the Dorian race settled in Libya."

Delos(?):

See Appendix I, no. **9**, and Appendix II, no. **28**, near end (Hesiod, fr. dub. 357 M-W).

Epidauros, Asklepieia:

See above, no. **4** (Plato, *Ion* 530a; Ion has just come from the *agōn mousikos* there, in which he won first prize for rhapsody).

Olympia:

See above, nos. **24** (Dicaearchus *ap*. Athen.), **25** (Favorinus *ap*. Diog. Laert.), and **27** (Diodorus Siculus).

Samos(?):

See Appendix I, no. **15**.

Sikyon:

See above, no. **3** (Herodotus).

Sparta(?):

See above, no. **35** (Maximus of Tyre).

Syracuse:

See above, no. **28** (schol. 1c on Pindar, *Nem*. 2).

Appendix III

The Kitharodes

A: Bibliographical Note

There is a fairly concise survey of this subject, extending over the entire Graeco-Roman period, by Abert, art. Κιθαρῳδία in *RE* vol. 21 (1921), cols. 530–34. For the kitharodic nome one may consult del Grande (1923) and Lasserre (1954), pp. 22–29, and for the semi-legendary kitharodes, the lengthy essay by Böhme (1953). On the manner and matter of the performances, two papers by West (1971 and 1981) are of the greatest interest. There seems to be no comprehensive recent survey of visual representations of the kitharodes, but some important examples are illustrated and discussed by Beazley (1922) and Holloway (1966); cf. also Plate II.

The testimonia presented in this appendix have been selected primarily to illustrate the manner and conditions of kitharodic performance. Section D, on the early history (if so it can be called) of the art, must be taken merely as a checklist of the principal ancient passages concerning the subject; to print and analyze the sources in full would require a lengthy and, alas, rather inconclusive monograph.

B: Pre-Hellenistic Testimonia on Performance

1. Homeric Hymn 4, To Hermes, lines 418–33: quoted above, Chapter 1, pp. 15–16.
2. Herodotus 1.23–24, on Arion's performance aboard ship: quoted and discussed above, Chapter 1, p. 16.
3. Aristotle(?), *Problems* 19.48, on the question of why the tragic choruses do not sing in the Hypodorian or Hypophrygian mode: "The Hypodorian is a majestic and steady mode; for which reason it is the most kitharodic of the modes." [See below, no. **11**, latter part, for Proclus's account of the character of kitharodic music. That passage,

as well as the tract attributed to Psellus (below, App. IX, no. 17), names the *Lydian* mode as appropriate to kitharody.]

C: Hellenistic and Later Testimonia on Performance
Not arranged by chronological order of source.

4. Proclus, *Chrestomathy*, *ap*. Photius, *Bibliotheca*, codex 239, 320a–b, ed. Henry, on the beginnings of the kitharodic nome: "The Cretan Chrysothemis was the first who, wearing a splendid robe and taking the lyre in imitation of Apollo, sang a nome solo. As a result of the fame which he thus achieved, this fashion of competing still remains."
5. Phillis of Delos *ap*. Athenaeus 1.21f, on the marching and dancing movements of the early kitharodes: quoted above, Chapter 1, p. 17, with note 28. [For the importance of body movements in performance, cf. below, no. 9.]
6. Pausanias 10.7.2, on the earlier phase of the Pythian kitharodic contests, before the reorganization of 582 B.C.: "They say that Eleuther won a Pythian victory merely by the power and sweetness of his voice, since the ode that he sang was not of his own composition."
7. Hesychius, *s.v.* Ōdeion, on kitharodic competitions in that building: see App. II, no. 30.
8. Plutarch, *Philopoemen* 11, on the Nemean festival of 207 B.C.: Philopoemen entered the theater during a kitharodic competition, "and it chanced that the kitharode Pylades began to sing the *Persians* of Timotheus, 'Building for Greece the great and splendid beauty of freedom.' The majesty of the poetry matching the brilliance of the voice, everyone in the theater turned to look at Philopoemen." [The same story is told in Pausanias 8.50.3, where the detail is added that Pylades had formerly won a Pythian victory.]
9. Auctor ad Herennium 4.47.60: a rich man of high rank, but without virtue or education, is like "a kitharode who steps forth brilliantly dressed in a gold-embroidered robe, with a purple cloak into which various colors are woven, wearing a golden crown bright with gleaming gems, and holding a highly ornate lyre inlaid with gold and ivory, being in his own person of a dignified figure, appearance, and height. Such a one will raise immense expectations among the audience; but if, when silence falls, he lets out a most raucous voice,

moving his body in the ugliest possible fashion, . . . he is thrown out with derision and contempt." [A very similar anecdote is told in Lucian, *Adversus Indoctum* 8–10, but in much more detail: the contestant is named Euangelos of Tarentum (otherwise unknown), and he is competing with two other kitharodes at the Pythian Games. The common source must be earlier than the Auctor ad Herennium (ca. 86–82 B.C.); how much earlier, there is no saying.]

10. Ovid, *Metamorphoses* 11.165–70: Apollo, as kitharode, competes with Pan: "His golden head is garlanded with Parnassian bay, and his robe, deep-dyed in Tyrian purple, sweeps the ground. On his left side he holds up a lyre inlaid with gems and the tusks of India, and his right hand took the plectrum; his was the very attitude of a musician. Then with his thumb he skillfully roused the strings." [This is only one of several Augustan descriptions of *Apollo Citharoedus*, inspired by Skopas's statue (fourth century B.C.) in the Palatine temple; see Abert, *RE* vol. 21, col. 534.]

D: The Principal Hellenistic and Later Passages Referring to the History of Kitharody
Not arranged by chronological order of source.

11. Proclus, *Chrestomathy*, *ap.* Photius, *Bibliotheca*, codex 239, 320b, ed. Henry: after discussing the earliest kitharody (above, no. **4**), Proclus proceeds: "It seems that Terpander was the first to perfect the nome, using the heroic meter; and that after him Arion of Methymna, being himself both a poet and a kitharode, made considerable additions to it; but that Phrynis of Mitylene altered it drastically, by joining the hexameter to free (*lelymenōi*) meter, and by using more than the traditional seven lyre-strings. It was Timotheus who afterwards brought it into its present shape. Now the dithyramb is agitated, and expresses much divine possession through the dance; it produces in the spectator the passions that are most appropriate to the god [Dionysos]; its rhythms are violent, and it is somewhat simple in its diction. The nome, on the other hand, because of its patron god [Apollo], is relaxed, orderly, and majestic, and makes use of a diction twice as rich [*diplasiais tais lexesin*; meaning uncertain; possibly 'compound words']. Furthermore, each makes use of its own special modes: the dithyramb is tuned to the Phrygian and Hypophrygian, the nome to the mode of the kitharodes, namely, the

Lydian." [There follow a few more remarks on the supposed origins, and the character, of the two forms. On the mode appropriate to the nome, see above, no. **3**, with note.]

12. Ps.-Plutarch, *De Musica*: this compilation is our richest source of information on the history of kitharody, but its treatment of the subject—to a considerable extent, it seems, based on the work of Heraclides Ponticus—is both lengthy and confusing. Here a couple of references must suffice; the reader is referred to the editions by Lasserre (1954) and Einarson and De Lacy (1967) for further information. 1132b *fin.*–e: an outline of the history of the kitharodic nome, not dissimilar to that given in Proclus (above, no. **11**), but adding a number of details. 1133b–d: more on the same, concentrating on the period from Terpander to Phrynis.

13. Pausanias 10.7.2–8, on the early history of kitharody at Delphi (cf. App. I, no. **10**).

E: The Setting of Homer to Music

See, in particular, West (1981). Two of the relevant ancient sources (Heraclides Ponticus *ap.* ps.-Plut. *Mus.* 1132c, and ps.-Plut. ibid. 1132d) are cited above, Chapter 1, p. 19. The others—none of which is likely to inspire great confidence—are: (1) Athenaeus 14.632d: Homer's "acephalous" lines result from his practice of setting all his verses to music [this looks like the desperate theory of some philologist or metrician]. (2) Timomachus, *Cypriaca*, *ap.* Athenaeus 14.638a: Stesandros of Samos "was the first at Delphi to sing to the lyre (*kitharōidēsai*) the battles according to Homer, beginning from the *Odyssey*." [Timomachus may have been earlier than Aristotle (Laqueur in *RE*, art. Timomachos 4); Stesandros is otherwise unknown (*RE*, *s.v.*). But the passage is suspect on several grounds, of which not the least is that in this context Athenaeus is discussing unaccompanied lyre-playing, not kitharody. Probably emendation is required.] (3) Chamaeleon, *ap.* Athenaeus 620c, "says that not only the poems of Homer were set to music, but also those of Herodotus [*sic*; "Hesiod" Valckenaer, "Herodas" Crusius] and Archilochus, and even those of Mimnermus and Phocylides."

Appendix IV

Choral Lyric Performance

A: Bibliographical Note

The only monograph on Greek choral performance in general that I have been able to find is Webster (1970A), *The Greek Chorus.* That work, however, covers choruses of every kind, dramatic as well as non-dramatic, and relies to a great extent on the archaeological evidence (notably vase-paintings) and on inferences from the texts of the dramatists. Here I attempt to put together the main literary sources for archaic and classical choral lyric performance; and for this task I can find few precedents. Pickard-Cambridge thoroughly discusses the literary evidence for the dithyramb and for dramatic choral performances in *DFA*[2], pp. 74–79 and ch. V respectively; and Ferri (1932) discusses the archaeological and literary evidence for ancient circular choruses in general.

B: Alcman

The internal evidence for the rehearsal and performance of Alcman's poems is discussed above, Chapter 1, pp. 20–24; and the external evidence on pp. 24–26.

C: Pindar and Bacchylides

See the general discussion of the performance of their poems above, Chapter 1, pp. 26–31. Here I enumerate the passages on which that discussion is based.

1. *Instrumental accompaniment*: Lyre alone mentioned: *Ol.* 1.17, 2.47 (cf. 1), 4.2, 6.97, 9.13; *Pyth.* 1.1, 2.70–71, 8.31; *Nem.* 4.5 (cf. 13–16, 44), 10.21, 11.7 (?—the reference is general, but might have a particular application to this ode); *Isthm.* 2.1–2 (?—a similar

case to the last). Three *enkōmia* are evidently to be sung to the *barbitos*: Pindar frr. 124d and 125, Bacchylides frr. 20B.1–2 and 20C.2. Oboe alone: *Ol.* 5.19 (the authenticity of this ode is doubtful), and perhaps *Pyth.* 12 (for the oboist Midas; see also lines 25–27); Bacchylides 2.11–14; the oboe is also mentioned as the accompaniment in Pindar's *Partheneion* 2, fr. 94b.14, and the variety of oboe called *Molossos* in fr. 107b. Both lyre and oboe: *Ol.* 3.8–9 (for Theron of Akragas), 7.12 (for Diagoras of Rhodes), 10.93–94 (for Hagesidamos of Lokroi Epizephyrioi); *Nem.* 3.12 and 79 (for Aristokleides of Aegina), 9.8 (for Chromios of Aitna). Lyre and oboe together are also mentioned in *Pyth.* 10.38–39 (for the Thessalian Hippokles), where they seem to accompany the choruses of the fortunate Hyperboreans; and in *Isthm.* 5.26–27 (for Phylakidas of Aegina), where they are played in honor of the warlike heroes of old.

2. *Indications of the kind of music to which the ode was to be performed*: *Ol.* 1.100–103 (for a Syracusan), "him I must crown with the horseman's nome, in Aeolian song"; *Ol.* 3.4–6 (for an Acragantine), the singer has found a new style, which consists in "fitting the glorious voice of the revel to the Dorian measure" [not a certain instance; the reference might be to *meter*]; *Ol.* 5.19 (not certainly by Pindar; for a Camerinan), "with Lydian oboes"; *Ol.* 14.17–18 (for an Orchomenian), "singing in the Lydian fashion"; *Pyth.* 2.67–69 (for a Syracusan), "this song is being sent across the gray sea like Phoenician merchandise; look willingly on the Kastor song set to Aeolian strings"; *Nem.* 3.79 (for an Aeginetan), a song "set to the Aeolian breath of oboes"; *Nem.* 4.45 (for an Aeginetan), the lyre is to play "in the Lydian mode"; *Nem.* 8.15 (for an Aeginetan), the singer offers "a Lydian headband embroidered with sound." The case of *Isthm.* 1.15–16 (for a Theban) is doubtful: "for I wish to fit him, the victor, into a hymn of Kastor [cf. *Pyth.* 2.69] or Iolaos." [Such "musical directions" occur in other lyric poets, e.g., Stesichorus fr. 212 *PMG*, line 2; Lasus, fr. 702.3; the list could no doubt be extended.]

3. *References to the performers of the epinician odes*: The performers are referred to collectively as a *kōmos* in *Ol.* 6.98, 8.10, 14.16; *Pyth.* 3.73, 5.22, 8.20 (?); *Nem.* 3.5; *Isthm.* 8.3; Bacchylides 11.12; cf. the adjectives *enkōmios* at *Ol.* 2.47, *Pyth.* 10.53, *epikōmios* at *Pyth.* 10.6 and *Nem.* 8.50, *aglaokōmos* at *Ol.* 3.6, and the verb *kōmazein* at *Isthm.* 7.20. They are never referred to as a *choros*. On

all occasions they appear to be men; at *Pyth.* 5.103, *Nem.* 3.5 and 66, *Isthm.* 8.2, Bacchylides 6.9, and Bacchylides 13.190, they are described as young. The following passages refer to them as singing: *Pyth.* 5.103, "in the singing (*aoidāi*) of youths"; *Pyth.* 10.6, "the glorious voice of men in revelry (*epikōmiōn*)"; *Nem.* 3.4–5, "young men, masters at the craft of sweet-voiced *kōmoi*"; Bacchylides 6.6–9, "the young men, their hair flowering with garlands, sang" of a victory at Olympia. In *Ol.* 8.10 the performance is "a *kōmos* and carrying of a garland" (*stephanaphorian*; this might possibly refer to the crowning of the victor, but compare the preceding item); in *Ol.* 14.16–17 the *kōmos* "steps springily"; in Bacchylides 11.10–12 (a passage which, indeed, may not refer to epinician odes as such), "*kōmoi* of fair-limbed young men" in Metapontum celebrate the Pythian victory. Finally, we should recall the four passages referring to music, song, and dance that were quoted above, Chapter 1, p. 29: *Ol.* 2.1, *Ol.* 3.6–9, *Pyth.* 1.1–21, and Bacchylides 4.7.

D: The Poet as "Didaskalos" (Select Examples)

4. *Dithyrambic poems*: Herodotus 1.23, "Arion of Methymna, . . . second to none of the kitharodes of his day, and the first of all men known to us to have composed and named and produced (*didaxanta*) a dithyramb in Corinth"; Simonides(?), Epigrams XXVII and XXVIII ed. Page (1975), *didaxamenos choron andrōn* and *amphi didaskaliēi*, respectively; Aristophanes, *Wasps* 1411, "Lasus was once producing in competition (*antedidaske*) with Simonides." [This last example is perhaps not totally certain, since dithyrambs are not specifically mentioned; but Lasus was best known as a dithyrambist, and the dithyramb is the only kind of poem that Simonides is known to have produced in Athens. Many more examples of *didaskalos, didaskō* in connection with the dithyramb could be cited from the fifth century and later.]

5. *Poems other than dithyrambs*: Alcman, fr. 10 *PMG* (= *POxy* no. 2506, quoted above, Chapter 1, p. 24 (Alcman as *didaskalos* of the Spartan choruses of maidens and youths); Eumelus is recorded by Pausanias, 4.4 *init.*, as having produced (*didaxai*) a chorus in honor of Apollo at Delos; Pausanias 5.25.2 (see further below, no. **13**) mentions the *didaskalos* of a boys' chorus, about 500 B.C.; the scholia on Pindar, *Ol.* 6.148a and 149a Drachmann refer to Pindar's emissary

Aineas as *ton chorodidaskalon* and *ho tou chorou didaskalos*, respectively. Finally, we may recall that *didaskō* and its related words are regularly used of a poet's production of tragedy and comedy in all our ancient sources, including those that appear to derive from the official archives. It is applied, for example, to Thespis in the Parian Marble entry (discussed above, Chapter 4, p. 87), and to the competing tragic and comic poets in the *Fasti* inscription *IG* II² 2318 (reproduced for the most part in the appendix to ch. II of *DFA*²); and Herodotus applies it to the dramatic activity of Phrynichus (6.21.2, *poiēsanti . . . kai didaxanti*).

E. Select Testimonia on Dithyrambic Choruses

The Athenian dithyrambic choruses receive more attention than any other kind of nondramatic choral performance in our ancient literary sources, for the obvious reason that they figured annually in one of the city's most spectacular official celebrations; it was far otherwise with, say, a Pindaric epinician ode performed at a gathering of family and friends in Orchomenos. In this case almost alone, therefore, the sources provide us with a fairly clear notion of the circumstances of a Greek choral lyric production. For further details, see *DFA*², cited in the Bibliographical Note.

6. Antiphon, *Oration* 6.11–13 (probably datable to 419 B.C.): the speaker says that being appointed choregos for the Thargelia and having had one Pantakles allotted to him as *didaskalos* (i.e., poet), and the tribe Kekropis along with his own, "I first of all set up a *didaskaleion* [training quarters] in that part of my house which was best suited for the purpose; here, also, I used to train choruses (*edidaskon*) when I was choregos for the Dionysia." The speaker then assembled a chorus of the very best boy-singers, without having to fine their parents and without making any enemies (an interesting detail, this). When the boys arrived, he appointed four deputies to take charge of them, including one Philippos, "whose orders were to buy anything and to make any expenditures required by the *didaskalos* or any of the deputies for the best possible training and equipment of the boys."
7. Demosthenes, *Oration* 21.16 (*Contra Meidiam*; one of the matters at issue was Demosthenes' dithyrambic choregia for the Great Dionysia of 348 B.C.): as choregos, Demosthenes has had a gold-

smith make a cloak for him, "and the gold garlands, as an adornment for the chorus"; according to sec. 22 (an ancient interpolation), the cloak was for Demosthenes to wear in the *pompē* of the Dionysia. The second Argument to the same oration (p. 16, ed. Humbert-Gernet) further informs us that the dithyrambic choregoi were appointed eleven months before the celebration of the Dionysia —an indication of the amount of preparation required for one of these productions. [This Argument, it should be noted, contains a great deal of misinformation on the Athenian festivals; but this particular detail hardly looks like an invention.]

8. Antiphanes, the poet of the Middle Comedy, fr. 204K, lines 5–6: an unfortunate individual "chosen as choregos, having provided golden cloaks for the chorus, is himself reduced to wearing rags." [The chorus is not specified as being a dithyrambic one; but cf. no. 7.]
9. Posidonius *ap.* Athenaeus 4.152b, describing the feasts of the Kelts: "they sit in a circle; and in the middle is the noblest of them . . . , like the *koryphaios* (leader) of a chorus." [Since the formation is circular, Posidonius's reference is almost certainly to a dithyrambic chorus. This is the only passage I have found that mentions the position taken up by a lyric koryphaios.]
10. Xenophon, *Oeconomicus* 8.20: on the importance of orderliness in the arrangement of household goods: "thus even the space between the utensils seems beautiful, when each is set separate from the other; just as a cyclic [i.e., dithyrambic] chorus is not merely a beautiful sight in itself, but also the space in the middle of it seems beautiful and pure." [Cf. the same treatise, 8.3, on the discipline and order of a good choral dance; the reference there, too, may well be to the dithyramb.]
11. Ps.-Plutarch, *De Musica* 1141c–d: "Of old, up to the time of Melanippides the composer of dithyrambs [first half of the fifth century], it had been the practice for the oboists to receive their salary from the poets, for clearly the *poetry* took the leading role, and the oboists were subservient to the *didaskaloi*; afterwards, however, this practice too vanished." [Cf. Athenaeus 14.617b–c, on Pratinas's indignation "because the oboists were not playing to accompany the choruses, as ancestral custom required, but the choruses were singing to accompany the oboists." Athenaeus, to illustrate this, quotes Pratinas fr. 708 *PMG*; this, however, is a hyporcheme, not a dithyramb.]

F: Select Testimonia on Nondithyrambic Choral Lyric (see also above, nos. **1–3** and **5**)

12. *Numbers of choreuts recorded* vary from 100 (Herodotus 6.27.2: a chorus of Chiote youths sent to Delphi), through 50 (the regular number for an Athenian dithyrambic chorus—see, e.g., "Simonides," epigram XXVIII in Page [1975])—to 11 or 10 (implied by Alcman, fr. 1.98–99 *PMG*, with schol. A, and Herodotus 5.83.3), and 10 (inscription recording a contest in the Soteria at Delphi in 268 B.C., Dittenberger [1915–1924], no. 424). See also no. **13**.

13. Pausanias 5.25.2–4: "The people of Messina on the Sicilian strait, by ancient custom, used to send to Rhegium a boys' chorus numbering 35, and a *didaskalos* and an oboist with them, to take part in a local festival of the people of Rhegium. On one occasion a disaster befell them: not one of those whom they sent came back home, but the ship carrying the boys vanished." Pausanias adds that the Messinans set up bronze statues of the chorus, the *didaskalos*, and the oboist in the sanctuary of Zeus at Olympia; these statues were the work of Kalon of Elis. [This sculptor worked about 500 B.C.; see *Kleine Pauly*, *s.v.* Kalon no. 1. The number 35 for a chorus is unparalleled; cf. Mosino (1977).]

14. Proclus, *Chrestomathy*, *ap*. Photius, *Bibliotheca*, codex 239, 319b–322a, ed. Henry: this passage is the longest systematic account of Greek lyric poetry that has survived from classical antiquity. Unfortunately, it gives relatively little information about the conditions of performance. Those parts of it that refer to kitharody have been quoted above, Appendix III, nos. **4** and **11**. Here may be added: "The *prosodion* [processional] was uttered when they went to the altars or temples, and it was sung to the oboe during the procession; the *hymnos* proper, however, was sung to the kithara, while the chorus remained stationary" (319b). The *daphnephoric* songs are a species of partheneion, performed at Apollo's temples in Boeotia every eighth year: a staff of olive wood is decorated with bays, flowers, and bronze spheres, and then "a boy with both parents surviving leads the *daphnēphoria*, and his nearest relative carries the decorated olive wood, which they call the *kōpō*. The *daphnēphoros* [bay bearer] himself comes next, with his hand on the bay; his hair flows free, he wears a gold garland and is dressed in a brilliant robe that falls to his feet, and he is shod with *epikratides*[?]. Behind him follows a chorus of maidens, holding out branches before them in supplication and singing a hymn. Now they sent the *daphnēphoria* procession to the temple of Apollo Ismenios and Chalazios" (321b).

"The *ōschophoric* songs were sung among the Athenians. Two young men of the chorus led the festival, dressed as women, and carrying a vine branch laden with ripe grapes; this branch was called *ōschē*, whence the name of the songs. . . . The Athenians made this procession from the temple of Dionysos to the sacred precinct of Athena Skiras. Behind the young men came the chorus, singing these songs" (322a). [For the *daphnēphoria*, compare Pindar's second *Partheneion*, discussed above, Chapter 1, pp. 26–27. There is no extant example of an oschophoric song; the ceremony associated with it is discussed in detail by Parke (1977), pp. 77–80, with references to the other ancient sources in n. 82.]

15. Aristophanes, *Tagenistai*, *ap.* Athenaeus 15.677b–c (= fr. 491K): "What are we to do, then? We ought to take white cloaks, and then take Isthmiac garlands, as the choruses do, and sing an *enkōmion* to our master." [For the garlands, cf. above, nos. **3** and **7**, and below, no. **16**. The context does not make it clear whether the white cloaks are to be thought of as part of the regular dress of an encomiastic chorus, but this seems not unlikely.]

16. Plutarch, *Nikias* 3.4–5, on Nikias's choral production at Delos in 417 B.C. (for the date and circumstances cf. Kagan [1981], pp. 153–54): "Formerly the choruses which the cities sent to sing for the god used to sail up to the island in no fixed order. A crowd would at once meet their ship, and they would be urged to begin singing in much confusion; they would disembark in haste and without discipline, in the very act of putting on their garlands and changing their costumes. When Nikias conducted the sacred mission, however, he disembarked at Rheneia, together with the chorus, the sacrificial victims, and the rest of the equipment. He had brought with him a bridge made to the correct measurements in Athens and brilliantly decorated with gilding, colors, festoons, and draperies. With this he spanned the strait between Rheneia and Delos, which is not a wide one, during the night. Then, just at dawn, he sent the procession over the bridge together with the chorus, already richly adorned and singing."

17. Aristophanes, *Clouds* 1355–58: Strepsiades reports on his son's behavior after dinner: "First I told him to take the lyre, and sing a poem of Simonides, on how the Ram (*Krios*) was shorn. But he at once began to say that it was out of date to play the lyre and sing over the wine, like a woman grinding barley." [The schol. ad loc. say that the poem by Simonides was an epinician ode for the wrestler Krios of Aegina (fr. 507 *PMG*). This seems to be the only certain instance of a solo rendering of an epinician, although one might suspect that the line from another Simonidean epinician, *πῖνε πῖν' ἐπὶ συμφοραῖς* (fr. 512 *PMG*), reproduced by the Chorus at Ar. *Knights* 406, may also have been a favorite in Athenian symposia.]

18. Eupolis, *Helots*, *ap.* Athenaeus 14.638e (= fr. 139K): "It's out of date to sing the songs of Steisichorus and Alcman and Simonides, when one can listen to Gnesippus." [Comparison with no. **17** suggests that, again, the context of the singing mentioned here may be the symposium. Stesichorus and Simonides are also mentioned as being sung at symposia in schol. Ar. *Wasps* 1222.]

19. Athenaeus 14.628c–631e contains much information on choral dancing, both lyric and dramatic. Unfortunately, little of it really helps us in the attempt to envisage a choral lyric production specifically. Some notable passages are: "In dancing, as in walking, gracefulness and decorum are beautiful, disorder and vulgarity are ugly. For this reason the poets from the beginning composed their dances for free men, and used the dance figures simply to express what was being sung, always keeping nobility and manliness in them—whence they called such dances *hyporchēmata* [this is an attempt, probably mistaken, to etymologize the word as 'dances subordinate to (words)']. But if anyone failed to observe due measure in setting out his dance figures or, on coming to compose his songs, did not make the words correspond to the dance, he was in disgrace. Hence Aristophanes (or Plato) in the *Skeuai*, according to Chamaeleon, said: 'So that if anyone danced well, it was a real sight to see; but now [the choreuts] do nothing, but stand stock still as if paralyzed, and howl'" (628d–e). "The statues made by the ancient sculptors are relics of the dancing of early times; for this reason special care was taken with the arm movements" (629b). [The meaning of the second clause is mysterious (see Gulick ad loc.).] "In ancient times satyric poetry consisted entirely in choruses, as did the contemporary tragedy; hence they didn't even have actors. Dramatic poetry has three kinds of dance: tragic, comic, satyric. Likewise lyric poetry has three: *pyrrhic*, *gymnopaidic*, *hyporchematic*. The *pyrrhic* is like the satyric, for both are performed at speed; and the *pyrrhic* is evidently a war dance, being danced by armed boys. . . . The *gymnopaidic* is like the tragic dance called *emmeleia*, for in both of them is seen gravity and solemnity. The *hyporchematic* is akin to the comic dance called *kordax*, both being playful" (630c–e). "The *gymnopaidic* is like the dance called *anapalē* by the ancients. All the boys dance naked, carrying out certain rhythmic movements and figures of their arms in a supple way[?], so as to render certain effects of the palaistra and the pankration, moving their feet in rhythm. *Oschophoric* and *Bacchic* dances are varieties of this dance, so that it too can be traced back to Dionysos" (631c). "The *hyporchematic* is a dance mode in which the chorus sings while it dances. . . . In Pindar, this is danced by Laconian men; the *hyporchematic* is a dance for both men and women. And the best of the [poetic] kinds are those that are danced. They are these: *prosodiac*, *apostolic* (these are also called *parthenian*), and their like. Of hymns, some were danced and some were not . . . and the paean likewise" (631c–d; this passage is much corrupted in the original).

G: The "Sending" of Lyric Poems

(Here, for convenience, I group all the instances known to me, including one or two cases where the lyric concerned was certainly or probably monodic.)

20. Herodotus 5.95.2; after describing the defeat of the Mytilenaeans by the Athenians at Sigeum and Alcaeus's loss of his armor in that battle, the historian says: "These events Alcaeus made into a poem and sent to (*en melei poiēsas epitithei es*) Mitylene, reporting his misfortune to his friend Melanippos." [The only comparable usage of *epititheēmi* in Herodotus is at 3.42.4: Polykrates writes down on papyrus all that has happened to him, "and after writing, he sent it to (*epethēke es*) Egypt." The almost certain inference is that Herodotus thought Alcaeus's poem had been written down and sent like a letter; whether or not he was correct, the passage shows that by the third quarter of the fifth century an investigator exceptionally learned in archaic Greek literature and history could envisage a poem designed for singing, a *melos*, as being sent by mail.]

21. Pindar, *Ol.* 6 (for Hagesias of Stymphalos and Syracuse), lines 87–100: "Aineas! Urge on your companions first of all to hymn

Hera Parthenia [an Arcadian cult name] . . . for you are an honest messenger, a message stick (*skytala*) of the lovely-haired Muses, a sweet mixing-bowl of loudly uttered songs; and tell them to remember Syracuse and Ortygia, which Hieron rules. . . . May he [Hieron] welcome the *kōmos* for Hagesias when it reaches him from the walls of Stymphalos, from one of his homes to another, leaving the mother-city of Arcadia rich in sheep." [The scholia on lines 87–88 (148a, 149a, Drachmann) take Aineas to be a *chorodidaskalos* or chorus trainer whom Pindar has deputized to produce this ode on his behalf. In this very reasonable interpretation they seem to be followed by all modern scholars. Pindar's words suggest that Aineas can be trusted to reproduce exactly the poet's intentions in the performances at Stymphalos and Syracuse, at least so far as the music and poetry go—and presumably (although Pindar makes no explicit reference to this) the dance, too. One might further infer from the passage that the *kōmos* that Aineas is to direct consists of Syracusan friends of the victor, who will travel home *via* Stymphalos.]

22. Pindar, *Isthm.* 2 (for Xenokrates of Akragas), lines 47–48: "Nikasippos! Impart all this, when you reach my honored friend." [On these, the final words of the ode, the scholiast comments: "Pindar sends (*pempei*) this hymn for Xenokrates to Akragas *via* Nikasippos, to Thrasyboulos (the victor's son)." Nikasippos occurs nowhere else in the ode, or indeed in history. One may conjecture that his status resembles that of Aineas in no. **21**.]

23. Pindar, *Pyth.* 2 (for Hieron of Syracuse), lines 67–69 (cf. above, no. **2**): "This song is being sent (*pempetai*) across the gray sea like Phoenician merchandise; look willingly on the Kastor song set to Aeolian strings!" [Note that this same sentence contains an indication of the musical mode in which the ode is to be performed; cf. above, no. **2**.]

24. Pindar, *Pyth.* 3 (for Hieron of Syracuse), lines 68–79: if he could, the poet would have crossed the Ionian sea to Syracuse, bringing Hieron *health*, as well as the news of his victories at the Pythian games; as it is, he will offer vows for him at the neighboring sanctuary of the Great Mother. [The implication clearly is that Pindar is for some reason immobilized at Thebes, just as Hieron is immobilized at Syracuse by ill-health. We must therefore assume that the script of *Pyth.* 3 will be performed in Syracuse, but not under the poet's personal direction. Since Wilamowitz ([1900], p. 48; [1922], p. 280), it has become almost de rigueur to describe this ode as a "poetical epistle" (cf. Burton [1962], p. 78; Bowra [1964], p. 408), as if it were some composition by Horace; Nisetich (1980), p. 168, however, rightly recognizes it as a performed ode.]

25. Pindar, *Nem.* 3 (for Aristokleides of Aegina), lines 76–80: "This I send (*pempō*) to you . . . , this draught of song, set to the Aeolian breath of oboes, late though it is." [Cf. above, no. **23**, with note there.]
26. Pindar, fr. 124a.b (*enkōmion* for Thrasyboulos of Akragas), lines 1–2: "I send (*pempō*) you this vehicle of lovely songs as dessert for your dinner."
27. Bacchylides 5 (epinician ode for Hieron of Syracuse), lines 10–14: "The glorious servant of the golden-tiara'd muse Ourania, and your friend, sends (*pempei*) this hymn from the sacred island [i.e., Keos] to your famous city." [Cf. line 197: "to send (*pempein*)" the poem to Hieron.]
28. Bacchylides, fr. 20B (*enkōmion* for Alexander, son of Amyntas, of Macedon), lines 1–4: "*Barbitos* [harp]! No longer hang on your peg, keeping your seven-noted voice silent! It is my will to send (*pempein*) a golden wing of the Muses to Alexander."
29. Bacchylides, fr. 20C (*enkōmion* for Hieron of Syracuse), lines 2–7: "I am about to send (*pempein*) the flower of the Muses to Hieron . . . and his guests in the symposium, at Aitna." [*pempein* (line 6) is restored from the single initial letter *pi*, but almost certainly correctly.]
30. Pausanias 9.16.1 mentions that Pindar "sent off" (*apepempse*) a hymn for Ammon at his shrine in Libya.

Appendix V

Performance of Other Kinds of Greek Poetry

Note: I include in this appendix only those items of evidence that seem to provide *explicit* information about the performing conditions of the kinds of poetry concerned: elegiac, iambic, and monodic. More such information can be inferred with varying degrees of probability (a) from the poetic texts themselves, e.g., Solon fr. 1W, Theognis 237–40, Sappho fr. 118, Alcaeus 70.3, Anacreon frr. 373, 374 (on these last three see Campbell [1982], p. ix); and (b) from allusions in later authors to the musical activities of the early poets, e.g. Neanthes *ap.* Athenaeus 4.175e (Ibycus invents the *sambyka*, Anacreon the *barbitos*), or Horace, *Odes* 2.13.24–26 (Sappho and Alcaeus singing to their lyres). After experiment, however, I decided not to include this material; not merely is it voluminous and endlessly repetitive, but it adds almost nothing of substance to what can be learned from the evidence given here.

A: Testimonia on Elegiac Performance
(cf. Campbell [1964], Rosenmeyer [1968], and West [1974], ch. I)

1. Ps.-Plutarch, *De Musica* 1133f–1134a: "And there is another ancient nome called the *Kradias*, which Hipponax [fr. 153W] says Mimnermus performed on the oboe; for in the beginning the aulodes performed elegiac verse set to music, as is shown by the *graphē* of the Panathenaia which concerns the musical contest." [Much is doubtful here, notably the nature of the *graphē*, of which this is the only ancient mention (for discussion, see Davison [1958], pp. 39–40). The statement that elegiacs were performed to the oboe on certain (mostly public?) occasions in early times may possibly be supported by the following passages: *Souda s.v.* Tyrtaios (this poet was *elegopoios kai aulētēs*); Strabo 14.643 (Mimnermus was *aulētēs hama kai poētēs elegeias*); ps.-Plut. *Mus.* 1134a (immediately fol-

lowing the passage quoted here on the Panathenaic *graphē*: Sakadas of Argos was a *poiētēs melōn te kai elegeiōn memelopoiēmenōn*, and was also a good oboist, appearing thrice as victor in the Pythian records.]

2. Diogenes Laertius 1.18: Xenophanes "rhapsodized" his own works. [Cf. Appendix II, no. **34**. A doubtful instance; although Xenophanes composed much in elegiacs, he also composed in hexameters and iambic trimeters.]

3. Plato, *Timaeus* 21b–c, on the "rhapsodizing" of Solon's poetry at an Attic family festival in the mid fifth century. [Cf. Appendix II, no. **8**; again, a doubtful instance, since Solon composed in elegiacs, tetrameters, iambics, epodes, and possibly hexameters (fr. 31W, of doubtful authenticity). Many of his most famous poems, however, were in elegiacs.]

B: Testimonia on Iambic Performance
(cf. West [1974], ch. II)

4. Aristotle(?), *Problems* 1336b: "And one must legislate that the younger people should not be spectators (*theatas*) either of iambics or of comedy until they reach the age at which it is already permissible for them to take part in the banquet and in the drinking." [This passage is cited by West (1974), p. 23, as an indication that iambics were recited "as a public spectacle in the fourth century." Compare also Appendix II, nos. **22** and **23**.]

5. Phillis of Delos *ap.* Athenaeus 14.636b, giving a catalogue of various special kinds of stringed instrument: "those to the accompaniment of which they chanted (*ēidon*) the iambics, they called *iambykas*." [There is no way of identifying the persons called "they" here. The statement looks suspiciously like a Hellenistic philologist's attempt to answer the question, "why the *iamb-* in the word *iambykē*?" And suspicion grows when we find that on the only occasion when the word appears in high classical Greek (Eupolis, fr. 139K) it evidently refers to an instrument accompanying a lover's serenade. Perhaps, however, we cannot exclude the possibility that the *iambykē* was used to accompany "iambics" in the wider sense of "epodes"; cf. sec. C, below.]

C: Testimonia on the Performances of Archilochus

Nos. **6** and **7** indicate performance to instrumental accompaniment (see also Appendix VII, nos. **13** and **14**); nos. **8–10**, rhapsodic delivery. As was suggested above, Chapter 1, p. 39, the apparent contradiction is probably to be solved on the assumption that the performance style varied according to the metrical form.

6. Inscription of Mnesiepes in the *Archilocheion*, Paros, ed. Kontoleon (1952) pp. 40–41, cf. Lasserre and Bonnard (1958), p. cv: on Archilochus's initiation by the Muses, who told him that in exchange for the cow he was driving they would give him a fair price: "and after this was said, neither the Muses nor the cow were to be seen any more, but he saw, lying before his feet, a lyre." [Mnesiepes' inscription dates from the third century B.C., but a similar story may already have been known to the painter of the mid-fifth-century Attic vase, below, no. **23**. Archilochus is also associated with the lyre in *Anth. Pal.* 7.664 (attributed to Theocritus or Leonidas), line 6 (he is clever at "making verses and singing to the lyre"), and in one of the scholia to Pindar, *Ol.* 9.1 (he was "one of the lyric poets").]

7. Ps.-Plutarch, *De Musica* 1140f–1141b, on the musical and metrical innovations of Archilochus: "Also, Archilochus invented recitative (*parakatalogē*), and the instrumental accompaniment that goes with it. . . . Further, they say that Archilochus introduced the practice of speaking some iambics to instrumental accompaniment, but of singing others (*ta men legesthai para tēn krousin, ta de aidesthai*); and that the tragedians then adopted a similar practice, and that Crexus took it and applied it to the dithyramb. They also think that he first discovered accompaniment higher than the song, whereas the ancient poets always accompanied [the song] in unison." [On *parakatalogē*, and on some other questions presented by the present passage, see *DFA*[2], pp. 156–64; and, on *legesthai para tēn krousin*, Dale (1968), p. 208.]

8. Plato, *Ion* 531a and 532a, suggesting that Archilochus was part of the rhapsode's repertoire.

9. Clearchus *ap.* Athenaeus 14.620c, recording "rhapsodic" delivery of Archilochus in the theaters at some period before ca. 300 B.C.; see Appendix II, no. **22**.

10. Heraclitus, no. 22 D-K, B42, perhaps implying rhapsodization of Archilochus at *agōnes mousikoi*; see Appendix II, no. **33**.

D: Testimonia on Performances of Monodic Lyric
(cf. Campbell [1982], p. ix; and in general
Kirkwood [1974].)

11. Aristophanes, *Daitaleis*, *ap*. Athenaeus 15.694a (= fr. 223K): "Take and sing me a skolion from Alcaeus or Anacreon." [The *Daitaleis* was produced in 427 B.C.; skolia were regularly sung at symposia, and presumably that is the occasion here. It is not clear from Athenaeus's excerpt what object is to be supplied after "take" (*labōn*), but *Clouds* 1355–56 ("I told him to *take the lyre* and *sing a song* by Simonides") suggests that a lyre may be meant. *Clouds* 1364–65 ("I told him *to take a myrtle branch* and *speak* something from Aeschylus") might suggest that the myrtle branch was reserved for unaccompanied recitations at the symposia.]

12. Athenaeus 15.694f–695f gives a general account of the skolia sung at Attic symposia, with a large number of actual examples (frr. 884–908 *PMG*). The contents of some of them, and the fact that several are already quoted by fifth- and fourth-century B.C. authors (especially Aristophanes, *Wasps* 1219–47), suggest that Athenaeus has here preserved an Attic songbook dating from the classical period. One of the songs appears to have been taken from the works of Alcaeus (fr. 891 *PMG*), and two from Praxilla (frr. 897, 903); another (fr. 890) is attributed in some sources to Simonides.

13. Aelian, *ap*. Stobaeus, *Florilegium* 29.88, on the performance of a song by Sappho at an early Athenian symposium: quoted and discussed above, Chapter 1, p. 35.

E: Archaeological Evidence
(i) Poetry in Performance in Fifth-Century Symposia
(all the examples except nos. **14–15** are Attic).

14. London, British Museum, Boeotian red-figured stemless cup: Lullies (1940), pp. 6–8, with Taf. 3, Campbell (1964), p. 66. A, symposium with standing servant and three reclining revelers, of whom the left-hand one plays the lyre; from the mouth of (apparently) the right-hand one issue the words *φασὶν ἀληθῆ ταῦτα*, which "look like the introduction to a maxim and may well have been in elegiac metre" (Campbell; note, however, his reservations, p. 66, nn. 13 and 14). Lullies dates the vase to about 470 B.C.

15. The same vase: B, again a symposium with three reclining figures; the left-hand one is lifting a cup to his lips; the central one plays the oboe (although a lyre is hanging conveniently on the wall behind him); next to the right-hand one is inscribed *ὦ διὰ τῆς θυρίδος*. This is surely to be identified with the couplet by Praxilla of Sikyon beginning *ὦ διὰ τῶν θυρίδων καλὸν ἐμβλέπουσα*, fr. 754 *PMG* (where Page gives further references).

16. Rome, Villa Giulia, fragment of rhyton, *ARV*², p. 872, no. 26 (manner of the Tarquinia Painter): upper part of a singer, reclining with his head thrown back; from his open mouth proceed the words *σοὶ καὶ ἐμ[οί* (so restored by Beazley). Beazley, *AJA* 58 (1954) 190 (cf. pl. 31, fig. 5) compared *Theognidea* 1058, where the same words are found; Mabel Lang (cited in the *ARV*² entry) noted that they also occur in Mimnermus fr. 8W. Unfortunately, the fragment is very small, and we have no way of telling whether an instrumental accompaniment was originally shown.

17. Copenhagen, kalyx-krater, *ARV*², p. 185, no. 32 (very early Kleophrades Painter), Immerwahr (1965), *CVA* Denmark VIII, plates 331–33, Webster (1972), pp. 54–55. The largest fragment shows a lyre-player reclining at a symposium (*CVA*, pl. 331.1a, with detail on pl. 332.1a); above the lyre is an inscription which Immerwahr restores *π]ενίης* and with which he compares *Theognidea* 1129 *ἐμπίομαι· πενίης θυμοφθόρου οὐ μελεδαίνω*. The word and the dialect are certainly consistent with gnomic elegiacs, even if the precise identification is unprovable. See also below, no. **29**.

18. Munich, kylix, *ARV*², p. 437, no. 128 (Douris), Furtwängler and Reichhold (1904–32), pl. 105 with text volume II, pp. 230–32. The tondo shows a standing youth playing the oboes to a man reclining on a couch and holding a kylix. The man's head is thrown back, and he sings *ουδυναμου* (i.e., *οὐ δύναμ' οὐ*?), which has been compared with *Theognidea* 939 *οὐ δύναμαι φωνῇ λίγ' ἀειδέμεν* (see Furtwängler and Reichhold, pp. 230–31). The case seems uncertain.

19. Athens, National Museum, kylix, inventory no. 1357, *CVA* Athens i, III Ic, pl. 3.1, 3.3, Campbell (1964), p. 66. The tondo shows a man reclining against a striped pillow of the kind regularly used in symposia; in his left hand he holds a pair of castanets, with his right he caresses a hare that crouches below his couch. His mouth is open, and from it proceeds the inscription ὦ παίδων κάλλιστε, which may well be identifiable with *Theognidea* 1365, a line which opens with the same words. [It should perhaps be noted that the absence of any instrumental accompaniment—except for the castanets—may not prove that no such accompaniment was envisaged by the painter of the scene. The tondo clearly provides room only for an *extract* from the symposium, and we cannot be sure what is to be imagined as lying outside its circular frame.]

20. Boston, Museum of Fine Arts, on loan from private collection: fragmentary kalyx-krater by Euphronios, published by Vermeule (1965); cf. Page, *SLG*, fr. S317. A, symposium with five figures, all inscribed; one of them, a girl named Syko, in profile toward the right, plays the oboes; the second figure from her to the right (and on the extreme right of the whole group), is a man named Ekphantides, who is reclining, facing toward her. His head is flung back, his lips are open; and in the space between him and the youth reclining next to him are inscribed the words ὤπολλον σέ γε καὶ μάκαι[. Vermeule supplies μάκαι[ραν, which seems almost certain; after that she suggests Λατὼ or Ἄρτεμιν. Clearly we have here an Aeolic line of the type favored by the monodists; it could be a glyconic (with overlap into a second line) or a hipponactean. The line is not preserved in the literary tradition, but Vermeule notes that it seems to have been well known at the time (cf. no. **21**, below), and she raises the possibility of an attribution to Anacreon.
21. Paris, Cabinet des Médailles, fragmentary kylix, *ARV*², p. 372, no. 26 (Brygos Painter), referred to by Vermeule (1965), p. 38, and illustrated in her plate 13.4. We see the upper part of a symposiast reclining in very nearly the same pose as Ekphantides on no. **20**; from his parted lips comes the inscription ΟΠΟΛΟΝ, which might be the beginning of the same line as that which Ekphantides is singing.
22. Boston, Museum of Fine Arts, kylix, *ARV*², p. 1567 ("somewhat akin to the early work of Douris"). In the tondo, an elderly man sings to the lyre, with an inscription proceeding from his mouth: ἐ]ς Πανιωνίην, so restored by Beazley, *AJA* 31 (1927), 348–49; cf. idem, *AJA* 33 (1929), 364. As Beazley observes in the former of

those passages, the words might be part of a glyconic line. The Ionic case-ending might recall Anacreon.

F: Archaeological Evidence
(ii) Monodic Poets Shown on Athenian Works of Art in the Sixth and Fifth Centuries.

For a list of portraits of the Greek poets from all periods in antiquity, with copious illustrations, see Richter (1965), vol. I, pp. 45–78. For the representations of Anacreon and Kydias on Attic red-figure vases, see Webster (1972), pp. 53–55.

23. *Archilochus*(?): Boston, Museum of Fine Arts, white ground pyxis, *ARV*², p. 774, no. 1 (Hesiod Painter), Caskey and Beazley (1931–63), no. 37, Richter (1965), p. 58. A good, if not quite certain, case has been made for interpreting the scene as the initiation of Archilochus (cf. the Mnesiepes inscription, above, no. 6); a rustic youth with a cow is seen in the presence of seven Muses. The vase is dated by Richter to ca. 460–50 B.C.
24. *Sappho*: Warsaw, hydria in Six's technique, *ARV*², p. 300, bot., Beazley (1928), pp. 8–9, Richter (1965), pp. 70–72. A woman inscribed ΦΣΑΦΩ holds a lyre and poises the plectrum. The vase is dated by Richter to ca. 510–500 B.C.
25. *Sappho*: Athens, hydria, *ARV*², p. 1060, no. 145 (group of Polygnotus), Richter (1965), pp. 70–72. A woman inscribed as Sappho sits facing right, reading a scroll with an only partly decipherable verse written on it (see fr. 938*d PMG*; it is there classed among the *Fragmenta Adespota*). Left of her, a standing woman holding a garland over her head; immediately to her right, a standing woman holding out a lyre toward her; extreme right, another standing woman. The vase is dated by Richter to ca. 440–420 B.C.
26. *Sappho and Alcaeus*: Munich, kalathos-psykter, *ARV*², p. 385, no. 228 (Brygos Painter, very late), Richter (1965), pp. 69–70. On the left, Alcaeus, his lyre at the ready, his right hand holding the plectrum; he faces toward the figure on the right, Sappho, who half-turns toward him, her lyre dropped to a horizontal position, her right hand also holding the plectrum. Both figures are inscribed with their names. The vase is dated by Richter to ca. 480–70 B.C.
27. *Anacreon*: London, British Museum, kylix, *ARV*², pp. 62–63, no. 86 (Oltos), Richter (1965), p. 77, Webster (1972), p. 54. On side B is

a *kōmos*: Anacreon (so inscribed), in a dancing posture with two males, also dancing; he wears a simple *himation* and is playing the lyre. The vase is dated by Richter to ca. 515 B.C. See Plate III of this book.

28. *Anacreon*: Syracuse, lekythos, *ARV*², p. 36, no. 2 (Gales Painter), Richter (1965), p. 77, Webster (1972), p. 54. Anacreon (so inscribed) "walks with his lyre leaning backwards, between two boys, one with a skyphos and the other with a stick. Anacreon wears a long chiton, himation, perhaps shoes and sakkos. This is Anacreon in Maenad dress" (I quote the description by Webster, since this vase-painting is hard to make out in photographs, and I have not seen it). On the "Maenad dress," see the references given below, no. **31**. The vase is dated by Richter to ca. 500–490 B.C.

29. *Anacreon*: on the fragmentary kalyx-krater in Copenhagen (see above, no. **17**) appears part of a figure playing the lyre; one of the uprights of the instrument is inscribed ANAKPE (*CVA*, pl. 333.1a). On a fragment that belongs close to that figure is a man wearing a sakkos, carrying a parasol, and evidently dancing (*CVA*, pl. 333.1b; Webster [1972], p. 54). The vase is dated by Webster to a little before 500 B.C.

30. *Anacreon*: there exist several copies (some inscribed with the poet's name) of a statue of Anacreon, the lost original of which is dated by Richter ([1965], pp. 76–77) on stylistic grounds to ca. 440 B.C. The most famous, and best-preserved, example is that in the Ny Carlsberg Museum. It represents a bearded man who has a short cloak draped around his shoulders but is otherwise naked, with his arms in the position of one playing the lyre. The lost original has been plausibly, if not quite certainly, identified with the statue of Anacreon in the posture of "a man singing in a state of intoxication" seen by Pausanias (1.25.1) on the Athenian Acropolis; it stood next to a statue of Perikles' father, Xanthippos.

31. *Anacreon*(?): besides the Attic vases inscribed with Anacreon's name (above, nos. **27–29**), some thirty other vases have been thought to show figures identifiable with Anacreon on the ground of their resemblance to the inscribed representations (the "Maenad dress," mentioned under no. **28**, above, has been an important, but perhaps not very safe, criterion here). All but one of them are later than Anacreon's death (ca. 487 B.C.); see Webster (1972), pp. 54–55, Snyder (1974), and Slater (1978).

32. *Cydias* (for whom see frr. 714–15 *PMG*): London, British Museum, psykter, ARV^2, p. 31, no. 6 (Dikaios Painter), Webster (1972), pp. 53–54. A bald-headed, bearded man, inscribed as *Kydias*, is playing the lyre as he takes part in an energetic *kōmos*. The vase is dated by Webster to ca. 510 B.C.

33. *Cydias*: Munich, kylix, ARV^2, p. 173, no. 2 (Ambrosios Painter), Webster (1972), pp. 53–54. Again a *kōmos*, in which a youthful oboist inscribed as *Kydias* is seen between a castanet player and a lyre player. [Either nos. **32** and **33** refer to different individuals or, as Webster observes, "one of these painters did not know what Kydias looked like."] The vase is dated by Webster to ca. 510 B.C.

Appendix VI

Texts in Archaic and Classical Times, Down to the Beginning of the Peloponnesian War

This appendix has the strictly limited aim of documenting certain statements made in Chapter 2 (especially on pp. 45–46) concerning the existence of book texts in the archaic and earlier classical periods and the locations in which they seem normally to have been preserved. I do not attempt to deal with the complicated and obscure question of textual transmission in that era, and I have not included the testimonia concerning the "Peisistratean recension" of Homer and related problems (see Davison [1955] and [1962, *Comp.*], p. 220) in which I, for my part, have searched for light in vain. I have also omitted most of the testimonia that relate to the Peloponnesian War period and the fourth century, when our information about the existence and circulation of book texts becomes relatively much more abundant (see Turner [1952] and [1975]).

A: Sanctuaries as Repositories of Texts

1. Pausanias 9.31.4: "The Boeotians who dwell around Helikon say that there is a traditional belief that Hesiod composed no other poem than the *Works*. Even of this, they treat the proem as spurious, saying that the passage about the two Strifes is the beginning of the poem; and they showed me a piece of lead where the spring [Hippokrene] is, to a great extent ruined by time, and on it is written the *Works*." [On this problematical document, cf. West (1978), p. 137.]
2. *Certamen Homeri et Hesiodi*, ed. Allen in the OCT of Homer, vol. V, p. 237, lines 319–21: Homer recites the Hymn to Apollo at the panegyris at Delos, whereon "the Delians wrote the verses on a white board, and dedicated them in the temple of Artemis."
3. Diogenes Laertius 9.6, on Heraclitus's book: "and he dedicated it in the temple of Artemis." [It is natural to assume that the shrine

concerned was the famous Artemisium in Heraclitus's native city, Ephesus.]

4. Gorgon *ap*. schol. Pindar, *Ol*. 7 *init*. (Drachmann vol. I, p. 195.13–14): "Gorgon says that this ode is laid up as a dedication in the temple of the Lindian Athena, in golden letters." [Gorgon was a Rhodian historian, perhaps of the first century B.C.]
5. Pausanias 9.16.1: "Pindar also sent off to the Ammonians of Libya a hymn to Ammon; and even until my day this hymn existed on a triangular stele, by the altar which Ptolemy son of Lagos dedicated to Ammon." [Pausanias is describing the temple of Ammon in Boeotian Thebes. Considering the circumstances, one would imagine that the inscribed stele as well as the altar was likely to date from the period of Ptolemy I.]
6. (?) Choeroboscus, commentary on Hephaestion 13.4: on an anonymous lyric line (fr. 1031 *PMG*) cited by Hephaestion: "The present example is from the so-called *Delphika*, which do not have the poet's name." [Wilamowitz (1900), p. 38 with note 3, inferred from this, perhaps rather adventurously, the existence of an archive of poems at Delphi. Compare the end of the note on the following item.]
7. *Inscriptions de Délos 1400–1496*, ed. Félix Durrbach and Pierre Roussel (Paris 1935) no. 1400, line 7, and no. 1409 Ba II, line 39: "A triangular box containing books (*byblia*) of Alcaeus." [The wording is identical in both the inscriptions cited, which are inventories, datable to some year not long after 166 B.C., of the Building of the Andrians on Delos. It may be noted in this connection that Wilamowitz (1900), pp. 38–39, with note 4, inferred the existence of an archive of poems in the Delian sanctuary from a combination of several passages in Pausanias and from an obscure clause in Strabo 15.3.2, "as Simonides has said *en Memnoni dithyrambōi tōn Dēliakōn*." He himself, however, subsequently felt doubts, which the rest of us may well share: see Pickard-Cambridge, *DTC*², p. 17, n. 1.]
8. The *Archilocheion* on Paros (see, e.g., Kontoleon [1964]) may deserve a mention in this place. This shrine, with its inscribed memorials of Archilochus's life and poetry, is, as we have it, clearly the product of Hellenistic antiquarianism, having been constructed from the mid third century B.C. onward; yet it may suggest the possibility that here, and in other home cities of famous Greek poets, the poets'

texts may have been preserved from a much earlier date. Already in the fourth century B.C. Aristotle remarks (*Rhet.* 2.1398b) how honors are paid to Archilochus in Paros, to Homer in Chios, and to Sappho in Mitylene.

B: Texts in Family Archives

9. Plato, *Critias* 113a–b: Critias tells how he has heard from his grandfather of the same name, who in turn heard from *his* grandfather Dropides (a kinsman and friend of Solon, cf. *Timaeus* 20e), that Solon had inquired about the meaning of the names in the story told by the Egyptians, "meaning to make use of it for his own poetry." Solon then "turned the meaning into our own language and committed it to writing (*apegrapheto*). These writings (*grammata*) remained with my grandfather and still remain with me at this time; and I have given them careful study in my boyhood." [Cf. above, Chapter 2, p. 46, with note 12.]
10. Plutarch, *Lycurgus* 4.4: the Spartan lawgiver travels in Asia Minor, "and there, it seems, he first met with the poems of Homer, which were being preserved by the descendants of Kreophylos . . . and he eagerly wrote them down and assembled them, in order to bring them to Greece." [Kreophylos was supposed to have been a *xenos* of Homer's; cf. Callimachus, *Epigram* 7, Strabo 14.638, etc. For many reasons, the tradition here recorded by Plutarch is most unlikely to be accurate in itself; but it could incorporate a memory of the general conditions under which poems were preserved in the archaic period.]

C: Schoolteachers' Collections of Texts

Most of the passages given here refer, in fact, to the late fifth century or even to the fourth century. The vase-paintings, however, show that poetic texts were to be found in Athenian classrooms from at least as early as ca. 490; see Beazley (1948) for examples, of which the most notable are the famous "school cup" by Douris in Berlin (Boardman [1975], fig. 289) and the lekythos in the Seyrig collection (Beazley [1948], pl. XXXIV), on which a seated boy holds a papyrus roll inscribed with the first two words of the eighteenth Homeric Hymn.

On the conditions in the early schools in general, cf. Marrou (1965), pp. 81–83.

11. Plato, *Protagoras* 325e–326b: "And when they [the children] have learnt their letters (*grammata*), and are ready to understand written works (*ta gegrammena*) just as in the earlier stage they understood the spoken word, the schoolmasters put beside them on their benches the poems of good poets to read aloud (*anagignōskein*) and compel them to learn them by heart. In these poems are many counsels, and many stories, and praises and panegyrics of the noble men of old, so that the child may admire them and imitate them and may be eager to become like them. The lyre teachers follow much the same practice. . . . When the children have learnt to play the lyre, they teach them the poems of yet other good poets, namely, the lyricists, accompanying them with the lyre, and making the rhythms and tunes [or 'modes': *harmonias*] familiar to the minds of the children." [It will be noted that although Protagoras's account of the schoolmasters' work emphasizes the use of written texts—apparently of many different kinds of poem—there is not a word about written materials in his description of the lyre teaching; the implication surely is that written scores were not in use. Aristophanes' account of lyre teaching under the regime of the Old Education (*Clouds* 964–71) similarly gives the impression that musical instruction was purely a matter of ear and memory.]
12. Plato, *Laws* 7.810e–811a: the Athenian is speaking: "Now I tell you that we have many poets in hexameter verse, and in trimeters, and in fact in all the meters that are uttered, some of them aiming at seriousness and others at laughter. Thousands upon thousands of people say that those of the young who are rightly educated must be nourished, and indeed sated, with these poets: that we must make them listen much to readings of them (*polyēkoous en tais anagnōsesin*) and acquire great erudition in them, learning whole poets by heart. And there are people who select the most important passages from all the poets, and gather certain entire speeches (*rhēseis*) into a single collection, and maintain that we must make [the pupils] learn them by heart and store them in their memories."
13. Xenophon, *Symposium* 4.27: Charmides reproaches Socrates for discouraging his friends from associating with handsome boys: "But I have seen you yourself at the schoolmaster's (*grammatistēs*) when

you and Kritoboulos were searching for something in the same book, head to head and bare shoulder to bare shoulder."

14. Plutarch, *Regum et Imperatorum Apophthegmata* 186D: Alcibiades "went to a school and asked for a canto (*rhapsōidia*) of the *Iliad*. The schoolteacher said that he had nothing by Homer, whereupon Alcibiades gave him a punch and moved on."
15. Alexis, *Linus*, *ap.* Athenaeus 4.164b–d (= fr. 135K), lines 1–7: one of the great educators of Greek myth, Linus, is examining his new pupil, Herakles, and in order to find out his interests tells him to choose a book: "Go on, take any book you like from here, and then you shall read it aloud (*anagnōsei*); look around, calmly and at your leisure, telling them from the titles. Orpheus is in the collection, and Hesiod, and tragedies, and Choerilus, and Homer, and Epicharmus, and treatises of every kind." [Since the play belongs to the Middle Comedy and the pupil is Herakles, we are not surprised that the hero finally selects a cookbook.]

D: The "Sending" of Lyric Poems

See Appendix IV, section G, for the instances. It seems likely that in most, if not all, of them a written text of the poem concerned was involved.

E: Miscellaneous

16. Herodotus 5.90.2 and 7.6.3, taken in combination, show that the Peisistratid family possessed a collection of written oracles by the end of their reign. The former passage describes how the family owned certain anti-Spartan oracles, of which the Spartans were ignorant until King Kleomenes brought them home with him: "and Kleomenes acquired these oracles from the Acropolis of the Athenians; the Peisistratids had formerly possessed them, but on being expelled they left them in the temple." The latter passage describes the journey of the Peisistratids to Sousa at the beginning of Xerxes' reign: "they took with them Onomacritus, an Athenian oracle-expert (*chrēsmologos*) and the arranger (*diathetēs*) of the oracles of Musaeus, having first ended their enmity with him; Onomacritus had been expelled by Hipparchos the son of Peisistratos, because he had

been caught red-handed by Lasus of Hermione in the act of interpolating into the Musaeus collection an oracle that said that the islands off Lemnos would vanish under the sea." [It is difficult to decide how far this evidence of a library—and even of editorial activity—on the Peisistratid Acropolis was responsible for the later stories concerning Peisistratos's collection of books and recension of Homer. On them see Davison, cited in the preliminary note to this appendix.]

The following two references to archaic poetic texts are included for the sake of completeness; neither seems particularly trustworthy.

17. Ptolemaeus Hephaestion *ap*. Photius, *Bibliotheca*, codex 190, 151a, ed. Henry: "the *Kolymbōsai* of Alcman (cf. fr. 158 *PMG*) were found at the head of Tynnichos [?—the name is conjecturally restored]" after his death.
18. Valerius Maximus 6.3. ext. 1: "The Lacedaemonians ordered the books of Archilochus to be expelled from their city, because they considered the reading of them to involve too much immodesty and indecency."

Appendix VII

Re-performances of Nondramatic Poetry

A: Evidence for Re-Performances Probably or Certainly Earlier than ca. 300 B.C.

For rhapsodic re-performances, see Appendix II.

(i) *Sparta*

1. Athenaeus 14.632f: a general statement on the Spartans' devotion "even now" to their ancient music and songs, quoted above, Chapter 2, p. 48.
2. Plato, *Laws* 1.629b: the Athenian begins to discuss a poem by Tyrtaeus (fr. 12W) and remarks to the Cretan: "I imagine that you, too, have heard these poems; for our friend here [the Spartan] must be saturated in them, I should think." The Spartan agrees, and the Cretan adds: "Yes, they have reached us Cretans too, having been brought from Sparta."
3. Lycurgus, *In Leocratem* 107, on the contemporary Spartan custom of reciting Tyrtaeus's poems on campaign: quoted above, Chapter 1, p. 33.
4. Philochorus, *ap.* Athenaeus 14.630f, on the Spartan contests in reciting Tyrtaeus when on campaign: quoted above, Chapter 1, p. 33.
5. Athenaeus 14.630f, immediately before no. 4, but without reference to any source: "The Spartans themselves in their wars recite the poems of Tyrtaeus from memory, moving in time with them."
6. Sosibius, *ap.* Athenaeus 15.678b–c (= *FGrH* 595 Sosibios, fr. 5), on performances of Thaletas, Alcman, and Dionysodotos at the Gymnopaidiai, quoted above, Chapter 1, p. 25.
7. Plutarch, *Lycurgus* 28.4–5, on the Spartans' harsh treatment of the helots: "and they used to order them to sing odes, and to dance dances, which were ignoble and ridiculous, but to abstain from the odes and dances of the free men. Hence they say that at a later time, during the Theban expedition into Laconia, the helots who were taken captive, being told to sing the poems of Terpander, Alcman,

and Spendon the Laconian, said that their masters would not allow it." [The three Theban incursions into Laconia took place between 370 and 367. The implication of the story is clearly that the works of the three poets named were regularly re-performed by free Spartans at that period.]

(ii) *Fifth-Century Athenian Symposia*

See Appendix V, no. **12**, for the skolia songbook preserved by Athenaeus. From that source, from the vase-paintings, and from the playwrights of the Old Comedy we learn that among the works re-performed in the symposia were:

Alcman; see App. IV, no. **18**.

Sappho(?); see App. V, no. **13**.

Alcaeus; see App. V, nos. **11** and **12**.

Stesichorus; see App. IV, no. **18**.

Theognidea; see App. V, nos. **16–19**.

Anacreon; see App. V, no. **11**.

Unidentified monodic lyric; see App. V, no. **20**.

Simonides; see App. IV, nos. **17** (an epinician) and **18**; and App. V, no. **12** (not certain).

Praxilla; see App. V, no. **12** (two instances).

(iii) *Elsewhere*

8. Plato, *Ion* 534b: mention is made of the only important poem composed by Tynnichus of Chalcis (datable not later than the lifetime of Aeschylus, and probably much earlier): "that paean which everybody sings, which is perhaps the finest of all songs."
9. Eupolis, *ap.* Athenaeus 1.3a (= fr. 366K) "says that the works of Pindar are already consigned to silence (*katasesigasmena*) because of most men's failure to appreciate beauty." [Eupolis's career as a playwright began in 429 B.C. and ended about 412. The reference may well have been to re-performance in symposia (cf. Eupolis's fragment cited in Appendix IV, no. 18); that Pindar's music continued to be known to professional musicians is clear from Aristoxenus, below, no. 17.]

B: Select Examples of Re-performances later than ca. 300 B.C.

10. For the re-performances of Timotheus's poems in the Hellenistic period, see above, Chapter 7, p. 151, with note 2.
11. Polybius 4.20.8: "It is a fact known and familiar to everyone that the Arcadians are almost alone in having their children trained from infancy, by law, to sing the hymns and paeans with which each community honors the local heroes and gods according to ancestral custom. After that the children learn the nomes of Philoxenus and Timotheus and dance them with much competitiveness each year for the Dionysiac oboists in the theaters; the boys compete in the boys' contests and the young men in what they call the men's. Similarly throughout their lives they entertain themselves at their parties not by bringing in outsiders to sing for them but from their own resources, calling on one another to sing in turn." [To judge by this account of Arcadian customs in the second century B.C., the people of that remote and rather backward area still retained some of the practices of the song-culture era, which had disappeared from most other Greek communities in the course of the fourth century.]

C: Fifth- to Fourth-Century Passages Indicating the Writers' Familiarity with Earlier Greek Music

12. Glaucus of Rhegium *ap.* ps.-Plutarch, *De Musica* 1133f: "That the *Harmatios Nomos* is the work of Olympus, one might learn from Glaucus's treatise on the ancient poets; and one might further discover that Stesichorus of Himera imitated neither Orpheus nor Terpander nor Archilochus nor Thaletas, but Olympus, since he [Stesichorus] used the *Harmatios Nomos* and the dactylic species of rhythm." [Olympus is universally put at or near the beginning of the recorded history of Greek music in the ancient sources; he may have lived in the eighth century B.C. Glaucus of Rhegium seems to have worked at the turn of the fifth and fourth centuries; see *OCD*[2] *s.v.*, no. 5.]
13. Glaucus of Rhegium *ap.* ps.-Plutarch, *De Musica* 1134d–e: "Glaucus, who says that Thaletas was later than Archilochus, asserts that

he [Thaletas] imitated the songs of Archilochus, but that he increased the length, and incorporated the paeon and the cretic rhythm into his musical compositions. Archilochus had not used these rhythms, nor had Orpheus or Terpander; it was from Olympus's oboe music, they say, that Thaletas developed them, thus becoming known as a fine composer."

14. Plato, *Laws* 7.798d–803b, contains a discussion of the music and dance to be prescribed for the city. At 802a the Athenian says: "We must make the following arrangements for songs and dances. There exist many fine ancient compositions (*poiēmata*) in music by the men of old, and likewise dances for the body; there will be no objection to our selecting from these anything that it is fitting and suitable for the city we are establishing."
15. Aristotle, *Politics* 8.1340a, on the effect of music on our character: "That we are in fact disposed one way or another [by music] is clear from many cases, and particularly from the melodies of Olympus. Everybody agrees that these make our souls ecstatic (*enthousiastikas*)."
16. Aristoxenus *ap.* ps.-Plutarch, *De Musica* 1142b–c (= fr. 76 Wehrli), on his contemporary Telesias's essays in musical composition first in the style of Pindar and later in the style of the New Music: quoted above, Chapter 2, pp. 48–49. [Aristoxenus was a pupil of Aristotle, and wrote in the second half of the fourth century B.C.]
17. Aristoxenus *ap.* ps.-Plutarch, *De Musica* 1134f–1135a (= fr. 83 Wehrli): "Olympus, as Aristoxenus says, is thought by the students of music to have been the inventor of the enharmonic genus, since all music before him was diatonic and chromatic. . . ." [There follows a long technical description of the manner in which Olympus was thought probably to have made his discovery, working from the diatonic genus.]

Appendix VIII

Nondramatic Poems Apparently Composed for Two or More Voices

1. Sappho fr. 114 *PLF* and Campbell (1982), dialogue between a bride and Maidenhood; discussed above, Chapter 2, p. 56.
2. Sappho fr. 140a *PLF* and Campbell (1982), dialogue between some girls and Aphrodite; discussed above, Chapter 2, pp. 56–57.
3. Sappho frr. 104a, 105a, 105c *PLF* and Campbell (1982), hexameter fragments of an epithalamion or epithalamia; Page (1955), pp. 121–22 tentatively raises the possibility that they may "come from a composition similar to the sixty-second poem of Catullus, in which some of them are imitated, a dialogue between a choir of young men and a choir of young women at the ceremonial banquet." The conjecture is attractive but, as Page notes, cannot be shown to be correct on the evidence we have.
4. Sappho fr. 137 *PLF* and Campbell (1982) is alleged by Stephanus, the Byzantine commentator on Aristotle, to represent a dialogue between a wooer and a girl. The case seems possible; see Page's discussion (1955), pp. 106–9 (as he there remarks, the lovers' dialogue in Horace, *Odes* 3.9 might have had a precedent in Lesbian lyric).
5. *Carmina popularia* fr. 870 *PMG*: Plutarch's description of the three choruses at Sparta, consisting severally of old men, mature men, and boys, each group chanting an iambic line appropriate to its time of life. The performance was also known to the historian of Spartan poetry and antiquities Sosibius (see Page's testimonia to this fragment); cf. also above, Chapter 1, p. 25. A passage in Pollux (4.107) attributes a similar triple chorus to Tyrtaeus.
6. Bacchylides, *carm.* 18 Sn., the dithyramb *Theseus*; the four stanzas of this monostrophic poem are to be sung alternately by a chorus impersonating Athenians and a singer impersonating Aegeus. The only nondramatic Greek poem remotely resembling this that I can find is no. 2, above (Sappho); there also a group (impersonating Nymphs?) addresses and is answered by the impersonator of a

mythological character (Aphrodite). There are, of course, many comparable scenes in Attic tragedy, e.g., Aeschylus, *Persians* 908–1077. It seems impossible on our evidence to decide whether Bacchylides 18 continues a much older tradition of lyric composition (of which the only other trace would be the Sappho fragment) or whether the poet has here been influenced by the already fairly mature art of tragedy (for a possible instance of this, see Snell-Maehler, p. XXII, citing D. S. Robertson).

7. *Carmina popularia*, fr. 879(1) *PMG*: a ritual song at the Lenaia festival, with speeches divided between a *daidouchos* and the bystanders.
8. *Carmina popularia*, fr. 879(2) *PMG*: a libation song, divided between (apparently) one speaker and the rest of the company present.
9. For the sake of completeness we may add certain children's songs, recorded by Pollux: frr. 875 *PMG*, 876a, 876c. They cannot be exactly dated, but the simplicity and elegance of the meter and even the diction might suggest that they are pre-Hellenistic.

Appendix IX

Passages Illustrating Ancient Views on the Relationship Between Tragedy and Nontragic Poetry

A: The Playwright as *Poiētes*:

The most notable ancient passages in which the tragedian is ranked firmly among the *poiētai* are referred to above, Chapter 4, p. 81, and Chapter 5, pp. 104–5. Many further instances could be added from all periods of antiquity, but to detail them would add enormously, and unnecessarily, to the length of this appendix. It may suffice to mention that I have found not a single passage in which the tragedian *in the exercise of his craft* is described as priest, shaman, or cultist of any kind.

B. Homer and Tragedy

Most of the relevant passages have been discussed above, Chapter 6; here, for convenience, I assemble the references to them, and add some further instances.

1. Aristotle, *Poetics*, passim; see the discussions in Chapter 6, pp. 133–35 and 141. Aristotle's examination of the relationship between Homeric epic and tragedy is by far the most comprehensive that antiquity has left us. The general idea, however, was by no means new when he wrote the *Poetics*, as nos. 2 to 8 will illustrate.
2. Plato, *Republic* 10.595b–c: "I have to speak my mind, even though I am held back from speaking by a certain love and veneration for Homer which I have had since boyhood; he seems to have been the first trainer (*didaskalos*) and leader of all these glorious tragedians of ours."
3. Plato, *Republic* 10.598d–e: "Next, then, we must take a careful look at tragedy and its leader, Homer, since some people tell us that these men understand all arts and all human things that have to do with virtue and vice."
4. Plato, *Republic* 10.602b: the practitioner of a mimetic art knows little or nothing about the objects he represents, "and those who at-

tempt tragic poetry, both in iambics and in heroic verse, are representers par excellence."

5. Plato, *Republic* 10.605d–e: "You know that the very best of us, when we listen to Homer or some other of the tragic composers (*tragōidopoioi*) representing one of the heroes in his grief, declaiming a long speech of lamentation or even singing and beating his breast, feel pleasure and surrender ourselves, and we follow him with our sympathy and eagerness; and whoever best succeeds in putting us into that condition, him we praise as a good poet."
6. Plato, *Republic* 10.607a; quoted above, Chapter 5, p. 104.
7. Plato, *Theaetetus* 152e: all agree that the objects of sense perception cannot be described as "being," but as "becoming"; not only the philosophers, but also "the supreme masters in each of the two kinds of poetry: Epicharmus in comedy, Homer in tragedy."
8. Isocrates, *Ad Nicoclem* 48–49: quoted above, Chapter 5, p. 105.
9. Polemon of Athens *ap.* Diogenes Laertius 4.20, on Sophocles and Homer: quoted above, note 46 to Chapter 6. [This Polemon was head of the Academy from 313 to 270 B.C.]
10. Athenaeus 8.347c: Aeschylus's alleged remark about slices from the Homeric banquets: see above, Chapter 5, p. 104, with note 5; and note 55 to Chapter 6.
11. "*Commentarius in Melicos*," *POxy* no. 2506 (= fr. 217 *PMG*), on Homer, Hesiod, and Stesichorus in their relation to the tragic poets; see note 15 to Chapter 6.
12. British Museum, second-century B.C. relief of the "Apotheosis of Homer" by Archelaos of Priene, Richter (1965), vol. I, p. 54: Near the head of the procession of worshipers of Homer in the bottom register of the relief come "Poetry," "Tragedy," and "Comedy." Cf. Lesky, *TDH*[3], p. 48.
13. Euanthius, *De Fabula hoc est de Comoedia* 1.4–5 ed. G. Kaibel in his *Comicorum Graecorum Fragmenta*, vol. I, pp. 62–67: "Tragic subjects were invented long before comic. Although, therefore, as we unroll the pages of history back to the beginnings we find that Thespis was the first discoverer of tragedy, and although Eupolis, along with Cratinus and Aristophanes, is believed to have discovered the Old Comedy, yet after all Homer, that most generous fount of almost all the poetic art, provided the examples even for these poems, and as it were laid down a law in his own works; it can be shown that he composed his *Iliad* in the likeness of a tragedy, his

Odyssey to the pattern of a comedy." [Euanthius, who writes in Latin, is datable in the first half of the fourth century A.D.; see *Kleine Pauly*, *s.v.*]

C: Tragedy's Debt to Nondramatic Poetry in Music, Meter, etc.

See in general above, Chapter 5, especially pp. 105–111.

14. Aristophanes, *Birds* 745–51, on Phrynichus's apparent borrowings from songs to the Mountain Mother: above, p. 108.

15. Aristophanes, *Frogs* 1281–82, on Aeschylus's apparent borrowings from the kitharodic nome: above, pp. 107–8. Cf. also the following item:

16. Timachidas *ap.* schol. Aristophanes, *Frogs* 1282: "*From the kitharodic nomes*: Timachidas writes that [this is said] because Aeschylus used the Orthian or high-pitched nome." [For Timachidas of Lindos, see *OCD*², *s.v.*; he is datable ca. 100 B.C. In translating the passage, I have conjecturally emended the *anatetamenōs* of the manuscripts to *anatetamenōi*, taking the word to be an explanation of "Orthian."]

17. Psellus(?), *Peri Tragōidias*, lines 35–40, ed. Browning (1963): among the tragedians "it was Sophocles who first took to the Phrygian and Lydian modes. . . . Now the Lydian is more closely akin to the kitharodic fashion." [It is difficult to evaluate this item of information, as so much else in the treatise; for more detail see Browning's commentary. Even if the passage is correct in what it appears to say, however, it need not necessarily conflict with the evidence of Aristophanes, no. **15**; the reference there appears to be to the meters, not the mode, of Aeschylus's songs. Cf., further, Appendix III, no. **3**, with the note there.]

18. Aristophanes, *Frogs* 1296–97, the mysterious implication that Aeschylus has borrowed from Marathon and/or ropewinders: above, p. 107, with note 16.

19. Aristophanes, *Frogs* 849, the allegation that Euripides "collects Cretan monodies": see note 24 to Chapter 5.

20. Aristophanes, *Frogs* 1301–03, the allegation that Euripides garners his songs from a variety of vulgar and disreputable sources: above, p. 109, with note 24.

21. Ps.-Plutarch, *De Musica* 1140f–1141b, on Archilochus's practice "of speaking some iambics to instrumental accompaniment, but of singing others" and its application by the tragedians: see Appendix V, no. 7, for the passage in full.

22. Philodemus, *Peri Poiēmatōn* 2, fr. 29, p. 252, ed. Hausrath: "For the iambic poets compose tragically (*tragika poiousin*) and the tragic poets in turn iambically (*iambika*); and Sappho composes some poems in the iambic manner, Archilochus some not in the iambic manner. We should therefore not describe an iambic poet or a poet in any other genre as being such by nature (*physei*) but by convention (*nomōi*)."
23. Horace, *Ars Poetica* 79–82: "The rage of Archilochus armed him with the iambic meter appropriate to it; this foot was taken over by the comic slippers and by the magnificent *cothurni* of tragedy, suited as it was to the exchange of speeches, conqueror of the roar of the crowds, born for action." [This passage, like many in the *Ars Poetica*, has the air of standard Hellenistic doctrine, but no Greek source has so far been identified; cf. C. O. Brink's commentary on the poem, vol. II, p. 161.]
24. Aristoxenus *ap.* ps.-Plutarch, *De Musica* 1136c–d, on the tragedians' inheritance of the Mixolydian mode from Sappho: see above, pp. 109–110, with note 25.
25. Sch. Aeschylus, *Prometheus* 128a, ed. Herington, on the acquaintance between Anacreon and Aeschylus: see above, pp. 110–111, and Appendix X.
26. Athenaeus 14.630c–e, on certain affinities between choral and dramatic dancing: see Appendix IV, no. **19**.

Appendix X

Similarities Between the Meters of Anacreon and Aeschylus

A: Ionic-Anacreontic

In general, meters of the ionic variety are found throughout extant tragedy; it is a curious fact that the plays which make by far the most spectacular use of them fall at the beginning of the series and at the end, Aeschylus's *Persians* and *Suppliants* and Euripides' *Bacchae*. Fragment 14 (Snell) of Aeschylus's senior, Phrynichus, is also in ionics; it is not attributed to a specific play in the source, but if Crusius's fairly plausible attribution to the *Phoenissae* is right, this instance will antedate the *Persians*.

Pure ionic measures (of the form ⏑⏑––/⏑⏑––/. . .) are attested in Greek nontragic lyric from the earliest times; see, for instance, Alcman fr. 46 *PMG* (with Hephaestion's comment there) and Simonides fr. 543, lines 8 and 21. It is noteworthy that the fragments of Anacreon show a remarkably large number of pure ionic lines (e.g., frr. 351, 352, 409, 411b), but that would hardly be of much significance in itself for our present question. What does seem to be of significance is Anacreon's very extensive use of the line that was later named after him, the anaclastic ionic dimeter or "anacreontic," ⏑⏑–⏑–⏑––. Famous examples are the drinking-songs, frr. 356*a* (six straight anacreontics) and 356*b* (four anacr., one pure ion. dim.); and the song on approaching old age, fr. 395 (apparently in two stanzas, each consisting of four anacr., one ion. dim., and one anacr.). The other examples of the anacreontic line in his fragments (some not quite certain, for textual reasons) are at frr. 346.2, 5, 8, 10; 353; 354.2; 396; 397.2; 398.2; 399(?); 400; 401; 402*a* and *c*; 403.2; 404; and 405(?). Most of these fragments are quite short but, even so, in some of them the anacreontics are seen to be in juxtaposition with other kinds of line, often ionic dimeters.

This exceptionally catchy verse form (anacreontic lines, sung to the guitar, can still be heard with pleasure, as I have found by experiment) cannot be traced earlier than Anacreon; its employment in long runs cannot be paralleled elsewhere in archaic nondramatic poetry; and it is not even common as an isolated unit in that poetry (the only examples I can find occur in the informal songs, Bacchylides frr. 19 and 20A, and in the undated but presumably early fragment of a hymn to Aphrodite, *Carm. Pop.*, fr. 872.1 *PMG*). There seems much to be said for A. M. Dale's suggestion that this verse form was "possibly invented by" Anacreon (*Lyric Meters*, p. 121).

By contrast, tragic lyric, and notably Aeschylean lyric, shows very close parallels to Anacreon's usage. Phrynichus fr. 14, indeed, is not significant in this respect, since it consists merely of two ionic tetrameters catalectic (a measure that—if we can trust the Byzantine metrical writer, Trichas, cited by Snell ad loc.—Phrynichus "employed in many passages"). When we turn to Aeschylus, we find the following lyric passages composed wholly or partly in some variety of ionic:

Persians 65–114 (i.e., the first half of the *parodos* song); 649–50 = 654–55; 694–95* = 701–702.

Seven 321–22* = 333–34; 720–26 = 727–33.

Suppliants 165*; 840*; 869* = 879; 1018–61 (i.e., all of the *exodos* song except the final pair of stanzas).

Agamemnon 689–95 = 707–14; 744–47 = 757–60 (both in the "Helen ode").

Choephori 327–30 = 358–61; 790–91*; 807–8*, 827–29*.

Prometheus (?) 128–35 = 143–51; 397–405 = 406–14 [The meters of both passages are much disputed. Some interpret both as ionic-anacreontic, some as primarily choriambic. I am inclined toward the former view by two considerations: first, the close analogies with *Seven* 720–33, the ionic character of which cannot be doubted; second, the unconvincing colometry that results if one prints the *Prom.* passages as choriambics, as Page does in his *OCT.*]

Fragments (Mette) 103*, 104*, 337*, 472(?), 733*(?).

The starred passages in the above list are in pure, or almost pure, ionics; with the exception of fr. 103 (from the *Heliades*), they are very brief. *All* the other passages listed contain some admixture of anacreontics, and *Ag.* 689–95 = 707–14, *Cho.* 327–30 = 358–61, and the two *Prom.* passages show considerable runs of them; the longest unbroken runs—four anacreontics in a row—appearing in the *Cho.* passage and in the second of the *Prom.* passages.

I should perhaps add three footnotes to the above account, for the sake of completeness. First: I have left the poems attributed to Corinna out of consideration, since I am not yet convinced that they really belong to the archaic period (cf. C. P. Segal in *Eranos* 73 [1975], 1–8, for a good account of this problem); in any case, her long poem in ionic verse, fr. 654 *PMG*, contains no anacreontics. Second: although E. R. Dodds's theory (second edition of *Bacchae*, pp. 71–72) that the ionic meter is proper to Dionysiac cult hymns has certain obvious attractions, there is as yet no solid evidence for the existence of ionic hymns to Dionysos before the end of the fifth century, if then. Iacchos (*Frogs* 324–53, cited by Dodds) is Dionysos only in a very special aspect; and the Dionysiac Paean of Philodamos (also cited by Dodds) belongs to the late fourth century and is, in fact, predominantly glyconic. By contrast, the fragment of an ionic-anacreontic hymn in fr. 872 *PMG*, cited above, is a hymn to *Aphrodite*. Third: the only poem earlier than Anacreon that contains any element resembling the anacreontic line, so far as I know, is Sappho fr. 102, where the second half of each line is actually of the same quantitative pattern as an anacreontic. Page, however (1955, p. 320), is probably right in preferring a different analysis in this nonionic context.

B: Combinations of Glyconic and Pherecratean

Both the glyconic line (basic form ⏓⏓–⏑⏑–⏑–) and the pherecratean (⏓⏓–⏑⏑––) are attested from early times. There are already examples of the glyconic in Alcman (fr. 59*b*3; cf. fr. 161*c*, near end), Sappho (frr. 94, 96, 98), and Alcaeus (fr. 234); and of the pherecratean possibly in Alcman (frr. 38.2 and 100) and fairly certainly in Sappho. Thereafter we shall find isolated occurrences of each form in a good many archaic nondramatic poems: the glyconic, for instance, in Ibycus (fr. 321.3) and Simonides (fr. 542.15, 25, 35); the pherecratean in Simonides (fr. 542, in the penultimate line of the stanza). But it is Anacreon, so far as our record goes, who first systematically *combines* the two forms, building them (and them alone, without the admixture of any other kind of colon), into marvelously singable stanzas. The best-preserved examples are frr. 348, 357 through 362, and 373; the shorter frr. 363 through 371, and 374, may well come from similarly built poems. The commonest arrangement is a run of two, three, or even four (frr. 348, 357) straight glyconics, rounded off by a pherecratean clausula. In one fragment (373) Anacreon simply alternates glyconics and pherecrateans (in later times the combination glyc. + pher. was recognized as a specific colon and given the name *priapean*, but here the glyc. and pher. are separated by word end and must probably be felt as distinct cola). The corrupt fr. 371 probably contained two successive pherecrateans. Finally, it should be noted that Anacreon shows a strong tendency to make both the first two syllables of his glyconics and pherecrateans *long*, and of course admits no resolutions at any point; the result is a markedly firm and clearly articulated rhythm.

Once again, the only close parallels to these procedures, in all extant Greek poetry before the late fifth century, occur in the tragedies of Aeschylus and his successors. It is true that the two lyric poets who flourished in Aeschylus's lifetime, Pindar and Bacchylides, also make some use of glyconics and pherecrateans in various combinations, and occasionally in short runs (see Snell's Pindar, vol. II, pp. 168–73, and the Bacchylides of Snell-Maehler, pp. xxxii–iv, for the instances). But one has only to listen momentarily to, say, *Nem.* 2.1–5, or Bacchylides 2.4–5 = 9–10, to recognize the profound difference from either Anacreon or the tragic poets in this matter. The cola of the two choral lyricists are more often than not heavily resolved, and tend to flow into each other, without being marked off by word end or syntactical pause, to the extent that it is often difficult to recognize them for what they are.

In Aeschylus both cola are quite common in isolation from each other; the following list confines itself to those passages in him where pher. and glyc. predominate in various combinations:

Persians 568–72 = 576–80: three pher., glyc., aristophaneus (with interjections separating the first four cola from each other).

Suppliants 630–709: this hymn of benediction to the Argives contains six refrains (639–42, etc.), all in the form pher., pher., glyc. + pher. (the last two cola, in every refrain except the first, should properly be called priapeans, since they are not separated by word end). The wording is different in each refrain.

Agamemnon 367–487: this chorus contains six refrains (381–84, etc.), which metrically are the same as the refrains in *Suppliants* 630–709. 717–26 = 727–36: two glyc., pher.; then three lines which Page interprets as variants of pher.; then two resolved lecythia; finally glyc. + pher. (= priapean).

Choephori 608–11 = 619–22: glyc., pher., glyc., pher., all separated by word end.

Fr. 252M (*Phryges?*), lines 2–9: glyc., pher., glyc., pher. (all separated by word end), iambic dimeter, pher. + pher.

Fr. 474M (*Diktyoulkoi*) Silenus's song in lines 802–11 = 812–20: this is the longest and metrically the simplest of all such passages in Aeschylus, each stanza being composed almost entirely of glyc. and pher. (the solitary exception, the phalaecian in the third line of each, is in fact merely an extended variety of glyc.); all the cola are separated by word end. The scheme is two pher., phalaecian, three glyc., three pher.

One should also, perhaps, note the remarkable runs of six pure pherecrateans in *Persians* 584–89 = 591–96 and *Seven* 295–300 = 312–17; in both passages all the cola are separated by word end.

It may seem to other hearers besides myself that the resemblances between two such passages as those that I am about to quote are too strong to be explained by mere coincidence: that the composer of the second most likely had been influenced metrically by the composer of the first.

ὦ παῖ παρθένιον βλέπων,
δίζημαί σε, σὺ δ' οὐ κλύεις,
οὐκ εἰδὼς ὅτι τῆς ἐμῆς
ψυχῆς ἡνιοχεύεις (Anacreon fr. 360)

ἵξῃ παιδοτρόφους ἐμὰς
ὦ φίλος χέρας εὐμενής,
τέρψῃ δ' ἴκτισι καὶ νέβροις,
ὑστρίχων δ' ὀβρίχοισι (Aeschylus, *Diktyoulkoi*, fr. 474.806–9M)

Here, too, a footnote seems desirable. It has more than once been suggested that these rhythms, especially in the forms that they take in the refrains of *Suppliants* 630–709 and *Agamemnon* 367–487, were characteristic of ritual songs to various deities (Wilamowitz on *Herakles* 348ff., a chorus that contains a series of very similar refrains; Fraenkel, *Agamemnon*, vol. II, p. 186; Dodds on *Bacchae* 862–911, esp. 908–11). Some color is given to this theory by the apparent occurrence of one, or the other, or both measures in fr. 871.3 and (?)5 *PMG* (the Elean women's hymn to Dionysos), fr. 934.6, 15, 24 (the Erythraean paean to Asklepios), fr. 997 (nine lines on an epiphany of Apollo, entirely glyconic-pherecratean), and fr. 1029 (three glyconics, perhaps by the poet Glycon, concerning the death of Adonis). Lines 1 and 2 of fr. 882 (the herdsmen's begging song), lines 3 and 4 of fr. 892 (an Attic skolion), and possibly fr. 938*b* as restored (a vase inscription) might further suggest that these cola had a long history in popular, subliterary song. We thus cannot exclude the possibility that Anacreon himself was influenced by ritual or popular models in devising his glyconic-pherecratean songs.

C: Conclusion

In the fragmentary state of our evidence, both for early Greek lyric and for Attic tragedy, one must concede that absolute proof of Anacreon's direct influence on the formation of tragic lyric (and Aeschylean lyric in particular) can scarcely be hoped for. To the present writer, however, it seems that the metrical facts adduced in section A of this appendix quite strongly support this supposition, and those adduced in section B only slightly less so. In connection with them we have also to bear in mind the evidence (discussed earlier in this book) for Anacreon's presence in Athens during the formative period of tragedy, and the evidence of the scholium on *Prometheus* 128.

The possibility might be worth considering that certain other metrical patterns which seem to have been either first developed, or first brought to a fine art, by Anacreon may also have directly influenced Greek tragedy. I refer in particular to trochaic dimeters (Anacr. fr. 347, cf. 422 and, in part, 417; and *Prom.* 415–17 = 420–22) and choriambic-iambic measures (Anacr. frr. 382–89; and many Aeschylean passages, e.g., *Agam.* 218–27 = 228–37). But here certainty would be much harder to attain on the evidence we have.

Notes

1. Poetry as a Performing Art

[1]The quotation is from Sharp (1932), p. xxv. For a recent general survey of oral cultures, see Finnegan (1977).

[2]A general bibliography on the subject of this section, with select ancient testimonia, will be found in Appendix I.

[3]Surviving samples of such purely *ritual* songs are to be found in *PMG* (*Carm. pop.*) frr. 854–55, 862, 868, 871, 879; add the Cretan song for Diktaian Zeus, for example, as edited by Wilamowitz (1921), pp. 499–502.

[4]The distinction here drawn between strictly religious ritual on the one hand, and artistic or athletic activities more or less loosely attached to a god's festival on the other, will be familiar enough to any student of the Greek cults; compare, for example, Nilsson (1906), pp. v and 159. It seems worth emphasizing once again, however, since it has been so often completely ignored in discussions of the dramatic contests at the Great Dionysia.

[5]For a survey of the meanings and applications of the word *agalma*, see Bloesch (1943).

[6]Records of the musical-poetic contests were certainly kept at Delphi from early times; they must underlie, for instance, at least some parts of Pausanias's account, 10.7.2–7 (the earliest specific date there cited is 582 B.C.). Equally, the now-lost *Karneonikai* of Hellanicus (Athenaeus 14.635e), which included victors as far back as Terpander, must have been based on some kind of official archive. The antiquity of the list (*anagraphē*) of poets preserved at Sikyon is uncertain; but it cannot be later than the sophistic period (Jacoby, *FGrH* vol. IIIb, pp. 476–7) and could be much earlier, so far as the scanty evidence goes (ps. Plut. *Mus.* 1131f and 1134b; cf. Lanata [1963], pp. 282–83). Another such record may have been the "Panathenaic *graphē* concerning the musical contest" (ps. Plut. *Mus.* 1134a, the sole mention), but this is much less certain; for an alternative view, see Davison (1958), pp. 39–40.

[7]"Set up their gathering" is perhaps the more likely translation of *stēsōntai agōna* in line 150, but I do not think that we can absolutely exclude the meaning "set up their contest"; compare the survey of the history of the word *agōn* in Duchemin (1945), pp. 11–12.

[8]This passage, the only surviving fragment of Polykrates (no. 588 in Jacoby, *FGrH*, vol. IIIb), was quoted from his *Lakonika* by Didymus, who is in turn

preserved by Athenaeus, 4.139d–f. Of Polykrates' date all that can be said is that he probably belonged to the Hellenistic period, and presumably wrote before the *floruit* of Didymus (ca. 40 B.C.). Even if he lived relatively late in the Hellenistic period, however, Sparta's ritual and musical conservatism was such that he could well have witnessed a celebration of the Hyakinthia in much the same form that it would have had in classical times. The attempt by Farnell (1896–1909), vol. IV, pp. 264–66, to challenge the veracity of his account—at least in regard to the number of days occupied by the celebration—does not seem to rest on clear enough evidence.

[9] I have not translated the words πρὸς αὐλὸν ᾄδοντες, which occur at this point in the transmitted text of Athenaeus (vol. I in Kaibel's edition, p. 316, lines 20–21): they seem to be corrupt or interpolated, since they conflict with the mentions of *lyres* in the earlier part of the sentence. Wilamowitz's conjecture πρόσοδον ᾄδοντες is ingenious, but this theatral setting does not seem to be the right context for a *prosodos*-song.

[10] It is sometimes forgotten that the word and concept *theatron* was by no means associated only with the drama; quite possibly, indeed, it antedated the drama. Herodotus (6.67.3) uses it to describe the site of another Spartan festival-performance, the Gymnopaidiai, with reference to an incident which took place about 491 B.C. (cf. also Plutarch, *Agesilaos* 29, with reference to an incident in 371 B.C. at the same festival).

[11] Athenaeus's text is very doubtful here: in translating, I adopt Kaibel's guess (ed. Athen., vol. I, p. 317).

[12] The sacrifices, followed by a general banquet, which concluded the second day can hardly be counted as a strictly ritual element. They fall rather into that category of sacrifice which was really a kind of butchery in religious disguise, for which see Parke (1977), p. 19. We have no information about the events of the third day.

[13] Sporadically, the poetic events also included *aulody*, or solo singing to another performer's oboe accompaniment. Little is known about this kind of performance, which in any case seems to have been less popular than the others. At Delphi, it was dropped from the program within a few years of its introduction (Pausanias 10.7.5, cf. Appendix I). At the Panathenaia, where it was included at least by the time of the prize inscription *IG* II^2 2311 (first half of the fourth century B.C.), the aulodes rated fewer and much less valuable prizes than did the kitharodes; see that inscription, and also Parke (1977), p. 35.

[14] *Poet.* 1462a 6–7. The rhapsode Sosistratos is otherwise unknown, and our only clue to his date is the past tense here used by Aristotle, which suggests that he was no longer performing at the date of the *Poetics*.

[15] Similar alternations between *aidein* and a verb for "speaking" will be found in the allusions to rhapsodic recital at *Ion* 536b6–7 (*phtheggesthai*), 537a5 (*eipein*), *Timaeus* 21b–c (*legein*). In imperial-period Greek writers, it is true, *aidein* may lose the implication of singing or intoning (thus Lucian, *Herodotus seu Aetion* 1, where it is used of a recital of Herodotus's *Histories*!), but I can find no certain case of this in classical Attic. Aristophanes, *Clouds* 1371 (*aidein* with reference to a private recitation of a rhesis of Euripides) is a

possible exception, but this passage is problematic: for all we know, a tragic rhesis may well on occasion have been intoned in the rhapsodic manner rather than delivered as ordinary speech (the emendation to a part of *agein*, proposed by Borthwick and accepted by Dover [1968], *ad loc.*, seems rather venturesome for this reason). The scholium on Eur. *Hippol.* 58 (discussed by Lesky, *TDH*³, p. 40), where *aidein* and *legein* are both used of the same tragic passage, is probably too late in date to be of significance in this context. Most recently, West (1981), esp. pp. 113–115, has accounted for the problem by a quite different and very interesting line of argument.

[16]The dramatic date of the *Ion* cannot be exactly determined, but most would probably put it at some period during the Peloponnesian War. For a full discussion of the rather ambiguous data, see Flashar (1958), pp. 98–100; I find it difficult, however, to accept his conclusion that the dramatic date is 394 B.C., five years after the death of Socrates.

[17]Xenophon, *Symposium* 3.6, *Memorabilia* 4.2.10, both quoted in Appendix II.

[18]Many samples could be given from each of these fields, but here only a brief indication is possible. In metrics, we may cite the rapidly increasing freedom of Euripides' verse during the latter part of his career (cf. Webster [1967] passim, esp. pp. 2–3); for the breakdown of musical conventions during the same period, compare the Epilogue to the present volume; for the change to a freer acting style, see Ar. *Poet.* chap. 26, with the commentators; in the visual arts, one need only compare (e.g.) the Meidias or Reed Painters with the Achilles Painter, or the Nike balustrade with the Parthenon frieze.

[19]The last four sentences in this paragraph are based primarily on my own practical experience in the delivery of Homer aloud. For a *theoretical* inquiry which arrives at much the same results, the reader may consult Bölte (1907); largely through an analysis of metrical pauses and sense pauses in the Homeric speeches, he concludes (p. 581) that the chief characteristic of rhapsodic delivery was "strongly mimetic expression, which characterizes the persons themselves and their dispositions through the modulation of the voice and through the tone and tempo of the utterance." No one, of course, will deny that this kind of inquiry is in the last resort subjective. As an example of the opposite view one might cite the interesting work of Nutzhorn (1869), especially the chapter entitled "Die Unzulänglichkeit der Rhapsodenvorträge" (pp. 74–99); his view, in brief, is that the Homeric epics were not designed originally for such wild performances as those described in Plato's *Ion*, but for quiet readings in aristocratic family circles. Although I doubt if many people nowadays would be inclined to accept that result, Nutzhorn's able discussion of the evidence is still worth reading.

[20]Beazley, *ARV*², p. 183, no. 15: amphora with twisted handles, British Museum E270.

[21]The words are not found, in fact, anywhere in extant Greek poetry (do we have here the traces of a lost epic account of the deeds of Tydeus or Diomede, the lords of Tiryns?). The observation that for this reason the rhapsode shown on the vase cannot be competing at the Panathenaia (since we have express evi-

dence that the *Iliad* and *Odyssey* were the poems performed there) is due to Davison (1958), p. 37, n. 22. Davison's idea, however, that the words shown are not even metrical is refuted by Beazley, *ARV*², p. 1632.

[22] Very many examples of such walking sticks will be found on the vases of the ripe archaic period (that is, the period of the Kleophrades Painter). Here I may simply cite from the convenient anthology of pictures in Boardman (1975): figs. 33.2, 48.3, 51.2, 92, 125, 175, 234, 238, 239, 251.1–2, 254, 259–60, 264, 272, 289, 377, 379.2.

[23] So far I have been unable to find any vase painting, apart from the one under discussion, that quite certainly represents an epic rhapsode. Webster (1972), p. 171, cites two other putative representations: Beazley, *ABV* p. 386, n. 12, and *ARV*², p. 272, no. 7. Each shows a draped figure, carrying no staff, standing on a platform; there seems no way of deciding in either case whether we have to do with a rhapsode or (e.g.) a singer or an orator. Webster's suggestions (ibid., pp. 61 and 171) that the oboist on the reverse side of the Kleophrades Painter's vase may be accompanying the rhapsode's recital seems doubtful. First, there is no evidence elsewhere for oboe accompaniment to heroic verse; and second, the oboist, like the reciter, is mounted on a low platform, as if he were giving a solo performance in his own right.

[24] Hermes presents his new invention to Apollo toward the end of the poem (lines 464–96). The absolute date of the Homeric Hymn to Hermes cannot be fixed with any degree of exactness; most commentators agree on linguistic, and also partly on archaeological, grounds that it must come *relatively* late in the older group of Homeric Hymns, and some have even placed it in the fifth century B.C. For a recent summary of opinions see Càssola (1975), pp. 173–74.

[25] In line 427 the meaning of the word *krainōn* is debated; rather than leave a blank, I have accepted the most basic, sensuous meaning of the verb, translating "he wrought [*i.e.* in his song] the undying gods and the black Earth." This cannot be taken as certain, but perhaps is no more unlikely than the suggestions offered in LSJ, *s.v.*, II. Another Greek passage which evokes the moment when the lyre (but not the accompanying voice) was first heard on earth is Sophocles, *Ichneutai* 79–259; no doubt inspired by our Homeric Hymn, but very different, and in its own way no less magical.

[26] So Heraclides Ponticus *ap.* ps.-Plut. *Mus.* 1131f–1132a; for this and other ancient passages on the prehistory and early history of kitharody, see Appendix III.

[27] Arion's apparent need, even under the extraordinary circumstances, to put on his singing robes in order to perform may remind us of the attitude of the Appalachian cowherd cited at the beginning of the present chapter.

[28] Phillis of Delos (on whom see *RE*, vol. 19. col. 2430), *ap.* Athenaeus 1.21f. By "ancient," *archaious*, Phillis probably referred to the kitharodes who antedated the great revolution in the art of the latter half of the fifth century B.C.; cf. ps.-Plut. *Mus.* 1133b.

[29] Beazley, *ARV*², p. 197, no. 3: one-piece amphora, New York, Metropolitan Museum, 56.171.38. Beazley (1922) discusses the vase at length.

[30] For this practice in athletic contests, see Herodotus 8.59. There may per-

haps be an allusion to a similar practice in Aristophanes, *Frogs* 1024, where Dionysos, who is judging an *agōn mousikos* between Aeschylus and Euripides, says to the former, "for that, take a beating!" Are we to imagine Dionysos as carrying a judge's wand in this scene, and occasionally tapping the contestants with it? It should be noted, however, that Beazley (1922), p. 73, interprets the figure on the reverse of the New York amphora as a *trainer*, beating time to the kitharode's music.

[31] In this respect his equipment (and that of the other publicly performing kitharodes shown on the Attic vases) differs from the simpler lyre described in the fourth Homeric Hymn (47–54) and commonly seen in Attic symposium scenes, etc.

[32] There are many examples on the vases; two are figured by Holloway (1966), figs. 1–2. A detail in Herodotus's story of Arion (1.24.4–5) may imply that he (or his source) envisaged the early kitharodes, also, as performing on platforms: it is noteworthy that Arion stipulates that he should perform "standing on the poop-deck," while the audience of sailors is to withdraw into the waist of the ship. The use of platforms both by the rhapsodes and by the kitharodes may perhaps (as Professor Thomas Rosenmeyer has recently pointed out to me in correspondence) provide some support to those who argue for the existence of a low stage already in the sixth- and fifth-century dramatic performances.

[33] "The contests," presumably, would be those held at the Spartan Karneia (cf. Hellanicus *ap.* Athenaeus 14.635e) and at the Delphic Pythia (cf. ps.-Plut. *Mus.* 1132e, etc.).

[34] For other evidence to the effect that the Homeric poems were occasionally set to music by the early kitharodes, see Appendix III.

[35] One need here only recall the titles by which they were known in antiquity (see the edition of Stesichorus in *PMG*; e.g. *Geryoneis*, *Iliou Persis*, *Nostoi*), and Quintilian's famous judgement: (*Stesichorum*) *maxima bella et clarissimos canentem duces et epici carminis onera lyra sustinentem* (*Inst. Or.* 10.1.62).

[36] His *Oresteia* occupied at least two "books" in the Alexandrian scholars' texts (frr. 213, 214 *PMG*); and cf. West (1971), p. 302.

[37] West (1971); to which article the reader must be referred for the detailed arguments in favor of this hypothesis.

[38] There is considerable evidence that Stesichorus's poems, and perhaps his music also, were familiar to fifth-century Athenians; see the passages cited in *PMG* frr. 217 (Aeschylus's knowledge of him), 193 and 202 (Euripides), 210–12 (Aristophanes, in the *Peace*). One source of this familiarity might be the Athenian schoolmasters, but another might well be the kitharodic performances at the Panathenaia. I have not been able to verify the statement in Webster (1974), p. 103, that the vase paintings show that Stesichorus's work "was well known in Athens in the second half of the sixth century," since he does not give specific examples; presumably the reference is to vases showing themes known to have been treated by Stesichorus.

[39] By the end of Pindar's lifetime the traditional choral lyric poetry, as well as the traditional lyric music, were disintegrating fast. We know of only one

post-Pindaric epinician ode, that which Euripides composed for Alcibiades (frr. 755–56 *PMG*). The future lay with the New Music, and above all with the New Dithyramb; by the time that Aristotle was composing his *Poetics*, about 330 B.C., the dithyramb seems to have been the only kind of choral lyric that was still alive enough to deserve his notice in that work.

[40] Alcman's date remains uncertain, although ancient and modern authorities are generally agreed that he must have lived at some time within the seventh century B.C. In spite of a persistent rumor in the ancient sources that he was born at Sardis in Lydia, there can be no doubt that his working career was spent almost entirely at Sparta. The problems of his date and of his origin are discussed by Page (1951), appendices I and II respectively; the subsequently discovered papyrus evidence, published by Page in *PMG* frr. 10 and 13, is unfortunately not decisive for either of them.

[41] Alcman, second column of the fifth fragment of fr. 10 *PMG* (on p. 31): remains of a song in which a chorus leader named Hagesidamos is addressed in the vocative by a chorus which seems to describe him and another chorus leader as "young men who are of our own age and are our friends" (lines 16–17). It seems more likely that a Spartan chorus which so speaks will be composed of young men rather than of young women, although the matter is not certain. In Thebes, a couple of centuries later, a young man undoubtedly heads a chorus of girls in procession (*Partheneion* by Pindar, fr. 94b.66–70Sn.), and the unattached scrap of papyrus commentary published by Lobel in *POxy* Part XXVI (London 1961), p. 6 expressly states (on what authority we do not know) that some of the Pindaric *Partheneia* were performed by "mixed choruses of men and girls."

[42] Page (1951), pp. 2–3. He there remarks on the possibility that one column, only, has been lost from the Louvre papyrus of the poem before the extant column i; this would result in a poem consisting of ten stanzas in all, the transition from the heroic narrative to the chorus talk falling at what would then be the sixth stanza. As Page points out, there is no way of verifying this conjecture, but it is certainly attractive.

[43] Almost all the details of this sketch of *Partheneion* 1 are subject to learned dispute, and understandably. A dialogue among intimates, such as this poem is, is never easy for an outsider to interpret under the best of circumstances; and we are at the further disadvantage that this particular dialogue is wafted to our ears from a time and place, seventh-century Sparta, of which we have very little other knowledge. I have simply stated what seem to me the likeliest interpretations. Even if they should be incorrect in this feature or that—if, for example, the clothes and jewelry mentioned really belong to the rival chorus, or if (as some have thought) there is no rival chorus at all—that should not really affect the essential point that is being made here: the last five stanzas of the poem are a vivid dramatization of the circumstances in which it is being sung.

[44] Only a word or two is missing from the papyrus at this point, almost certainly in the genitive plural. We should probably, then, supply the name of the kind of bird whose "delicate wing" is mentioned in the preceding line.

[45] The exact sense of "the liquid charm of Kinyras" is uncertain (here again,

we have to remind ourselves that we are complete outsiders, briefly overhearing an intimate seventh-century conversation). The context, however, suggests that perfume of some sort is meant, and the name of Kinyras, the legendary king of Cyprus, suggests that the perfume is a Cyprian import.

[46] "Tongued" is the literal meaning of Alcman's epithet here, *geglōssamenon*, and I prefer to translate it literally because no one seems sure of the exact nuance intended. LSJ's "tuneful" seems to read more into the word than is actually there; did Alcman perhaps mean "articulate"?

[47] Fr. 40, it should be noted, comes to us without a context. We cannot know whether the first person in it is a dramatized Alcman, or a chorus; but the ultimate effect of the message will be the same in any case.

[48] There are further references to the lyre in frr. 41 and 140, and fr. 101 mentions another variety of stringed instrument, the *magadis* or psaltery.

[49] Again if we can trust the ancient sources of the fragments, Alcman's poetry contained a number of other passages in which he dramatized himself, but this time in various nonartistic capacities. His interest in girls qua girls was allegedly attested in frr. 34, 59a, 59b; his extravagant passion for eating and drinking, in frr. 92–94, 95a, 96. All these might conceivably have been misinterpreted by our sources, but in two further passages, frr. 17 and 95b, he mentions himself by name as possessing a gluttonous desire for hot soup and as organizing a dinner, respectively. How far all this was strictly autobiographical, how far a fictional dramatization, who can tell? Similar doubts have arisen, in ancient as well as in modern times, with regard to fr. 16, where somebody is addressed as having originated in "the heights of Sardis"; on this see Page (1951) p. 168 (where it is referred to by its number in Diehl's collection: fr. 13).

[50] Page re-edited the papyrus in *POxy* Part XXIX (London 1963), no. 2506. The authorship and even the general purport of the treatise remain doubtful, but it certainly dealt with various aspects of the lives and works of Alcman, Stesichorus, Sappho, and Alcaeus. In *PMG* the parts relating to Alcman are printed as fr. 10; the passage mentioned in my text will be found on p. 30 of *PMG*.

[51] Page holds, reasonably, that the very fragmentary line 29 must have had the sense of the words here given in parentheses.

[52] The gaps in the papyrus before and after the phrase "but not yet to engage in contests" (= lines 34–35), make it impossible to determine its syntactical relationship to the context.

[53] For *didaskein* and related words in connection with choral lyric and drama, see Appendix IV.

[54] Plutarch, *De Audiendo* 46b. Another ancient passage that describes a tragic rehearsal is Aristophanes, *Thesm.* 25–265, but here it is very doubtful whether the tragedian is actually "teaching" his chorus; see the discussion in Chap. 2, p. 47.

[55] See Jacoby, *FGrH*, vol. IIIb, no. 595 Sosibios; the fragment which concerns us here is fr. 5 (= Athenaeus 15.678b–c). I have followed Jacoby's somewhat skeptical account of Sosibius's nationality and date; for a more positive view, see G. L. Barber in *OCD*^{2}, *art.* Sosibius. There is some reason to suppose that

the festival described in this fragment, though concurrent with the Gymnopaidiai, is actually the Parparonia; see Jacoby's commentary.

[56] The phrase "on the right, old men" was supplied by Kaibel conjecturally, but with great probability. It is recommended not merely by the context in Sosibius, but also by the parallel account of a trio of Spartan choruses (complete with a quotation from their songs) printed in *PMG*, fr. 870; Sosibius is among the sources named for this, and it seems quite possible that the performance was identical with that described in the passage which we are now discussing. For the Cretan poet Thaletas, or Thales, see Edmonds (1928) vol. I, pp. 34–37; the ancient sources put him very early, and he has left no fragments. Of Dionysodotos, nothing seems to be known apart from this passage (Crusius in *RE s.v.* Dionysodotos, no. 2).

[57] This is by no means to say that Pindar does not dramatize himself; but he does so in his capacity of poet and sage, not of *didaskalos*. Cf. Lefkowitz (1963).

[58] *Pindarou apophthegmata*, p. 4, lines 3–5 Drachmann (vol. I). Similarly, schol. *Ol.* 6.148a and 149a Drachmann claim that Pindar employed a *chorodidaskalos* because he was "thin-voiced," *ischnophōnos*.

[59] The story is in fact rather difficult to reconcile with another story (in the ancient *Life of Pindar*, Drachmann, vol. I, p. 1, lines 11–15) to the effect that in early youth he was entrusted with the *didaskalia* of a dithyramb in Athens; this will be further discussed in Chap. 4, pp. 95–96.

[60] Dionysius of Halicarnassus, *De Demosthene* 39: the *Partheneia* alone do not display that *austēra harmonia* which otherwise characterizes Pindaric poetry.

[61] Bowra (1964), pp. 363–64: Lefkowitz (1963), pp. 190–92.

[62] Fr. 94bSn. = 84 Bowra; translation in Sandys (1919), pp. 568–75.

[63] This line (= line 14 in the Greek) is not easy to put into English. Literally it means "to the tune of lotus-wood oboelets"; I do not know whether the diminutive form *aul-iskos* here (a conjecture, but an almost certain one) merely expresses the singer's playful affection for the accompanying instrument, or whether it actually means some kind of miniature—and presumably high-pitched—oboe.

[64] I am not confident about our ability to identify these two persons by name: for proposals, see Sandys, p. 569, and Snell, vol. II, p. 92.

[65] *bainousa pedilois*, "marching with sandals," says the text, with devastating simplicity. It will not do to gloss over the strangeness of the phrase, as Sandys does, by translating "advancing with her feet" (by what other means *could* she advance?). Clearly the poet has some reason for stressing the presence of sandals; perhaps because of their ceremonial importance (cf. the passage from Proclus adduced by Slater [1969], *s.v.* pedilos)?

[66] I can see no certain reference to Pindar himself, in any capacity, in the second *Partheneion*. Lefkowitz (1963), in her discussion of this song (pp. 188–90), finds a mention of him at lines 56–58 Bowra (= 76–78 Sn.); but the correct restoration of this very fragmentary passage seems too doubtful to allow any certainty.

[67] *Paeans* 2 (Abderites) and 4 (Keians): cf. Lefkowitz (1963), pp. 186–87 and 183–84, respectively.

[68] I have searched the Pindaric scholia in vain for any information about the original performance or delivery of the odes that has even a prima facie claim to authenticity. The probability is that the Hellenistic scholars whose work, however mutilated and confused, underlies these notes, could themselves find no information of this kind; for there is evidence that some of them, at least, went to a great deal of trouble to discover any documents that might throw light on the circumstances of Pindar's work. They carefully consulted the victor lists at the great athletic festivals in order to establish a chronology for the epinician odes (cf., e.g., *Nem.* 7 inscr., *Nem.* 9 inscr., Drachmann). Similarly, as we now know, they checked the records of the dithyrambic contests at Athens (*POxy* no. 2438, lines 8–10). On occasion somebody even took the pains to seek out the victor's statue in the sanctuary concerned (*Ol.* 7, *Pyth.* 9, inscrr.). Where the victor happened to be a major historical figure in his own right, the appropriate literary sources were exploited (*Ol.* 2 inscr. and sch. on lines 15 and 16, for Theron of Acragas: *Ol.* 7 inscr., for Diagoras of Rhodes). When these, as it were, public sources failed them, even the most learned Alexandrians were reduced to disarray (see Aristarchus at sch. *Ol.* 3. 1a, or Eratosthenes at sch. *Ol.* 9. 1k). We must therefore conclude that neither oral tradition nor private sources such as family archives were available to them concerning the performance or delivery of a given song; our only recourse, in trying to reconstruct these matters, must be to analysis of the Pindaric texts themselves.

[69] Or a few years later, if one assumes that this passage could have been one of the parts of the *Clouds* that were rewritten for a revival (cf. Dover [1968] pp. lxxx–xcviii).

[70] We are probably safe in assuming that by this date Simonides would long have been incorporated in the curriculum of the Athenian music teachers. Other allusions to his songs in Old Comedy are: *Knights* 405–6 (a quotation, this time in the mouth of a chorus, from another epinician, fr. 512 *PMG*); and Eupolis, *Helots* fr. 139K. Compare also sch. *Wasps* 1222 for the performance of songs by Stesichorus and Simonides at dinner-parties.

Unfortunately no reliance can be placed on Cicero's statement (*De Oratore* 2.86) that Simonides in person was performing one of his own songs at dinner with Skopas on the notorious occasion when the roof fell in; see Page's collection and discussion of the various ancient versions of this anecdote in fr. 510 *PMG*.

[71] Not only the lengths of these odes, but also the locations and statuses (where known) of the addressees, may suggest that these were de luxe performances. Three of the addressees are Western Greeks (and of them, two are Sicilian dynasts); another is the famous Diagoras of Rhodes; in only one case, that of the otherwise unknown Aristokleides of Aegina (*Nem.* 3), have we no prima facie evidence for supposing that the addressee was unusually wealthy.

[72] This ode commemorates a victory in an oboe-playing competition, and the instrument is emphatically praised in lines 25–27. The oboe alone as an accom-

paniment is also mentioned once by Bacchylides (*Carm.* 2, a very short epinician ode for a fellow Keian).

[73] To bring out in English the full meaning of Pindar's Greek is one of the most difficult of tasks. Even at what we moderns should call its most metaphorical level, there is a kind of sensuousness in it that defies a language anaesthetized by centuries of dead metaphor. At the cost of clumsiness, I have here tried to bring that sensuousness out, but the cost may be worth paying. For instance, Pindar's phrase *chaitaisi . . . zeuchthentes epi stephanoi* is emasculated in the standard English prose translation to "the crowns that are about my hair"; the yoke is lost, and its weight, its tightness, the urgency of its reminder. I have at least tried to keep that yoke in place. But in truth, no translation will satisfy. "The lyre with her intricate voice" loses the iridescence inherent in Pindar's epithet *poikilogaryn*, and the simplicity of the noun which I have rendered "placing," *thesin*, defies our tired language. One thinks of bricklaying, or of the image used by a Roman poet: *lexis compostae ut tesserulae omnes / Arte pavimento* (Lucilius 84–85 Marx).

[74] In Bacchylides (4.7–8) the word is not certain, but is restored with much probability. His ode commemorates a victory of 470 B.C; *Ol.* 2 was occasioned by a victory of 476.

[75] Homeric Hymn 4 (Hermes) 480–81. Hermes offers the newly invented lyre to Apollo, that he may carry it "to the rich banquet, and the lovely *choros*, and the glorious *kōmos*." On the use of *kōmos* in Pindar's epinician odes, cf. Adrados (1975), pp. 38–39; I must admit that I cannot follow him in the conclusions that he there draws from it.

[76] Above, pp. 43–45. As will be seen there, I can find no certain example or mention of a musical score of any kind before the mid fourth century B.C.; and even thereafter the musical notation is so primitive that it could only serve as an aide-memoire to a performer already acquainted aurally with the music concerned.

[77] The two exceptions are *Ol.* 9, for a victor in Opous, and *Ol.* 14, for one in Orchomenos, both places being not more than forty miles from Thebes by the ancient roads. Perhaps we should also count as exceptions the four "overseas" odes that are destined for nearby Aegina. But in all such cases the explanation for such built-in directions on performance might be that Pindar was unable for some reason (travel abroad, for an important client? pressing business in Thebes?) to supervise the productions concerned in person. Somewhat comparable to Pindar's practice is the tragedians' practice of incorporating implicit "stage directions" in their poetic texts: cf. Loehrer (1927), pp. 23–25, Taplin (1977), pp. 28–31, 75–79. Here, however, the intention would be to provide not so much for the first production of the play in the Theater of Dionysos at Athens (which, presumably, the tragedian would normally direct in person), as for productions later, or elsewhere.

[78] *Pyth.* 5.103, *Pyth.* 10.6, and *Nem.* 3.4–5 (cf. 66) all seem to refer to singing voices in the *plural*, although in no case is it absolutely clear that those voices will sing in unison through the entire ode (cf. the following note). Cf. Bacchylides 6.6–9.

[79]Since the early nineteenth century scholars have occasionally advocated the theory that the delivery of the odes, or some of them, may have been divided between more than one singer; cf. Floyd (1965), on the eighth *Pythian*. This theory seems far from impossible, but I have discovered no passage in Pindar that quite certainly substantiates it (*pace* Floyd, whose case seems very interesting, but not compelling).

[80]*Od.* 8.256–65 (Demodokos and the Phaeacian dancers); compare *Od.* 4.17–19 (the bard and the two tumblers), and perhaps also *Il.* 18.604–605, although this case is less clear.

[81]The next step would have to be into pure fiction; any reader who cared to go that far might consult a story called "Song for Sale" in *Arion*, n.s. 2 (1975), pp. 92–95.

[82]This estimate is based on my repeated experience that Greek hexameter verse, delivered aloud at a fairly leisurely pace, runs at the rate of about ten lines to a minute; thus, for example, two separate performances of Hesiod's *Works and Days* were each found to occupy about one hour and twenty minutes. Most of the verse units employed in the poetry to be considered in the present section were either no longer than a hexameter line or considerably shorter. Even if we make all proper allowances for dramatic pauses in delivery, for variations in tempo, and (in the monodic lyrics) for instrumental preludes and intermezzi, the estimates given in the text should not be too far out.

[83]Frr. 856–57 *PMG*, both Spartan war songs in anapaestic rhythm (the former is named an *embatērion* in the source), have been thought to be by Tyrtaeus himself; but in default of reliable evidence Page was surely right to place them among his anonymous *Carmina popularia*.

[84]Although only eight lines of this poem actually survive (frr. 1–3W), its original length is known from Plutarch, *Solon* 3.

[85]See Plutarch, *Solon* 8.1–3 and Diogenes Laertius 1.46.

[86]Fr. 1W. The second line of this extract contains some corruption, but it seems to be limited to the single word *ōidēn*, in which case the general sense is scarcely affected. See Westman (1974), who very plausibly suggests that *ōidēn*, as a gloss on *kosmon epeōn*, has ousted some epithet attached to the latter word, e.g., *ligeōn*.

[87]At least one poem of this kind *may* have been in trochaic tetrameters: fr. 35W (with West's apparatus).

[88]Fränkel (1960), pp. 75–76.

[89]Cf. West (1971–72), vol. II, pp. 144–45. The poems mentioned are of course in elegiacs, like the bulk of Solon's nonpolitical poetry. There are, however, three nonpolitical iambic fragments (38–40W), mostly concerned with *food*; here one thinks back to Alcman (cf. n. 49 to this chapter), forward to the innumerable similar passages in Epicharman and Attic comedy.

[90]The eyewitness account of a sung performance of poems by Anacreon, Sappho, and some more recent composers in Aulus Gellius, *Noctes Atticae* 19.9, probably does not count as evidence for the classical Greek circumstances of performance; at most it will have been an archaizing revival, rather than a direct descendant in unbroken line from classical practice. It is noteworthy that

the one extract from the performance cited verbatim by Gellius as "Anacreon" turns out to be from the much later *Anacreontea* (Poem 4). Comparable performances of Sappho and Anacreon at Roman wine parties are mentioned by Plutarch, *Quaest. Conv.* 7.8.2.

[91] This is obviously true of the Praxilla vase, since the singer there is male. In the other vase, where the singer is inscribed "Ekphantides," I suppose we cannot rule out the theoretical possibility that he is also the composer of the verse—a poet who has disappeared from our literary records. This, however, seems less likely.

[92] There is little doubt, in fact, that this figure is to be thought of as present in a symposium, his solitude in the painting being dictated simply by the tondo form.

[93] Cf. Campbell (1964), Rosenmeyer (1968), and West (1974), chap. 1.

[94] We can hardly make much use, in this context, of the observation by J. Boehlau (*Philologus* 60 [1901], p. 329, with photographs opposite p. 480), that the graffito on the foot of a fifth-century Attic kylix formerly in Berlin appears to be part of a line by Hipponax (fr. 119W). The identification does not seem to be absolutely certain; the surviving phrase ε]ἴ μοι γένοιτ[ο is sufficiently commonplace, and could have occurred in many other contexts, besides that of Hipponax's line. Furthermore, the mere fact that the graffito happens to be found on the type of vessel normally used in Attic symposia is no guarantee that the verse itself is to be associated with a symposium.

2. Text and Re-performance

[1] Wade-Gery (1952), esp. p. 39.

[2] For the editorial work of the Alexandrians in general the reader is referred to part II of Pfeiffer (1968), the standard treatment of the subject. Only on one significant point would I venture to disagree with his account; see below, p. 43.

[3] *Dionysii Thracis Ars Grammatica*, ed. Uhlig, p. 6. On Dionysius and his book, see Pfeiffer (1968), pp. 266–72. Rutherford (1905), pp. 97–156, gives abundant illustrations of the perpetuation of the doctrine of *hypokrisis* in the scholastic tradition.

[4] Stanford (1967), chap. 1, esp. pp. 1–3, collects references to the silent reading of literary texts in the late fourth century A.D. Even in these instances, however, none of the texts concerned is a *poem*, and one may surmise from the scholiasts (cf. Rutherford, cited in n. 3) that the reading aloud of poetry may have continued in the schools for several centuries longer. The main exception in antiquity to the rule that poetic texts should be read aloud is found in a special class of learned poetry, the *Technopaignia*, as early as the Hellenistic period (see Maas [1962], p. 12). These poems, the ancient equivalent of twentieth-century "concrete poetry," are designed to be appreciated, in part at least, as visual patterns.

The silent reading of *nonliterary* texts is a totally different matter: Knox

(1968) shows that this must have been a common practice in antiquity at all periods, from at least the late fifth century B.C. onward.

[5] Pfeiffer (1968), p. 181; his view is to some extent anticipated by Wilamowitz (1922), p. 92. Most authorities on Pindar that I have consulted assume without question—but, so far as I can discover, without evidence either—that Pindar's original manuscripts were musically notated. Some add that there were choreographic indications also. See, for example, Wilamowitz (1900), p. 48; Irigoin (1952), esp. pp. 5–8 (a highly circumstantial account); Nisetich (1980), p. 5.

[6] Immerwahr (1964), p. 46; idem (1973), p. 143.

[7] Henderson (1957), p. 338, with her note 2. The passage in Aristoxenus is *Harmonics* 39–41, but even this appears to contain no reference whatever to musical notation *as a device for the practical performer of music.* Rather, Aristoxenus is here attacking, with his customary acerbity, those musical theorists who make use of musical notation *in order to clarify the theory of harmonics* either to themselves (which, says Aristoxenus, merely demonstrates their ignorance) or to their lay pupils (which, he says, is a proof of their extreme absurdity). On the absence of Greek evidence for the teaching of practical notation see, further, Marrou (1946).

[8] The two certain examples are: (1) the Vienna papyrus of Euripides *Orestes* 338–344: see Lesky, *TDH*[2], p. 458, n. 309, and Feaver (1978); (2) Euripides *Iphigeneia in Aulis* 784–792; see Jourdain-Hemmerdinger (1973) and Comotti (1977). Some other tragic musical texts, apparently of Hellenistic date or later, are enumerated and discussed in Winnington-Ingram (1955), Pöhlmann (1970), and Neubecker (1977), p. 150.

[9] A discussion of Timotheos will be found in the Epilogue, Chapter 7.

[10] If the theory outlined in the above paragraph is correct, it will follow that the musically notated papyri of the *Orestes* and *Iphigeneia* (above, n. 8) may well preserve a memory of the actual melodies composed by Euripides (since there is no evidence that scores of any kind were known in the late fifth century), but will themselves be memoranda made in Hellenistic times, based on a Hellenistic reperformance by a troupe which still preserved, by aural tradition, the Euripidean music. The same might apply to the score of *Orestes* which was evidently known to Dionysius of Halicarnassus in the late first century B.C. (*Comp. Verb.*, 11 and 19).

[11] The only possible Homeric allusion to writing of any kind is of course that at *Il.* 6.168–70 (cf. 176–79), the *sēmata* given to Bellerophon by Proitos. The passage is endlessly debated, but at least one point is certain: even if the *sēmata* are indeed alphabetic (or syllabic?) characters rather than pictographs, they convey a message, not a poem.

[12] See Plato, *Critias* 113a–b, quoted in Appendix VI. To accept this passage as good evidence for the existence of family archives in classical Athens is not necessarily, of course, to accept the reality of the particular *grammata* there mentioned by Critias; these look, indeed, very like a Platonic fiction. But Plato would scarcely have introduced them into his dialogue if the preservation of writings in a family archive from Solon's time down into the late fifth century B.C. had seemed improbable in itself.

[13] Most notably the "Artists of Dionysos," who are fully discussed in Pickard-Cambridge, *DFA*², chap. 7. The exact status of the "Homeridai," for whom see Pfeiffer (1968) pp. 11–12, is disputed; but it seems not impossible that these men already constituted something resembling a guild in archaic and classical times.

[14] Even this, of course, cannot be proved on our present evidence. The inscriptions of the archaic and classical periods by no means always respect the line ends of stichic meters; but it might be argued that in inscriptions (as in the representations of written papyrus rolls on the vase paintings) the size and shape of the area to be written on would be chiefly responsible for this neglect.

[15] In the *Poetics*, 1455a22–34, Aristotle gives an actual example of what such exclusive concentration on the *words* of a dramatic composition might lead to: Carcinus (perhaps the younger, fourth-century tragedian of that name) was hissed off the stage by reason of his failure to visualize his stage action. This whole Aristotelian passage seems to bear a close relationship to the doctrine expressed by the Aristophanic Agathon in *Thesmophoriazusae* 146–56 (the question is discussed in an as-yet-unpublished Yale dissertation by Joseph Gannon, to whom I am much indebted).

It is perhaps not enough noticed that even Aristotle's *Poetics*, just like the two Aristophanic scenes which we have been discussing, contains not a single direct reference to writing as an element in the process of tragic composition (or of epic either, unless we agree with the minority who take *egrapsen* in 1460b32 to mean "wrote" rather than "painted"). Indeed, the only passage that implies a written text at any point in a tragedy's existence is 1462a12–18, on reading tragedies aloud as opposed to seeing them acted.

[16] See Pickard-Cambridge, *DFA*², p. 84.

[17] Page (1964), pp. 161–63, offers some interesting speculations about the manner in which Archilochus may have composed. He supposes that in this case, too, the process of composition was essentially independent of writing, while allowing that Archilochus might well have set down his own poems at some subsequent stage.

[18] I deliberately confined the selection to examples securely datable no later than the fourth century B.C. Many more could be adduced from subsequent centuries in classical antiquity, but their credibility becomes progressively harder to estimate.

[19] There is no way of telling from the text whether "now" refers to Athenaeus's own time or to that of an unnamed source.

[20] The emphasis in this passage is of course my own. For the songs quoted here by the Just Logos, see fr. 735 *PMG*. Page there discusses the perplexing question of their authorship: Stesichorus? Lamprocles? Phrynichus? Cydias? On any assumption, however, the author or authors will have lived at least two generations before the production of the *Clouds*.

[21] For Douris's school cup, see Beazley, *ARV*², p. 431, no. 48. It has often been illustrated, for example in Boardman (1975), fig. 289. On the "old education" generally, see Marrou (1965), pp. 80–83.

[22] This question will be looked at more closely in Chapter 3.

[23] Friedman (1956), p. ix.

[24] I have experimented in this way (sometimes, I fear, to the bewilderment of the neighbors) with large parts of Homer, with the *Works and Days* and *Theogony*, and with a fair selection of the iambic and elegiac fragments, above all those by Archilochus and Solon.

[25] *Poetics*, 1448a20–22, 1448b35–36, 1460a5–11.

[26] Cf. Bölte (1907).

[27] A practical hint to would-be declaimers of Homer: a long staff, such as the ancient rhapsodes seem to have carried from Hesiod onward, can be of very great advantage to one's act—and not merely in the scepter passage just cited.

[28] We have information (see Appendix II) that Xenophanes' poetry also was performed rhapsodically. Since, however, it refers only to performances by the poet himself, it is not relevant to the present discussion.

[29] See no. 31 Empedocles in D-K, frr. B112–15, 117–18, 131, 136, 139, 141, 145, for speeches in either or both the first or second persons. (It is true that we cannot be sure in all these cases whether the "I" is the poet's or some other character's, but the long opening fragment, B112, for instance, leaves no room for doubt). Empedocles' *Peri Physeōs* was also addressed in the second person to one Pausanias (fr. B1), but the second person does not surface very often in the fragments from the bulk of the poem.

[30] My consideration of Archilochus as a performer owes its inspiration primarily to the study by Dover (1964), to which the reader should certainly refer; if I have contributed anything in this matter, it is only a slight change of perspective and a detail or two. Some interesting remarks on the dramatic quality of Archilochus's work will further be found in Wilamowitz (1913), p. 305, end of n. 2, Kirkwood (1974), pp. 46–48, and Nagy (1979), pp. 247–49.

[31] Even if the Cologne papyrus (Page, *SLG*, fr. S478) is considered spurious, such fragments as 39–43W will suffice to prove the existence of this kind of subject matter in Archilochus's poetry; add the reproach of Critias (see Archilochus fr. 295W) that Archilochus's verses had revealed him, among other things, as *lagnos* and *hybristēs*.

[32] Here in particular I am indebted to Dover (1964), esp. pp. 206–10.

[33] The instances are frr. 19W, 24, 25 (lines 5–6), 122, 168, 172, 182, 188, 197; of these, only the two-line fr. 182 contains no first or second person. One may also note that all but four of Horace's seventeen *Epodes* (which, at least on the face of it, are dependent on Archilochus) contain a first or second person within their first four lines. The exceptions are *Epodes* 2, 3, 10, 16.

[34] Either alternative seems possible, as Dover (1964), pp. 207–208, remarks.

[35] Cf. Dover (1964), pp. 208–11.

[36] As Dover observes, the Critias passage (Archilochus fr. 295W) shows that at least one well-educated Greek of the late fifth century B.C. took the "I" of the poems to be Archilochus himself. This might just indicate that by that time, at any rate, the rhapsodes were delivering them in the assumed character of Archilochus.

For possible instances of impersonations in *monodic lyric* poetry similar to those just discussed, see Dover (1964), pp. 207 and 210. He cites Alcaeus fr. 10 *PLF* and Anacreon fr. 385 *PMG*, in both of which, interestingly, the character impersonated is feminine; and also Anacreon frr. 376, 378 *PMG*. To these one might add the anonymous "Locrian song," fr. 853 *PMG*, where again the first person is feminine.

[37] The grounds for this assumption have been given in the preceding section.

[38] This latter alternative perhaps deserves more consideration than it has received since Page (1951), p. 64, discussed and rejected it. Even then, a prima facie case, if an insufficient one, could be made for supposing that some of the names in *Partheneion* I had been devised to suit the poem's circumstances: Hagesichora, "chorus leader"; Agido, apparently "leader"; Nanno, apparently a pet name for a flute girl in Mimnermus (to Page's instances we may add the diminutive Nannion, a hetaira in Anaxilas com. fr. 22.15K, *ap*. Athen. 13.558c). Since that time, the publication of the second *Partheneion* (fr. 3 *PMG*) has added another candidate, Astymelousa, "concern of the town," which Alcman himself seems to interpret by *melēma dāmou* (line 74); and it may be added that fr. 107, on the man Pollalegon and his wife Pasicharea, shows that Alcman was perfectly capable of inventing *redende Namen* when he felt like it. On the other hand, we have to note that the names in the Pindaric *Partheneia* (see the following paragraph in the text) must almost certainly belong to real individuals; there is no reason to doubt the historicity of the Theban house of Aioladas, for instance.

[39] For the statement that Pindar's poetry was no longer being performed, see Eupolis fr. 366K (reproduced in Appendix VII).

[40] See *Isthm*. 6, lines 3–9 (the family), 19–56 (the isle of Aegina and its patron-heroes, the Aiakidai), 60–65 (the family), 65–66 (the city), 66 ff. (Lampon, father of the victor). If epigraphs really have to be written to the Pindaric odes, I should prefer to write in this case: "FOR THE PSALYCHIDAI AND THE AEGINETANS, ON THE OCCASION OF YOUNG PHYLAKIDAS' VICTORY IN THE PANKRATION." It must be emphasized that this very recently composed epigraph, whatever its merits, will be of exactly equal authority with the epigraph inserted by the Alexandrians: neither derives from Pindar, each is based simply on a later scholar's inspection of the poetic text.

[41] The instance is not quite certain because the source, Demetrius (*De Elocutione* 140), does not state expressly that the two lines appeared consecutively in his text of Sappho. He is discussing the figure *anadiplosis* and illustrates it by our passage, "where the bride says to Maidenhood, '*Parthenia* (etc.),' and she answers with the same figure, '*ouketh' hēxō* (etc.).'" thus the possibility is open that Sappho composed introductory narrative lines for each utterance, which Demetrius did not need to quote for his purposes.

The textual and metrical difficulties in the fragment do not seem to affect our present problem. I have adopted Blomfield's *apoichēi* for codd. *oichēi* in line 1, and have translated what is almost certainly the general drift of line 2 (where, at least, Demetrius's words guarantee the redoubling of the phrase "I'll not come").

[42] Most recent treatments of Sappho fr. 140*a* seem to assume without much question that it is a true dialogue between separate voices: Page (1955), p. 127; Webster (1970), p. 73; Alexiou (1974), p. 55; Campbell (1982), p. 155.

[43] For a list of other early Greek songs (mostly either quasi-ritual songs or

children's play songs) that seem to be designed for delivery by two or more voices, see Appendix VIII.

3. The Forests of Myths

[1]Archilochus, fr. 1W; Sappho, frr. 127, 128, 193 *PLF*; Ibycus, fr. 282*a* *PMG*, line 23; Anacreon, eleg. fr. 2W, line 3; see also, for a traditional association of Archilochus with the Muses, the story of his initiation into the poet's craft inscribed on the Archilochus monument in Paros, Lasserre and Bonnard (1958), p. cv (cf. ibid., p. lxxiii, for the Boston vase-painting which seems to show that this tradition existed at least as early as the mid–fifth century). A full collection of passages in Greek poetry which bear on the Muses, along with other passages which throw light on the Greek poet's conception of his craft, is to be found in Lanata (1963). Murray (1981) offers a very useful inquiry into the relationship between poet and Muse.

[2]"The devotion of the Pagans was not incompatible with the most licentious scepticism," as Edward Gibbon neatly formulated the matter (in his treatment of Julian the Apostate, *Decline and Fall*, chap. 23). Fully to appreciate this truth is one of the hardest tasks of any classical student who has been raised in the Judaeo-Christian tradition.

[3]E.g. *Od.* 8.580; Hesiod, *Theogony* 31–32 and *WD* 3–4; Ibycus, fr. 282*a* *PMG*, lines 47–48; Pindar, *Nem.* 4.6–8. A similar claim is made very forcefully, but this time in sarcasm, by Xenophanes, fr. 6W, lines 3–4; in this passage (which could be a kind of parody of *Theognidea* 251–52, quoted just above in my text) the poet threatens that he will make the *kleos* of a certain person's stinginess reach "all Hellas, and it shall never wane, so long as there shall be singing of the Hellenic kind."

[4]Simonides himself attributes the epitaph to the sage Kleoboulos of Lindos, who flourished perhaps a century earlier. Others even attributed it to Homer (*Vita Herodotea*, pp. 198–99 in T. W. Allen's Oxford Text of Homer, vol. V; *Certamen*, ibid., pp. 235–36).

[5]Mimnermus, fr. 6W; Solon, fr. 20W, cf. fr. 21.

[6]For example, Archilochus's allusions to the Homeric poems, frr. 110–11W, 127, 131, 132, 134, 189. A comprehensive survey of such cross-referencing between the archaic poets, although laborious to compile, might throw interesting light on the song culture—and perhaps also on the course of certain poets' transmission.

[7]A single semantic detail may illustrate this difference in attitudes between the song culture on the one hand and the new culture which emerged in the late fifth century (and our own culture, too) on the other. Only toward the middle of that century did the Greek words for "old" come to acquire the scornful significance "outmoded," one of the earliest instances of this being Aeschylus, *Prometheus* 317. Cf. Herington (1970), pp. 95–96.

[8]No one will doubt that specialized collections of texts existed in the archives of temples, great families, school teachers, and professional poets and

rhapsodes (above, pp. 45–46). Some truth could even underlie the relatively late stories that the tyrants Polykrates and Peisistratos possessed general collections of texts (Athenaeus 1.3a; cf. Davison [1962], p. 152). But it is to be noted that both those tyrants were particularly keen on encouraging the poetic art, and the function of their collections is likely to have been more like that of a modern collection of musical scores or discs than that of a *library* as we have understood the term since the Alexandrian period. Even if we were privileged to look into the putative library of Peisistratos, it seems extremely improbable that we should find the texts arranged chronologically. The Alexandrian scholars themselves, though going to considerable lengths to discover the dates of their texts where possible, were not yet so "chronology conscious" as to catalogue the works of any given author by date in their editions. One thinks of their dispositions of the Pindaric epinicians (by the Great Games concerned), of the Simonidean epinicians (by athletic events), or of the works of the tragedians (by play title in crude alphabetical order).

[9] An example (admittedly from the period when the song culture was approaching total collapse, but when the rhapsodes were still regularly performing at the Panathenaia) might be Socrates' transfiguration of the scene between Achilles and Thetis in the eighteenth *Iliad*, which superimposes a quite new scheme of values on the Homeric verses (Plato, *Apology*, 28b–d).

[10] For the rest of this chapter, and in several passages later in the book, I shall use "myth" as a convenient shorthand symbol for the entire body of narrative material that formed the normal subject matter of the Greek artists, poets, and tragedians: religious myths in the strict sense, heroic sagas, and ancient *Märchen*. In many kinds of investigations it is obviously necessary to keep these categories distinct, but this does not seem to hold here, where we are concerned primarily with the ways in which the poets and their publics used and perceived that material.

[11] "Even the well known [myths] are known to few." There seems no reason to distrust this statement, as for instance Lucas (1968) does in his commentary ad loc. Even a superficial comparison of the artifacts of the mid–fifth century B.C. with those of ca. 330, when the *Poetics* was being composed, will show how both the range and the intensity of the Athenian public's interest in the mythical world have decreased. Fr. 191K of the Middle Comic poet Antiphanes (cited by Lucas) hardly invalidates Aristotle's remark. He produces the stories of Oedipus and Alcmeon as examples of plots so well known to the audiences that the tragedian's task, as opposed to that of the unhappy comedian, is made easy for him. But these particular legends had been treated very often indeed by the fifth- and fourth-century tragedians (cf. Nauck's index of tragic titles and *Poet.* 1453a18–21), and the mid-fourth-century audience would have been dim indeed if it had had no notion whatever of the probable course of a play announced as *Oedipus* or *Alcmeon*. Cf. also Pickard-Cambridge, *DFA*², p. 276.

[12] Clearly it is not practicable here to give an adequate bibliography of this vast subject, but some idea of the richness and variety of the mythological scenes to be found on the archaic vase paintings—to mention no other works of art—may be gained from: Boardman (1974), chap. 13; idem (1975), chap. 8;

the indices to mythological subjects in Beazley's *ABV* and *ARV*[2]; and Brommer (1973).

[13] Lines 3–4 of "Correspondances" in *Les Fleurs du Mal*: "L'homme s'y passe à travers des forêts de *symboles* / Qui l'observent avec des regards familiers."

[14] For example, in the early hymn, fr. 29Sn., and the opening stanza of *Isthm.* 7. That the extemporizing effect produced by such passages was no doubt consciously planned by the composer himself, with a priamel effect in mind, is not significant for our present argument, which concerns the enormous range of myth immediately available both to poet and audience in archaic times.

[15] Pindar, *Ol.* 9; the verbatim quotation is from line 94.

[16] For a survey of certain mythological "*paradeigmata*" of that kind in Homer, see Willcock (1964). Willcock's point there, that Homer will often himself introduce considerable modifications in the myths to suit his own context, is very well taken. Even the eight examples which he discusses, however (including *Il.* 24.602–17 in the total), leaves us in no doubt that in most cases the general *outline* of the story concerned must have been pre-Homeric. Some further instances of Homeric *paradeigmata* are *Il.* 18.117–19 (Herakles), 19.95–133 (Zeus and Ate), *Od.* 8.224–28 (Eurytos), 20.66–78 (daughters of Pandareos), 21.295–304 (Centauromachy).

[17] "Sage setzt Ruinen voraus," as Lesky (1966B), p.30, concisely put it.

[18] Some idea of the complexity and extent of the relationship between archaic Greek lore and that of other and earlier peoples may be conveniently obtained from West (1966), pp. 1–31, and idem (1978), pp. 3–30.

[19] Cf. above, p. 59, with n. 2.

[20] The Corinthian vase-painting: column-krater in the Vatican, Arias and Hirmer (1962), plate xi; compare Payne (1931) p. 98 for the probable connection of this painting with a lost earlier Corinthian work, the Cypselid Chest.

The Aeschylean passage referred to is *Seven Against Thebes* 568–625; Plato's citation of it (with a paraphrase of line 592 and a direct quotation of 593–94) occurs at *Rep.* 3.362a.

[21] Famous examples of these are the Deception of Zeus (*Il.* 14), the tale of Ares and Aphrodite (*Od.* 8), the Thersites episode (*Il.* 2), the Elpenor episode (*Od.* 10). To the examples from non-Homeric poems given in my text, one might add the lost Homeric hymn on the chaining of Hera and the return of Hephaistos. The erstwhile existence of this poem had long been conjectured from the vase paintings and from certain literary indications. An actual fragment of it may be preserved in *POxy* no. 670; see Merkelbach (1973), who describes it (p. 213) as "eine Art Komödie."

[22] Eustathius ad *Od.* 10.552 (= *Margites*, fr. IV Allen). My slightly inelegant English version reproduces a corresponding inelegance in Eustathius's Greek at this point.

[23] Embryonic spy stories are found, for instance, in *Iliad* 10 (complete with double cross!), *Odyssey* 4.242–64, *Little Iliad* p. 107.4–7 and p. 107.7–8 Allen. For tales of the supernatural that might bear comparison with Poe or James, see *Odyssey* 16.161–63, 19.36–40, and above all 20.345–70. Less hair raising, but still impressive, is the apparition of Patroklos at *Iliad* 23.57–107

(there were evidently other such apparitions in the *Little Iliad* and the *Nostoi*, pp. 106.30–33 and 108.25–26 Allen). Approaches to science fiction include the workshop of Hephaistos in *Iliad* 18.373–79, 417–21, 469–73; and the self-guided Phaeacian ships in *Odyssey* 8.556–63.

[24] This aspect of the Epic Cycle is thoroughly discussed by Griffin (1977), esp. pp. 40–42.

[25] But it was not, of course, transmitted by the poets alone. In a comprehensive consideration of the transmission of myths during the song-culture period we should also have to take into account the parts played by the visual artists at all levels from potter to architectural sculptor and (above all in the earlier stages) by a vast undercurrent of continuing oral transmission. By its nature, the latter is scarcely recoverable at this late date, but it certainly existed. One thinks of "the battles of Titans, Giants, and Centaurs, fictions of our ancestors," which were narrated at some symposia around 500 B.C. to the disapproval of Xenophanes (fr. B1D–K and W); or of the Athenian women, on a visit to Delphi, identifying a sculpture of Iolaos, "whose tale is told among our looms" (Euripides, *Ion* 196–97).

[26] 68 Democritus fr. B21 D-K. The interpretation of the phrase, especially the word *kosmon*, is in fact debatable (Diels translated "einen wohlgeordneten Bau mannigfaltiger Verse," cf. Pindar fr. 194.2–3 Sn.), but "universe" seems to be among the legitimate overtones. The similar phrase in Solon fr. 1W (above, p. 34, with n. 86) has a quite different sense.

[27] For example Tyrtaeus fr. 12W, lines 4–8 (glancing allusions to no less than seven mythical figures, in priamel fashion, to reinforce the overriding importance of valor); *Theognidea* 541–42 (the lyrics of the Centaurs), 699–718 (multiple allusions, especially to Sisyphos, in order to illustrate the power of wealth), 1123–28 (the endurance of Odysseus and Penelope).

[28] Stobaeus, *Florilegium* 88.14, there cited as from "Xenophon, *On Theognis*." Nothing else has been preserved of this treatise and Xenophon's authorship of it has been doubted, but one seems to hear a familiar accent in it—that of Xenophon the conservative, the cavalry colonel, the not-always-too-perceptive listener to Socrates.

One might, of course, cite many more passages of the same tenor from authors of the late fifth century onward. A few examples are the famous passage in Aristophanes, *Frogs* 1008–76 (where it is common ground to both Aeschylus and Euripides that the poet's duty is to "make the people in the cities better"); Isocrates 2, *Ad Nicoclem*, 41–49; or, long after, Iamblichus, *Vita Pythagorae* 164 (the Pythagoreans used passages from Homer and Hesiod "to straighten souls").

[29] And that even in its earliest traceable phase: "All methods of imposing an order upon discourse by means of rhythm that are known to us from other literatures are on a lower level, from the point of view of metric, than the oldest type of Greek verse, the Homeric hexameter," Maas (1962), pp. 1–2. To this Dale (1968), p. 9, adds, of Greek *lyric* meter: "[It] has a variety enormously exceeding that of any known body of verse in any language."

[30] The quotation is taken from my verbatim notes of Frost's talk given at

Smith College, April 16, 1961. If the nature of English metrics is to be summarized in a simple sentence, that does not seem to be a bad attempt. For a more expansive treatment of the question, I refer to a *libellus vere aureus*, Hollander (1981), esp. pp. 4–11.

[31] Zelter to Goethe, quoted by Wilamowitz (1921), p. viii: "Sie (die Philologen) sollten merken, 'dass Metrum ein Werk des Pulses ist.'"

[32] "The very beauty of the name has gone / Into my being," *Endymion* I.36–37.

[33] Above, p. 56.

[34] A full discussion of the New Music lies outside the chronological scope of this book, but something will be said of it in the Epilogue, Chap. 7.

[35] Lucilius 84–85, Marx; cf. above, Chap. 1, end of n. 73.

[36] "Iambics" in the early, wide sense of the term, which includes trimeter, trochaic tetrameters, and epodic verse forms.

[37] Interestingly, this practice of composing elegiac verse on the side, as it were, was continued by a number of fifth-century tragedians: Aeschylus, Sophocles, Euripides, and Ion of Chios.

[38] They are collected in vol. V of Allen's Oxford Text of Homer, pp. 152–59 (since Allen's time, *POxy* no. 2309 has contributed another fragment); and West (1971–72), vol. II, pp. 69–76.

[39] Nor is that picture affected by the occasional minor *jeu d'esprit*, such as Simonides, fr. 17W (hexameter and trochaic tetrameter, both composed of the identical words placed in different order), or Critias, fr. 4W (trimeter obtruded into an elegiac poem, in order to accommodate the name Alcibiades). For *extensive* polymetric nondramatic poems we have to await the fourth century B.C. (Ar. *Poet.* 1447b21, 1460a2, on the *Kentauros* of Chaeremon; but even this seemed eccentric to Aristotle, as the second of his references shows).

[40] The situation was only saved, if saved it was, by the advent of the New Music in the late fifth century, with its revitalization of the nome and the dithyramb.

[41] The verses cited are from the poem "Dead Letter" in Scully (1971), p. 41.

[42] Eliot (1961), p. 96.

4. Poetry in Sixth-Century Athens

[1] For example, by Wilamowitz (1921), p. 206.

[2] This is not the place to investigate at length the Athenian tendency to syncretism in many departments of life, which is no doubt attributable in part to Athens's geographical position at the intersection of the main Greek land and sea routes, and to her long maritime tradition. But it may here be worth recalling just one striking comment on the phenomenon, by the Old Oligarch: "Furthermore, hearing as they do every kind of dialect, they selected one feature from this, another from that; and whereas the Greeks in general each tend to use their own separate dialect and lifestyle and dress, the Athenians use a mixture of them, derived from all the Greeks and the barbarians" (ps.-Xenophon, *Resp. Ath.* 2.8).

[3] Wilamowitz (1910), pp. 35–37; idem (1921), pp. 41, 206, etc.; Else (1957) and (1965). Compare also Maas (1962), p. 10; Dale (1968), p. 18.

[4] Adrados (1975), p. 7.

[5] See Snell, *TrGF* I, no. 1 Thespis, T2. Thespis is also alluded to as *poiētēs* in T11, and in the papyrus which preserves his putative fr. 2; add T9 (*poieō*) and T14 (*poēmata*). His other designations in the ancient sources are *tragikos, tragōidopoios* (T3, as restored), and "[the molder of] tragic song" (T8).

[6] See, for example, the Attic items in the extensive list of such representations given by Wegner (1968), pp. 69–84; some are illustrated in his plates Ib, IIab, IIIb, VIab.

[7] The chronology of Solon's life is not quite certain, even the exact date of his archonship (generally put at 594/3 B.C.) being disputed; see Cadoux (1948), pp. 93–99. The only pre-Solonian Attic poems that are attested with reasonable certainty are the anonymous dirges whose existence is implied by Solon's law forbidding *to thrēnein pepoiēmena* (Plutarch, *Solon* 21.4).

For completeness, it should be added that certain ancient sources attribute Athenian birth to the legendary poet Musaeus (D-K 2 Musaios A4, cf. A1, A9; *OCD*², *art.* Musaeus), and to the historical poet Tyrtaeus (Plato, *Laws* 1.629a, and a number of later writers, for example, Pausanias 4.15.6). The former story—one variant among many—looks like a mere fiction of Attic pride. It seems not impossible that Tyrtaeus could have been an Athenian born, as Plato says; but all his poetic career seems to have been spent in Sparta, and several students (e.g. Bowra, *OCD*², *art.* Tyrtaeus) have found it hard to believe that a native Athenian could ever have reached the high position in the Spartan polity held by Tyrtaeus.

[8] That is as far back as the literary record will take us, but few will doubt nowadays that the metrical forms concerned had a very much older preliterate history.

[9] For the Dipylon jug graffito and its date see Jeffrey (1961), p. 68, and Snodgrass (1971), p. 352. Watkins (1976), pp. 437–38, notes (following Notopoulos) the resemblance to Homeric diction in the first line of the graffito, an undoubted dactylic hexameter. His extremely interesting suggestion that the following short line was intended as an adonic colon, and that the graffito as a whole is therefore to be taken as a scrap of *lyric* verse, is not, I fear, susceptible of proof.

[10] On the Demeter hymn see Richardson (1974), esp. pp. 52–56; he concludes that Athenian composition cannot be proved on the linguistic evidence, although that evidence does suggest Athenian transmission. On the Athena hymn see Wilamowitz (1931–32), vol. II, p. 164.

[11] The exact chronology of Peisistratos's tyrannies and exiles is uncertain; for an account of the question see Berve (1967), vol. II, pp. 544–45.

[12] Here I do not attempt detailed discussion of the relationship between events at Corinth and Sikyon and the "Origin of Tragedy," a topic with which this book is not directly concerned. Studies of the question will be found in Pickard-Cambridge, *DTC*², pp. 97–101, and Patzer (1962), pp. 89–127, for Corinth; and in *DTC*², pp. 101–107, for Sikyon.

[13] The primary evidence (Hdt. 1.23, *Souda s.v.* Arion; Proclus, *Chresto-*

mathia 12, and John the Deacon, *Comm. in Hermog.*) is assembled in Pickard-Cambridge, *DTC*², pp. 97–98. None of the sources expressly states that Periander patronized Arion's dithyrambic productions, but the Herodotean account makes this likely. Berve (1967), vol. I, p. 67, notes the resemblance between Periander's (assumed) patronage of Arion, and the patronage certainly given by the Peisistratids to the dithyrambist Lasus of Hermione.

[14] Hdt. 5.67. There is no other primary testimony to these events, unless one counts Themistius (*Or.* 27, p. 406, cited in *DTC*², p. 101, n.); but that looks very like an inference from Herodotus.

[15] See Davison (1958), p. 28; he is rightly cautious about accepting the date 566/5, since it depends on a combination of two not very satisfactory texts: Marcellinus, *Vit. Thuc.* 3–4, and Eusebius (Jerome), *Chron.*, *Ol.* 53.3–4.

[16] The references to the ancient sources here named are: 323a Hellanikos F2 in Jacoby, *FGrH*; Apollodorus, *Bibl.* 3.14.6; Pausanias 7.2.1 (for this, cf. sch. Plato, *Parm.* 127a). These passages, with others concerning the history and composition of the festival, are collected and well analyzed by Davison (1958). I have accepted his major conclusions, although there are some details about which I have been unable to agree with him. Other treatments of the Panathenaia will be found in Ziehen (1949), and Mikalson (1976).

[17] For this *xoanon*, see in particular Apollodorus, 3.14.6, and Pausanias 1.26.6; there is a discussion of the evidence for its nature and appearance in Herington (1955), especially pp. 16–26. Since such a venerable and primitive-looking object (Pausanias says that it was believed to have dropped from heaven) could scarcely have been fabricated in the sixth century, I am inclined to doubt Davison's conjecture ([1958], pp. 25–26) that the famous peplos ceremony dated only from the Peisistratean era; the *xoanon*, if rightly reconstructed, must *always* have required draping with a peplos.

[18] See n. 15 to this chapter.

[19] Davison (1958), pp. 26–27.

[20] In the event, of course, the Panathenaia never achieved parity with the Great Four. None the less, they were by no means merely a parochial meet, as is shown by the wide distribution of the find-places of the Panathenaic amphoras (see n. 21), and by the odes of Pindar. The latter mentions Panathenaic victors who came from Rhodes, Opous, Corinth, Aegina, Argos, Akragas, and Thebes.

[21] Boardman (1974), pp. 167–70, gives a useful brief account of the Panathenaic amphoras. Much information about the numbers of such amphoras awarded in the games is preserved in the fourth-century inscription *IG* II², no. 2311(= Dittenberger, [1915–1924], no. 1055); the winner in the chariot race would be faced with the transportation (or disposal in some manner) of no less than 140 of these sizeable vessels, all filled with Attic oil.

[22] Sch. Aristides, III.123 Dind., cited and discussed by Davison (1958), p. 24. A further link between Peisistratos and the Panathenaia has been seen in Plutarch, *Solon* 1.4, which mentions his consecration of the statue of Eros in the Academy, where the torches were lit for the Panathenaic torch race; see Parke (1977), p. 45. Berve (1967), vol. I, p. 59, is thus in error when he states that there is no ancient evidence connecting Peisistratos with the festival.

[23] Marcellinus, *Vit. Thuc.* 2–4; Davison (1958), p. 28. The Marcellinus pas-

sage is textually corrupt, but Davison's solution to the problem seems convincing.

[24] D. L. 1.57. Although this passage does not refer to the Panathenaia by name, its wording (Solon "moved a law," *gegraphe*) indicates that an official, public occasion was involved. The only such occasion known to have existed in Athens is the Great Panathenaia, as all our other sources indicate.

[25] *Hipparchus* 228b. The consensus of modern students seems to be that this dialogue was probably composed in the fourth century B.C.; see Davison (1958), p. 38, n. 16. It should thus be a reliable witness to the practice of the Panathenaic rhapsodes toward the end of the city-state period ("now," at the end of the quotation). How far it can be trusted as an authority for the early history of the rhapsode contests remains in doubt. Its mention of Hipparchus as "eldest" of Peisistratos's sons (228b6; *contra*, Thuc. 6.42.2) is not reassuring, in spite of Davison (1955), pp. 10–11. One may also be inclined to suspicion by a certain simple-minded hyperbole in this passage: Hipparchus is "eldest *and wisest*" of the sons; he "first brought" the Homeric poems to Attica; he "compelled" (*ēnagkase*!) the rhapsodes to recite them by turns.

[26] The clearest evidence is to be found in *IG* II^2 2311 (see n. 21); the same four events are probably to be inferred from the language of Plutarch, *Pericles* 13.6 (see n. 27).

[27] Davison (1958), pp. 36–41. Davison seems to succeed in showing that Plutarch's statement (*Pericles* 13.6), to the effect that the Panathenaic *agōn mousikos* was instituted *for the first time* by Pericles, cannot be accurate in light of the monumental evidence. He suggests that Plutarch or his source may have misunderstood a decree *reorganizing* the contests.

[28] That the normal reward for musical victories consisted of crowns or cash is inferred: (a) from the inscriptions *IG* II^2 2311 and *IG* II–III^2 1388, line 36; (b) from Ion's remark in Plato, *Ion* 535e5–6; and (c) from Aristotle, *Ath. Pol.* 60.3. Panathenaic amphoras were not normally awarded officially for these events; unofficial Panathenaic amphoras showing musical events are not uncommon, however, and provide a significant proportion of the evidence for Davison's supposition ([1958], pp. 36–38, with list on p. 42) that the musical contests were in being by the mid sixth century B.C. The Leningrad amphora of the third quarter of the fifth century, inscribed with the regular official inscription "from the contests at Athens," and showing a kitharist or kitharode (Beazley, *ABV*, p. 410, no. 2; Davison, pp. 37–38) indicates that on occasion a musical victor might be rewarded (on request, perhaps?) with Panathenaic amphoras. The majority, no doubt, being migrant professionals, preferred to take their winnings in more portable form; cf. Ion's remark, cited at the beginning of this note.

[29] One should here note the evidence assembled by Johansen and others regarding the extreme rarity of Iliadic scenes on the Attic vase paintings before ca. 530 B.C., and the great increase in such scenes toward the end of the century: see Davison (1958), p. 39, and Richardson (1974), p. 6, where further references will be found. I am not certain, however, whether this evidence is quite decisive on the question of the date when the rhapsode contests may have been introduced.

[30] See above, n. 20, for the wide geographical distribution of the athletic contestants in the Panathenaia by the early fifth century B.C. We have very little information about the *musical* contestants in the same early period; it is noteworthy, however, that the oboist Midas of Akragas in Sicily (Pindar, *Pyth.* 12, commemorating his Pythian victory of 490 or 486) is said by the scholiast also to have won a victory at the Panathenaia (Davison [1958], p. 39).

[31] The date of this important event rests on three testimonies (the Parian Marble, the *Souda* entry on Thespis, and possibly Eusebius, *Chron.*); all converge toward the years between 541 and 533 at the outside. For discussions of the problem, see Jacoby's comment on Epoch 43 of the Parian Marble (no. 239 in *FGrH*, vol. IIb), and Lesky, *TDH*³, pp. 49–50.

[32] All these titles, or slight variations on them, are found in the classical inscriptions as well as in the literary documents; see Pickard-Cambridge, *DFA*², p. 56, nn. 1–3.

[33] The evidence is printed in Pickard-Cambridge, *DTC*², pp. 69–72, and analyzed on pp. 72–95. I refer to *DTC*², here and elsewhere, because the first edition of the book is no longer easy to obtain. Those who have access to it, however, are recommended to consult it on this point, because the analysis in the second edition seems to me to reach more positive results than the evidence will justify. Particularly surprising is the claim in *DTC*², p. 96, that "we have definite evidence" that "the dithyramb was sometimes sung by men dressed as satyrs." This conflicts with the much more cautious statements to the same effect on pp. 34 and 98, and the only basis for it seems to be the two vases in which satyrs are shown bearing lyres—but the dithyramb was normally accompanied by the *oboe.*

[34] I translate as literally as possible, marking with square brackets those passages which have been restored by modern students from illegible or mutilated passages on the marble. With some hesitation, I have adopted the text given by Snell, *TrGF*, vol. I, p. 61, as probably representing the consensus of the experts. But collation of the versions of the Parian Marble published in this century (Hiller von Gaertringen [1903], Jacoby [1904], and Jacoby, *FGrH* no. 239 [publ. 1929]) does not give me great confidence. I am not convinced, for example, that B. Keil's supplement *hypekrinato*, "acted," in the first clause, is absolutely certain; the published evidence does not seem to exclude, for example *ēgōnisato*, "competed." Perhaps the moment has arrived for a thorough reexamination of the marble by an epigraphic specialist.

[35] These are assembled in Snell, *TrGF* I, pp. 3–52, with addenda in vol. II, pp. 325 ff.; cf. also Pickard-Cambridge, *DFA*², pp. 101–125. On the history of the verb *didaskō* in connection with choral lyric, see above, pp. 24–25; it may confirm the belief that the earliest tragic performances were predominantly choral.

[36] This clause looks as if it has been spliced in by the compiler of the Parian chronicle from some other source, probably a literary one. The definite article, *ho tragos*, with its implication of "the goat we have all heard about," deserves attention (the translation given in *DTC*², "a goat," misses this nuance); that is not the language one would expect from an archive dating from the institution

of the tragic contests. Further, the clause is closely paralleled in the Parian Marble's entry on the institution of comedy, "and as prize was set up a basket of dried figs and a measure of wine" (Epoch 30; Jacoby, in his commentary in *FGrH*, there remarks "auch das *athlon* ist erfunden"). Burkert, in a now famous article (1966), supports the authenticity of the goat prize; but although he has much of great interest to say on the nature of sacrifice and of tragedy, this fundamental premise really seems very doubtful. The facts remain that: (a) apart from the Parian Marble (which actually says nothing about the *sacrifice* of a goat), the authorities are late, and mostly Roman; and (b) there is no trace in fifth- or fourth-century B.C. literature or inscriptions of a goat as the prize for tragedy; indeed, such little evidence as we have (*DFA*², pp. 90, 98) suggests prizes of quite a different nature.

[37] The scanty remains of this temple do not permit a precise archaeological dating. Estimates have varied from ca. 575 to ca. 520–510 B.C., according to Boersma (1970), p. 19. Pickard-Cambridge (1946), p. 3, allowed even more latitude: "anterior to the Persian Wars and almost certainly of the sixth century B.C."

[38] See Boersma (1970), esp. pp. 11–24, for a survey of Attic building projects datable to the age of Peisistratos and his sons. Out of a list of some thirty projects, six are expressly attributed to a member of the family in the ancient literary sources—an impressive proportion, if one bears in mind how scanty these sources are where the sixth century is concerned. We have already seen the evidence that both Peisistratos and Hipparchos had some connections with the Great Panathenaia; it may be added here that Hippias and Hipparchos appear as conducting a Panathenaic procession in the ancient accounts of Hipparchos's assassination (Thuc. 6.57.1, Hdt. 5.56.2, Ar. *Ath. Pol.* 18.3); cf. Berve (1967), vol. I, p. 59, and Parke (1977), pp. 128–29.

[39] *The Dramatic Festivals of Athens*; I quote the revised edition by Gould and Lewis throughout.

[40] *DFA*², pp. 19–25. The quotation translated in my text is from ps.-Demosthenes, *In Neaeram* 76. Another ancient source of great importance is Thuc. 2.15.3–6.

[41] *DFA*², pp. 1–19.

[42] *DFA*², pp. 25–42.

[43] See especially p. 35 in *DFA*².

[44] The evidence, which consists entirely of vase-paintings, is discussed in *DFA*², pp. 30–34. Compare also Dodds (1960), p. xxii: among all the Athenian Dionysos festivals, "only the Lenaia may perhaps have kept something of the original fervour which its name betokens and which we may recognize on some of the so-called 'Lenaia-vases.'"

[45] *DFA*², p. 35; Pickard-Cambridge treats this passage (sch. Clem. Alex. *Protrept.* 1.2) with a well-justified caution.

[46] *DFA*², p. 51; pp. 42–56 contain the discussion of the Rural Dionysia.

[47] For a reconstruction in detail, see *DFA*², pp. 57–70.

[48] *DFA*², p. 58; the information on the duties of the *archōn basileus* is from Ar. *Ath. Pol.* 57.

[49] The image of Dionysos Eleuthereus is called a *xoanon* and an *agalma* by Pausanias (1.38.8 and 1.29.2 respectively); Philostratos, *Vit. Soph.* p. 549, calls it a *hedos*. *Agalma* can be used indifferently of any statue of any date, but *xoanon* and *hedos* usually imply a primitive image. For the strong possibility that it was kept in the archaic temple in the Theater precinct, see Pickard-Cambridge (1946), p. 4. Simon (1982), p. 4 (with further references in her note 9) holds that it was actually pillar-shaped. This is possible, although the evidence does not seem to me quite conclusive. It consists (a) of Attic vases, such as the famous cup by Makron (Boardman [1975], fig. 311), which show the worship of a pillar-shaped Dionysos; and (b) fragment 203 Nauck² of Euripides' *Antiope* (a play which is known to have been set in or near Eleutherai), mentioning an ivy-covered "pillar of the Euian God."

[50] Pickard-Cambridge (*DFA*²) pp. 59–60, with p. 60 n. 1 and p. 65, tentatively suggests that the proceedings with the *xoanon* were in some sense distinct from the City Dionysia; in this suggestion he is followed, more decisively, by Parke (1977), p. 127. The only evidence for it is the ephebic inscription, *IG* II² no. 1006, which certainly mentions, as if they were two separate events, (a) the escorting of the image, and (b) the escorting of a bull "for the Dionysia, which bull they [the ephebes] also sacrificed at the sanctuary at the *pompē*." This indeed makes it clear that the two ceremonies were felt as distinct, like acts in a play. The *xoanon*'s final destination, however—in the front row of the Theater—should not be overlooked. One might perhaps equally regard it as the bond which united the opening and closing elements in the lengthy festival as a whole.

[51] Pickard-Cambridge discusses the ceremony in *DFA*², pp. 57–60. He offers no speculations about the dates either of the original importation of the *xoanon* from Eleutherai, or of the institution of its *pompē* in Athens, for which dates there is, indeed, no solid evidence. All we have is a tradition that the former event was linked to a secession of the people of Eleutherai to Athenian jurisdiction, but that in itself cannot be dated. I therefore cannot accept the suggestion of Farnell (1896–1909), vol. V, pp. 226–29, followed by Parke (1977), p. 126, that all the events referred to took place in the sixth century B.C. That is not impossible, on the evidence; but the consideration stated in the sentence of my text to which the present note refers seems to make it rather unlikely.

[52] Parke (1977), p. 127. The *pompē* and *kōmos* are treated on pp. 61–63 of *DFA*².

[53] *DFA*², p. 67, with n. 2 (citing the *Souda*, *s.v. katharsion*, and Pollux 8.104).

[54] *DFA*², p. 59; some of these provisions were not peculiar to the Great Dionysia, but applied also to, for example, the Panathenaia and to Apollo's festival, the Thargelia.

[55] *DFA*², pp. 58–59.

[56] Most of these establishments or reorganizations are inferred, with reasonable probability, from the extensive building activity at the shrines of the gods concerned during the Peisistratean period: most notably at Eleusis (Mylonas [1961], chap. 4), at Delos, and at the Olympieion in Athens (Parke [1977],

p. 144). For a well-referenced account of the building programs in general, see Boersma (1970). Andrewes (1956), pp. 111–14, and Berve (1967), vol. I, pp. 59–67, offer surveys of the tyrants' religious policies.

[57] Ps.-Plato, *Hipparchus* 228b. The most likely occasion for this incident is the fall of the Samian tyrant Polykrates, in whose court Anacreon formerly worked (an early witness to this is Hdt. 3.121.1). Polykrates' fall is datable in about 522 B.C. (cf. Barron [1964]).

[58] *Hipparchus* 228b. The substance of this passage (and also of 228c–229b) is reproduced by Aelian, *Var. Hist.* 8.2, with no significant changes except some abbreviation here and there.

[59] Ar. *Ath. Pol.* 18.1: *τοὺς περὶ Ἀνακρέοντα καὶ Σιμωνίδην καὶ τοὺς ἄλλους ποιητὰς οὗτος ἦν ὁ μεταπεμψάμενος.* In translating, I have omitted the first two words (which in normal Greek of course, would mean "*the circle of* Anacreon"), because in Aristotelian idiom this usage often seems to be redundant; see the parallels cited by Sandys (1912) ad loc.

[60] The suggestion that Lasus could have been meant among the "other poets" in *Ath. Pol.* 18.1 is due to Sandys (1912) ad loc. For a full discussion of him and his work, see *DTC*², pp. 13–15.

[61] Herodotus 7.6.3–4: the anecdote of Lasus's discovery of Onomacritus in the act of interpolating Musaeus's oracles. It is noteworthy that Hipparchus, not his elder brother Hippias, is the tyrant who takes the initiative of banishing Onomacritus on this occasion; one has the impression that his role in the regime was that of Minister for Cultural Affairs.

[62] *Hipparchus* 228c–29b. I have quoted only the essentials of this long passage.

[63] See Peek (1935). The implications of these monuments for the question of the extent of literacy in Attica during the last quarter of the sixth century B.C. have perhaps not been sufficiently considered.

[64] One has to allow for some exaggeration in this dialogue (cf. n. 25), and also for a not very successful attempt to reproduce Socratic irony. The emphasis on Hipparchus's *sophia* throughout the passage seems to be an example of the latter. Also Socratic, rather than Hipparchan, is no doubt the emphasis on *paideia* and on the notion of educating one's subjects to be "as good as possible."

[65] The evidence is collected in the apparatus to *PMG* fr. 703.

[66] See *DTC*², pp. 13–15. The evidence consists of (*a*) Aristophanes, *Wasps* 1410, *Λᾶσός ποτ' ἀντεδίδασκε καὶ Σιμωνίδης*: here the verb certainly implies a dithyrambic contest, but we learn nothing of the date, nor even of the place (although Athens would certainly be most likely); (*b*) the *Souda*, *s.v.* Lasos; here the transmitted text seems unambiguous, "and he introduced dithyramb into the contest," *καὶ διθύραμβον εἰς ἀγῶνα εἰσήγαγε*. Garrod's conjecture, however, *καὶ διθυραμβώδεις ἀγωγὰς εἰσήγαγε*, deserves serious consideration in the light of the parallel passage in ps.-Plut. *Mus.* 1141c, *Λᾶσος . . . εἰς τὴν διθυραμβικὴν ἀγωγὴν μεταστήσας τοὺς ῥυθμούς.*

[67] On the date, see *DTC*², p. 15, n. 2. The year 510/509 has also been sug-

gested; but in that case we should have to suppose *both* a mistake about the archon's name on the part of the inscriber of the Parian Marble, *and* the institution of the contests in a year of extraordinary political turmoil. The dithyrambic contests at the City Dionysia remained by far the most important of such contests throughout the classical period; we have a little evidence for the existence of others during the fifth century at the Thargelia and the Lesser Panathenaia (*DTC*², p. 37), and it has been conjectured that they also took place at the Anthesteria (below, n. 70).

[68] On the introduction of the comic contests, see *DFA*², p. 82, with n. 6.

[69] Parian Marble, Epoch 46. Pickard-Cambridge has remarked on the importance of the dithyrambic contests for the attraction of foreign poets in *DTC*², p. 31, and *DFA*², p. 76.

[70] *POxy* Part XXVI (1961), no. 2438, col. i, lines 9–10. On the question of the precise year of Pindar's dithyrambic victory, see Lobel's commentary ad loc., and E. G. Turner in *CR* 77 (1963), p. 268. On Pindar's Athenian dithyrambs: frr. 74a–77 Sn., and possibly fr. 78. Hooker (1957) has suggested that fr. 75 may have been composed for the Anthesteria, not the City Dionysia, but I do not find his thesis completely persuasive. First: it is not even certain that there were any dithyrambic contests at the Anthesteria. Johansen's ingenious argument that they may have existed (see *DFA*², pp. 16–17) depends on no documentary or inscriptional evidence, but on an interpretation of two vase paintings which, to me at least, are highly enigmatic. Second: Hooker's acute observation that the abundance of *flowers* in fr. 75 would be more appropriate for the Anthesteria than for the City Dionysia scarcely seems decisive. On the whole, it seems safer to suppose that Pindar would have performed at the most prestigious of Athenian dithyrambic contests.

[71] Parian Marble, Epoch 47.

[72] Parian Marble, Epoch 54; for the same victory see the Simonidean epigram 28 in Page (1975), p. 20, which, whoever its composer may have been, looks as if it is based on a genuine didascalic record. The fifty-six dithyrambic victories which Simonides (?) claims in the epigram *Anth. Pal.* 6.213 (= no. 27 in Page) cannot all have been gained in Athens. Not merely is chronology against that possibility, but also lines 1–2 of the epigram: "six and fifty bulls and tripods did you win, Simonides." Since bulls were not awarded as prizes in the Athenian contests, whereas tripods notoriously were (*DFA*², pp. 77–78), I would interpret these words to mean that Simonides won a total of 56 dithyrambic victories, part of them in Athens and part elsewhere in the Greek world.

[73] Bacchylides, Carm. 18 and 19 Sn.; Snell (p. XLIX) dates 18 approximately to the seventies of the fifth century, although the evidence for this is not very strong. Another non-Athenian poet whose dithyrambs (frr. 740–41 *PMG*) might well have been performed at Athens is Ion of Chios.

[74] Even of these three Agathocles is not expressly attested as an Athenian, although his strong Athenian connections make this likely (Graf, *art.* Agathokles no. 22 in *RE* 1, col. 758); and it has even been questioned whether he was actually a dithyrambist (Schwenn, art. Pindaros in *RE* 40, col. 1611). For

Lamprocles' dithyrambs see fr. 736 *PMG*, and for his Athenian birth (or at least citizenship), ps.-Plut. *Mus.* 1136d. A third possible Athenian dithyrambist, Apollodorus, is discussed below, (pp. 95–96 and n. 81).

[75] The ancient sources place Aeschylus's first *appearance in the contests* in ca. 499/8 B.C., and Phrynichus's first *victory* in 511–508 (Snell, *TrGF* I, p. 3, with references there).

[76] See below, pp. 138–44, esp. 138–39.

[77] That tradition (the main ancient source for which is ps.-Plut. *Mus.* 1132f–1133a) is admittedly confused and difficult to evaluate.

[78] See above, p. 91.

[79] *Vita Thomana* of Pindar in Drachmann's ed. of the Pindar scholia, vol. I, p. 4, lines 16–17.

[80] Eustathius, *Prolegomena in Pindarum* 25 (Drachmann, vol. III, p. 296, lines 17–20). The *megalophōnia* or *megalēgoria* of Aeschylus was something of a cliché in later antique criticism: see Schoell (1875), nos. CXXI (Horace's *magnumque loqui*), CLXXVIII, CLXXIX, CLXXX. No doubt Aristophanes' *Frogs* was an important influence on this tradition.

[81] *Bios Pindarou* in Drachmann, vol. I, p. 1, lines 11–15. Wilamowitz (1922), p. 90, with n. 1, is inclined to accept the truth of this story, thinking that the names and circumstances are not likely to have been invented, but may have been handed down among professional musicians. The Apollodorus named in it is mentioned in no other source; for Agathokles see above, n. 74.

[82] On the numbers of performers involved in the dithyrambic choruses, see *DFA*², pp. 66 and 75, with n. 1; all were citizens (ibid., p. 76). In this calculation I assume that the arrangements from the beginning were similar to those existing in the second quarter of the fifth century (see especially the *Fasti* inscription, *IG* II², no. 2318). Our source for the earliest official contests under the democracy (Parian Marble, Epoch 46) mentions only *men's* choruses, but the context does not necessarily imply that there were no *boy's* choruses.

[83] This calculation is based on the assumptions (*a*) that three tragedians competed from the institution of the contests onward, and (*b*) that the number of singers in a tragic chorus was at no date less than twelve (*DFA*², pp. 234–36). I have not taken into account the satyr dramas; the date of their introduction is uncertain, although few would set it later than the first appearance of Pratinas in the contests (i.e. in 499–496).

[84] At a later period the dramatic choristers, like athletes in the gymnastic competitions, tended to become professionals; see *DFA*², p. 90.

[85] In the course of the fifth century the number of choristers required annually will have greatly increased. From about 486 B.C. we have to add as many as 120 for the comic choruses (for details, see *DFA*², pp. 83 and 236). From about 440 B.C. we must figure in the tragic and comic choruses of the Lenaia festival (*DFA*², p. 125). By the end of the century there were also tribal dithyrambic contests at the Thargelia (*DTC*², p. 37), and dithyrambic performances of some kind at the Lesser Panathenaia (Davison [1958], p. 25).

On the question of the numbers of *tragic* choristers required at Athens in any one year and the effects of this on the audiences, see Sedgwick (1947). He estimates (pp. 6–7) that by the time of the *Frogs* "there might be several thousand spectators who had actually learnt the words and music of a whole trilogy." Dover (1957), p. 98, is certainly right to question the magnitude of this figure, on the ground that many singers might serve several times over in different performances. Even so, if we survey the entire scene (including the dithyrambic choruses), the probability remains that a high proportion of any given audience had had some experience in the public performance of nondramatic or dramatic poetry. It is unlikely, at least, that anyone would be called on to sing among the 500 *boy* dithyrambists on more than a couple of occasions.

[86] Snell, *TrGF* I, pp. 61–64; these testimonies are translated in *DTC*[2], pp. 69–72, and evaluated on pp. 72–97.

[87] Parian Marble, Epoch 43; cf. above, n. 5.

[88] From a choice of any number of histories of the film-making art, I refer to the concise account of the early years in Sklar (1975), pp. 6–29; from which the details given in the present paragraph are taken.

[89] Ar. *Poet.* 1449a19–20.

[90] Ps.-Plato, *Minos* 321a. It is noteworthy that the unknown author, like the real Plato and so many other ancient writers, subsumes tragedy under poetry, *poiēsis*. Aristotle's account of the controversy between those who preferred epic and those who preferred tragedy (*Poet.* 1461b26 ff.) implies that quite a number of people in the fourth century B.C. shared this attitude toward tragedy.

[91] It is noteworthy that the earliest tragedies about which any reliable information has survived are all concerned with some aspect of the Persian threat to Greece: Phrynichus's tragedy on the taking of Miletus (the city was sacked ca. 494 B.C.); the same poet's *Phoenissae* (produced certainly before Aechylus's *Persians*, and quite probably in 476); and Aeschylus's *Persians* (472).

5. Some Features of Tragic Music and Meter

[1] Eliot (1951), p. 43.

[2] It has already been touched on above, p. 81; compare, further, Scott (1921–1922).

[3] The only apparent exception to this rule that I can recall is the famous passage in Aristotle (*Poet.* 1449a11) where tragedy is derived from "those who led off the dithyramb." But even if (a) the early dithyramb was regarded as *Dionysiac ritual* rather than simply as a species of poem, and (b) Aristotle is not simply theorizing from the analogy of classical dithyrambs such as poem 18 of Bacchylides, or the heavily dramatized poems of the New Musicians—neither of which assumptions seems quite certain—the remark seems still only to apply to the remote prehistory of tragedy, not to the tragedy of the fifth and fourth centuries. Herodotus's equally famous story of Kleisthenes of Sikyon and the choruses honoring Adrastos (5.67.5) has also been interpreted in modern times to indicate a ritual origin for "tragedy." The passage is mysterious in many

ways, but one thing Herodotus does *not* say in it is that Attic tragedy, as he knew it, was derived from the performances at Sikyon—whatever their status as rituals or performances may really have been.

[4] Hdt. 2.156.6. Herodotus also uses *poieō* of Phrynichus's composition about the fall of Miletus (*poiēsanti kai didaxanti*, 6.21.2).

[5] Athenaeus 8.247e (for comments, see Lanata [1963], p. 141). On the meaning of the word which I have translated "slices," *temachē*, see Radin (1921/22) and LSJ, *s.v.* There seems little question that the normal meaning in pre-Hellenistic Greek was "slices *of fish*," but whoever coined the remark quoted by Athenaeus, whether or not it was Aeschylus himself, can hardly have intended this sense; notoriously, fish banquets were alien to Homer. The translation by Lloyd-Jones (1971), p. 89, as "slices of *dried* fish" (my italics) seems unwarranted, especially in this context. On Eustathius's gloss on Aeschylus's supposed remark, see below, Chap. 6, n. 55.

[6] This passage was emphasized by Wilamowitz (1910), p. 95, but has not been much noticed since.

[7] For a recent assessment, see Silk (1980).

[8] Fraenkel (1962), chap. 10, has much of great interest to say on Aristophanes' parodies of the choral lyricists. Examples of the parodies or imitations alluded to in my text are: Alcman, *Lys.* 1248–1320 passim; Stesichorus, *Peace* 796 ff.; Anacreon, *Birds* 1373–74; Archilochus, *Ach.* 120; *Birds* 967–88.

[9] In the *Frogs*, the regular word for the art of tragedy is (*hē*) *technē*: lines 93, 766, 770, 780, 786, 793, 811, 831, 850, 939, 961, 973, 1369; compare *antitechnos* 816 and *syntechnos* 763. *Tragōidia* is used with this meaning in 95, 798, 862, 1120; in 1495 we have *hē tragōidikē technē.*

[10] Notably 797–801 (building), 819–20 (woodworking and architecture), 881 (woodworking), 1004 (architecture). The visual culmination of the debate on *technē*, the pair of scales, evokes even more prosaic skills: butchery (798) and grocery (1369).

[11] Group I of the samples extends from 1264 to 1277, and includes *Ag.* 104; Group II extends from 1285 to 1295, and includes *Ag.* 109 and 111. (The sample quoted at line 1291 presents a puzzle. It also is attributed to *Ag.* by schol. RV, but there is no place for it in the *Ag.* which we have. Probably the safest course is to follow Wellauer and Mette [fr. 198] in supposing that an original *Memnon* has been corrupted to *Agamemnon* in our present texts of the scholia.)

[12] *Frogs* 1281–82. One can only guess at the meaning of the word *stasin* in 1281; the scholiast's attempt to connect it with *stasimon* is surely misguided, but modern commentators have produced no parallels to its use in such a context as this. I have simply translated its basic etymological meaning "stand," bearing in mind such English usages as "a stand of wheat."

[13] Dactylic or iambo-dactylic meters are certainly *not* typical Aeschylean meters, so far as one can judge from the extant plays and fragments; the only extensive examples are the opening triad of the *Agamemnon* parodos, and *Persians* 852–906. One may suspect that the samples cited here in the *Frogs*

represent practically all such passages that Aristophanes was able to recall in the plays of Aeschylus known to him; it may be significant that he has recourse no less than three times to the relatively short iambo-dactylic passage near the opening of the *Agamemnon*. Even if he has slanted the evidence in this way, however, his underlying sense that Aeschylean meters are on the whole distinguished from those of the later tragedians by their simplicity and clarity will be shared even by a modern hearer.

[14] Although (especially in view of 1281–82) no one can doubt that this charge is being made, the commentators differ widely in interpreting the details of 1264–95. To me the following assumptions seem probable. (1) Euripides' parody is sung throughout to oboe accompaniment. Whether or not the *parepigraphē* in the manuscripts after 1263 can be accepted as preserving a genuine tradition about the performance, almost all we know about tragic instrumental accompaniment suggests that it has hit the truth. (2) It will be for that very reason that in Group II of the samples Euripides resorts to a *verbal* imitation of lyre playing, and its effect, against the real oboe accompaniment, will be all the funnier. (3) Since lines from the *parodos* of *Agamemnon* appear in both groups, we have to suppose that both are felt to be examples of the same kind of music. In that case Euripides' words at 1281–82 mean ". . . yet another stand of songs contrived [like the former one] from the kitharodic nomes," and not "another stand of songs, [this time] contrived from the kitharodic nomes."

[15] For this argument compare Fraenkel (1918), p. 321 and n.; idem (1962), pp. 209–12; and Fleming (1977), esp. pp. 226–28.

[16] I have no confidence about the details of the obscure passage 1296–97. One may perhaps reasonably assume (1) that the reference to Marathon (as in *Knights* 781) will carry the implications of being sadly out of date; (2) that *himoniostrophos* can hardly mean anything but a "ropewinder"; (3) that if observation of a modern ropewalk is anything to go by, this allusion should concern Aeschylus's repetitive and seemingly endless metrical structures, as Euripides has made them appear in the parody just preceding.

[17] Denniston (1954), p. 442.

[18] See Snell, *TrGF* I, 3 Phrynichos T9, T10b, c, d, g; and on the same poet's choreography. T13, 15, 16 (also 1 Thespis T11).

[19] *Birds* 745–51, with Fraenkel (1962), pp. 209–12.

[20] Snell, *TrGF* I, 3 Phrynichus, T1 (= the *Souda*).

[21] Some further *possible* examples of Phrynichus's metrical borrowings will be noted below in nn. 41 and 42 (from Spartan march songs?) and 46 (from the Aeolic poets?).

[22] Snell, *TrGF* I, pp. 3–4.

[23] Above all, of course, in Timotheus's *Persians*; see the Epilogue, Chap. 7.

[24] *Frogs* 1301 is corrupt. In translating it, I have followed Stanford (1963) in adopting *meli* (A. Palmer) for codd. *men*, and *pornōidiōn* (Meineke) for codd. *pornidiōn*. Further, the implications of *choreiōn* 1303 are unclear; I presume, however, that the reference must be to some kind of popular song and dance, and have accordingly translated "dance halls."

Another possible reference to Euripides' borrowings from nondramatic poetry is found at *Frogs* 849, "O collector of Cretan solos!," but the precise reference is disputed (see Radermacher [1967], p. 266).

[25] Aristoxenus, fr. 81 Wehrli = ps.-Plut. *Mus.* 1136c–d. Lasserre (1954), pp. 20, 30, 164, expresses some doubts about this passage, but I cannot see any convincing grounds for them. On the question of how Aristoxenus might have known Sappho's music, see above, pp. 48–49.

[26] For the vase paintings relating to Anacreon, see Webster (1972), pp. 54–55, Snyder (1974), and Richter (1965), vol. I, pp. 75–78. The impression made in Athens by Anacreon lasted long after his death (which on our evidence should have occurred in ca. 487 B.C.: cf. Barron [1964] p. 221). Witness the statue of him playing the lyre which was raised on the Acropolis about 440 B.C. (Richter, op. cit., p. 77), and Kritias's admiring poem about him, preserved in Athenaeus 13.600d–e. For interesting conjectures on the nature of Anacreon's symposiac activities—which will have come rather close to a kind of drama in themselves—see Slater (1978).

[27] Sch. *Prom.* 128a Herington (1972), lines 1–8 (the following three lines of the scholium were probably in origin a separate entry: they refer to a quite different topic, the staging of the scene). It is greatly to be hoped that the researches of Dr. Ole Smith into the Aeschylean scholia will throw more light on the readings here; I was able to find five manuscripts, besides the Medicean, which contained this scholium, but they helped little.

[28] Anacreon's close connection with Critias and his house is attested by Plato, *Charmides* 157e, and perhaps is implied by Critias the Tyrant's poem (above, n. 26). The author of sch. *Prometheus* 128a could just conceivably have deduced his information from these passages; but he gives me the impression that he is not the sort of person to make mere guesses.

[29] That example is also corrupt, since as it stands it does not illustrate the meter which is under discussion. The simplest and most satisfactory emendation of it that I know is Edmonds's *μεθύοντ' ἀπ' οἴκαδ' ἐλθεῖν*, (1928), vol. II, p. 158.

[30] *καὶ ἠράσθη λίαν τοῖς μέλεσι τοῦ τραγικοῦ*, cod. M; the later manuscripts read *ἠράσθην*. Almost certainly the verb must have been a part of *areskō*, and Dindorf's emendation *ērest̄hē* is palaeographically easy. That still leaves us, however, with a sentence ("Anacreon was greatly pleased by the songs of the tragedian") that contradicts the tenor of the passage as a whole. There is much to be said, therefore, for reconstructing it along the lines proposed by Weil: *ἠρέσθη λίαν τοῖς μέλεσιν αὐτοῦ ὁ τραγικός*, or, perhaps better, *ἠρέσθησαν . . . οἱ τραγικοί*. For the purely metrical evidence which seems to support such a reconstruction, see below, p. 115, with Appendix X.

[31] In preparing this survey I have taken into account the plays and fragments of Aeschylus, and the fragments of the other tragedians from the beginnings to about the middle of the fifth century (nos. 1 to 20 in Snell, *TrGF* I). I have not, however, accepted as genuine the alleged verbatim fragments of Thespis (cf. Snell, op. cit., p. 65n.). Nor have I made reference to the so-called Gyges drama

(cf. Lesky, *TDH*³, pp. 62, 536–37; Kannicht and Snell, *TrGF* II, fr. 664); in the present state of our knowledge—and especially of our metrical knowledge—it is impossible to be confident that this play dates from earlier than the fourth century B.C.

[32] Pickard-Cambridge, *DFA*², pp. 156–67, collects the ancient evidence for the three levels of tragic delivery, and for the meters associated with each. The only serious doubts in this matter seem to be, first, the exact nature of the style of delivery called *parakatalogē* and usually translated as "chant" or "recitative"; for our purposes, however, it is enough to constate that it stood somewhere between unaccompanied speech and fully melodic song. Second, and more difficult, is the question whether trochaic tetrameters catalectic were normally delivered in speech, like the trimeters, or in recitative. The main, if not the only, evidence for supposing that they were delivered in recitative is Xenophon, *Symp.* 6.6, where a character says to Socrates: "Would you like me to converse with you to oboe accompaniment, just as Nikostratos the actor used to recite tetrameters to the oboe?" The passage is enigmatic, but to me, at least, its most likely implication is that Nikostratos's performance was regarded as something unusual.

[33] Iambic trimeters are already found in the fragments of Choerilus (no. 2 in *TrGF* I, F2) and Phrynichus (no. 3, F8 etc.). Most scholars (e.g., Lesky *TDH*³, p. 59) have identified trochaic tetrameters catalectic in Phrynichus F10a, but there are uncertainties here (Drew-Bear [1968], pp. 90–91); cf. also below, n. 41.

[34] Page (1964), p. 145.

[35] The skyphos from Pithekoussai (Ischia), with the graffito about Nestor's cup; the date in my text is that proposed by Snodgrass (1971), p. 352.

[36] Examples of trimeters are: the song sung by the three choruses at Sparta, fr. 870 *PMG*; the phallophoric song, fr. 851*b*; the line chanted at the Anthesteria, fr. 883; and the play song, fr. 876*c*. Tetrameters: the farmer's proverb, fr. 874. For relatively early *inscribed* examples of trimeters, see Hansen (1975) nos. 28, 52, 318, 437, 469.

[37] Trimeters: Archilochus frr. 18–87W; Semonides, apparently all the verbatim fragments; *Margites* frr. 1W, 5, 7; Anacreon, iamb. fr. 1W (conjecturally attributed). Tetrameters: Archilochus, frr. 88–167W; Anacreon, iamb. fr. 2–4W; Demodocus of Leros, fr. 6W. One should also note the large output of choliambics by Hipponax and Ananius, both of whom also wrote "limping" tetrameters on occasion (Hippon. frr. 120–27W, Anan. fr. 5).

For the rare trimeter oracles attributed to Delphi, see Parke and Wormell (1956) nos. 24, 63, 91, 329, 420; the earliest example that has a reasonable chance of being authentic, no. 91 to the Knidians, refers to the mid–sixth century.

[38] Above, pp. 34–35.

[39] Such metrical modifications as the tragedians did make are surveyed below, pp. 117–118.

[40] Cicero, *Tusc. Disp.* 2.16.37: *Spartiatarum . . . procedit ad modum acies ac*

tibiam, nec adhibetur ulla sine anapaestis pedibus hortatio (cf. Valerius Maximus 2.6.2). References to anapaestic song in early Sparta are found in Pausanias 4.15.6 (*ta epē . . . ta anapaista* of Tyrtaeus) and Polykrates (on the Hyakinthia festival; cited above, n. 8 to Chap. 1) and Hephaestion, *Ench.*, p. 25 Consbruch (cited in *PMG* fr. 161*b*: songs by Alcman). Verbatim samples are *Carm. Pop.* frr. 856, 857 *PMG*. Most modern authorities on Greek metric seem to accept without question the Spartan origin of the "marching anapaests" in Attic tragedy; see Wilamowitz (1921), pp. 366–67, Schroeder (1930), p. 40, Dale (1968), pp. 47–48, Korzeniewski (1968), p. 95.

[41] A probable anapaestic dimeter is found already in Phrynichus (fr. 2 Snell). If the Byzantine tract published by Browning (1963) is to be trusted, Phrynichus also experimented with anapaestic tetrameters catalectic (Phrynichus T12, Snell; cf. perhaps the *Souda*'s allusion to his discovery of "tetrameters" in T1?); but Snell is probably right to question this. That measure was characteristic of Sicilian and Attic *comedy*, and it is all too likely that at some stage in the tradition which underlies T12 (and T1?) the Old Comic poet Phrynichus has been confused with the tragedian.

[42] It is perhaps worth observing that Spartan troops (presumably chanting their anapaestic war songs) were on Attic soil four times during the archaic period: in 510 (the expeditions of Anchimolios and Kleomenes), 508 (Kleomenes' second expedition), and 490 (the belated arrival of the contingent at Marathon). The expeditions of Kleomenes, in particular, fell just at the period when Phrynichus was beginning to succeed in the Athenian theater (we have seen that he won his first victory in 511–508 B.C.); and the popular appeal of catchy wartime tunes, from *Lilliburlero* to *Lilli Marlene*, is notorious. Could this be another instance of Phrynichean borrowing?

[43] For a brief account of the facts, see Smyth (1956), pp. 3–4, 14–15; for an extensive inquiry, see Björck (1950), and the comments by Lesky, *TDH*³, p. 46. I use the term "Doric alpha" with reluctance, and only because it is too well established to be dropped. In fact, the phenomenon to which it refers is by no means confined to Dorian speakers; see below.

[44] Cf. Björck (1950), p. 358.

[45] Cf. Björck (1950), p. 359, and Snell-Maehler, *Bacchylides*¹⁰ pp. xvii–xix. In his solo party lyrics (frr. 17 and 19, if the latter is really his), Bacchylides might lapse more frequently into his native Ionic *ē*'s; Anacreon, of course, preserves them throughout his poems.

[46] Cf. e.g., Maas (1962), p. 10. His remark there that "the longer types of aeolic line were rejected" by the tragedians "after a brief period of trial" should be modified. To his instances (Phrynichus fr. 6 Sn., and Sophocles fr. 223 Nauck) we should probably add at least lines 175–76 and 186–87 of Sophocles' *Philoctetes* (409 B.C.) as analyzed by Dale *ap.* Webster (1970B) ad loc.; cf. 715 = 726 in the same play.

[47] This is, if not the basic, at least the most memorable form of the dochmiac, which adds to its other peculiarities an amazing diversity of shapes: see Conomis (1964), who catalogues no less than thirty-two of them.

[48] In their editions of the *Persians* both Groeneboom and Broadhead also take 1077, the final line, as *dochmiac plus iambic metron*, but I am not sure of this analysis: *spondee plus lecythion* (a favorite combination in Aeschylus) seems at least equally likely.

[49] For instance, Wilamowitz (1921), pp. 307 and 404 (dochmiacs in Simonides, Pindar, Bacchylides); Schroeder (1930), pp. 35–36 (Pindar); Gerber (1970), p. 317 (Simonides, fr. 541 *PMG*). So far as I can see, however, there are no absolutely undisputed isolated dochmiacs in the corpus of archaic non-dramatic poetry—still less, dochmiacs in lengthy sequences.

[50] Else (1965), p. 71. He attributes this theory to Wilamowitz (1921), p. 208, but in that passage Wilamowitz does not allude specifically to dochmiacs.

[51] Dale (1968), p. 104. Korzeniewski (1968), p. 170, opposes this view on the ground that dochmiacs are also found in certain Greek proverbs; that indeed suggests that the rhythm had a long popular history behind it, but does not prove the early existence of sustained dochmiac *lyrics*.

[52] See above, pp. 110–11. Wilamowitz (1910), p. 37, has already remarked that in metrical technique "allerdings Aischylos bei Anakreon nachweislich gelernt hat." To him, evidently, the matter seemed as clear as it seems to me, but the *Nachweis* is perhaps worth supplying, and I attempt to do so in Appendix X. A similar suggestion, but again without supporting evidence, was made by Schroeder (1930), pp. 84 and 132.

[53] A brief but authoritative analysis of the dactylo-epitrite meter is given by Maas (1962), pp. 40–42; for a longer account see Dale (1968), chap. 11.

[54] See Dale (1969), p. 57—the paper concerned was first published in 1950—Merkelbach (1963); Haslam (1974) and (1978). The suggestion by Maas (1962), p. 40, that Pindar may have invented the meter has now been rendered obsolete by the publication of the Stesichorus papyri.

[55] For details, see Snell-Maehler, *Pindar*[5], vol. II, pp. 161–68; Snell-Maehler, *Bacchylides*[10], pp. xxii–xxxi. Other composers of dactylo-epitrite who belong roughly to the same period are Cydias of Hermione (fr. 714 *PMG*) and Timocreon of Rhodes (fr. 727).

[56] Snell actually uses the description "dactylo-epitrite" only in his heading to fr. 9 of Phrynichus: in the other fragments named he simply uses D-E notation in his metrical analyses. Fr. 13 of Phrynichus seems equally analyzable as an example of the dicolon already found in Archilochus, frr. 168–71W (i.e., "enoplian" plus ithyphallic). Two other early fragments to which Snell applies D-E notation in part are Pratinas fr. 4 (but that is surely an Alcaic hendecasyllable), and Pratinas fr. 3 (but that is neither certainly from a drama nor consistently D-E).

[57] Dale (1971) includes *Persians* 852–906 and *Suppliants* 40–175 among the dactylo-epitrite choruses of surviving Greek tragedy. Neither of these, however, is dactylo-epitrite even in the widest sense in which the term is used by modern students; the *Persians* chorus contains no epitrites at all, the *Suppliants* chorus only two (line 43 = 50). They clearly belong to a different kind of music from that found in the dactylo-epitrite odes of Pindar and Bacchylides, and the

Prometheus odes. A couple of Aeschylean fragments, 109 and 355.7M, have been or might be interpreted as dactylo-epitrite, but there can be no certainty; and neither is dactylo-epitrite in the strict, Pindaric-Bacchylidean sense.

[58] Dale (1968), p. 179. She refers of course only to the strophe and antistrophe of this ode, the epode being primarily iambic. Her remark will also, in fact, apply to the *first* stanza pair of the preceding ode, *Prom.* 526 ff. (its *second* stanza pair is not strictly dactylo-epitrite at all except in the last line of each stanza; see Dale's analysis on p. 193).

[59] If the composer was Aeschylus, the *terminus ante* is of course fixed by his death in 456/55 B.C. Griffith (1977), who questions that attribution, seems inclined to date the *Prometheus* a decade or so after the middle of the century (pp. 225, 226, 253).

[60] For details of the later modifications see Dale (1968), chap. 11. Most notable is the introduction of the ithyphallic colon, –⏑–⏑––.

[61] The scholiast's generalization is no doubt too bold, to judge by our extant evidence (see Appendix X). It does seem to be true, however, that ionic-anacreontics are quite often used in mournful or sinister passages (e.g. *Seven* 720 ff., *Cho.* 327 ff.), and rarely if ever in moments of unmixed joy. The only exception that I can recall is only an apparent one, since it occurs in a satyr play: Eur. *Cyclops* 495–518, a song which marvelously catches the manner of Anacreon himself in its sympotic content as well as in its metrical form.

[62] For a concise account of this matter see Korzeniewski (1968), pp. 45–60. The most notable tragic modifications in the iambic trimeter are: the occasional use of the so-called *caesura media* in lieu of the regular caesuras; the abandonment of "Knox's law"; and a very great increase in the frequency of resolution. In prosody, we note the tragedians' occasional treatment of a short vowel followed by mute plus liquid as a short syllable—apparently a feature of native Attic prosody, and at any rate never found in the Ionian iambists (Maas [1962], pp. 75–77).

[63] Ar. *Poet.* 1449a19–28.

[64] The Aeschylean passages referred to are *Persians* 155–75, 215–48, and 697–758 (apart from the lyric at 700–702); *Agamemnon* 1344, 1346–47, and 1649–73. In the fragments, trochaic tetrameters are found in fr. 17M, lines 22–26 and 39–46 (the satyric *Theoroi*), fr. 380 (*Sisyphos*), and possibly fr. 74 (*Edonoi*). Drew-Bear (1968) gives a complete list of the tetrameter passages in extant tragedy, with discussion.

[65] Aeschylus's tragic predecessors, of course, had already employed the iambic trimeter; see above n. 33.

[66] Hipponax fr. 25W: "May Artemis damn you!—And may Apollo damn *you*!" For dialogues within Archilochus's poems, see frr. 23 W, 176–78, 181, 187, and the Cologne papyrus S478 in *SLG*; and compare the remarks in Lasserre and Bonnard, p. xxxviii.

[67] Dactylic *lyrics*, of course, are fairly common in the tragedians (Aeschylus and Euripides especially), and here and there, naturally, dactylic hexameters occur among them, for example, *Ag.* 104 and 122. Hexameters used stichically, however, are rare in tragedy, and then used only for special purposes. There are

no examples in the extant plays of Aeschylus (although stichic hexameters appear in fr. 355M, lines 16–39, apparently sung; the verses show the "Doric alpha"); examples in Sophocles and Euripides respectively are *Philoctetes* 839–42, *Troades* 598–600 = 604–607. The dactylic hexameter's closest relation, the elegiac couplet, occurs only at one point in all Greek tragedy, Euripides *Andromache* 103–117; here again there seems to be a special dramatic purpose, which Herbert Golder examines in his as-yet-unpublished Yale dissertation on the play.

[68] Cf. Aristotle, *Poetics* 1449a23–28.

[69] One can hardly suppose that Phrynichus's play on the taking of Miletus (late 490s B.C.?) and his *Phoenissae* (between 478 and 473 B.C., probably 476) lacked passages of narrative poetry, considering their known subject matter. Further, his fr. 10a in *TrGF* I might well be an extract from a messenger's narrative in tetrameters; and his fr. 16a (inc. fab.), ἐσθλῶν ἀπαγγελτῆρα μᾶλλον ἢ κακῶν, might well come from the opening of an iambic messenger speech (cf. e.g., *Ag.* 636–49).

[70] On the whole question of messenger speeches see Bremer (1976), with bibliography on his p. 19.

[71] And possibly, in the earlier stages, the trochaic tetrameter; see above, n. 69, on Phrynichus fr. 10a.

[72] Many earlier students have suggested that the occasional omission of syllabic augment in tragic messenger speeches may be a carryover from the language of epic. This theory, while interesting, does not seem provable on our rather scanty available evidence; see Bergson (1953). On the manner in which the narrative speeches of tragedy may have been delivered there is almost no positive evidence. The Queen's command to the Messenger in *Persians* 295, *lexon katastas*, may supply a hint: the nearest parallels to *katastēnai* (Hdt. 1.152.1 and 3.46.2) suggest that the words mean "take up your stance"—as it might be, in the fourth position of dancing?—"and speak." Similarly, the detached tone of almost all tragic messenger narratives, and the lack of characterization in the messengers themselves (the Guard in *Antigone* and the Messenger in *Bacchae* 600 ff. are only mild exceptions) suggest that the manner of delivery may have been perceptibly different, approaching that of a rhapsode reciting a narrative passage from the epics.

[73] Fr. 857 *PMG*: "Onward, armed youths of Sparta, to the war god's dance!"

[74] The fragment reads: σῶμα δ' ἀθαμβὲς γυιοδόνητον τείρει. Snell is probably right in interpreting it (with a cautious question mark) as a complete anapaestic dimeter followed by the first word of another.

[75] The examples of more or less certainly pretragic anapaests are collected in n. 40 above. Here I would note that the only nondramatic anapaestic dimeters of any date in which I have noticed dactylic substitution are *Carm. pop.* frr. 863.3 and 865.3 *PMG* (both allegedly herald's cries, both preserved in authors of Roman imperial date.) It may or may not be mere coincidence that there are no dactylic substitutions in the anapaestic fragments of Epicharmus (109, 114 Kaibel), or in the probably spurious fragment attributed to his predecessor in Sicilian comedy, Aristoxenus (Kaibel, p. 87).

[76] Choral entrances: *Persians*, *Suppliants*, *Agamemnon*, *Myrmidons* (fr. 213 M), probably *Nereides* (frr. 237–238), *Prometheus Unbound* (frr. 320–323; note Procopius's statement in fr. 322*b*). Choral exits: *Choephori* 1065–76, and quite probably *Diktyoulkoi* (fr. 474, lines 821 ff.). I take the present ending of the *Seven* (1054–78) probably to be non-Aeschylean; the finale of the *Prometheus* (1043–93), although anapaestic, is divided between two actors and the chorus, and no marching seems to be involved.

[77] Entrance of an actor (or actors): *Agamemnon* 783–809, and perhaps *Seven* 861–74 (athetized by many editors, from Bergk to Page); in *Persians* 140–54 the Queen enters *during* an anapaestic chant by the Chorus. Exit of an actor: *Suppliants* 966–79, the departure of Pelasgos; *Agamemnon* 1331–42 and *Choephori* 719–29 and 855–68 are chanted either during or immedately after the exit of an actor.

[78] *Prometheus* is remarkable for the number of such passages that it contains: 284–97, Ocean's entrance chant; 561–65 and 876–86, the entrance and exit chants of Io. In the rest of the Aeschylean corpus there is only one parallel, Xerxes' entrance chant at *Persians* 908–917.

[79] The other instances in Aeschylus are *Persians* 623–32, *Seven* 822–31 (athetized by some), *Suppliants* 625–29, *Agamemnon* 355–66, *Choephori* 306–315 (introducing the kommos), *Eumenides* 307–320. At *Choephori* 476–78 alone anapaests are used to *conclude* a sung passage, namely the kommos (*Ag.* 783–809 rather opens a new episode than concludes the preceding song). It is, indeed, possible that some marching movement was involved in these passages, though perhaps not very likely.

[80] See the entire passage, *Agamemnon* 1372–1576—marvelous in many ways, but not least in its calculated gradations of meter. Anapaests—again, so far as one can see, involving no *physical* movement—recur within the great kommoi of the *Choephori* (306–478) and of the *Eumenides* (916–1020).

[81] For the striking metrical differences between the anapaests of the *Prometheus* and those of the rest of the Aeschylean corpus, see Griffith (1977), chap. 4; add the observation by Herington (*AJP* 100 [1979] 420) that the *Prometheus* is unlike the rest in that it admits paroemiac lines only at the ends of its anapaestic systems, never within them.

[82] Snell-Maehler, *Bacchylides*[10], pp. xxii–xxiii. There may have been examples of such mixed poems in Alcman; see fr. 161*a PMG*, where Hephaestion says that Alcman on occasion wrote poems of fourteen stanzas, seven in one meter and seven in another (unfortunately he does not say exactly what the meters were).

[83] On *Ol.* 13 see Dale (1969), pp. 63–64; she remarks that in this poem the strophe "melts into orthodox dactylo-epitrite in the middle of the sixth period," while the epode is in dactylo-epitrite throughout. In the same place she adds two or three much less striking examples of Pindar's blending of dactylo-epitrite with other meters.

[84] The following studies may be mentioned here; most of them contain references to the earlier literature on the question concerned. On *thrēnos*, prayer-

hymn, kommos, and stichomythia: Else (1977). On the *agōn* form: Duchemin (1945). On the pairing of strophes in tragic lyric: Webster (1974). On the *thrēnos*: Lesky, *TDH*[3], p. 44, Duchemin (1974), and in general Alexiou (1974).

6. Old and New in Early Tragedy

[1]See the family tree in Snell, *TrGF* I, p. 88. It has often been remarked (e.g., by Welcker [1839–1841], pp. 891–93) that the Attic tragedians, to an even greater extent than the great eighteenth-century musicians such as J. S. Bach, tended to run in dynasties. Once more we are reminded of the importance of sheer craftsmanship, *technē*, in the formation of an Attic tragedian, as in the formation of a Baroque composer.

[2]Snell, *TrGF* I, 60 Astydamas II, T2a (on the date, see T6).

[3]Cf. Stanford (1942), pp. 48–50, on the presumed influence of colloquial Attic on Aeschylus. A recent survey of Aeschylean style in general: Rosenmeyer (1982), chaps. 4 and 5.

[4]In his poem prefixed to the First Folio of Shakespeare; for the long tradition underlying the phrase, see above n. 80 to Chap. 4.

[5]*Eumenides* 585–613. Comparable passages, from this point of view, are *Choephori* 753–57 (from the Nurse's speech), and several stretches of the messenger speeches in the *Persians*.

[6]The quotation is from Mark Pattison, *art.* Macaulay in the eleventh edition of the *Encyclopaedia Britannica*, vol. XVII, p. 196. A convenient survey of certain or probable Aeschylean borrowings from the earlier Greek poets is given by Stanford (1942), chap. 2. Since the publication of that book more has been done on this aspect of Aeschylus (notably by Sideras [1971]), and more could yet be done.

[7]This analogy might repay further study by Homerists. Although we know little enough in detail about the formation of the *tragic* composite dialect, we are at least in a position to locate the process exactly in space, and with reasonable accuracy in time also: it seems to have come about within a single community, Athens, and within less than a hundred years.

[8]The Aristophanic Aeschylus had already seen this point (*Frogs* 1060–61).

[9]See Parry (1971), pp. 365–75, "The Traditional Metaphor in Homer"; Moulton (1979) offers some important qualifications in detail to Parry's view.

[10]Examples of lengthy formal similes in elegiac verse: Solon, fr. 13W, lines 19–24, *Theognidea* 449–52; but such passages are very rare and, when they occur in an elegiac context, all the more striking. One should add that a full treatment of comparisons in the elegists and iambists would necessitate several qualifications to the generalization in my text. For example, Semonides' long poem on women, fr. 7W, is *de facto* a string of extended similes; and the elegists and iambists provide many examples of those special varieties of metaphor: personification, allegory, animal fable.

[11]The most spectacular Aeschylean example is surely the great vulture simile

in the parodos anapaests of the *Agamemnon*, lines 49–60. For two general considerations of Aeschylus's imagery (on which there is now a vast bibliography), see Stanford (1942), chap. 4, and Rosenmeyer (1982), chap. 5.

[12] I have translated the text of the *Poetics* as it stands in the manuscripts. Something is amiss with it, and Else may well be right in denying to Aristotle all the words following "*Little Iliad*." The information contained in them, however, is presumably ancient and based on solid evidence which we no longer have.

[13] Athenaeus 7.227e; from Athenaeus's preceding words it is evident that by the "Epic Cycle" he here means not only the cyclic poems on the Matter of Troy but also, at the least, the *Titanomachy*. There is a useful survey of Sophocles' epic sources in Pearson (1917), vol. I, pp. xxii–xxxii. I have not run into any comparable treatment of the sources of the other two tragedians later than that of Welcker (1839–41). Although many details in that work naturally require correction in the light of more recent information, Welcker's general picture of the dependence of the tragedians on the Epic Cycle seems still acceptable. The tables on his pp. 29–31 (Aeschylus), 59–62 (Sophocles), 437–40 (Euripides) and 873–80 (all three) offer a useful conspectus of his results.

[14] It is true that in most of these instances not enough survives either of the epic or the play concerned for us to be altogether certain that the one derives its story directly from the other, but the probability is there. Themes of Aeschylean tragedies apparently anticipated in the *Eoiai* include the story of Perseus and Danae in the chest, in the satyric *Diktyoulkoi* (cf. *Eoiai* fr. 135M-W); *Atalanta* (frr. 72–76M-W); *Kallisto* (fr. 163M-W); *Niobe* (fr. 183M-W).

[15] Most notable is the passage from a papyrus commentary first published by Page (fr. 217 *PMG*, and subsequently in *POxy*, Part XXIX [1963], no. 2506, fr. 26, col. ii). Page thus paraphrases its mutilated beginning: "poetis plurimis fons erat Stesichorus; post Homerum Hesiodumque cum illo praecipue concinunt." The commentator then instances the recognition by means of the lock of hair in the *Choephori*, Orestes' receipt of a bow from Apollo in Eur. *Or.*, and possibly the luring of Iphigeneia to Aulis in Eur. *I.A.*

[16] In the *Aitnaiai*, the legend of the Palikoi (frr. 27–28M); in the *Glaukos Pontios*, the legend of the marine seer which Pausanias (9.22.5–7 = Aesch. fr. 54M) says that both Aeschylus and Pindar learned from the people of Boeotian Anthedon. A further exception to the rule may be the Antigone story as we know it from the extant tragedians: see the ancient Hypothesis to *Antigone*, with pp. ix–x of Jebb's edition of the play.

[17] Euripides, *Archelaos* frr. 228–64N, with Austin (1968), pp. 14–21 and Webster (1967), pp. 252–57.

[18] Lembke and Herington (1981), pp. 9–12. On the somewhat comparable "mythologizing" of another relatively recent oriental story (that of Croesus) in Bacchylides and Herodotus, see Fränkel (1975), p. 465, n. 47.

[19] Cf. above, pp. 63–64. The tragedy concerned was Agathon's *Anthos* (*Antheus*?), of which the only surviving record is in Ar. *Poet.* 1451b19–23. The context there, and also the wording of 1459a34–b1, suggest that Aristotle

knew of a few other tragedies wholly or partially resembling the *Anthos* in free invention.

[20] Cf. Snell (1957).

[21] Cf. Wartelle (1971), chap. 16. It is noteworthy that the only extant Attic tragedies that were *not* filtered through the late antique selection process, but reached us quite by chance—the "alphabetic plays" of Euripides in codd. LP—include all three of the so-called romantic melodramas, and the satyric *Cyclops*.

[22] Biffi (1961) lists the comic or quasi-comic features to be found in the extant tragedies and in the fragmentary *Telephos* of Euripides.

[23] Athenaeus preserves most of our information about the kind of tragic passage now to be discussed. The majority of his examples are from Aeschylus. He cites two from Sophocles: fr. 355P, a paederastic allusion in the *Colchides*, and fr. 565P, a description of a chamber pot in the *Achaiōn Syndeipnon* (this passage is evidently modeled directly on Aeschylus fr. 486M). Euripides he adduces once only in this context, at 10.428f (a general reference to his having brought drunken characters onstage). It need scarcely be said that such passages were common in the *satyr plays* of all the tragedians: one recalls the drunkenness and homosexual byplay in Euripides' *Cyclops*, or the moment in Aeschylus's *Diktyoulkoi* (fr. 474M, line 31) where, it seems, the baby Perseus innocently reaches out for Silenus's phallus.

[24] Welcker attributed this fragment with much probability to the *Ostologoi*. Those who infer from its mention of a chamberpot that the play must necessarily have been satyric overlook the fact that the word here employed, *ouranē* instead of *amis*, is specifically said by Pollux to have occurred in tragedy (Pollux 2.224, cited by Mette on fr. 486).

[25] The grandeur of this couplet is hard to reproduce in English. Literal translation: "Had you no respect for the hallowed majesty of [our?] thighs, O ill repayer of our many kisses?" Fr. 229M ("and reverent communion with your thighs") may well come from the same scene.

It must be noted that not all the instances of the *aprepes* given in my text are certainly from tragedies. Some scholars have assumed that some or all of the plays concerned, with the exception of the *Myrmidons*, were satyr plays—but purely on the ground of their undignified content. How unsafe an argument this is is shown not merely by the *Myrmidons* passage, but also by the already-mentioned speech in *Choephori* 752–60, where the Nurse describes her labors over the still not toilet-trained infant Orestes. By the same reasoning this passage, if transmitted as an isolated fragment, would surely have been adjudged satyric. Preserved in its context it makes good tragic and human sense, heightening the pathos and irony of the scene.

[26] Cf. Griffin (1977).

[27] For example, Sophocles' *Inachos* (which, in spite of all the fragments that have now accumulated, still cannot be proved to have been a satyr play: cf. *POxy*, Part XXIII [1956], p. 58, and Radt in *TrGF* IV, pp. 247–48), *Manteis* or *Polyidos*, and the very early *Triptolemos* (which last, like the Prometheus plays, contained substantial passages of "romantic geography"); and Euripides'

Aeolus (Webster [1967], pp. 157–60), the plot of which was founded on mass incest between the sons and daughters of the island king.

[28] Ar. *Poet.* 1453b32.

[29] Aeschylus, *Thrēissai* fr. 292M.

[30] Aeschylus, *Laios*, frr. 171 and 173 (as emended, with probability, by Reitzenstein).

[31] Euripides, *HF* 843–58.

[32] For the marble *hippalektryon*, see Schrader (1939), plate 145, with text-volume pp. 239–40. Also interesting from our present point of view is *Frogs* 937–38, where Euripides tells Aeschylus: "Well, I didn't compose cockhorses and goatstags as you did—things they paint on Median curtains!" The visual world of Aeschylus evidently reminds him of the monster haunted art of the Near East—an art which of course had still heavily influenced the Greek artists in Aeschylus's youth, but was totally out of fashion in the late fifth-century Athens.

[33] Snell, *TrGF* I, 3 Phrynichus F1 (*Aigyptioi*), F4 (*Danaides*).

[34] On the question of the total number of Aeschylus's plays, see the discussion in Mette (1959), pp. 256–60. The *Souda*'s figure of ninety may well be approximately correct; even if one hesitates to trust that, the number of Aeschylean titles now actually preserved amounts to 80 (see Mette, p. viii–ix; I exclude from this count the highly conjectural titles *Kyknos* and *Tennēs*). Aeschylus's Dionysiac titles are: the tetralogy of the *Lykourgeia* (consisting of *Edonoi*, *Bassarides*, *Neaniskoi*, satyric *Lykourgos*); and *Bakkhai*, *Pentheus*, *Semelē*, *Trophoi*, *Xantriai*.

[35] The list of fifth-century Dionysiac tragedies, apart from those by Aeschylus (see n. 34) is as follows:

THESPIS: A *Pentheus* was attributed to him (F1c in *TrGF* I); but all the fragments and titles attributed to Thespis are under suspicion, particularly because Hellenistic forgeries are known to have been in circulation (T24 in Snell; Lloyd-Jones [1966], pp. 18–19, takes a slightly more favorable view of the *titles*).

PRATINAS: His *Dymainai* or *Karyatides* is thought to have had Dionysiac connections (Lesky, *TDH*[3], p. 63); but we cannot even be certain that this work was a drama (cf. fr. 711 *PMG*).

POLYPHRASMON: *Lykourgeia* tetralogy, produced in 467 B.C. (Hypoth. to *Seven Against Thebes*, lines 8–9, Page).

MESATOS seems to be credited with a *Bakkhai*, produced in competition with Aeschylus's *Suppliants*, in the papyrus hypothesis fr. 122M, *TrGF* I DID C6 (but there are many doubts about this: see Snell ad loc.).

SOPHOCLES touched the theme only in a satyr play, *Dionysiskos*. (Welcker's conjecture that his *Hydrophoroi* also concerned Dionysos seems to have been generally abandoned).

EURIPIDES, again, touched the theme only once, in his *Bakkhai*.

The remaining fifth-century examples all seem datable to the last third of the century (in which period a revival of interest in Dionysiac themes can also be traced in the vase-paintings): *TrGF* I 22 Iophon F2, *Bakkhai*; 33 Xenocles I, FI, *Bakkhai* (produced 415 B.C); 40 Spintharus, TI, *Semelē Keraunoumenē*.

[36] Cf. Dodds (1960), pp. xxix–xxxiii, and, in particular, xxxvii–xxxviii.

[37] Euripides, *Bakkhai* 266–327, esp. 274–85 (with Dodds's commentary).

[38] Longinus, *On the Sublime* 15.6.

[39] For all these likenesses and differences, see above all the twenty-fourth chapter of the *Poetics*; many of them are also noted or implied in several passages elsewhere in the treatise.

[40] For Aristotle Homer is also the poet of the *Margites*, which (1448b28–1449a5) stands to comedy as the *Iliad* and *Odyssey* stand to tragedy. Unfortunately the full discussion which he presumably devoted to that poem must have vanished with the second book of the *Poetics*.

[41] This idea is implied throughout the *Poetics*; it becomes almost explicit in the passage cited in n. 40.

[42] Supremely great as the *Poetics* is, it is yet the product of a particular method, a particular thinker, and a particular epoch—the thirties or twenties of the fourth century B.C., when the transition from the song culture to the book culture was nearing completion. The treatise inevitably takes little or no account of many aspects of the fifth-century tragic art that might seem of the utmost significance to a practicing fifth-century dramatist like Aristophanes (whose views were considered in Chap. 5), or to a modern critic. See, e.g., Lucas (1968), p. xxii.

[43] We can still check for ourselves the utterly un-Homeric designs of the extant Hesiodic poems (and also of the fragmentary *Eoiai*), which are, of course, a function of their un-Homeric contents and aims. To judge by Proclus's prose summaries of the Trojan Cycle, the poems constituting it were simply segments of the heroic annals in chronological sequence; the narrative certainly contained its high points, such as the death of Achilles or the taking of the city, but *focal* incidents or characters are hard to discern. There is less evidence about speeches, or characterizations by speech, in the early non-Homeric epics. Dialogues in the *Theogony* are few, short, and cast in symmetrical, almost antiphonal form (164–67 and 170–72; 543–44 and 548–49; 644–53 and 655–63); there are indications, however, of longer and more sophisticated dialogues in the fragmentary Hesiodic works (e.g. fr. 280M-W, from the *Peirithoou Katabasis*). Few examples of dialogue, or of speeches generally, have survived among the scanty verbatim fragments of the other early epics (see, e.g., *Little Iliad* fr. II Allen, Eumelus frr. 9, 11 Kinkel). But I find no certain traces of anything resembling the Homeric speech and dialogue techniques.

[44] The only Greek poems that approach them in technique, at least so far as characterization by speech is concerned, are the longer Homeric Hymns; but none of these is of such a scale as to be counted as "epic" in the Aristotelian or modern senses.

[45] Welcker (1839–41), pp. 29–31; Mette (1959), pp. vii–ix. One must be warned, of course, that both tables rest on a considerable proportion of conjecture in detail.

[46] A selection of other ancient opinions on the subject is given by Pearson (1917), pp. xxiii–iv; for example, the famous (but a little too contrived?) saying of the Academic philosopher Polemon, that "Homer was an epic Sophocles, Sophocles was a tragic Homer." The full collection of such testimonia is printed in Radt, *TrGF* IV, p. 75.

[47] Duchemin (1945); cf. above, pp. 51–52.

[48] I have not checked the entire Homeric corpus for examples, but here is a selection from the first half of the *Iliad*: 1.53–305 (four human speakers; Athena's intervention is no part of the debate itself); 1.533–611 (three speakers); 2.278–398 (three); 4.1–72 (two); 6.312–69 (three); 7.345–79 (three). A curious instance is the long debate in Achilles' lodging, 9.193–657, in which four speakers take part but Patroklos, though present throughout, says not a word; one is almost reminded of the *kōpha prosōpa* in tragedy. The most important exception to the Homeric "four-actor rule" that I have noticed is the great debate in the Ithacan Assembly, *Od.* 2.6–256 (seven speakers).

[49] The modern perception of many Euripidean plays (above all the so-called romantic melodramas) may well have been distorted by the ingrained belief that tragedy, to be a real tragedy, must necessarily have an *Iliadic* tone and outcome even though it may admit those *Odyssean* plot complexities, the peripety and the anagnorisis. The trouble seems to date back to the critics of the Renaissance; Aristotle's taste was more catholic (see esp. *Poetics* 1459b13–16, quoted above, p. 134).

[50] Duchemin (1945), pp. 73–105 and 117–23 on Euripides.

[51] Much more, I think, might be said on this last question; and also on the question, how far even Euripidean cosmic irony has been anticipated by Homer. But that, as Aristotle might put it, "belongs to another method."

[52] Cf. above, p. 98.

[53] *Poetics* 1449a15–19. On points like this—points that could be verified from the dramatic texts and from the official records of the contests, both of which sources were familiar to him—Aristotle's authority may count as absolute. The information which these combined sources afforded him extended back, at the very least, to the first years of the fifth century. Compare 1449a37–1449b1, where he remarks that the early evolution of tragedy is known, but not that of comedy, "for it was only at a late stage that the archon granted a comic chorus"; what Aristotle considered a "late stage" can be dated with some precision to the year 486 B.C., fully fourteen years before our first extant tragedy.

[54] The fifth-century sources are Aristophanes, *Frogs* 1004–1005 and Pherecrates, *Krapataloi* fr. 94K. Many of the later sources no doubt depend on one or other of these (e.g., the ancient *Vita* of Aeschylus, sec. 2), but certainty is not easily obtained in such matters. The most interesting of them, apart from the *Vita*, are Dioscorides in *Anth. Pal.* 7.411, and Quintilian 10.1.66.

[55] Cf. above, p. 104, with n. 5 there. One cannot, unfortunately, give any credence to Eustathius's words (on *Il.* 23.256): "the noble Aeschylus, who said

that his tragedies were slices from the mighty feasts of Homer—because he so brilliantly *took as his model* (*apomattesthai*, literally 'molded impressions from') *the Homeric methods*." The last clause here is a mere gloss on the original Aeschylean saying (which Eustathius almost certainly took from Athenaeus, one of his favorite sources), concocted out of (a) *Frogs* 1040 *apomaxamenē*, and (b) the remark about Sophocles in *Vit. Soph.* 20, "taking as model (*ekmattomenos*) the Homeric charm."

[56] We have to admit that the record is very incomplete, yet enough titles survive to have perhaps some statistical value for our purposes. Here is the list (omitting the Aeschylean titles, and satyr play titles). *TrGF* I, 1 Thespis: *Athla Peliou* or *Phorbas*, *Hiereis*, *Eitheoi*, *Pentheus* (on the question of the authenticity of these titles, see above, n. 35, *ad init.*). 2 Choerilus: *Alope*. 3 Phrynichus: *Aigyptioi*, *Aktaion*, *Alcestis*, *Antaios* or *Libyes*, *Danaides*, *Dikaioi* or *Persai* or *Synthōkoi* (alternative titles for *Phoenissae*?), *Phoenissae*, a play on the taking of Miletus, *Pleuroniai*, *Tantalos*. 4 Pratinas: *Dymainai* or *Karyatides*, *Perseus*, *Tantalos*. 7 Polyphrasmon: *Lykourgeia* tetralogy. 9 Aristias: *Antaios*, *Atalante*, *Kēres*, *Orpheus*.

[57] The Aeschylean *Iphigeneia* might possibly be added to the list of plays concerning prominent figures of the Trojan Cycle, but we really know nothing of its contents. I should emphasize that all the instances of possible trilogies mentioned in my text are conjectural, but in varying degrees. That the three Achilles plays formed a connected trilogy is likely both on internal grounds and on the evidence of vase paintings (cf. T. B. L. Webster in *Hermathena* 100 [1965], p. 22); the supposed Ajax trilogy seems likely on internal grounds; the remaining instances are less certain. Even so, the total of *individual tragedies* on the heroes of the Trojan War remains impressive.

[58] The *Oresteia* contains 3,842 lines; *Iliad* 1–5, 3,902 lines; *Odyssey* 1–8, 3,979 lines (the count is based on the Oxford Text of each work). These and similar figures seem often to be overlooked in discussions about the practicability of delivering the Homeric epics complete on any one occasion. The *Iliad* (16,193 lines) might indeed tax the endurance of a modern audience; but I calculate that even during the Peloponnesian War period, when the number of comedies was cut from five to three, the *Athenian* audiences routinely listened to a total of some 17,000 dramatic lines within three days. (If one assumes three tragic trilogies of the length of the *Oresteia*, three satyr plays of the length of the *Cyclops*, and three comedies of the length of the *Acharnians*, one has in fact a total of 17,355 lines).

[59] For the Achilles trilogy, see frr. 211–59M, Snell (1964), chap. 1; and Lesky, *TDH*[3], p. 149. The interpretation of the titles and fragments of the Odysseus plays (frr. 475–90M), I must stress, is uncertain, but such evidence as there is seems to favor the sequence printed in Mette: *Psychagōgoi* (fr. 478, the prophecy of Odysseus's death, might be spoken by Teiresias in Hades, cf. *Od.* 11.134–36); *Penelope* (with fr. 483 compare *Od.* 19.171–84); *Ostologoi* (frr. 485–86 were presumably spoken by Odysseus at some time after he had revealed himself to the Suitors). Any further conjectures as to the contents will depend entirely on the meaning assigned to the title, compare Smyth [1957],

vol. II, p. 440; but perhaps the "Bone Collectors" of the Chorus are most likely to have been the kinsmen of the deceased Suitors). The satyric *Kirke* could have rounded off the tetralogy.

[60] The general abandonment of the connected trilogy after the lifetime of Aeschylus meant that dramatic compositions covering large areas of the Homeric subject matter were ruled out in any case. But in fact, as Aristotle remarked (*Poet.* 1459b2–4) there were relatively few tragedies that attempted to confront any part of the *Iliad* or *Odyssey* at all. Neither Sophocles nor Euripides seems ever to have chosen an Iliadic theme, but we hear of plays entitled *Achilles* by Aristarchus of Tegea and by Iophon. From the *Odyssey* must have derived Sophocles' *Nausikaa*, and possibly his *Phaiakes* (the statement in the *Vita Sophoclis* 20, "he copies the *Odyssey* in many dramas," whatever it implies, can scarcely refer to subject matter); and also the *Aeolus* of Euripides. That seems to be the total of certain fifth-century instances: for the sake of completeness we may add the *Rhesus* (early fourth century?); then, certainly in the fourth century, the *Achilles* and the *Hector* of Astydamas II, the *Odysseus* of Apollodorus, the *Achilles* of Carcinus II, and a few other instances by poets of even lesser note (see nos. 71, 77, 85 in Snell *TrGF* I).

[61] The Achilles trilogy required two actors (*Myrmidons* fr. 223M, plus Bartoletti [1966]; *Phryges* fr. 243a, *fin.*), but we do not know at what period before 472 Aeschylus introduced the second actor. Perhaps it is worth remarking that the high proportion of choral song to speech in the *Myrmidons* is noted in the *Frogs*, 914–15 and 924; that might conceivably be taken in conjunction with Aristotle, *Poetics* 1449a15–18 (quoted above, p. 138) as evidence for a relatively early date.

[62] Lesky, *TDH*³, p. 61, with bibliography on the question in n. 15.

[63] Snell (1964), chap. 1, esp. pp. 1 and 14; and *Phryges* fr. 254M.

[64] Else (1965), p. 82 (he is actually speaking there of Homer's religious, moral, and political attitudes, but the application of the remark may be extended, as we shall see); compare ibid. pp. 5, 32, 84 for the experimental nature of Aeschylus's art in general.

[65] The inference that those tragedies which contained comic, bawdy, or otherwise *aprepeis* elements mostly belonged to an early stage in Aeschylus's career, before his realization of the possibilities of Homeric artistry, is obviously attractive; but we are in no position to confirm it.

[66] Above, p. 129.

[67] The *Eumenides* is perhaps only a superficial exception. In spite of the plot's wide range in space and time the entire action converges, again, on a single crucial point: the reconciliation between men and gods. In the text I have spoken only of individual plays. An Aeschylean *trilogy*, to judge (if one dare) by the solitary extant example, consisted of a sequence of three such crucial episodes in the saga of which each was self-contained aesthetically; but the first and second were incomplete thematically and morally.

[68] It is no part of our present business to inquire how far such a plot structure is based on the way in which great events (above all, wars) tend to structure

themselves in reality, or how far our pleasure in a plot of this kind is related to our actual life experience.

[69] Glaucus (of Rhegium?) in the Hypothesis to the *Persians* (= Phrynichus, fr. 8 in Snell, *TrGF* I). Cf. Lesky, *TDH*[3], p. 59, Lembke and Herington (1981), pp. 14–15, and below, p. 145. For the presumed date of 476 B.C., see Phrynichus T4 in Snell, with note; even if it is not accepted, the outside chronological limits for the *Phoenissae* seem to be 478–73 B.C.

[70] Duchemin (1945), pp. 46–55.

[71] The quotation is from Ireland (1974), p. 509. On stichomythia, cf. above, pp. 123–24.

[72] When all is said, the differences between the Eteocles of the *Seven* and (say) the Sophoclean Ajax are more than the likenesses. The Aeschylean figure, who carries, as it were, within himself a beleaguered city, that city's gods, and a strange and terrible heredity, seems incommensurate with the monolithic individualist created by Sophocles.

[73] It is difficult, however, to use this indisputable fact as an argument against the play's authenticity. Prometheus's presence throughout the work is obviously a function of the playwright's initial choice of mythical theme; and so too perhaps, is Prometheus's lonely defiance. Nor can we neglect the evidence in the *Oresteia* (most notably the employment of a third actor) which suggests that in his last years Aeschylus was perfectly capable of learning from his younger competitor.

[74] Just how original and how daring an achievement it was will be realized by anyone who cares to contemplate as a whole the history not merely of archaic Greek literature but also of archaic Greek architecture and sculpture.

[75] By the time of Aeschylus's extant plays we have to reckon with yet a further disguise—that of the facade of the *skēnē*, the stage building behind the dance floor. It is certain that in the *Oresteia* this structure is already treated as if it were a palace (or, in the *Eumenides*, a temple), as in so many plays by the subsequent tragedians; how far the actual physical disguise went beyond the piercing of the facade with apertures to represent doors we do not know. Opinions vary sharply over the scenic arrangements of the rest of Aeschylus's plays, and over such questions as stage machinery and scene painting; on all this the reader will find ample information and discussion in Taplin (1977).

[76] Glaucus, in the Hypothesis to the *Persians* (cf. above, n. 69). It seems a curiously cozy opening for a tragedy: one recalls the openings of so many English light comedies of the years around 1900, where the curtain rises on a butler or parlormaid tidying the drawing-room before the arrival of the main characters. Aeschylus never made a mistake like that, at least in the plays and fragments that have survived to us.

[77] Phrynichus T 8–11 in *TrGF* I, esp. T 10 (the references to Phrynichus's music by Aristophanes).

[78] Complete, that is, as a *tragic* statement; the lost satyr drama *Proteus* must have played its part—a part scarcely imaginable now—in the statement of the *Oresteia* as a whole. The other extant dramas of Aeschylus (the *Persians* ex-

cepted) all apparently belonged to connected tragic trilogies the other members of which are now lost; and are therefore very much harder to analyze from our present point of view, or indeed from any point of view. Least difficult is the *Seven Against Thebes*, since it was the final play of a trilogy (*Laios*, *Oedipus*, *Seven*) whose plot can in some degree be reconstructed from our general knowledge of the legend and from certain allusions within the extant tragedy. Here the visual climax to the entire sequence of plays was surely the procession bearing the corpses of the two brothers (848–60), the last generation of an illustrious and tormented line. The *Suppliants* was certainly, the *Prometheus* probably, the first play in its trilogy; and, as we shall see in the following discussion of the *Agamemnon*, the visual statement of a first play may be ambivalent in itself and may offer no clue at all to the trilogy's subsequent visual development.

[79] She may first sense out the Palace Guilt as early as 1087–88; she sees it with increasing clarity at 1095–97, 1186–97, 1217–22.

[80] It seems arguable that the moment of transition between the Troy Guilt and the Palace Guilt as dominant themes is deliberately signaled by the emphatic juxtaposition in the Chorus's address to Agamemnon at his entrance (782–83): ἄγε δή, βασιλεῦ, Τροίας πτολίπορθ', 'Ατρέως γένεθλον: "Come now, King, *city-sacker of Troy, offspring of Atreus!*" This is the first passage in the play where Agamemnon individually is characterized as *offspring of Atreus*, although the traditional patronymic *Atreides* is several times applied to him, or to him and Menelaus together, in the earlier scenes (3, 44, 124, etc.), and the two brothers are described as *Atreōs paides* in line 60.

[81] Scully and Herington (1975), p. 97.

[82] The stichomythia in 908–30, where Orestes drives Clytaemnestra at swordpoint step by step, iambic line by iambic line, toward her death within the palace seems to me one of the most effective harmonizations of visual poetry with an apparently highly artificial verbal convention ever achieved in Greek drama. The stichomythia seems to continue as long as the pair are in sight; we are all but drawn into the palace door, to witness the final sword thrust.

[83] If the *Choephori*'s credentials as an Aeschylean work were not so impeccable as they happen to be—if, for instance, we knew only the *Persians*, the *Seven*, the *Suppliants*, and the *Choephori*, bereft (as it still is) of its ancient Hypothesis—I imagine that more than one excellent scholar would have athetized it out of hand. The grounds for the athetesis would, I think, be at least as impressive as some of those on which the *Prometheus* has been damned; most notably, the fact that its dramaturgy could be paralleled nowhere else in extant Aeschylus, but repeatedly in Sophocles and Euripides.

[84] Characteristically, these powers are introduced to us in a riddling metaphor, "your mother's spiteful hounds" (*Cho.* 924, cf. 1054). They are not actually identified as Erinyes until *Eumenides* 331: Orestes, seeing them in his mind's eye at *Cho.* 1048 ff., still cannot make out what creatures they are, but gropes helplessly for comparisons; even the Delphic priestess, after actually seeing their physical presence in the Temple, can still only compare them to better-known archaic monsters, Gorgons or Harpies (*Eum.* 57–59). This par-

ticular progression from verbal ambiguity to the visual clarity of the Furies' actual appearance onstage (*Eum.* 117 ff.) is a very fine example in miniature of Aeschylus's technique.

[85] Every beginning student of the *Oresteia* in Greek must have sensed the ever-growing simplicity of Aeschylus's language, as he passes from the dense verbal texture of the *Agamemnon*, through the *Choephori* (where the language retains its Agamemnonian complexity mostly in the *kommos* and the choral odes), into the *Eumenides* (where even the choral singing is now relatively simple and extrovert). It is true that the modern reader—and not merely the beginning reader—would be able to see and delight in this progress much more easily if he were not harassed at every point in the trilogy by lexical and textual dubieties; but that is not due to any fault in Aeschylus's art.

[86] Even Aristotle, probably with the stricter standards of fourth-century drama in mind, is easy-going enough in this matter: he seems satisfied with tragedy's practice of "*trying* to keep within a single revolution of the sun, more or less" (*Poetics* 1449b12–13). On the whole, the fifth-century tragedians—including Aeschylus himself, in the first part of the *Eumenides*—felt a great deal freer than that: a choral ode, in particular, may often cover a considerable lapse of dramatic time.

7. Epilogue: The Enactment of a Greek Lyric Poem

[1] The papyrus of Timotheus's *Persians* was first edited by Wilamowitz (1903); his book remains indispensable for the study of Timotheus. There are subsequent editions by Edmonds (1928), vol. III, Diehl (1925), vol. II, and Page (frr. 788–91 *PMG*); I adopt the fragment- and line-numbering of this last. Edmonds provides an almost complete collection of the ancient testimonia. *In the notes to the present chapter, I refer to these testimonia simply by the abbreviation "E 298" (etc.),* which means that the text and full reference of the testimonium concerned will be found on p. 298 (etc.) of Edmonds. Two important modern studies on the poet are those by Maas (1937; *RE* article) and Lesky (1966A) pp. 415–16; the latter notes the possibility that the Timotheus who appears on the Aixone inscription *IG* II/III^2, no. 3091 (dated ca. 380 B.C.) as a tragedian could perhaps be identifiable with our poet.

[2] Plutarch, *Philopoemen* 11 (E 304), Pausanias 8.50.3; see App. III, no. 8. Other known re-performances of works by Timotheus are: the boys' dithyrambic contest at the Great Dionysia of 319 B.C. (the poem was *Elpenor*: inscr., E 298); at Knossos, about 170 B.C. (unidentified poems with lyre accompaniment: inscr. no. 190 in Schwyzer [1923]); in Arcadia, in the second century B.C. (Polybius, Appendix VII, no. **11**); at the Isthmian, Nemean, and other (unnamed) contests, in the first half of the second century A.D.; and probably at the Great Didymeia in Miletus, ca. 200 A.D. For the inscriptions recording these events, see Latte (1954) and (1955). The poems are not named; in the first in-

stance, at least, new music had to be composed for them, and it is therefore to be presumed that Timotheus's original music had by now disappeared from memory.

[3]The date and even the place of performance have been much debated: see Wilamowitz (1903), pp. 61–64; Bassett (1931), pp. 153–58; and Maas (1937), col. 1332. If we can accept the statement of Satyrus (papyrus *Life* of Euripides, E 282, cf. Plut. *An Seni* 23, ibid.) that Euripides helped Timotheus compose the *Persians*, plus the evidence (see next note) that it was performed in Athens, then we have a *terminus ante* in the year 408, when Euripides left Athens for Macedon. I can see no solid evidence for a more exact dating than that, although there is something to be said for Bassett's conjecture: between 412 and 408.

[4]The evidence cited in note 3 alone would make this seem likely (although theoretically Euripides might also have associated with Timotheus in Macedon), but we have also an express statement that the *Persians* was performed in Athens; see the anecdote in Müller's *Mélanges*, E 308. From that source, plus Satyrus, we further learn that the performance won the prize. Since the *Persians* is a kitharodic nome, we infer that the occasion was a contest in kitharody.

[5]The Panathenaia fell at the end of Hekatombaion: late July or early August (Parke [1977], p. 33).

[6]This is a probable inference both from the very name of the Odeion and from Plutarch, *Pericles* 13.5–7 (although that passage presents certain difficulties; see Davison [1958], pp. 33–36). In general cf. Holloway (1966) on kitharodic performances at Athens.

[7]Satyrus's *Life*, and Plutarch *An Seni*; see above, n. 3.

[8]We know that at any rate in the first half of the fourth century B.C. the contestants in kitharody numbered five; see the Panathenaic prize inscription, *IG* II^2, no. 2311 (= Dittenberger [1915–1924], no. 1055). Elsewhere than Athens, the usual number seems to have been three: *IG* XII.9, no. 189 (Eretria, mid-fourth century B.C.); Lucian, *Adversus Indoctum* 9 (the Pythian contests at Delphi).

[9]His red hair: Pherecrates fr. 157K, line 21 (E 284). His pugnacity and egoism: frr. 796 and 802 *PMG*, and the *sphragis* of the *Persians* itself.

[10]That much may, I think, be safely inferred from *Persians* 206–212. The comic stories about the Spartans' treatment of the four extra strings on Timotheus's lyre in Plutarch, Pausanias, and Artemon *ap*. Athenaeus (E 286–88) may perhaps be unhistorical in detail, but they also point to performances at Sparta; Plutarch specifies the occasion as the Karneia.

[11]Plutarch, *An Seni*, plus Satyrus: above, n. 3.

[12]*αἰσθόμενος ἡλίκος ἐστὶν ἐν τῷ γένει*, Satyrus.

[13]The authority, again, is Satyrus.

[14]*Kainotomia* and similar words are applied to Timotheus's art in Satyrus, Plutarch, and ps.-Plut. *Mus.* (E 282–86); cf. his own use of the word *kaina* in fr. 796, line 2.

[15]Timotheus was in fact not the first musician thus to multiply the traditional number of strings (see Wilamowitz [1903], pp. 68–78), but his eleven-stringed

instrument was particularly notorious; compare the testimonia cited in note 14, plus Nicomachus (E 288–90). In *Persians* 230 he proudly alludes to it himself.

[16] Dionysius of Halicarnassus (E 364) is the main source for this, but cf. also *exarmonious* in Pherecrates, fr. 157K, line 25 (E 286).

[17] Here I quote the translation of an expert on this difficult passage: Düring (1945), p. 195.

[18] Plutarch, *Philopoemen* 11 (E 306, top).

[19] See the testimonia to frr. 785, 792, and 793 (= Ar. *Poet.* 1461b30) in *PMG*.

[20] *Probl.* 19.15 (E 294).

[21] Fr. 788 *PMG*. It is not, indeed, quite certain that this was the very first line in the poem: see Bassett (1931), p. 157, and Korzeniewski (1974), pp. 38–39.

[22] Fr. 735 *PMG*, with Aristophanes, *Clouds* 967–68.

[23] Ps.-Plut. *Mus.*, chap. 4 (E 290).

[24] Frr. 789 *PMG* (where this interpretation is made certain by the words of the source, Plutarch), and 790 (where it is probable, but not certain).

[25] There can, of course, be no absolute certainty about the length of the *Persians* as it originally stood, but the calculations of Bassett (1931) on mechanical grounds correspond remarkably well with those of Korzeniewski (1974) on thematic grounds; they would suggest a length of about 700 lines. An evenly paced oral delivery of the best preserved part of the poem (lines 60–240) takes about twelve minutes. Allowing, as one probably should, for considerable variations in tempo and perhaps even pauses for miming during Timotheus's original performance, one arrives at a running time of about thirty-five or forty minutes for the poem as it stood complete.

[26] Lines 26–28.

[27] Lines 31–39; I have accepted, rather doubtfully, Wilamowitz's supplement *ammig[a autis]* in 36.

[28] Korzeniewski (1974), p. 37, has well conjectured that these frantic *Persian* speeches may have balanced and contrasted with the steady and determined *Greek* speeches in the first part of the narrative (cf. frr. 789 and 790).

[29] That he is a magnate is clear from lines 41–42; that he is a Persian (rather than a Phrygian, as he is in Wilamowitz's restoration of 40) seems likely on that very account.

[30] See especially lines 61–71 and 82; one recalls here the birth cries in the *Semelēs Ōdis*, for instance (fr. 792 *PMG*).

[31] Korzeniewski (1974).

[32] This effect is heightened by the quotation (or unconscious echo?) of Aeschylus's *Choephori*, line 50, in the King's opening words, ἰὼ κατασκαφαὶ δόμων (*Persians* 178).

[33] Wilamowitz (1903), p. 36.

[34] Korzeniewski (1974), p. 24.

[35] In Timotheus's Greek the final word, which I have ambiguously translated "harmony," is *eunomiai*. Bassett (1931) and Korzeniewski (1974) have both suggested, I think rightly, that it is meant to involve a play on both the separate

senses of the word from which it derives, *nomos*: "law," and "musical nome."

[36] For the evidence, see above, n. 4.

[37] See, especially, Bassett (1931), pp. 159–61; he names Euripides' *Antiope*, *Hypsipyle*, and *Phoenissae*, besides *Orestes*. Perhaps the most remarkable parallel to which he points is the verbal and metrical correspondence between *Orestes* 1397 Ἀσιάδι φωνᾷ βασιλέων and line 147 of Timotheus's poem, Ἀσιάδι φωνᾷ διάτορον. All this may lend some credibility to Satyrus's story about the collaboration of the two poets (E 282).

Bibliography

Abbreviated Titles

ABV: Beazley, J. D., *Attic Black-Figure Vase-Painters*, Oxford 1956.

*ARV*²: Beazley, J. D., *Attic Red-Figure Vase-Painters*, ed. 2, 3 vols., Oxford 1963.

*DFA*²: Pickard-Cambridge, Sir Arthur, *The Dramatic Festivals of Athens*, ed. 2, revised by John Gould and D. M. Lewis, Oxford 1968.

D-K: Diels, Hermann, and Kranz, Walther, eds., *Die Fragmente der Vorsokratiker*, ed. 7, 3 vols., Berlin 1954.

*DTC*²: Pickard-Cambridge, Sir Arthur, *Dithyramb Tragedy and Comedy*, ed. 2, revised by T. B. L. Webster, Oxford 1962.

FGrH: Jacoby, Felix, ed., *Die Fragmente der griechischen Historiker*, 14 vols., Berlin and Leiden 1923–1958.

K: Kock, Theodor, ed., *Comicorum Atticorum Fragmenta*, 3 vols., Leipzig 1880–1888.

Kleine Pauly: Zeigler, Konrad, and Sontheimer, Walther, eds., *Der Kleine Pauly: Lexikon der Antike*, 5 vols., Stuttgart 1964–1975.

LSJ: Liddell, H. G., and Scott, R., *A Greek-English Lexicon*, ed. 9, revised by Stuart Jones, H., Oxford 1940.

M: Mette, H. J., ed., *Die Fragmente der Tragödien des Aischylos*, Berlin 1959.

M-W: Merkelbach, R., and West, M. L., eds., *Fragmenta Hesiodea*, Oxford 1967.

*OCD*²: Hammond, N. G. L., and Scullard, H. H., eds., *The Oxford Classical Dictionary*, ed. 2, Oxford 1970.

PLF: Lobel, Edgar, and Page, Denys, eds., *Poetarum Lesbiorum Fragmenta*, Oxford 1955.

PMG: Page, D. L., *Poetae Melici Graeci*, Oxford 1962.

POxy: *The Oxyrhynchus Papyri*, London 1898 to present.

RE: Wissowa, G., ed., *Paulys Real-Encyclopädie der classischen Altertumswissenschaft: neue Bearbeitung*, Stuttgart 1894–1959.

SLG: Page, Denys, ed., *Supplementum Lyricis Graecis*, Oxford 1974.

Sn.: (1) *Bacchylides*, post B. Snell edidit H. Maehler, Leipzig 1970. (2) *Pindarus*: Pars Prima, Epinicia, post B. Snell edidit H. Maehler, Leipzig 1971; Pars Altera, Fragmenta, edidit Bruno Snell, Leipzig 1964.

*TDH*³: Lesky, Albin, *Die tragische Dichtung der Hellenen*, ed. 3, Göttingen 1972.

TrGF: *Tragicorum Graecorum Fragmenta*, Vol. I, ed. Bruno Snell, Göttingen 1971; Vol. II, ed. Richard Kannicht et Bruno Snell, Göttingen 1981; Vol. IV, ed. Stefan Radt, Göttingen 1977.

W: West, M. L., ed., *Iambi et Elegi Graeci ante Alexandrum cantati*, 2 vols., Oxford 1971–1972.

JOURNALS: The titles of journals are for the most part abbreviated on the model of the list given in *The Oxford Classical Dictionary* (see above, *OCD*²), pp. ix–xxii.

AUTHORS

Adrados, F. Rodriguez (1975): *Festival, Comedy, and Tragedy. The Greek Origins of Theatre*, translated by C. Holme. London.

Alexiou, Margaret (1974): *The Ritual Dirge in Greek Tradition*. Cambridge.

Andrewes, A. (1956): *The Greek Tyrants*. London.

Arias, P., and Hirmer, Max (1962): *A History of 1000 Years of Greek Vase-Painting*. New York.

Austin, Colin, ed. (1968): *Nova Fragmenta Euripidea in Papyris reperta*. Berlin.

Barron, J. P. (1964): The Sixth-Century Tyranny at Samos, *CQ* 14, 210–229.

Bartoletti, V. (1966): Un Frammento dei "Myrmidones" di Eschilo, *American Studies in Papyrology*, 1, 121–23.

Bassett, S. E. (1931): The Place and Date of the First Performance of the *Persians* of Timotheus, *CP* 26, 153–65.

Beazley, J. D. (1922): Citharoedus, *JHS* 42, 70–98.

——— (1928): *Greek Vases in Poland*. Oxford.

——— (1948): Hymn to Hermes, *AJA* 52, 336–40.

———. *See also ABV* and *ARV*², under "Abbreviated Titles," above.

Bergson, L. (1953): The Omitted Augment in the Messengers' Speeches, *Eranos* 51, 121–28.

Berve, Helmut (1967): *Die Tyrannis bei den Griechen*, 2 vols. Munich.

Biffi, Lydia (1961): Elementi comici nella tragedia greca, *Dioniso* 35, 89–102.

Björck, G. (1950): *Das Alpha impurum und die tragische Kunstsprache*. Uppsala.

Bloesch, H. J. (1943): *῎Αγαλμα als Kleinod, Weihgeschenk, und Götterbild*. Bern.

Boardman, John (1974): *Athenian Black Figure Vases*. London.

——— (1975): *Athenian Red Figure Vases: The Archaic Period: A Handbook*. London.

Boersma, J. S. (1970): *Athenian Building Policy from 561/0 to 405/4*. Groningen.

Böhme, R. B. (1953): *Orpheus: Das Alter des Kitharoden*. Berlin.

Bölte, F. (1907): Rhapsodische Vortragskunst. Ein Beitrag zur Technik des homerischen Epos, *Neue Jahrb*. 19, 571–81.

Bowra, C. M. (1964): *Pindar*. Oxford.
Bremer, J. M. (1976): Why Messenger-Speeches?, in *Miscellanea Tragica in honorem J. C. Kamerbeek*. Amsterdam.
Brommer, Frank (1973): *Vasenlisten zur griechischen Heldensagen*, ed. 3. Marburg.
Browning, Robert (1963): A Byzantine Treatise on Tragedy, in ΓΕΡΑΣ: *Acta Universitatis Carolinae*. Prague. (Reprinted in Robert Browning: *Studies in Byzantine History, Literature, and Education*, London 1977).
Burkert, W. (1966): Greek Tragedy and Sacrificial Ritual, *GRBS* 7, 87–121.
Burton, R. W. B. (1962): *Pindar's Pythian Odes*. Oxford.
Cadoux, T. J. (1948): The Athenian Archons from Kreon to Hypsichides, *JHS* 68, 70–123.
Campbell, David A. (1964): Flutes and Elegiac Couplets, *JHS* 84, 63–68.
——— (1967): *Greek Lyric Poetry*. London and New York.
——— (1982): *Greek Lyric*, Vol. I (Sappho, Alcaeus). Cambridge, Mass., and London (Loeb Classical Library).
Caskey, L. D., and Beazley, J. D. (1931–1963): *Attic Vase-Paintings in the Museum of Fine Arts, Boston*, 3 vols. plus plates. London and Boston.
Càssola, Filippo, ed. (1975): *Inni Omerici*. Florence.
Comotti, G. (1977): Words, Verse, and Music in Euripides' "Iphigeneia in Aulis," *Museum Philologum Londinense* 2, 69–84.
Conomis, N. C. (1964): The Dochmiacs of Greek Drama, *Hermes* 92, 23–50.
Dale, A. M. (1968): *The Lyric Metres of Greek Drama*, ed. 2. Cambridge.
——— (1969): *Collected Papers*. Cambridge.
——— (1971): *Metrical Analyses of Tragic Choruses: Fasc.* 1: *Dactylo-Epitrite*. London (University of London Institute of Classical Studies, Bulletin Supplement No. 21.1).
Davison, J. A. (1955): Pisistratus and Homer, *TAPA* 86, 1–21.
——— (1958): Notes on the Panathenaea, *JHS* 78, 23–42.
——— (1962): Literature and Literacy in Ancient Greece, *Phoenix* 16, 141–56 and 219–33.
——— (1962, *Comp.*): The Transmission of the Text, *and* The Homeric Question, in *A Companion to Homer*, ed. Alan J. B. Wace and Frank H. Stubbings, London and New York, pp. 215–33 and 234–65.
Del Grande, C. (1923): Nomos Citarodico, *Rivista Indo-Greca-Italica* 7, 1–7.
Denniston, J. D. (1954): *The Greek Particles*, ed. 2. Oxford.
Diehl, E., ed. (1925): *Anthologia Lyrica Graeca*, 2 vols. Leipzig.
Diels, Hermann. *See* D-K, under "Abbreviated Titles," above.
Dittenberger, Wilhelm, ed. (1915–1924): *Sylloge Inscriptionum Graecarum*, 4 vols. Leipzig.
Dodds, E. R., ed. (1960): *Euripides: Bacchae*, ed. 2. Oxford.
Dover, K. J. (1957): Aristophanes 1938–1955, *Lustrum* 2, 52–112.
——— (1964): The Poetry of Archilochus, in *Archiloque*, Vandoeuvres-Geneva (Entretiens Hardt, Vol. X).
———, ed. (1968): *Aristophanes, Clouds*. Oxford.

Drachmann, A. B., ed. (1903–1927): *Scholia Vetera in Pindari Carmina*, 3 vols. Leipzig.
Drew-Bear, Th. (1968): The Trochaic Tetrameter in Greek Tragedy, *AJP* 89, 385–405.
Duchemin, Jacqueline (1945): *L'ΑΓΩΝ dans la Tragédie grecque*. Paris.
——— (1974): Du Lyrisme à la Tragédie: Reflexions sur l'*Agamemnon* et les *Perses* d'Eschyle, in *Serta Turyniana*, ed. John L. Heller and J. K. Newman, Urbana, Chicago, and London.
Düring, I. (1945): Studies in Musical Terminology in Fifth-Century Literature, *Eranos* 43, 176–97.
Edmonds, J. M. (1928): *Lyra Graeca*, revised and augmented edition, 3 vols. Cambridge, Mass., and London (Loeb Classical Library).
Einarson, Benedict, and De Lacy, Phillip H., eds. (1967): Pseudo-Plutarch, *De Musica*, in Plutarch's *Moralia*, Vol. 14. Cambridge, Mass., and London (Loeb Classical Library).
Eliot, T. S. (1951): *Poetry and Drama*. Cambridge, Mass.
——— (1961): The Three Voices of Poetry, in *On Poetry*. New York.
Else, G. F. (1957): The Origin of *τραγῳδία*, *Hermes* 85, 17–46.
——— (1965): *The Origin and Early Form of Greek Tragedy*. Cambridge, Mass. (Martin Classical Lectures, Vol. 20).
——— (1977): Ritual and Drama in Aeschyleian [*sic*] Tragedy, *Illinois Classical Studies* 2, 70–87.
Farnell, Lewis Richard (1896–1909): *The Cults of the Greek States*, 5 vols. Oxford.
Feaver, D. D. (1978): A New Note, Omega, in the Orestes Papyrus? *AJP* 99, 38–40.
Ferri, Silvio (1932): *χορὸς κυκλικός*: Nuovi documenti archeologici e vecchia tradizione letteraria, *Riv. del R. Instituto d' Archeologia e Storia dell' Arte* 3, 299–330.
Finnegan, Ruth (1977): *Oral Poetry: Its Nature, Significance, and Social Context*. Cambridge.
Flashar, Helmut (1958): *Der Dialog Ion als Zeugnis Platonischer Philosophie*. Berlin.
Fleming, T. J. (1977): The Musical Nomos in Aeschylus' *Oresteia*, *CJ* 72, 222–33.
Floyd, Edwin D. (1965): The Performance of Pindar, *Pythian* 8.55–70, *GRBS* 6, 187–200.
Fraenkel, Eduard (1918): Lyrische Daktylen, *Rh. Mus.* 72, 161–97 and 321–52.
——— (1962): *Beobachtungen zu Aristophanes*. Rome.
Fränkel, Hermann (1925): Griechische Wörter, *Glotta* 14, 1–13.
——— (1960): Eine Stileigenheit der frühgriechischen Literatur, in *Wegen und Formen frühgriechischen Denkens*, ed. 2. Munich.
——— (1975): *Early Greek Poetry and Philosophy*. Oxford.
Friedman, Albert B., ed. (1956): *The Viking Book of Folk Ballads of the English-Speaking World*. New York.

Furtwängler, A., and Reichhold, K. (1904–1932): *Griechische Vasenmalerei*, 3 vols. plus plates. Munich.
Gaertringen, Hiller von (1903): edition of the *Marmor Parium* in *IG* XII.5, no. 444.
Gerber, Douglas E. (1970): *Euterpe*. Amsterdam.
Griffin, Jasper (1977): The Epic Cycle and the Uniqueness of Homer, *JHS* 97, 39–53.
Griffith, Mark (1977): *The Authenticity of "Prometheus Bound."* Cambridge.
Hansen, P. A. (1975): *A List of Greek Verse Inscriptions Down to 400 B.C.* Copenhagen.
Haslam, M. W. (1974): Stesichorean Metre, *QUCC* 17, 7–57.
——— (1978): The Versification of the New Stesichorus, *GRBS* 19, 29–57.
Henderson, Isobel (1957): Ancient Greek Music, *The New Oxford History of Music*, ed. Egon Wellesz, Vol. I, chap. 9, pp. 336–403. Oxford.
Herington, C. J. (1955): *Athena Parthenos and Athena Polias*. Manchester.
——— (1970): *The Author of the "Prometheus Bound."* Austin and London.
———, ed. (1972): *The Older Scholia on the "Prometheus Bound."* Leiden (Mnemosyne Supplement 19).
Hollander, John (1981): *Rhyme's Reason*. New Haven and London.
Holloway, R. Ross (1966): Music at the Panathenaic Festival, *Archaeology* 19, 112–19.
Hooker, G. T. W. (1957): Pindar and the Athenian Festivals of Dionysos, *PCA* 54, 35–36 (résumé).
Immerwahr, Henry R. (1964): Book Rolls on Attic Vases, in *Classical, Mediaeval, and Renaissance Studies in Honor of Berthold Louis Ullman*, ed. Charles Henderson, Jr., Vol. I. Rome, pp. 17–48.
——— (1965): Inscriptions on the Anakreon Krater in Copenhagen, *AJA* 69, 152–54.
——— (1973): More Book Rolls on Attic Vases, *Antike Kunst* 16, 143–47.
Ireland, Stanley (1974): Stichomythia in Aeschylus: The Dramatic Role of Syntax and Connecting Particles, *Hermes* 102, 509–24.
Irigoin, Jean (1952): *Histoire du Texte de Pindare*. Paris.
Jacoby, Felix (1904): *Das Marmor Parium*. Berlin.
———. *See also FGrH*, under "Abbreviated Titles," above.
Jeffery, L. H. (1961): *The Local Scripts of Archaic Greece*. Oxford.
Jourdain-Hemmerdinger, D. (1973): Un nouveau papyrus musical d'Euripide (Présentation provisoire), *Comptes Rendus de l'Académie des Inscriptions et Belles Lettres*, 1973, 292–302.
Kagan, Donald (1981): *The Peace of Nicias and the Sicilian Expedition*. Ithaca and London.
Kinkel, G., ed. (1877): *Epicorum Graecorum Fragmenta*, Vol. I (no further volumes were published). Leipzig.
Kirkwood, G. M. (1974): *Early Greek Monody: The History of a Poetic Type*. Ithaca and London (Cornell Studies in Philology, Vol. 38).
Knox, B. M. W. (1968): Silent Reading in Antiquity, *GRBS* 9, 421–35.
Kock, Theodor. *See* K, under "Abbreviated Titles," above.

Kontoleon, Nikolaos M. (1952): Νεαὶ ἐπιγραφαὶ περὶ τοῦ Ἀρχιλόχου ἐκ Πάρου, *Archaiologike Ephemeris*, 32–95.
——— (1964): Archilochos und Paros, in *Archiloque*, Vandoeuvres-Geneva (Entretiens Hardt, Vol. X).
Korzeniewski, Dietmar (1968): *Griechische Metrik. Einführung in Gegenstand, Methoden, und Ergebnisse der Forschung.* Darmstadt.
——— (1974): Die Binnenresponsion in den *Persern* des Timotheos, *Philologus* 118, 22–39.
Lanata, Giuliana (1963): *Poetica Pre-Platonica: testimonianze e frammenti.* Florence.
Landels, J. G. (1968): A Newly Discovered Aulos, *BSA* 63, 231–38.
Lasserre, François, ed. (1954): *Plutarque, De la Musique.* Olten and Lausanne.
Lasserre, François, and Bonnard, André (1958): *Archiloque: Fragments.* Paris.
Latte, K. (1954): Zur Geschichte der griechischen Tragödie in der Kaiserzeit, *Eranos* 52, 125–27.
——— (1955): Noch einmal die Themisoninschrift, *Eranos* 53, 75–76.
Lefkowitz, Mary R. (1963); ΤΩ ΚΑΙ ΕΓΩ: The First Person in Pindar, *HSCP* 67, 177–253.
Lembke, Janet, and Herington, C. J. (1981): *Aeschylus: Persians.* New York and London.
Lesky, Albin (1966A): *A History of Greek Literature,* translated by James Willis and Cornelis de Heer. London.
——— (1966B): Der Mythos im Verständnis der Antike, I: Von der Frühzeit bis Sophokles, *Gymnasium* 73, 27–44.
———. *See also TDH*[3], under "Abbreviated Titles," above.
Lloyd-Jones, H. (1966): Problems of Early Greek Tragedy. Pratinas, Phrynichus, the Gyges Fragment, in *Estudios sobre la tragedia griega*, Cuadernos de la Fundacion Pastor XIII, Madrid, pp. 11–33.
——— (1971): *The Justice of Zeus.* Berkeley (Sather Classical Lectures, Vol. 41).
Loehrer, R. (1927): *Mienenspiele und Maske in der griechischen Tragödie.* Paderborn (Studien zur Geschichte und Kultur des Altertums, XIV.4/5).
Lucas, D. W., ed. (1968): *Aristotle: Poetics.* Oxford.
Lullies, R. (1940): Zur boiotisch rotfigurigen Vasenmalerei, *AM* 65, 1–27.
Maas, Paul (1937): *art.* 9. Timotheos in: *RE* Vol. II.6.2, cols. 1331–37.
——— (1962): *Greek Metre*, translated by Hugh Lloyd-Jones. Oxford.
Marrou, H.-I. (1946): ΜΕΛΟΓΡΑΦΙΑ, *L'Antiquité Classique*, 15, 289–96.
——— (1965): *Histoire de l'éducation dans l'antiquité*, ed. 6. Paris.
Meier, P. J. (1894): *art.* Agones, in *RE* Vol. I, cols. 836–67.
Merkelbach, R. (1963): Zwei metrische Beiträge, *Maia* 15, 165–67.
——— (1973): Ein Fragment des homerischen Dionysos-Hymnus, *ZPE* 12, 212–15.
Mette, H. J. *See* M, under "Abbreviated Titles," above.
Mikalson, J. D. (1976): Erechtheus and the Panathenaia, *AJP* 97, 141–53.
Mosino, F. (1977): Lirica corale a Reggio. Una notizia trascurata, *QUCC*, no. 26, 117–19.
Moulton, Carroll (1979): Homeric Metaphor, *CP* 74, 279–93.

Murray, Penelope (1981): Poetic Inspiration in Early Greece, *JHS* 101, 87–100.
Mylonas, George E. (1961): *Eleusis and the Eleusinian Mysteries*. Princeton.
Nagy, Gregory (1979): *The Best of the Achaeans*. Baltimore and London.
Nauck, August, ed. (1889): *Tragicorum Graecorum Fragmenta*, ed. 2. Leipzig.
Neubecker, A. J. (1977): *Altgriechische Musik. Eine Einführung*. Darmstadt.
Nilsson, Martin P. (1906): *Griechische Feste von religiöse Bedeutung*. Leipzig.
Nisetich, Frank J. (1980): *Pindar's Victory Songs*. Baltimore and London.
Nutzhorn, F. (1869): *Die Entstehungsweise der homerischen Gedichte*. Leipzig.
Page, Denys L. (1951): *Alcman: The Partheneion*. Oxford.
——— (1955): *Sappho and Alcaeus*. Oxford.
——— (1964): Archilochus and the Oral Tradition, in *Archiloque*, Vandoeuvres-Geneva (Entretiens Hardt, Vol. X).
——— (1975): *Epigrammata Graeca*. Oxford (Oxford Classical Texts).
———. *See also PLF*, *PMG*, and *SLG*, under "Abbreviated Titles," above.
Parke, H. W., and Wormell, D. E. W. (1956): *The Delphic Oracle*, 2 vols. Oxford.
Parke, H. W. (1977): *Festivals of the Athenians*. Ithaca.
Parry, Milman (1971): *The Making of Homeric Verse: The Collected Papers of Milman Parry*, edited by Adam Parry. Oxford.
Patzer, H. (1952): ῬΑΨΩΙΔΟΣ, *Hermes* 80, 314–25.
——— (1962): *Die Anfänge der griechischen Tragödie*. Wiesbaden.
Payne, Humfry (1931): *Necrocorinthia*. Oxford.
Pearson, A. C., ed. (1917): *The Fragments of Sophocles*, 3 vols. Cambridge.
Peek, Werner (1935): Eine Herme des Hipparch, *Hermes* 70, 461–63.
Pfeiffer, Rudolf (1968): *History of Classical Scholarship from the Beginnings to the End of the Hellenistic Age*. Oxford.
Pickard-Cambridge, A. W. (1946): *The Theatre of Dionysus in Athens*. Oxford.
———. *See also DFA*[2] and *DTC*[2], under "Abbreviated Titles,"
Poehlmann, E. (1970): *Denkmäler altgriechischer Musik*. Nuremberg, n.d. [1970].
Radermacher, Ludwig, ed. (1967): Aristophanes' 'Frösche,' ed. 3 with additions by Walther Kraus. Graz, Vienna, and Cologne.
Radin, Max (1921/22): Homer and Aeschylus, *CJ* 17, 332–34.
Reisch, Emil (1885): *De Musicis Graecorum Certaminibus*. Vienna.
Richardson, N. J., ed. (1974): *The Homeric Hymn to Demeter*. Oxford.
Richter, Gisela M. A. (1965): *The Portraits of the Greeks*, 3 vols. London.
Rosenmeyer, T. G. (1968): Elegiac and Elegos, *California Studies in Classical Antiquity* 1, 217–31.
——— (1982): *The Art of Aeschylus*. Berkeley, Los Angeles, and London.
Rutherford, W. G. (1905): *A Chapter in the History of Annotation*. London.
Sandys, John Edwin, ed. (1912): *Aristotle's Constitution of Athens*, ed. 2. London.
——— (1919): *The Odes of Pindar*, ed. 2. Cambridge, Mass., and London (Loeb Classical Library).
Schadewaldt, W. (1959): *Von Homers Welt und Werk*, ed. 3. Leipzig.
Schmid, Wilhelm, and Stählin, Otto (1929): *Geschichte der griechischen Literatur*, Vol. 1, pt. 1. Munich (Handbuch der Altertumswissenschaft, 7.1.1).

Schoell, F. (1875): De Aeschyli Vita et Poesi Testimonia Veterum, in *Aeschyli Septem Adversus Thebas*, ed. F. Ritschl, Leipzig, pp. 1–52.

Schrader, Hans (1939): *Die archaischen Marmorbildwerken der Akropolis*, 2 vols. Frankfurt am Main.

Schroeder, O. (1930): *Grundriss der griechischen Versgeschichte*. Heidelberg.

Schwyzer, Eduard (1923): *Dialectorum Graecarum exempla epigraphica potiora*. Leipzig.

Scott, John A. (1921–1922): Whom Did the Greeks Mean by "The Poet"?, *CJ* 17, 330.

Scully, James (1971): *Avenue of the Americas*. Amherst, Massachusetts.

———, and Herington, C. J. (1975): *Aeschylus: Prometheus Bound*. New York and London.

Sedgwick, W. B. (1947): *The Frogs* and the Audience, *Classica et Mediaevalia* 9, 1–9.

Sharp, Cecil J. (1932): *English Folk Songs from the Southern Appalachians*, second edition, ed. Maud Karpeles. London.

Sideras, Alexander (1971): *Aeschylus Homericus*. Göttingen (Hypomnemata, No. 31).

Silk, Michael (1980): Aristophanes as a Lyric Poet, in *Aristophanes: Essays in Interpretation*, ed. Jeffrey Henderson. Cambridge (Yale Classical Studies, Vol. 26).

Simon, Erika (1982): *The Ancient Theater*. London and New York.

Sklar, R. (1975): *Movie-Made America: How the Movies Changed American Life*. New York.

Slater, William J. (1969): *Lexicon to Pindar*. Berlin.

——— (1978): Artemon and Anacreon. No Text Without a Context, *Phoenix* 32, 185–94.

Smyth, Herbert Weir, ed. (1957): *Aeschylus*, 2 vols., ed. 2, with appendix edited by Hugh Lloyd-Jones. Cambridge, Mass. (Loeb Classical Library).

——— (1959): *Greek Grammar*, revised by Gordon M. Messing. Cambridge, Mass.

Snell, Bruno (1957): Das Heitere im frühen Griechentum, *Antike und Abendland* 6, 149–55.

——— (1964): *Scenes from Greek Drama*. Berkeley and Los Angeles (Sather Classical Lectures, Vol. 34).

———. *See also* Sn. and *TrGF*, under "Abbreviated Titles," above.

Snodgrass, A. M. (1971): *The Dark Age of Greece*. Edinburgh.

Snyder, J. M. (1974): Aristophanes' Agathon as Anacreon, *Hermes* 102, 244–46.

Stanford, W. B. (1942): *Aeschylus in His Style*. Dublin.

———, ed. (1963): *Aristophanes: The Frogs*, ed. 2. London and New York.

——— (1967): *The Sound of Greek*. Berkeley and Los Angeles (Sather Classical Lectures, Vol. 38).

Taplin, Oliver (1977): *The Stagecraft of Aeschylus*. Oxford.

Tarditi, G. (1968): Sull' origine e sul significato della parola "rapsodo," *Maia* 20, 137–45.

Turner, E. G. (1952): *Athenian Books in the Fifth and Fourth Centuries.* London.
——— (1975): I libri nell' Atene del V e IV Secolo A.C. (translation of the preceding item, with updated notes), in *Libri, Editori, e Pubblico nel Mondo Antico*, ed. Giuglielmo Cavallo. Bari.
Uhlig, Gustavus, ed. (1883): *Dionysii Thracis Ars Grammatica.* Leipzig.
Vermeule, E. (1965): Fragments of a Symposion by Euphronios, *Antike Kunst* 8, 34–39.
Wade-Gery, H. T. (1952): *The Poet of the "Iliad."* Cambridge.
Wartelle, A. (1971): *Histoire du texte d'Eschyle dans l'antiquité.* Paris.
Watkins, C. (1976): Syntax and Metrics in the Dipylon Vase Inscription, in *Studies . . . Leonard R. Palmer*, ed. A. Morpurgo Davies and W. Meid. Innsbruck.
Webster, T. B. L. (1967): *The Tragedies of Euripides.* London.
——— (1970A): *The Greek Chorus.* London.
———, ed. (1970B): *Sophocles: Philoctetes.* Cambridge.
——— (1972): *Potter and Patron in Classical Athens.* New York.
——— (1974): Dithyramb, Tragedy, and Comedy, in *Serta Turyniana*, ed. John L. Heller and J. K. Newman. Urbana, Chicago, and London.
Wegner, M. (1968): *Musik und Tanz.* Göttingen (Vol. III U of *Archaeologia Homerica*).
Welcker, F. G. (1839–1841): *Die griechischen Tragödien mit Rücksicht auf den epischen Cyclus*, 3 vols. Bonn (Rheinisches Museum Supplementband II).
West, M. L., ed. (1968): *Hesiod: Theogony.* Oxford.
——— (1971): Stesichorus, *CQ* 21, 302–14.
——— (1974): *Studies in Greek Elegy and Iambus.* Berlin.
———, ed. (1978): *Hesiod: Works and Days.* Oxford.
——— (1981): The Singing of Homer, *JHS* 101, 113–29.
———. *See also* W, under "Abbreviated Titles," above.
Westman, R. (1974): Ein überdecktes Wort in Solons Salamis-Elegie, *Arctos* 8, 187–93.
Wilamowitz-Moellendorff, Ulrich von (1900): *Die Textgeschichte der griechischen Lyriker.* Berlin (Abhandl. der Königl. Gesellschaft der Wissenschaften zu Göttingen, Phil.-Hist. Klasse, N. F. Band IV, nr. 3).
———, ed. (1903): *Timotheos: Die Perser.* Leipzig.
——— (1910): *Einleitung in die griechische Tragödie*, ed. 3. Berlin.
——— (1913): *Sappho und Simonides.* Berlin.
——— (1921): *Griechische Verskunst.* Berlin.
——— (1922): *Pindaros.* Berlin.
——— (1931–1932): *Der Glaube der Hellenen*, 2 vols. Berlin.
Willcock, M. M. (1964): Mythological Paradeigma in the *Iliad*, *CQ* 14, 141–54.
Winnington-Ingram, R. P. (1955): Fragments of Unknown Greek Tragic Texts with Musical Notation, *Symb. Osl.* 31, 29–87.
Ziehen, N. L. (1949): art. *Panathenaia* in: *RE* Vol. 36.2, cols. 457–89.

Index

Designer: Adapted from design by William Snyder.
Compositor: G&S Typesetters, Inc.
Printer: Braun-Brumfield, Inc.
Binder: Braun-Brumfield, Inc.
Text: 10/13 Sabon
Display: Garamond